Meeting Human Needs

Meeting Human Needs

Toward a New Public Philosophy

Jack A. Meyer, editor

American Enterprise Institute for Public Policy Research
Washington and London

Library of Congress Cataloging in Publication Data
Main entry under title:

Meeting human needs toward a new public philosophy.

    1. Industry—Social aspects—United States—Addresses,
essays, lectures. 2. Trade-unions—Social aspects—
United States—Addresses, essays, lectures.
3. Associations, institutions, etc.—United States—
Addresses, essays, lectures. I. Meyer, Jack, 1944–
HD60.5.U5M427   1982   361.7'0973   82-11399

ISBN 0-8447-1358-9   (pbk.)
ISBN 0-8447-1359-7

Printed in the United States of America

Contents

PART FOUR

PRIVATE INITIATIVES AND PUBLIC POLICY REFORM IN SELECTED SECTORS

Preface

This book, the joint product of eighteen contributors, is a milestone for the American Enterprise Institute. It is, however, neither the beginning nor the end of our work on private sector initiatives: Our research on private responses to human needs began in 1976, and we expect it to continue.

Peter L. Berger and Richard John Neuhaus's *To Empower People: The Role of Mediating Structures in Public Policy* marked the beginning of this endeavor. Their thesis is straightforward: Society's "mediating structures"—neighborhoods, churches, families, voluntary associations, ethnic groups—are the vital element in the battle against social problems. Private institutions, which stand between the individual and the megastructures of society—the large bureaucracies, for example—have in many cases been supplanted by expensive and inflexible government programs.

Public policy, Berger and Neuhaus asserted, must avoid damaging mediating structures. "Wherever possible," they wrote, "public policy should utilize mediating structures for the realization of social purposes."

For more than five years, AEI has examined a wide range of mediating structures that successfully address human needs and the incentives that encourage private sector involvement in meeting them. Our studies, which have required a major commitment of human and financial resources, have kept AEI on the cutting edge of the public policy research debate.

The national elections of 1978 and 1980 and the changes in public attitudes they revealed hold a clear message for the future: the pendulum is swinging toward a greater role for the private sector in American life. The American people have raised fundamental questions about the relations between the public and private sectors, and their changing views will inevitably be reflected in public policy.

Because of our longstanding interest in this area, in 1981 we established the AEI Center for the Study of Private Initiative. President Reagan also asked AEI to analyze the potential of the private sector for meeting social needs, the barriers facing self-help efforts, and the incentives needed to encourage private sector initiatives. This volume, then, serves a twofold purpose: it responds to the president's request, and it broadens our exploration of the proper balance between the public and private sectors.

With this effort we enter uncharted territory in public policy research. In some of the areas examined in this volume, we are conducting the first systematic research. In others, we are mapping the terrain in a wholly new way, looking at relationships from a different perspective.

In education, for example, recent public policy debate has focused on the question of tuition tax credits and government support for private schools. In this book, we show that the private sector has a much greater role than providing education in traditional private schools. Business and industry are offering a veritable reeducation to the work force, one that could fundamentally change the way we allocate educational resources in the future.

Moreover, until now, the labor union has not been thoroughly examined as a provider of social services. Labor has been regarded generally in terms of large umbrella organizations like the AFL-CIO, the United Auto Workers, or the United Steelworkers of America. Union locals throughout America, however, provide extensive services, which have received little recognition.

In areas such as youth employment, housing, transportation, and neighborhood economic development, we have tried to identify new approaches and to show how they can be nurtured and allowed to grow—but we have only begun to explore this territory. More attention must be devoted to these novel ideas, by AEI and other institutions.

The material in this book forms the basis of a new agenda for reform. We have examined the historical and philosophical tradition of private sector initiatives; we have identified numerous options for the private sector and for public/private partnerships; we have highlighted examples of creative and effective local leadership in dealing with social problems; we have pointed out nagging administrative and regulatory barriers that stand in the way of privately initiated social programs.

Numerous case studies support the analysis—among them, in-depth analyses of two corporate community programs and descriptions of private sector and government programs in youth employment, aid to the elderly, health care, housing, and education.

In a larger sense, we have tried to challenge the conventional wisdom because we live in unconventional times. It is too easy for cynics to observe that money cut from federal social programs can never be "replaced." As Jack Meyer, editor of this volume, points out, "We should address the misleading, but prevalent notion that each dollar cut from federal government spending 'disappears' and must be 'replaced.' . . . The private sector neither can nor should re-fund the same programmatic structure de-funded by Congress." We are facing a conflict between our desire to help those in need and the limits on our resources for doing so. We need new ways of evaluating our strengths and building on them.

We are not suggesting that responsibility for meeting human needs be shifted from government to the private sector. We are convinced that government has an essential role in meeting social needs. Government's role and scope must, however, change as social needs change.

The new public philosophy that emerges from this volume transcends political parties and ideologies. It is based on a recognition of a fundamental change in the national mood, a desire to forge new relationships and to seek new and more effective solutions to our pressing social problems.

This book spans diverse disciplines and philosophies. It is appropriate that the authors disagree among themselves, for the competition of ideas is fundamental to a free society. As John Stuart Mill observed more than a century ago, "The work of a state, in the long run, is the work of the individuals comprising it."

WILLIAM J. BAROODY, JR.

Acknowledgments

This book is the result of a collaborative effort by numerous people at AEI. I would particularly like to express my appreciation to a few individuals who made very important contributions.

Ruth McKinnon, my project coordinator, did an excellent job of management, organization, and scheduling. In addition, she provided thorough research assistance, was a coauthor of two of the chapters, and was integrally involved in all phases of the project.

Sean Sullivan also made a vital contribution to the volume on several levels. He is the author of one chapter and coauthor of two others. He helped guide and review the writing of other chapters and provided useful advice on many aspects of the study.

I also relied on the expertise and judgment of Denis Doyle, Robert Woodson, John Weicher, and Marvin Kosters. Gretchen Erhardt participated in the planning and coordination of each phase of this undertaking; she typed most of the manuscript, assisted by Sylvia Catlett and John Kafka.

I would like to thank William Baroody, Jr., for his keen interest in this project. His ongoing desire to include diverse viewpoints about the proper balance between the public sector and the private sector encouraged me to amalgamate widely different perspectives in a single volume.

Jack A. Meyer

PART ONE

Conceptual Framework
and Historical Perspective

Private Sector Initiatives
and Public Policy:
A New Agenda

Jack A. Meyer

A Conceptual Framework for Analyzing Private Sector Initiatives

This study evaluates the potential of the private sector for delivering a wide range of human services to alleviate social problems. It also assesses the effect of government programs and policies on non-governmental organizations. Contributors to this volume analyze diverse private sector approaches to youth employment, child welfare, transportation, health care, education, housing, crime reduction, and business development. They focus on business and labor union activities, as well as volunteer and philanthrophic organizations and neighborhood groups. The study of business activities is not limited to corporate financial contributions to charitable groups or other non-profit organizations; it also includes the social programs established by businesses and their loans of talent and expertise to nonprofit groups and to government.

In a time when federal outlays for social programs are being scaled back, it must be stressed that notions of a slick transfer of funding responsibility from government to the private sector would be misleading and imprudent. This study does not advocate any target level of funding for private sector social programs. It features an objective assessment of the panoply of private sector activities to alleviate social problems—undertaken both by for-profit and by non-profit groups.

This book is not solely an evaluation of the impact of changing fiscal policy, though government expenditure and tax policies, as well as government regulations, form an important element of this analysis. The study primarily evaluates private sector efforts and assesses their relationship to government policies. Too often, government

3

policies stifle or eclipse private sector self-help efforts, though they could nourish and encourage these efforts. Government models of help have typically been overly rigid and structured along the lines of standardized frameworks. The huge social service bureaucracy has often been top-heavy and inefficient. Government service delivery has been over-professionalized, and it has imposed unwarranted "credentialing" requirements on alternative service delivery systems.

Private sector activities tend to be localized and varied, often reflecting the particular needs of a given area and the unusual skills of the leadership in that area. Such leadership, tailored to the unique circumstances of a community, should be fostered.

Participants in the AEI study selected examples of promising private sector activities that work with and through local leadership. The initiatives they cite tried not to repeat the mistakes of government in bypassing local leadership and imposing uniform program models "from the top down" on significantly different situations.

The Myth of the Disappearing Dollar. To begin with, we should address the misleading, but prevalent notion that each dollar cut from federal government spending "disappears" and must be "replaced." Neither the American business community nor the nonprofit portion of the private sector can or should try to compensate for the slowdown in the growth of federal social spending on a dollar-for-dollar "replacement" basis. It is important to avoid thinking of private sector initiatives as a "second-best" strategy where a return to expensive federal government programs is viewed as the ideal strategy. Private sector initiatives should not be depicted as a "filler" to be used until we can "afford" previous funding levels for federal programs.

There can be honest disagreement whether budget cuts were made in the right categories or in the right amounts, but not whether the reductions (compared with some baseline projection of what would have been spent) represent funds that have just disappeared. If taxes are left unchanged in the face of such budget cuts, then federal deficits will be smaller and pressure on interest rates and inflation will ease. A reduction in the federal deficit translates into a reduction in *public* borrowing, which, in turn, releases a portion of the pool of private savings for *private* borrowing. This spurs more private investment in plant and equipment, which improves productivity and facilitates consumer borrowing for home and automobile purchases or other forms of installment credit. If tax cuts corresponding to budget cuts are enacted (with deficits remaining about the same in the short run), then personal disposable incomes will rise. In neither event does a cut in government spending simply light a match to dollar bills; those dollars are transferred from the federal government to consumers, businesses, and state and local governments.

This point deserves emphasis as a rebuttal to the slick slogans and misguided shibboleths of two extreme points of view about private sector initiatives. According to one viewpoint, the budget cuts should be fully restored because a dollar cut from federal outlays reflects a dollar of unmet needs. According to the opposite notion, the budget cuts will be fully offset by increases in private outlays for social programs. The two views are equally misleading. The private sector neither can nor should re-fund the same programmatic structure de-funded by Congress. It is also true, however, that the money cut from federal social programs will not necessarily find its way from the private sector to the same social agenda addressed by those federal programs.

The budget and tax cuts enacted by Congress in 1981 reflected a consensus to trim certain social programs (and leave others untouched), in effect, to allow some of the resources spent on those programs to be retained by individuals and businesses to use as they see fit. Therefore, to ask corporations or individuals to "give more" because the government is spending less misses the point: in 1981 people expressed a desire to tilt the balance away from the public, and toward the private sector. When the American people believe that the balance has been tilted enough (and I believe we are approaching this point), the budget cutting will slow down.

A Sober View of the Role of Business. The facts about corporate giving presented in this study make it clear that business contributions to nonprofit organizations could not possibly compensate for federal budget cuts. And business should not be encouraged to sponsor programs that have failed under government supervision. Suggestions to the contrary would breed cynicism and distrust throughout the private sector.

To highlight the potential of the private sector is not to exhort corporations to dig deeper into their pockets. The main purpose of business is to produce goods and services that meet the needs of consumers and to generate wealth and income through growth. If ways can be found to increase the productivity of business, those who help the unfortunate or disadvantaged will have more resources to work with, and the disadvantaged will gain accordingly. For example, business, on average, gives about 1 percent of pre-tax profits to nonprofit organizations. If pre-tax profits rise 10 percent, business giving is likely to rise about 10 percent (other factors held constant),

5

without any increase in the proportion of profits donated. Obviously, a larger pie allows all to have a slightly larger slice. Some observers have, however, focused on redistributing the pie and, strangely, are looking to business to undertake this task. Thus, we hear calls for 2 percent clubs and 5 percent clubs, as if simply throwing more money at the problems will solve them. We have learned little if we think that corporate billions will accomplish what federal billions could not.

It must be acknowledged that the federal government has made great progress toward alleviating some very troublesome social problems. When President Franklin D. Roosevelt spoke of the need to end poverty among one-third of a nation, he was not using hyperbole. About one of every three Americans was poor fifty years ago, and that fraction has fallen steadily over the ensuing decades. Today 5 to 7 percent of Americans fall below the official government poverty line when a variety of cash and in-kind public assistance benefits are taken into account. While the strength of the American economy has played an important role in reducing poverty, an array of programs ranging from social security to food stamps and Medicare and Medicaid have helped. Many social problems remain, however, and new ones have developed. In this volume, the authors examine strategies for addressing these problems that seem to work, whether or not government funding is contributing to the success.

It is primarily the role of government, not of business, to carry out the people's desire to redistribute income to meet basic human needs.

In recent months, the debate over private sector initiatives has frequently taken the form of a contentious, polarized, and fruitless struggle between those who hold out an unrealistic vision of the private sector rushing in with checkbooks to fill the gap between continuing human needs and diminished federal resources and those who demand that federal spending cuts be restored. This dialogue pits those who see "privatization" as a blessing against those who see it as a curse. The truth surely lies in between. In this volume the authors develop an assessment of the role of the private sector in alleviating social problems that is sober and realistic, but not cynical.

To argue that federal spending cutbacks do not involve throwing money down a bottomless hole is not to deny that there will be problems in adjusting to new ways of meeting social needs. As government has pre-empted the delivery of many social services and the attempt to solve basic social problems, the role of private groups has atrophied, and individuals have held back, assuming that government would fill the void. Ironically, spending billions of dollars on stubborn social problems has often not filled the void, though government programs have helped to solve some specific problems. In many of the problem areas studied in this volume, such as youth crime, child welfare, and education, federal government programs are increasingly viewed as part of the problem rather than part of the solution.

As the federal role in providing human services is scaled back, we cannot expect the private role to be instantaneously augmented in the same proportion. There will be, and perhaps should be, a process of groping and experimentation, as the proper combination of a refashioned federal role, a more vibrant state and local government role, and an enlivened private sector role develops. The contributors to this volume hope to foster this development through a critical, objective study of the elements of successful private efforts and the ways in which the problems confronting those efforts were overcome.

The authors probe relations between the public and the private sectors and try to indicate where the proper balance should rest. They hope to emphasize the potential of grass-roots organizations that people turn to in time of need. These groups are usually small and nonbureaucratic, with low budgets. In contrast to the unwieldy organizations—public and private—that often skim over the real problems, these "mediating structures" often succeed where everything else has failed.

An objective study must contend with the notion that private sector initiatives are merely cheerleading campaigns to divert attention from the pains resulting from federal spending cutbacks. There is considerable suspicion within the private sector that the renewed interest in private sector approaches to social problems is a bread and circuses exercise. This notion must be expelled.

The authors of this study try to preclude such skepticism by spurning panaceas, placebos, and empty promises. They offer, instead, case studies of a wide variety of private sector initiatives combined with an analysis of public policy options and numerous policy recommendations. They evaluate the potential of private actions and relate them to government programs and policies. In fusing the studies of private programs with public policy analysis, the authors develop an agenda for reform that holds real promise of gradual improvement in areas such as health care, child welfare, education, housing, crime, and unemployment. By illustrating how broad and diverse private sector initiatives have been, and how innovative private efforts have successfully coped with society's most intractable problems in the harshest of environments, the participants in this study hope to point out alternatives to well-intentioned, but often costly and ineffective, government programs.

Perspectives on Private Sector Initiatives. In the past year the term "private sector initiatives" has entered the social policy lexicon in the United States. To some, it has meant a vision of a nostalgic return to the volunteer spirit of yesteryear, a clarion call for neighbors to help neighbors in time of need. Critics of this view have discredited and discarded such notions as sentimental, anachronistic, and diversionary and as attempts to gloss over the pains of cutbacks in the federal government's funding of social programs.

To others, private sector initiatives have meant partnerships between business firms or real estate developers, neighborhood groups, and local governments. These observers have highlighted the need for better cooperation between the public and private sectors.

To still others, private sector initiatives are associated with a movement to decentralize the power and authority of the federal government. These observers would allow more autonomy for state and local governments and more private involvement in government decision making that pertains to the private sector.

The concept of private sector initiatives need not be restricted to a retreat to the halcyon days of barn building, or to visions of downtown redevelopment, or to the new federalism; nor need it reject any of these. Voluntarism, partnerships, and the changing balance between levels of government deserve careful scrutiny. While these concepts of private sector initiatives are *included* in this analysis, they are not *featured* in the study. Rather, this study highlights the untapped potential of grass-roots neighborhood groups, business and labor unions, church and ethnic organizations, and family units for meeting people's needs largely without government assistance. We can stress the need to simplify and to relax government regulations that have stifled self-help groups and outline a new role for government as a catalyst, a leader, and a provider of incentives instead of a rigid, bureaucratic, and often ineffective service deliverer. Our viewpoint is derived from the basic conviction that society will suffer if it fails to capture the knowledge and creativity at the grass-roots level. By tapping such resources at the local level and building social strategies on the foundation of neighborhood strengths and talent, we can alleviate our most stubborn social problems. While a refashioned federal government role can contribute to this progress, no amount of federal dollars can substitute for creative energy and self-help efforts at the neighborhood level.

This study neither adopts any single, restrictive concept of private sector initiatives nor embraces one role for the private sector that excludes other roles. The authors start from the premises that (1) the proper balance between government programs, at any level, and private self-help efforts should be re-evaluated, and (2) the activities of what are called mediating structures have too often been overlooked in the debate over the role of the private sector.

Overview of the Volume. The organization of this book reflects the conceptual framework developed in this chapter. It is important to stress that some of the authors contributing to this volume might propose a different overview. This is a caveat, but not an apology; indeed, this book gains strength from diversity. In this volume I have attempted to bring together diverse viewpoints while preserving important differences in perspective. The fact that some authors might not accept the premises or agree with the conclusions of others does not rob the volume of coherence. In studying all of the chapters, I find common themes amid diversity, and in this section I note some of them, without attempting to compress all of the authors into the same mold.

In the next section of this chapter I analyze trends in government spending and discuss the effect of selected government programs on the incentives for individuals to trade dependency for participation in the labor force. In my view, the squeeze on federal funds for social programs, arising from public wishes to strengthen our defense posture while holding down the tax burden, heightens the need (1) to assess the potential of the private sector to help meet human needs; and (2) to devise more flexible, more efficient, and more humane designs for those programs that must be conducted by government.

A historical perspective for assessing the changing balance between the public and private sectors is provided by William Schambra. He presents a greater reliance on local community assistance to those in need as an alternative both to nationally imposed solutions—against which he believes the public will recoil—and to a mean-spirited attitude toward the needy, which he properly rejects. Schambra provides a bridge across time that complements the bridge I attempt to construct across the public and private sectors at present.

Part two features a cross section of activities of business, labor, and neighborhood groups that transcends individual problem areas and disciplines. The chapter on business initiatives by Ruth McKinnon, Patricia Samors, and Sean Sullivan presents two detailed case studies of companies involved in a range of activities, together with a survey of company-sponsored assistance programs in employment, housing, day care, and other areas.

In the chapter on the role of organized labor, Michael Balzano and Marlene Beck report on visits to labor-sponsored helping networks around the country. The authors trace the stages of development of these union activities and recount the lessons learned about strategies and structures that yield successful outcomes.

In his chapter on neighborhood groups operating at the grass-roots level, Robert Woodson also traces the evolution of successful programs and the barriers facing them in providing needed neighborhood services at a low cost. Woodson emphasizes the need for strategies that allow neighborhood residents to participate actively, rather than treat them paternalistically as passive dependents needing protection.

Although the specific formats of the business, labor, and neighborhood group programs differ substantially, there is a common tendency for successful initiatives to spring from the concerns of one individual for another—often involving people in the same family or neighborhood. Efforts initially geared to a single purpose frequently evolve into broader-based initiatives that transform an act of caring into a multipurpose program. This evolution, of course, does not and need not always occur. When it does, it is frequently plagued by "growing pains," which many of the authors discuss.

Part three begins with a map of the broad landscapes covered by private sector initiatives. Many of the key features of these landscapes are traced by Landrum Bolling. Rudolph Penner forges a link between the changes in macroeconomic policy and the prospects for meeting society's needs through the private sector. Penner evaluates present economic policies and suggests ways in which these policies, along with several long-term trends in our economy, are likely to affect private charitable contributions. Paul Pryde analyzes the key barriers to enterprise development in our economy. He provides guiding principles for a public policy that stresses the use of incentives and creative adaptation to a dynamic economy, rather than shortsighted efforts to forestall shifts in the economy.

Part four examines case studies of private sector initiatives—and accompanying public policy analysis—in specific problem areas. Many of the more successful private sector initiatives help to launch assistance programs, but do not fully direct such programs. One of the ingredients of success seems to be a sense of how to spark, guide, motivate, and educate people in such a way that those being helped are involved from the outset and take over the effort as soon as they can. Simply stated, successful programs seem to *help people help themselves*.

Sean Sullivan's analysis of the youth unemployment problem in the context of recent and proposed changes in the CETA program and of private sector programs in job counseling, placement, and training illustrates this point. Kenneth Orski provides many examples of private initiatives and public/private partnerships in the transportation sector. Patricia Samors and Sean Sullivan survey a variety of business, labor, and insurance industry efforts to contain health costs, particularly with regard to proposed market-oriented strategies. William Wardell and Nancy Mattison add a chapter on the potential role of the private sector in monitoring the safety of prescription drugs.

Denis Doyle and Marsha Levine explore new dimensions of the private sector role in education by assessing business efforts to improve the quality of education and to enhance the productivity of its work force. John Weicher describes long-term trends in housing, traces the dimensions of our current housing problems, and offers several models of private sector housing programs. Robert Woodson examines a way of reducing youth crime that relies on neighborhood groups working with the potential offenders. He criticizes government efforts that have foisted on local communities the ideas of national planners far removed from the problems. He also offers a poignant review of the tendency of foster care programs to keep children in high-cost institutions and to delay giving them the permanent family ties that can be vital to their well-being. Andrea Haines, Patricia Samors, and Ruth McKinnon review government social service programs, including work by charitable organizations to see that the basic human needs of low-income and disadvantaged Americans are met.

The authors writing in this section have combined case studies of promising private sector initiatives with a review of government programs. In constructing bridges between private sector initiatives and public policy, the authors hope to provide a policy agenda for public and private sector leaders. Government officials inclined to admonish the private sector to "do more" can gain credibility by practicing what they preach. We hope to help them achieve this credibility by providing both the broad contours of long-range policy reform and specific policy recommendations.

This volume does not attempt to catalog all private sector programs addressed to meeting human needs or to offer changes in government programs that might produce some sort of "instant relief." Rather, the authors feature private sector programs that illustrate the potential for successful outcomes, and they trace the basic elements of more promising government policies. In assessing both public and private programs, the authors suggest some common ingredients of success and some guiding principles for program development. We hope that those in the private sector who wish to help will benefit from reading a "menu" of alternative strategies addressed to our most troublesome social problems.

Changing Federal Budget Policy: Conflicting Needs and New Opportunities

The effort to meet basic human needs and to relieve persistent social problems in the United States has encountered increasing difficulties. Over the past two decades, enlarging federal outlays for social programs has been our answer to the social problems besetting us. A pattern has become established of initiating new government programs, broadening the coverage of existing programs, and increasing benefits per recipient. This pattern has been accommodated by the willingness of the American people to cut defense outlays as a share of gross national product (GNP) and to live with higher taxes and the adverse effects of large federal deficits. In recent years, however, public tolerance of all these ways of financing growth in social spending has been wearing thin.

A conflict results from the continuing need for human services, which may even accelerate as the elderly population increases, and the dwindling public willingness to meet these needs through some combination of cuts in real defense outlays, higher taxes, and larger deficits. In fact, the more we increase defense spending while holding down taxes, the more Draconian the cuts in nondefense outlays will have to be to avoid dangerously large federal deficits. In our low-savings economy, such huge deficits (now projected to be as much as 4–5 percent of GNP by the mid-1980s) would use up a very large portion of the available pool of savings and would surely limit capital formation and dampen productivity growth. Recent skirmishes over proposed cuts in social security, Medicare, Medicaid, Aid to Families with Dependent Children (AFDC), and food stamps dramatize these policy conflicts. Major battles loom as social needs collide with other national economic and foreign policy objectives.

Although the reduction in federal government funding of social programs leaves a void, it also creates an opportunity to devise new ways—more effective and less costly ways—of addressing and alleviating our social problems. As indicated in the section "A Conceptual Framework for Analyzing Private Sector Initiatives," it would be naive to think that the private sector will rush to fill this void, and it would be erroneous to argue that every dollar cut from federal spending must be matched elsewhere. Nonetheless, the scaling back of the federal government's social programs encourages us to examine the efforts of individuals and groups outside the public sector that are grappling with social problems.

In this section the nature and dimensions of the changing federal budget policy are analyzed. Ongoing federal budget trends require two strategies if we are to face up to the problems of those in need: (1) many federal government programs must be fundamentally restructured; and (2) private sector efforts must solve more problems by working through local leadership and directly involving people in the local community.

Through an expansion of social welfare spending, the United States has made implicit promises—and signed a kind of social contract—that it will find increasingly difficult to fulfill. The government has enacted and expanded an array of spending programs that cannot be fully financed *today*, given the upturn in real defense outlays, the limit on the federal tax burden, and the desire and commitment to reduce federal deficits.

Federal spending on social programs continues to rise sharply, often eclipsing alternatives in the private sector that are potentially more effective. I say this as one who is sympathetic with the aims of almost all of these government social programs. Indeed, many of them have effectively dealt with the problems toward which they were aimed; yet a considerable amount of mythology attributes to these programs evils they have not caused. The problem is that we can no longer afford the total cost of these programs as they are currently structured. Moreover, this sobering reality will not be significantly altered by an all-out attack on fraud and abuse. While I favor reducing fraudulent claims under government social programs, I am not as sanguine as some observers about the magnitude of the net savings likely to result from a "crackdown."

It is tempting to attribute the growth of overall federal spending on social programs simply to the initiation of new programs and the phasing in of beneficiaries under existing programs. In the 1960s and early 1970s these factors were important. If these were still the primary causes of outlay growth, we could stop initiating new programs or stop entitling new groups and presume that the spending growth would taper off. But in recent years the growth of spending on social welfare programs in the United States has resulted also from other factors, such as the following: demographic changes, which will accelerate, not taper off; faulty design, which builds excessive cost increases into some programs; and lax claims review processes. These factors, taken together, will continue to increase both the number of people eligible for benefits and the benefits per recipient, at least until fundamental changes in program design and administration are developed.

Recent data from the U.S. Office of Management and Budget illustrate the dramatic growth in social spending. Total federal outlays for social programs (including all payments to individuals and funds

13

TABLE 1

FEDERAL GOVERNMENT OUTLAYS FOR SOCIAL PROGRAMS AS A PROPORTION OF TOTAL FEDERAL SPENDING, FISCAL YEARS 1960–1981

Fiscal Year	Percent
1960	28.5
1967	33.4
1971	44.1
1981	55.5

SOURCE: Calculated from data compiled by the Office of Management and Budget, 1981.

for education and training programs and for social services) nearly doubled as a proportion of all federal outlays over the past two decades, rising from 28.5 percent in 1960 to 55.5 percent in 1981 (see table 1).

Figure 1 shows that the large increase in social spending occurred while defense spending fell as a proportion of all federal outlays (from about 10½ percent of our national output in the mid-1950s to about 5 percent in the late 1970s).

FIGURE 1

FEDERAL OUTLAYS FOR DEFENSE AND NONDEFENSE PURPOSES AS A PERCENTAGE OF TOTAL FEDERAL OUTLAYS, FISCAL YEARS 1940–1981

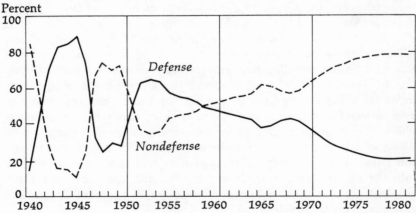

NOTE: Military retirement pay is excluded from defense spending and included in nondefense.
SOURCE: Calculated from data compiled by the Office of Management and Budget.

It is important to disaggregate nondefense federal outlays. One useful distinction isolates social programs from all other nondefense outlays.[1] Figure 2 reveals that over the past two decades the growth in nondefense outlays has stemmed primarily from the growth in social programs. The "all other" category was about the same percentage of total outlays and of GNP in 1980 as in 1960. Moreover, social programs are unlikely to bear the brunt of budget cuts in the early 1980s. Although some individual programs may be cut sharply, others that are much bigger, such as social security, will remain largely untouched. Spending on these programs as a whole, therefore, is likely to remain about the same proportion of all federal spending and of GNP in 1985 as in 1981. Under President Reagan's recent budget projections, for example, outlays for all entitlement programs would be 44½ percent of total federal spending in 1985, the exact proportion of outlays for entitlements in 1981.[2] Proposals currently under consideration in Congress could reduce this proportion. If entitlement spending remains at this level, however, and plans for defense spending remain intact or expand, then to prevent sharply rising deficits, cuts must come from the fairly small area of nondefense, nonentitlement programs, such as general revenue sharing, transportation, agriculture, and community development (see figure 2). In fact, in the Reagan administration's FY 1983 budget, the sum of national defense, social insurance, and net interest outlays will edge upward from 14.9 percent of GNP in 1981 to an estimated 15.8 percent in 1987. By contrast, the "all other" portion of the federal budget would be cut in half under the Reagan plan, from 8.1 percent of GNP in 1981 to 4.0 percent in 1987.

A further disaggregation of these federal outlay figures reveals that the surge in social spending over the past two decades occurred despite little if any growth since 1972 in programs targeted primarily to lower-income groups (see figure 3).[3] Programs accessible to all economic groups, which include various retirement programs and Medicare, have accounted for the surge in spending over the past decade.[4] Real outlays per capita for poverty programs rose steadily during the 1960s and early 1970s as new beneficiaries were phased into these programs, but are currently no higher than they were in 1972. Spending for social programs available to all income groups is scheduled to rise in the next three years while spending for poverty-oriented programs drops as a proportion of total federal outlays. It is worth noting, however, that the social security and Medicare programs, though available to all income groups, have helped to reduce poverty in the United States. Although these programs are now

15

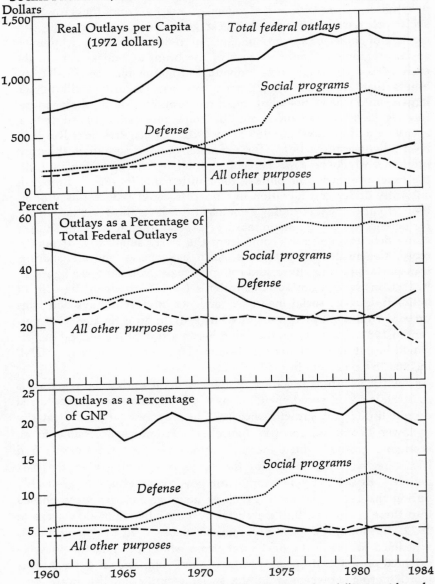

FIGURE 2

TOTAL FEDERAL OUTLAYS AND OUTLAYS FOR DEFENSE,
SOCIAL PROGRAMS, AND ALL OTHER PURPOSES, FISCAL YEARS 1960–1984

NOTE: Projections were made in 1981 and would be somewhat different with each subsequent updating.

SOURCE: Calculated from data compiled by the Office of Management and Budget.

16

FIGURE 3
FEDERAL OUTLAYS FOR ALL SOCIAL PROGRAMS, AND FOR "A" AND "P" PROGRAMS, FISCAL YEARS 1960–1981

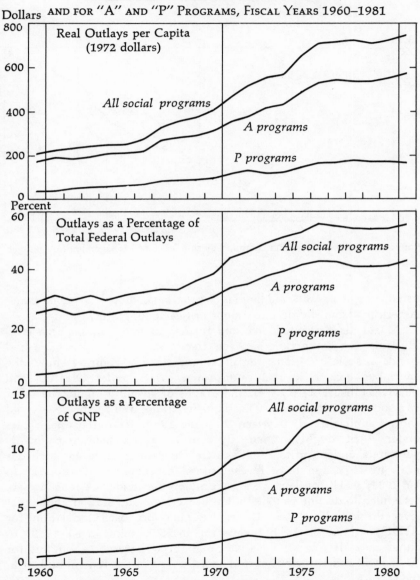

NOTE: "P" programs are keyed to the poverty group, and "A" programs are available to all income groups. These programs are listed in notes 3 and 4. Projections were made in 1981 and would be somewhat different with each subsequent updating.

SOURCE: Calculated from data compiled by the Office of Management and Budget.

FIGURE 4

OLD-AGE AND SURVIVORS INSURANCE, REAL OUTLAYS PER CAPITA, FISCAL YEARS 1940-1981
(1972 dollars)

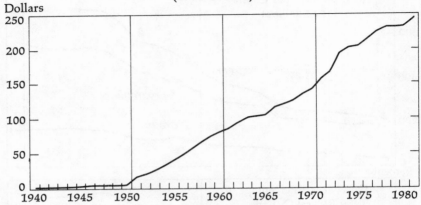

SOURCE: Calculated from data compiled by the Office of Management and Budget.

usually depicted as "middle class" programs, they have kept many Americans from sliding into a poor or near-poor status.

Data disaggregated one step further to the program area level illustrate the distinction between trends in poverty programs and trends in social programs for all income classes. Figure 4 shows the enormous growth in real outlays per capita under Old-Age and Survivors Insurance (OASI), and graphs of spending under the other two social security funds—Disability Insurance and Medicare—would show a similar trend. Between 1960 and 1980, *real* outlays per capita under OASI roughly *tripled*. By contrast, real assistance payments per capita under Aid to Families with Dependent Children reached a peak in 1972 and have leveled off since then (see figure 5). In FY 1981, AFDC outlays were $8.5 billion and under current law are scheduled to decline to $7.2 billion in FY 1983 and stay at about that level through FY 1985. Under Reagan's proposed legislation for AFDC, outlays for AFDC would fall to $5.9 billion in FY 1983. In either case, despite all the rhetoric about welfare costs, outlays for AFDC will constitute no more than 1 percent of the federal budget in the early 1980s.

The distinction between poverty social programs and other social programs breaks down, however, in the area of health care. Outlays under both Medicare and Medicaid have been doubling in nominal

FIGURE 5

AID TO FAMILIES WITH DEPENDENT CHILDREN,
REAL OUTLAYS PER CAPITA, FISCAL YEARS 1940–1981
(1972 dollars)

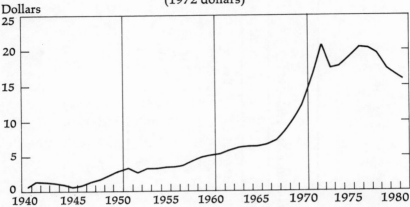

SOURCE: Calculated from data compiled by the Office of Management and Budget.

terms about every four years. Even after adjusting for inflation and population growth, federal outlays quadrupled under Medicare and increased more than fourfold under Medicaid between 1967 and 1981 (see table 2). The food stamp program was expanded in 1971, but as table 2 shows, real outlays per capita for this program have tripled since this date. Furthermore, this growth far exceeds the growth in the number of beneficiaries. The number of Medicaid recipients grew sharply in the early years (from 11.5 million in 1968 to 19.6 million in 1973), but the increase was quite small between 1973 and 1978 (19.6 million to 22.2 million). Yet real outlays per capita soared during this period, rising from $21.00 in 1973 to $31.50 in 1978. Thus, while the number of Medicaid beneficiaries rose by 13 percent during this period, real per capita outlays rose by 50 percent. Over half the growth in Medicaid outlays in recent years resulted from increased utilization by a fairly fixed population.

A number of our retirement programs, as currently structured, are like ticking time bombs. Failure to make any alterations in the benefit structure or in the financing mechanisms facing future retirees will lead, ultimately, to an explosion of costs. Proposals to bail out the OASI fund by borrowing from the Medicare fund are a classic case of "robbing Peter to pay Paul." If we continue to regard as sacrosanct the current age of retirement with full benefits, the cur-

19

TABLE 2

Growth of Federal Outlays for Selected Social Programs, 1967–1981

Fiscal Year	Food Stamps		Medicare		Medicaid	
	Real per capita dollars[a]	Percentage of total outlays	Real per capita dollars[a]	Percentage of total outlays	Real per capita dollars[a]	Percentage of total outlays
1967	0.70	0.1	21.50	2.2	7.40	0.7
1971	7.80	0.7	39.40	3.7	16.80	1.6
1981	22.20	1.6	84.40	6.3	33.00	2.5

[a] In 1972 dollars.
Source: Office of Management and Budget data.

rent indexing formula, and the current low limits on earnings allowed under social security, we will face a grim choice between bankrupt funds (reneging on our social contract with future retirees) or steeply rising payroll taxes. Indeed, by the year 2020, under the present benefit structure, social security taxes on employers and employees combined will reach a staggering level of about 21½ percent of payroll.[5] Effective, permanent reforms (instead of more stopgap remedies) need not rob current retirees of their benefits. Instead, they would arrest the process whereby each succeeding cohort of retirees receives a higher living standard than the preceding one. These changes could be phased in gradually without seriously affecting current recipients. Such reforms could include the phase-out of the limitation on the amount of earnings that is not subject to a corresponding reduction in social security benefits, a very gradual but steady increase in the retirement age and the early retirement age, a change in the treatment of federal workers, and a change in the method of calculating cost-of-living increases.

In the Federal Civil Service Retirement System, real outlays per capita have roughly tripled over the past twelve years and now account for an estimated 30.8 percent of payroll for federal civilian workers. But, according to the President's Commission on Pension Policy (1980), if this retirement system were funded according to the criteria established under the Employee Retirement Income Security Act—that is to say, if the federal government practiced what it preached—outlays for retirement would soar to an estimated 79.8 percent of payroll.[6] This figure is roughly double the proportion of payroll accounted for by *all* employee benefits, taken together, in the private sector.[7] The combination of fully indexed cost-of-living adjustments, early retirement with full benefits, the generous treatment of social security income for dual beneficiaries, and other factors has contributed to the disparity between retirement benefits in the federal and private sectors. That this situation represents a ticking time bomb is dramatized by the 1980 estimates of the President's Commission of the unfunded liability for accrued benefits under the Civil Service Retirement Fund—$304.8 billion. A more recent estimate by Congressman John Erlenborn places this figure at $469.5 billion. When all nine federal pension funds are aggregated, Erlenborn calculates an unfunded liability of $906.8 billion.[8]

The Reagan administration deserves some credit for addressing one aspect of this problem in its FY 1983 budget proposals. To correct the inequity of current retirees' having lower annuities than those of earlier retirees with the same work history, the Reagan budget plans would adjust future civil service retirement annuities by the lesser of the increase in the consumer price index or the increase in General Schedule pay for federal employees and would hold down future adjustments for these annuitants until they fall in line with the benefits of new retirees with comparable service.[9]

Regrettably, however, the latest Reagan proposal dropped the administration's 1981 request that federal pay determinations be broadened to include total compensation comparability rather than annual pay adjustments based on salary alone. Other reforms with support from the General Accounting Office and a series of presidential commissions, such as the broadening of the scope of the professional, administrative, technical, and clerical workers survey, are also missing from the administration's latest proposal.

The purpose of disaggregating the trend in overall federal government spending is to illustrate that the real growth areas of spending, such as programs geared to the elderly and national defense, are the sectors that are being treated as "untouchable." There is a lot of rhetoric about welfare spending, but my figures show that such programs are "under control" already and have actually not grown at all in real terms over the last decade.

Indeed, the resistance to cutting defense spending and social security, together with the uncontrollable nature of interest payments in the short run, leaves a small (and shrinking) piece of the federal pie available for budget cutting. In 1981 the share of the budget accounted for by national defense, social security, and net interest was 55.8 percent. Under the proposed FY 1983 Reagan budget, the corresponding figure in 1983 would be 64.8 percent, and by 1985, 68.5 percent. If Medicare were included in the 1985 projection, an estimated 75.8 percent of the federal budget would be in this "untouchable" category. This would leave only a fourth of the budget for cutting, and this one-fourth, which includes all of the social programs geared to the non-elderly, would require radical surgery indeed if we proceed with our current long-term defense and tax plans and still hope to avoid massive deficits. In my view, the burden should be spread more evenly.

These competing goals—holding down an increasing tax burden, reducing deficits to improve our chances for reducing inflation and interest rates, and increasing our defense capabilities—are not irreconcilable, but it may be extremely difficult (in both economic and political terms) to make significant progress on all three fronts simultaneously over a short period of time. It is vital (1) to establish priorities among these objectives, while indicating that none of the goals is being abandoned, and (2) to establish realistic timetables for these objectives to reduce the tensions between them.

The Need to Improve Work Incentives. In addition to a balanced approach to federal budget control, it is important to try to rid government programs of their work-discouraging features. In the long run there will be a healthier balance between the public and private sectors if government programs do not foster a state of permanent dependency among people who are able to work. A private initiatives strategy should encompass an effort to enable people to organize their lives as much as possible around their own initiatives, using government as a fallback during disruptive periods rather than as a crutch.

In poverty, income maintenance, and retirement programs, we should improve work incentives for able-bodied, healthy individuals. High effective marginal tax rates on earnings discourage work efforts. While the tax cuts enacted last year were addressed to this work disincentive factor, there are numerous features of government programs that discourage work, particularly for low-income individuals. Work incentives should not be limited to middle class and upper-income families. In a short-sighted attempt to save current outlays by sharply reducing benefits as earnings increase, the government has made people more dependent and, ironically, has probably boosted federal outlays over the long run.

Unfortunately, the recent Omnibus Budget Reconciliation Act of 1981 (P.L. 97-35) augmented some of the disincentives for welfare recipients to work, and the Reagan administration, which supported these changes, has proposed further steps in its FY 1983 budget that would exacerbate this problem. In the 1981 legislation, Congress effectively repealed the "$30 plus a third" rule, which at least provided some incentive for an AFDC beneficiary to increase work effort. Under this rule, AFDC beneficiaries were allowed to "disregard" a portion of their income for purposes of ascertaining the amount of benefits to which they were entitled. The first $30 per month of earned income was disregarded in the calculation of benefits (that is, benefits were not "docked" at all as a result of earnings up to $30); in addition, one-third of earnings beyond $30 per month was disregarded in this fashion. Thus, AFDC benefits were reduced by $2 for each $3 of earned income beyond $30, leaving the recipient with one-third of his or her earnings beyond $30 on a net basis. The combination of these two features meant that an AFDC beneficiary who worked got to keep a little over one-third of earnings, or, in effect, was "taxed" a little less than two-thirds of earnings. In addition, beneficiaries were allowed to deduct a certain amount of work expenses from earned income, including taxes and day-care costs for children. The dollar amounts of this work expense deduction varied by state and were increased periodically. This lowered the effective "tax rate" on earnings further. If taxes and other expenses took 15 percent of earnings, then this work expense allowance would have lowered the effective tax rate from about 67 percent to about 52 percent.

Under the new law, Congress placed a time limit on the work incentive bonus (the disregard) and a dollar limit on the work expense deduction. The $30 plus a third disregard may now be applied only for the first four months of employment. After four months, every penny of net earnings is subtracted from welfare benefits, negating any advantage of continuing to work. The work expense deduction for expenses other than day care was set at $75 per month and the child care deduction limited to $160 per month per child for full-time work throughout the month.

The 1981 law also imposed an eligibility limit restricting benefit payments to families whose gross family income does not exceed 150 percent of the states' standards of need. The act requires states to assume that eligible parents receive advance payment of the earned income tax credit (EITC); it tightens the family resource limits by lowering the cap on assets (other than a home and one car) from $2,000 to $1,000; and it allows states to consider as income the value of food stamps and rent or housing subsidies to the extent that these amounts duplicate food or housing components in the states' standards of need. The Reconciliation Act also institutes retrospective budgeting and monthly reporting and requires states to correct payment errors promptly.

With regard to the 150 percent limit for initial financial eligibility, a recent study by the Congressional Research Service (CRS) found that in more than one-half of the states, the new law's gross income limit is below the U.S. Census Bureau's 1980 poverty threshold of $548 per month.[10] A CRS survey of states showed that the new gross annual earnings limits would cut earned income limits by about a third. Additional changes in AFDC eligibility rules and program features are described in the chapter by Andrea Haines, Ruth McKinnon, and Patricia Samors on social service programs.

In evaluating the impact of the benefit reduction rate on labor supply, it is important to include not only the effect on the work effort of current recipients, but also the effect on families with slightly higher incomes who are newly qualified by the higher breakeven lines associated with lower effective tax rates, as well as the effects on the work effort of taxpayers who are supporting both groups. Studies of the labor supply within the AFDC program indicate that the higher effective tax rates have a negative effect on current recipients.[11] Two studies predict that increasing the tax rate by 10 percentage points would lower employment rates by an estimated 1.4–2.1 percentage points.[12] Studies that include the other groups are less conclusive, because the effects on labor supply of newly qualified AFDC recipients seem to offset the effects on existing recipients.[13]

A recent survey by Danziger, Haveman, and Plotnick of the literature on the work disincentives of social programs indicates that (compared with a hypothetical situation in which there are no public transfer programs) the combination of all social insurance and public assistance programs reduces the work hours of transfer recipients by 4.8 percent of the total work hours of all workers.[14] The authors suggest that this is likely to be an upper boundary because private transfers would have their own work disincentives. The extent to which this reduction in work by current recipients would be offset by the effects on the work effort of others is uncertain.

In evaluating program changes, we should understand that some changes may save the federal government a few dollars today, but could cost the taxpayers more tomorrow. Proponents of these changes argue that earlier incentives prompted few welfare recipients to "work themselves off welfare," but this is not the sole criterion. Many people who were still on welfare were less dependent on welfare as earnings from work provided a relatively larger proportion of their total incomes, and public assistance benefits provided a relatively smaller share of their total incomes. As taxpayers, we should not prefer a higher total welfare bill with a marginally smaller caseload to a lower total welfare bill with a marginally higher caseload. We should focus not on the number of people on welfare as much as on how many of those who are able to work are on the path toward a reduced dependency on the taxpayers and a greater—even if not yet total—reliance on their own work.[15]

A similar trend is evident in changes in the food stamp program where the earnings disregard was lowered marginally from 20 percent to 18 percent in 1981. A current proposal by the Reagan administration would eliminate the disregard altogether and increase the benefit reduction rate (the "effective tax rate") from 30 to 35 percent.

Congress could improve work incentives for current program recipients either by lowering the benefit reduction rate under individual programs like AFDC or food stamps or by capping the cumulative "tax rate" for those receiving benefits from more than one program. In addition, Congress could stimulate work effort by updating the EITC. By leaving the cap on the earned income tax credit

25

frozen at $500 per year (where it has been for three years), Congress has allowed any beneficial effect of the work incentives of this program to erode in real terms.

The 1981 Reconciliation Act also allows states to institute required "workfare" programs for AFDC recipients and authorizes states to offer a work supplement program. The administration and the Congress now seem to place more faith in *requiring* many AFDC recipients to work than in *motivating* them to work. It seems unfortunate and unfair for the federal government to reduce work incentives through changes in programs and then to tell the states to find a way to induce recipients to work.

The concept of workfare treats welfare benefits as a kind of stigma or punishment that must be worked off. In this sense, it is worth recalling that despite the popular mythology depicting lazy men refusing to work, only about 10 percent of all AFDC families have a father in the home. While twenty-six states offer the AFDC-Unemployed Parent (AFDC-UP) program for families with an unemployed father, only 5 percent of all AFDC families in December 1980 were covered under this program.

The judgment implicit in the 1981 act is that all women who head families with no children under three years old would spend their time more productively at work than at home. I question this premise. Society may save a few dollars in public assistance payments as these women work at low-wage jobs, only to lay out many more dollars through the juvenile justice system as children without much parental attention get into trouble. I would prefer that programs offer financial inducements to work; then those who wish to work could do so, while those who want to serve their family needs at home can postpone working. We should question a program that makes benefits contingent upon both unemployment or underemployment by a male head and employment by a female head.

Finally, other features of public assistance programs also damage work incentives. Medicaid and AFDC-UP end eligibility abruptly when a threshold is reached. This discourages full-time work by the father of a welfare family and can cause the loss of hundreds of dollars of medical benefits when one dollar is earned at the threshold. Employed applicants for public assistance are sometimes treated less generously than current recipients; AFDC denies the work incentive bonus to applicants. This work disincentive could be ended by extending AFDC eligibility to the break-even level of earnings for everyone; the full-time work disincentive under AFDC-UP could be reduced by a straight earnings test for two-parent families and by dropping the requirement that a father be unemployed in order to receive benefits.[16]

We should alter features of our welfare system that either encourage families to break up in order to receive assistance or encourage unemployment for program eligibility. Indeed, when one examines recent and proposed changes in programs such as AFDC, food stamps, EITC, Medicaid, and proposals that would limit job training under the Comprehensive Employment and Training Act to AFDC recipients and youths in very poor families, one wonders whether the working poor are not getting the short end of the public policy stick. One also wonders whether such people—if they cannot get marginal public assistance, food stamps, Medicaid, or job training—will not be induced to go on welfare. Surely, this should be neither the intent nor the effect of public policy.

Public assistance recipients are not the only federal beneficiaries to face stiff work disincentives. The strong penalty on earnings above $6,000 per year for social security recipients discourages the elderly who can work and wish to work. The Reagan administration had an effective plan for phasing out this earnings ceiling in its 1981 social security reform plan, but it met the same fate as the rest of the Reagan social security proposal.

Skilled workers in manufacturing industries also faced a strong work disincentive prior to 1981 from the cumulative structure of unemployment compensation, trade adjustment assistance, and private supplemental unemployment benefits. The changes proposed by President Reagan and adopted by the Congress helped reduce this work disincentive and prevent workers on layoff from receiving more after-tax income than they earned when working.

These penalties on work are not only penny-wise and pound-foolish from the perspective of the federal government, but also dispiriting to beneficiaries whose sense of self-worth and usefulness would be enhanced by work. A strategy for social problem solving that relies heavily on private initiative should encourage that initiative rather than penalize it. The federal government should thoroughly review a broad range of its own programs to remove as many disincentives as possible to active, voluntary participation in the work force.

A New Strategy: Program Redesign and Private Sector Initiatives. The conflict between ongoing social needs and the diminished capacity of the federal government to address these needs necessitates the development of fundamental reforms in the benefit structure and in the delivery and financing mechanisms of social programs and a greater reliance on private sector initiatives to alleviate social problems.

Program redesign. By delivering adequate social services at a lower resource cost, we can lessen the need to respond to the evaporation of available funds by (1) cutting eligibility, (2) reducing benefits per eligible recipient, and (3) putting price controls or rate ceilings on service providers that lead to a reduction in services. None of these strategies is desirable.

Regrettably, structural reforms in social programs often fall victim to short-term budgetary concerns. Long-term budgetary relief is sacrificed because of the reluctance of any regime to forgo short-term savings or to incur a temporary upturn in outlays. Over the past decade, for example, welfare reform proposals were dicussed and discarded. The plans entailed higher costs initially as benefit reduction rates (welfare "tax rates") would be lowered and benefits would be made more nearly equal across geographic areas. Eventually, however, welfare outlays would probably be lowered as improved work incentives encouraged welfare recipients to substitute work for dependency.

Other federal programs in areas such as health care, housing, employment, and education also need redesigning, and suggestions for major program reforms are contained in the chapters on these subjects that follow.

To the extent that these opportunities for reform are missed or postponed, efforts by the federal government to cap or to reduce its involvement in these programs will only shift to lower levels of government the difficult choices between tax increases, benefit reductions, and price controls. Numerous programs could be redirected from costly delivery mechanisms to more effective strategies that are also more consistent with consumer choice and the dignity of program participants.

Private sector initiatives. We are now facing a dilemma in social policy: the American people still want to pursue the basic social goals embodied in past government programs, but they are reluctant to continue paying for them. Moreover, as the people ratify government's pursuit of other goals (for example, returning the tax increases attributable to "bracket creep" and enhancing our defense posture), resources must be diverted from social programs, exposing a latent contradiction in public attitudes.

This dilemma may be resolved, in part, as elected officials perceive the public's desire to maintain the basic governmental role in meeting human needs and make smaller cuts in the budget. But this solution forces a choice between higher taxes and larger deficits, and larger deficits translate into either higher interest rates or higher inflation. As discussed earlier, a basic redesign of government programs is a promising way to ease the tensions between the public's desires, but reforms cannot be devised and implemented overnight. We therefore need to pay more attention now to the potential of private sector initiatives for alleviating our social problems.

I do not suggest turning over to the private sector the effort to assist low-income families in meeting such basic human needs as health care or nutrition; these basic needs for low-income people must be met primarily through government assistance. As I have indicated, we can effect long-term savings in government programs in these areas by redesigning the fundamental delivery and financing mechanisms and improving the work incentives of the programs. Moreover, I believe that meeting these basic human needs for the disadvantaged is the responsibility of the *federal* government. These problems are national in scope and will not be resolved by devolving them to lower levels of government. Such a step would foster an uneven access to basic social services across geographic boundaries. Although privatization of such vital human services is unrealistic, it is possible to build more market-oriented incentives into our federal human service programs.

In other nondefense program areas such as community development, housing rehabilitation, education, agriculture, and transportation, there is room for more local decision making and for private sector initiatives. We have relied too heavily on rigid, uniform federal programs in these areas that are more amenable to decentralized efforts tailored to local circumstances.

Concluding Remarks

It is worth reemphasizing that I view the increasing inability to fulfill our social contract with program beneficiaries as a major social problem in the United States. The enormous cost of fully meeting the government's expanded obligations to recipient groups is putting a strain on those who are paying the bill. This huge increase in social spending is not attributable primarily to welfare programs but rather to benefits available to all economic groups. And some beneficiaries are by no means impoverished.

Many of the benefits under social programs are indexed for inflation while most workers are not employed under contracts with cost-of-living escalator clauses.[17] Moreover, many of the benefits are tax-exempt while earnings from work are subject to income and payroll taxes. The typical worker in the private sector of the U.S. economy has experienced a decline in real income in recent years as higher taxes and accelerating inflation have eroded the purchasing power of employee compensation. Many program beneficiaries are insulated from this decline in real income by the indexation and tax-exempt status of their benefits.

An example of nonpoor groups protected by our social contract is auto and steel workers receiving Trade Adjustment Assistance while waiting to return to their former jobs. This program, originally designed to relocate workers from dying industries to more vibrant ones, has become largely an income maintenance program for middle-class manufacturing workers. I give this example not to argue that social programs serving nonpoor individuals lack justification entirely, but rather to show that raising the protective umbrella to cover more groups has led to the protection of some who are less needy—often with tax-free, inflation-proof benefits—by others who are more needy and more vulnerable to both higher inflation and higher taxes.

This disparity between those who are assisted and those who are assisting has diminished the willingness of workers to continue financing social programs and damaged the incentive of benefit recipients who are able to work to give up dependency for self-sufficiency. Indeed, the adverse work incentives of some overlapping benefit programs have probably increased unemployment. If ways are not found to ease the strain on the working population who must support both the dependent non-aged and the steadily swelling number of the aged, the result could be growing class and intergenerational conflicts in U.S. society.

In part, these conflicts could be eased by a relaxation or postponement of the commitments to increase our defense capability or to reduce inflation. A retreat from these objectives, of course, would bring other problems and conflicts to the foreground. I will let the reader decide how much emphasis or priority to give these different objectives. My main point is that they cannot all be achieved simultaneously in a brief period of time, and the resultant trade-offs must be soberly addressed. These trade-offs can, however, be reduced to the extent that we are willing to (1) remove the non-needy from income maintenance programs; (2) improve the work incentives of social programs; (3) tighten up claims review, returning programs to their original intent; (4) redesign programs with uncontrollable cost increases; and (5) rely to a greater extent on the resources of the private sector to meet our social needs.

Notes

[1] Social programs include all retirement programs (social security, railroad, federal employees, and military), unemployment compensation, medical care, housing assistance, food and nutrition assistance, public assistance, education and training, student assistance, veterans benefits, and all other payments to individuals. Other nondefense program areas include international affairs; general science, space, and technology; energy; natural resources and environment; agriculture; commerce and housing credit; transportation; community and regional development; administration of justice; general government; general purpose fiscal assistance; interest; and offsetting receipts.

[2] Office of Management and Budget, *The Budget of the United States*, FY 1983, pp. 3-21, 3-27.

[3] Programs targeted primarily to lower economic groups include Medicaid; housing assistance; food and nutrition assistance; public assistance; elementary, secondary, and vocational education; and training, employment, and social services.

[4] Programs that are accessible to all economic groups include social security and railroad retirement; federal employee and military retirement; unemployment compensation; medical care except Medicaid; assistance to students, including the GI Bill; higher-education and research and education aids; all other payments to individuals; and residual expenditures not included in payments to individuals.

[5] This figure is for Old-Age, Survivors, Disability, and Hospital Insurance. It is based on projections of the 1981 trustees of the Social Security Administration that assume for the long run an inflation rate of 4.0 percent, an unemployment rate of 5.0 percent, and real GNP growth of 2.7 percent. Less optimistic assumptions, of course, would mean that it would take an even steeper increase in payroll taxes to maintain the current benefit structure.

[6] President's Commission on Pension Policy, *Federal Pension Programs*, January 1981, pp. ii-iii, p. 8.

[7] This proportion was estimated to be 37.1 percent for 1980. See U.S. Chamber of Commerce, *Employee Benefits 1980*.

[8] Congressman John Erlenborn, *News Release*, January 19, 1982.

[9] See *Budget of the United States Government*, FY 1983, pp. 5-147–148.

[10] See Vee Burke, *AFDC FY 1982 Budget Cuts*, Congressional Research Service, February 1982, p. 6.

[11] See, for example, Irwin Garfinkel and Larry Orr, "Welfare Policy and Employment Rate of AFDC Mothers," *National Tax Journal*, vol. 27, no. 2 (June 1974), pp. 275-84; Robert Williams, "Public Assistance and Work Effort" (Princeton, N.J.: Industrial Relations Section, Princeton University, 1975); and Daniel H. Saks, "Public Assistance for Mothers in an Urban Labor Market" (Princeton, N.J.: Industrial Relations Section, Princeton University, 1975).

[12] Garfinkel and Orr, "Welfare Policy and Employment Rate of AFDC Mothers," and Williams, "Public Assistance and Work Effort."

[13] For a thorough review of the literature on this subject, see Sheldon Danziger, Robert Haveman, and Robert Plotnick, "How Income Transfer Programs Affect Work, Savings, and the Income Distribution," *Journal of Economic Literature*, vol. 19 (September 1981), pp. 975-1028.

[14] See Danziger, Haveman, and Plotnick, "How Income Transfer Programs Affect Work, Savings, and the Income Distribution," p. 996.

[15] For a comprehensive analysis of the issue of work incentives in social programs, see Vee Burke, "Work Disincentives in Income-Tested Programs," Congressional Research Service Report No. 80-158 EPW, October 24, 1980.

[16] See Burke, "Work Disincentives," pp. 83-84.

[17] About six out of every ten workers under major union contracts (1,000 or more workers) are covered by cost-of-living escalator clauses, but outside this sector—which is only about one-tenth of the U.S. work force—escalators are unusual. Moreover, escalator clauses in collective-bargaining contracts typically do not match the full increase in the consumer price index. The average "yield" or recovery was 58 percent of the consumer price index in 1980. See U.S. Department of Labor, Bureau of Labor Statistics, *Major Collective Bargaining Settlements in the Private Sector, 1980*, USDL: 81-59, January 26, 1981, p. 4.

From Self-Interest to Social Obligation: Local Communities v. the National Community

William A. Schambra

> *Our recent emphasis on voluntarism, the mobilization of private groups to deal with our social ills, is designed to foster [a] spirit of individual generosity and our sense of communal values.*
>
> PRESIDENT RONALD REAGAN

> *Reagan's cutbacks of government aid reflect an abandonment of notions of social obligation, if the words "social" and "obligation" have any nuance at all.*
>
> MICHAEL KINSLEY

The debate over President Reagan's effort to shift some social programs from the federal government to the private sector has tended to dwell, thus far, on immediate, practical questions of cost and efficiency—as most American political debates do, in their early stages. Supporters of private sector initiatives tend to argue that such initiatives will be less expensive and more effective than federal government programs. Opponents claim that the private sector cannot possibly replace all the services once performed by the federal government and that, besides, the private sector is disorganized and duplicative. Seldom does the debate touch the moral and political questions that are truly at the heart of the controversy: Which approach to social problems is an appropriate expression of our social obligation to assist others? Which set of programs nourishes and sustains that sense of obligation in the context of the American political order?

The issue of social obligation is critical for supporters of both federal government programs and private sector initiatives. Without a well-developed sense of obligation, Americans will not long support an active federal government program of social services. Such a program may be sustained for a while by bureaucratic inertia or budgetary momentum. In a democracy, however, voters will sooner or later find a politician ruthless enough to "adjust" government services to the level that accords with the popular sense of what is owed to others. Furthermore, unless Americans possess a sense of obligation, they will not volunteer the time and effort or contribute the funds necessary to sustain social programs within the private sector, thereby causing the failure of private sector initiatives.

When President Reagan reaches the deepest level of the debate over private sector initiatives, as in the speech from which the opening quotation is taken,[1] he makes us aware of this fundamental question of obligation at the center of the debate—a question far more important, ultimately, than matters of cost and efficiency. The president argues, in those moments, that voluntarism is necessary to foster individual generosity and communal values; it is the means by which we will rebuild a sense of social obligation in America. President Reagan apparently believes that social obligation is taught within the small local community, where individuals encounter public responsibilities in an immediate, concrete fashion. Only by associating with his fellow citizens, according to this view—only by deliberating about, and cooperating to solve common problems—will the individual begin to develop a sense of public-spiritedness, a sense that he is part of, and obligated to, a community. This truth by itself, in the president's view, justifies the effort to return responsibility for some important social programs to the local, private, voluntary sector, where they may begin to restimulate the sense of citizenly obligation. The encouragement of private sector initiatives, according to President Reagan, is not merely a "halfhearted replacement for budget cuts," but it is, in fact, "right in its own regard" because it is "part of what we can proudly call the 'American personality.'"[2]

Michael Kinsley and other Reagan critics are, to put it mildly, skeptical of this argument. Far from seeking to nurture social obligation, as Kinsley argues in the opening quotation, President Reagan is in fact abandoning it altogether.[3] As for the "mobilization of private groups to deal with social ills," Reagan is said to be simply "salving people's consciences with a lot of malarky about private initiative."

Behind Kinsley's skepticism of voluntarism lies the venerable liberal view that most important social problems today are national in scope and that our social obligation to deal with them is satisfied only by national programs. As the *Washington Post* put it some time ago, "there are certain . . . disadvantaged groups within the society whose troubles have their source in an array of national, not local, circumstances, and for whose improved welfare there is, correspondingly, a national responsibility." The social obligation expressed in national programs does, to be sure, require for its sustenance a sense of community. In the liberal view, however, the truly important community is to be found at the national—not the local—level. Indeed, the idea of the "great national community" is the central moral support of modern liberalism and its powerful central government. As the *Post* editorial noted, there was, until President Reagan appeared, "an evolving national consensus that the federal government, acting on a new-found sense of national community and of community obligation, was the proper instrument to deal with [national] problems."[4] It is especially the task of the American president, the liberal argument concludes, to forge and preserve the sense of national community and thereby to sustain the essential moral underpinnings of the active liberal state.

The lines are sharply drawn, then, between President Reagan and modern liberalism on the question: How do we nurture social obligation in America? It may not be too much of a simplification to say that the president believes this will happen only within the local community, whereas liberals maintain that it must be done at the level of the national community. As we shall see, however, liberalism attempts to build kinds of community and obligation that are inappropriate to the American regime and that are, therefore, impossible to sustain. The private sector initiatives program, by contrast, seeks to return to the American tradition of local community, best described long ago by Alexis de Tocqueville. Voluntarism nurtures and expresses a sense of obligation that is appropriate to the American regime and that is, therefore, likely to endure.

Self-Interest and Social Obligation

When we begin to search for a form of social obligation appropriate to the American regime, we quickly discover that our regime, at least in its theoretical foundations, is not particularly hospitable to notions such as social obligation, duty, compassion, or charity. The Declaration of Independence, our national credo, speaks of individual rights —to life, liberty, and the pursuit of happiness—but does not mention individual duties or obligations. Our Constitution nowhere speaks of citizenly duties or obligations to society, as do so many other constitutions in the world today. Rather, the Constitution's purpose is to "secure [those] rights" delineated in the Declaration of Independence. Our deepest political commitment has always been to liberty—to the idea that the individual, most of the time, is the best judge of what is in his own interest. Conditions have changed over two hundred years, and government has grown, but individualism remains a core principle of our regime.

Those who wish that America were more willing to fulfill its social obligations to the poor, sick, uneducated, and jobless have often complained about our national individualism—or, as it is then called, our selfishness. A review of welfare and values in America several years ago lamented that the American welfare system has "had to win its way in a struggle against American individualism" and has had to "confront the presumption in favor of 'taking care of one's own.' "[5] In 1980 President Carter's National Advisory Council on Economic Opportunity suggested that America's individualism had taken the form of a "way of life that worships wealth and power." This had, apparently, kept us from developing "an ethic of fairness and compassion in America."[6]

If advocates of social reform have been quick to perceive the harsh, ungenerous aspects of American individualism, however, they have been slower to acknowledge the tremendous benefits we have reaped from that tradition. In the political sphere, our individualism has assumed the form of a staunch defense of the rights of individuals —including the rights of the "poor, sick, uneducated and jobless," the first victims of regimes lacking a tradition of individualism. In the economic sphere, individualism has meant the unleashing of the productive and acquisitive energies of millions of people, creating in America a prosperity beyond the wildest fantasies of earlier men. The material precondition of any program of assistance (especially a generous program) to the poor, sick, uneducated, and jobless is precisely that prosperity—the product of selfish, ungenerous American individualism.

We may thank the Founding Fathers, of course, for erecting on the lowly foundation of individual self-interest a great regime of liberty and prosperity. In the Founders' view, self-interested individualism was an ineradicable part of human nature. It would do no good, they believed, to struggle against self-interest in the name of lofty virtues, as had earlier regimes. It was wiser to accept human nature as it was, to accept self-interest and try to nudge it into constructive channels like commerce, and thereby to wrest what decencies could be had from an often indecent human nature.[8]

One can prize the liberty and prosperity bequeathed to us by the Founders without being complacent about some of the uglier, and perhaps even dangerous, aspects of American self-interest. A regime grounded in self-interest does tend to be less generous or compassionate (at least in its official pronouncements) than, say, a Christian or socialist commonwealth founded on selfless ideals such as charity, benevolence, or universal brotherhood. Thoughtful students of American life have often observed that self-interest may make Americans petty, narrow-minded, and mean-spirited. On occasion, America has, of course, elevated mean-spirited self-interest to a kind of virtue. From time to time Americans have renounced the citizenly duty of assisting the less fortunate because poverty is viewed as a just result of the natural struggle for survival.

It would be a gross underestimation of the American people, however, to suggest that self-interest or its exaggerated form, Social Darwinism, is the sum of our political tradition. From the nation's beginning, Americans have held that self-interest is the necessary but by no means sufficient condition for a decent republic. At a minimum, it has always been understood that in times of grave emergency Americans must put aside self-interest and rush to the defense of the nation. There are also other times when self-interest must give way to the assistance of those in need. Americans have always realized that they have citizenly duties as well as individual rights.

The sense of citizenly duty, however, does not have the same sturdy roots in human nature as does self-interest. A sense of obligation to others does not come to us as easily as concern with self. Self-interest will flourish if we simply stand out of the way; duty and obligation, on the other hand, must be assiduously cultivated. Indeed, one of the great, enduring issues of American politics—the Founders had to struggle with it, as do present-day advocates of social reform—has been: How do we nurture and preserve some sense of citizenly duty, public-spiritedness, or social obligation within the American regime of self-interest? How in the name of community may we soften the harsh edge of American self-interest? We can now begin to understand the importance of the question at the heart of the debate over private sector initiatives, for it is the same question that has animated so much of our politics and our thinking about politics: How do we nurture a form of social obligation that is appropriate to America?

Liberalism, Self-Interest, and Community

The problem of taming self-interest in the name of community or citizenly obligation is at the center of modern liberalism. Liberalism today stands for an extensive federal social service program on behalf of the poor and helpless and supported by heavy taxation. American individualism, however, has always posed a great problem for this program. Self-interest tells the citizen that the suffering of the poor, usually "out of sight," in remote parts of the country, is none of his concern. The taxes and the programs they finance, therefore, come to be resented and possibly repealed.

Liberalism understands this, however, and so undertakes to replace self-interested individualism with a sense of obligation felt by each citizen toward every other. The citizen must come to feel that the suffering of the poor in every part of the country, however remote, is indeed his concern. This kind of obligation comes only when the citizen belongs to a genuine community—when he feels a oneness with his fellow citizens, including the poor and helpless. Ultimately, then, the essential moral underpinning for liberalism's extensive federal social service program is the "great national community"—the citizen's sense of belonging to one nation, and the feeling of obligation to help fellow citizens by means of national programs. To repeat the *Washington Post*'s summary of this notion: the doctrine that the federal government is the proper instrument for dealing with social problems rests on a "sense of national community and of community obligation."

The catalyst of the national community, in the liberal view, is the president—the galvanizing, unifying voice of all the American people. The presidency, as Franklin D. Roosevelt noted, is "not merely an administrative office. That's the least of it. It's predominately a place of moral leadership."[9] The progressive president, according to Michael Walzer, will use his office to "invoke the moral vision of a society whose citizens are committed to one another and willing to share the costs of commitment."[10] In short, the president will draw the American people together by using his office as a "bully pulpit" to preach selfless devotion to the national good.

The great prophet of this liberal vision for America was Herbert Croly. His book *The Promise of American Life*, published in 1909, is widely regarded as the theoretical underpinning for the strain of American liberalism running from Theodore Roosevelt's New Nationalism through Franklin D. Roosevelt's New Deal. The book is best remembered, perhaps, for its advocacy of a centralized, national government sufficiently powerful to deal with the new national problems created by the American industrial expansion of the nineteenth century.

The problem posed for American democracy by that expansion, according to Croly, was the gross inequality of wealth and power it had produced—an inequality that threatened to destroy the unity of the American nation. America had allowed the inequalities to develop without government intervention, he noted, because of its simple-minded devotion to the idea of individual rights, and the mistaken belief that public benefits followed from the unleashing of self-interest. "The existing concentration of wealth and financial power in the hands of a few irresponsible individuals is the inevitable outcome of the chaotic individualism of our political and economic organization, while at the same time it is inimical to democracy because it tends to erect political abuses and social inequalities into a system." American democratic unity could be restored, Croly believed, only if a powerful central government moved to control the industrial concentrations and reduce the inequalities—only if the "American state will [make] itself responsible for a morally and socially desirable distribution of wealth."[11]

Croly's powerful central government was but the instrument of a far larger project: the creation of a true national community, within which Americans would transcend self-interest altogether and bind themselves to the purposes of the nation. "The Promise of American Life is to be fulfilled—not merely by a maximum of economic freedom, but by a certain measure of discipline; not merely . . . by the satisfaction of individual desires, but by a large measure of individual subordination and self-denial." Americans must be brought to understand the "necessity of subordinating the satisfaction of individual desires to the fulfillment of a national purpose."[12] A people is "sincerely seeking the fulfillment of its national Promise" only if "individuals of all kinds will find their most edifying individual opportunities in serving their country."[13]

Croly knew that his program had to overcome some of the most cherished American political traditions, foremost among them the belief in individualism. A truly unified, coherent national community, however, could be achieved in no other way. American self-interested individualism "does not bind, heal, and unify public opinion," rather it is "confusing, distracting, and at its worst, disintegrating." It disturbs the "community of feeling," the "national consistency," the "solidarity," that the national community requires.[14] The new American democracy must transcend self-interest and be founded "essentially upon disinterested human action." Croly even hoped that Americans would eventually work, not for profit or money, but "from disinterested motives" and out of sheer love of excellence. Croly fully appreciated that, to overcome self-interest on behalf of "disinterested human action," human nature itself would have to be changed and perfected. Thus, "democracy must stand or fall on a platform of human perfectibility." It "cannot be disentangled from an aspiration toward perfectibility."[15]

The sense of obligation to be generated within Croly's national community was obviously an exalted one. For Croly, a "democratic scheme of moral values reaches its consummate expression in the religion of human brotherhood," and that "religion" "can be realized only through the loving-kindness which individuals feel toward . . . their fellow countrymen."[16] Within Croly's national community, social obligation would take the form of "loving-kindness" felt by each American for every other American.

Franklin D. Roosevelt was the first American president to preach Croly's doctrine of national community from the "bully pulpit" of the executive office. Roosevelt shared with Croly a deep suspicion of American self-interested individualism. In fact, he attributed the crisis of the Great Depression in large part to the narrow self-interestedness of American industrialists, who "know only the rules of a generation of self-seekers" and are caught up in the "mad chase of evanescent profits."[17] The depression had shown that "heedless self-interest" was "bad economics" as well as "bad morals."[18] Americans, therefore, needed to transcend self-interest, to see to it that "selfish purpose of personal gain, at our neighbor's loss, less strongly asserts itself."[19]

Roosevelt hoped to bring about this fundamental change in American morality with the doctrine that all Americans must be disciplined citizens of a great national community. Self-interest, he argued, must give way to national unity. In his first inaugural address, Roosevelt described the national community largely in military metaphors. He pointed out that "we have never realized before our interdependence on each other; that we cannot merely take but must give as well." Having realized these truths, however, Americans were now prepared to "move as a trained and loyal army willing to sacrifice for the good of a common discipline." We were "ready and willing to submit our lives and property to such discipline" and to pledge "that our large purposes will bind upon us all as a sacred obligation with a unity of duty hitherto evoked only in time of armed strife." Roosevelt was prepared to be the catalyst of this new sense of national oneness and to "assume unhesitatingly the leadership of this great army of our people dedicated to a disciplined attack upon our common problems."[20]

On other occasions, Roosevelt described the national community in terms of the principles of local community and neighborliness transferred to the national level: "We have been extending to our national life the old principle of the local community, the principle that no individual man, woman, or child has a right to do things that hurt his neighbors." Roosevelt added that "the many are the neighbors. In a national sense, the many, the neighbors, are the people of the United States as a whole. . . . We must think of them as a whole and not just by sections."[21]

The vision of the great national community, comprising citizens with a sense of neighborly obligations, became the essential moral underpinning of the New Deal. Roosevelt understood that only the moral doctrine of national oneness and neighborliness was adequate to sustain the vast expansion of national government programs undertaken by his administration. Citizens would continue to support national programs only if they possessed a truly national sense of obligation. And this idea of national community or national neighborly obligation remained the moral underpinning of strong national government programs for the next fifty years. The liberal vision of America and the national government that would make it a reality rested squarely on a citizenry always prepared, to paraphrase President Kennedy, to ask not what their country could do for them, but what they could do for their country.

The Problem of the National Community

The solid truth in liberalism's vision of national community is that there are, of course, times when we must and do pull together as one nation—when we must transcend self-interest, thinking first of the national good and the good of all our "neighbors." Such times were the Great Depression, the Civil War, and the two world wars. In moments of great crisis the gravity and proximity of national danger seem to transform the American people, to draw from them truly noble sacrifices. At such times it appears that national community *is* possible, that Americans *can* overcome their individualism, that human nature itself *can* be perfected.

Such self-transcendent, nation-forging moments are truly extraordinary, however, requiring extraordinary circumstances (such as war), which are not often desirable, and extraordinary leaders (such as Lincoln and Roosevelt), who are not often at hand. Indeed, this is the central dilemma confronting modern liberalism: it seeks to make permanent and ordinary a kind and degree of community possible only in transitory and extraordinary circumstances. It attempts to solve this dilemma by building a powerful, dynamic presidency (a sort of institutionalized Roosevelt), and by characterizing its programs as battles, campaigns, crusades, and wars. (One of the great humanitarian programs of our time was called a "war"—on poverty.) Liberal presidents must attempt rhetorically to re-create and perpetuate the extraordinary circumstances upon which the great national community depends. Each liberal president must cast about for a "moral equivalent of war."

This liberal project ultimately founders, however, because Americans cannot perpetually be kept on war footing—especially when the war being fought is but a moral stand-in for the real thing. American self-interestedness and individualism are too powerful, too rooted in our political traditions and institutions, to permit more than fleeting moments of self-transcendence and national neighborliness. Americans cannot forever be persuaded that their social obligation to fight poverty is of the same status as their social obligation to fight the nation's foreign enemies. The liberal vision runs against the fact that human nature cannot be changed or perfected, as the Founders had understood. Liberalism demands a form of social obligation that is, ultimately, inappropriate to the American regime of self-interest.

Thus it is that liberalism's great national community begins to disintegrate, and self-interest begins to reassert itself. Americans turn away from national neighborliness and social obligation, and as they do so, a gap grows between the citizen and his government. Once the moral underpinnings of the national community are shaken, the programs undertaken on its behalf lose legitimacy—they begin to seem oppressive, wasteful, irrelevant, and ultimately expendable.

Lest this seem an excessively harsh or pessimistic assessment of the prospects for national community, it should be recalled that President Carter was the preeminent spokesman for this point of view. It was, indeed, the centerpiece of his famous "malaise" speech of July 1979. The problem facing America, according to Carter in that speech, was far more than an energy problem—it was in fact the breakdown of the national community, a "loss of a unity of purpose for our Nation." In the wake of this loss, there had been a great resurgence of self-interest and petty materialism: "Too many of us tend to worship self-indulgence and consumption." Americans had become "too concerned with owning things and consuming things" and with "piling up material goods." America's turn inward was accompanied by "growing disrespect for government." Government seemed remote and irrelevant—"two-thirds of our own people do not even vote," and the federal government appeared "isolated from the mainstream of our Nation's life." President Carter's speech was, in effect, an admission that the liberal vision of national community was breaking down in America.[22]

President Carter, unhappily, had nothing to offer to remedy the situation beyond the now-tired device of a "moral equivalent of war." Energy, Carter argued, "will be the immediate test of our ability to unite this Nation"; "on the battlefield of energy we can win for our nation a new confidence." "We are the generation," he proclaimed, "that will win the war on the energy problem and in that process rebuild the unity and confidence of America." The profound repudiation of the Carter administration in 1980—and the election of the first administration in fifty years that spoke of local, not national, community—indicated that America was no longer prepared to transcend self-interest for the purpose of waging yet another moral equivalent of war.

President Carter was wise to be concerned about the disintegration of the sense of community and the resurgence of self-interest, even if his solution to the problem was unimaginative and ultimately unacceptable. Carter properly feared that national selfishness, malaise, and alienation would lead to abandonment of community and social obligation altogether—that we would choose the "path . . . to fragmentation and self-interest" rather than the "path of common purpose."

As our history demonstrates, there are times when Americans turn away from social obligation, when our individualism assumes a mean-spirited and destructive form. This danger is always with us and was obviously with us in the late 1970s. The tax revolts, for example, that swept America then seemed to be only the most obvious symptoms of such a rejection of community responsibility, on behalf of a narrow self-interestedness. Widespread, systematic, morally acceptable evasion of income taxes was another symptom. If Carter identified a real problem, however, what is the solution? As liberalism's national community erodes, how are we to avoid slipping into mean-spirited individualism? How can we begin to rebuild the sense of obligation in America?

Local Community and Social Obligation

These concerns lead us to a consideration of President Reagan's private sector initiatives program. President Reagan denies that he is a proponent of mean-spirited individualism, in spite of the uniform liberal opinion that he is, in Michael Walzer's words, "the chief spokesman for the ideology of selfishness, the American version of predatory politics."[23] In his speeches the president has agreed with liberals that we have a social obligation to the poor and helpless, and he has agreed that this obligation may be cultivated only within a true community, where citizens sense their oneness with other citizens. He denies, however, that it is possible to build this sense of community

43

or oneness on a national scale. In his view, it may be cultivated only within the small, local community. "It is . . . activity on a small, human scale that creates the fabric of community. . . . The human scale nurtures standards of right behavior, a prevailing ethic of what is right and wrong."[24]

Returning responsibility for some social programs to the local level—through private sector initiatives and the new federalism—will reinvigorate a true sense of community, according to Reagan, and thus "foster [a] spirit of individual generosity and our sense of communal values."[25] Social obligation may be restored, but only quietly, at the local level—not through a grand moral equivalent of war.

The Reagan position sounds radical to us, accustomed as we have become over the past fifty years to the notion that the only legitimate expression of social obligation is a national program undertaken on behalf of the national community. The private sector initiatives program is, however, a reflection of a longstanding American tradition of local community and voluntary activity that was, in fact, the undisputed basis for social welfare in this country prior to the New Deal. We cannot understand that tradition, or its resurrection in Reagan's program, until we have considered the unsurpassed theoretical treatment of it to be found in Alexis de Tocqueville's *Democracy in America*.

Central to Tocqueville's famous volume written in the 1830s is the same concern that lies at the heart of modern liberalism, and at the heart of the private sector initiatives debate: How do we cultivate a sense of obligation in naturally self-interested individuals? Tocqueville asked this question because he believed that democracy would soon sweep the world, and with democracy would come individualism. Individualism, for Tocqueville, presented all the dangers ascribed to it subsequently by modern liberalism. It would turn men into narrow-minded, petty, materialistic atoms of self-interest. It "disposed each citizen to isolate himself from the mass of his fellows and withdraw into the circle of family and friends." In individualistic democracies "each man is forever thrown back on himself alone, and there is the danger that he may be shut up in the solitude of his own heart."[26]

If there was hope for mankind in this democratic, individualistic age, according to Tocqueville, it could be found in America. Not only was America the first thoroughgoing democracy, but it was also, more importantly, a *decent* democracy, precisely because it had found ways to counteract the atomizing, isolating effects of individualism. America had discovered how to turn self-seeking individuals into public-spirited citizens.

Tocqueville found that America had countered the dangers of individualism by means of a series of devices—foremost among them administrative decentralization and voluntary association—that had in common a single principle. These devices all force the individual to assume responsibility for a small portion of the public business— business that affects his immediate self-interest and is therefore important to him, but that nonetheless compels him to interact with others and thus gradually to see beyond his immediate self-interest to the common good. These devices gently draw the individual out of the "solitude of his own heart" and thereby cultivate a citizen who bears some sense of public-spiritedness or social obligation.

Administrative decentralization is one of the most important tools for forging a responsible citizenry. Always a powerful tradition in America, local government had its roots in the New England town meeting. Even after the Union had been formed, however, Tocqueville notes, "the lawgivers of America did not suppose that a general representation of the whole nation would suffice" to ward off the dangerous tendencies of individualism. "They thought it also right to give each part of the land its own political life so that there should be an infinite number of occasions for the citizens to act together and so that every day they should feel that they depended on one another."[27] Citizens acting together and depending on one another thus develop a sense of obligation and come to form a genuine community.

Citizenly obligation can grow, however, only when it is immediately, tangibly clear to the individual that public matters affect his personal well-being. According to Tocqueville, social obligation cannot be cultivated by those devices that subsequently were to be so important to liberalism, such as high-flown appeals to national unity, patriotism, or morality—"it is difficult to force a man out of himself and get him to take an interest in the affairs of the whole state, for he has little understanding of the way in which the fate of the state can influence his own lot." In the regime of self-interest, public involvement and therefore social obligation are achieved only when the citizen experiences, in a concrete way, the connection between private interest and public affairs: "If it is a question of taking a road past his property, he sees at once that this small public matter has a bearing on his greatest private interests, and there is no need to point out to him the close connection between his private profit and the general interest."[28]

Once the individual enters the public realm to deal with the question of the "road past his property," he is forced to act together with others, and "as soon as common affairs are treated in common, each man notices that he is not as independent of his fellows as he used to suppose and that to get their help he must often offer his aid to them."[29] Although he entered the public realm out of self-interest, gradually he is habituated into thinking of the good of others; he acquires a sense of obligation. "At first it is of necessity that men attend to the public interest, afterward by choice. What had been calculation becomes instinct. By dint of working for the good of his fellow citizens, he in the end acquires a habit and taste for serving them."[30]

Private, voluntary associations operate in much the same way as administrative decentralization to produce a sense of citizenly obligation in the democratic individual. Americans, Tocqueville maintains, are instinctively joiners: "Americans of all ages, all stations in life, and all types of dispositions are forever forming associations."[31] Associations are formed to meet immediate, concrete problems that have a tangible bearing on individual self-interest. "If some obstacle blocks the public road halting the circulation of traffic, the neighbors at once form a deliberative body; this improvised assembly produces an executive authority which remedies the trouble. . . ."[32] As citizens associate, "pursuing in common the objects of common desire," they become accustomed to considering the interests of others as well as their own self-interest. "Feelings and ideas are renewed, the heart enlarged, and the understanding developed . . . by the reciprocal action of men one upon another" in associations.[33]

Voluntary associations and administrative decentralization are, then, democratic devices for taming the great problem of democracy —individualism. As Marvin Zetterbaum has noted, they are designed to accomplish "nothing less than the transformation of the atoms of democratic society into citizens, into men whose first thought is not of their private interest, but of the common good."[34]

It must be understood, however, that these devices do not raise men far above self-interest. The kind of morality they generate is best described as "self-interest properly understood"—the principle, according to Tocqueville, by which Americans enjoy explaining almost "every act of their lives." Americans take pleasure in pointing out "how an enlightened self-love continually leads them to help one another and disposes them freely to give part of their time and wealth for the good of the state." This is not an exalted morality—certainly not the kind of self-effacing morality so important to modern liberalism. It does not ask men to transcend self-interest altogether, to "forget oneself . . . and do good without self-interest."[35] Nonetheless, Tocqueville emphasized, this is the only kind of obligation possible in the new age of self-interested individualism. Like the Founders, Tocqueville believed that self-interest is an ineradicable part of human nature. Attempting to eliminate it so as to "perfect" human nature, as Croly hoped to do, would be foolish. Tocqueville agreed with the Founders that it was better to accept self-interest and to channel it into modest but attainable decencies, rather than to try to transcend it in the name of noble but unattainable virtues.

Tocqueville's gentle, realistic strategy for moderating self-interest on behalf of community and citizenly obligation is at the heart of today's private sector initiatives program. President Reagan's effort to revitalize local government and voluntary associations is nothing less than an attempt to resuscitate Tocqueville's citizen-forging devices in the context of the twentieth century. The president believes that, by returning some social programs to the local, voluntary sector, citizens will once again be confronted immediately and concretely with public responsibility. Individuals who volunteer and associate with one another, working to solve "common problems in common," will come to feel a sense of obligation to others. Within the small local community, citizens will once again be molded from self-interested individuals.

The private sector initiatives program, then, is one answer to the question raised by President Carter in his "malaise" speech: How are we to avoid the "path . . . to fragmentation and self-interest" and reinvigorate the sense of community and obligation in modern America? Whether the program will be a sufficient answer is, of course, not known, but there are reasons for encouragement. The devices that Tocqueville described and that Reagan would resurrect do not demand more than the American people can provide by way of obligation. These devices do not attempt to transcend self-interest altogether, in the name of community; rather, they attempt to tame and moderate self-interest and turn it to public use. They do not attempt to alter and perfect human nature; rather, they accept it as it is. The form of obligation thus nurtured is not, to be sure, the exalted, selfless kind that liberals prefer. It is modest—but it is enduring. It "does not inspire great sacrifices, but every day prompts some small ones."

Above all, however, Tocquevillian social obligation does not require extraordinary circumstances like war or rhetorical substitutes therefor. It in fact rests on the ordinary, everyday circumstances of local administration and citizenly participation therein. In short, we have some hope that private sector initiatives will begin to rebuild the sense of community in America, because the democratic devices described by Tocqueville seek to nurture a form of public-spiritedness or social obligation that is appropriate to the American regime. Liberalism's devices do not.

Conclusion

None of this is meant to suggest that we should abandon all, most, or even many social service programs at the federal level. Modern industrial civilization, of course, requires a far more powerful national government than the one Tocqueville saw in the America of the 1830s. The federal government, necessarily, is responsible for a much wider range of social services today. The extensive array of social services that seems to be demanded by modern circumstances, however, will not be provided by the American political system unless the American taxpayer/voter feels a sense of obligation to provide it. The argument that contemporary social problems are so widespread and complex as to demand national solutions may be absolutely, technically sound. That argument, however, will not coax from the electorate the dollars necessary to finance such solutions should the electorate decide, in a spasm of self-interest, that it owes little or nothing to the poor and helpless.

Liberalism's vision of the great national community, with its moral equivalents of war, no longer seems able to block those spasms of self-interest and to cultivate a sense of obligation in the electorate —as the experience of the Carter administration demonstrated. The self-interested character of the American voter must now be moderated by other means, and private sector initiative offers one such possibility.

Liberalism condemns this program, however, as an abandonment —not a cultivation—of social obligation. It steadfastly clings to the idea that national programs alone are an adequate expression of that obligation. By refusing to return any social programs to state, local, and voluntary agencies, however, we would stymie the ability of these critical "schools of citizenship" to nurture public-spiritedness. Social obligation would not thereby be saved, it would continue to erode. And Americans would, ultimately, no longer be willing to support *any* program of social services—least of all an extensive federal program. By continuing to demand too much of the American people, liberalism would wind up with nothing at all.

Private sector initiatives—far from being a mean-spirited rejection of social obligation—may in fact be the only way to rebuild that obligation in the wake of the collapse of liberalism's national community. By transferring some programs to the local, voluntary level, we may begin to reconstruct the sense of obligation ultimately required to support those programs we would leave at the federal level. Ironically, private sector initiatives may be the best way to save what is sound and necessary in modern liberalism.

Notes

[1] "International Association of Chiefs of Police: Remarks," September 28, 1981, *Weekly Compilation of Presidential Documents*, vol. 17, p. 1045.

[2] "National Alliance of Business: Remarks," October 9, 1981, *Weekly Compilation of Presidential Documents*, vol. 17, p. 1081.

[3] Michael Kinsley, "Waiting for Lenny," *Harper's*, March 1982.

[4] *Washington Post*, January 28, 1982.

[5] William Lee Miller, *Welfare and Values in America: A Review of Attitudes* (Durham, N.C.: The Institute of Policy Sciences and Public Affairs, Duke University, 1977), p. 45.

[6] Quoted in James T. Patterson, *America's Struggle Against Poverty: 1900–1980* (Cambridge, Mass.: Harvard University Press, 1981), p. 204.

[7] Kinsley, "Waiting for Lenny."

[8] The best account of the Founders' efforts to turn self-interest into constructive channels is to be found in the works of Martin Diamond. See especially "Ethics and Politics: The American Way," in *The Moral Foundations of the American Republic*, ed. Robert H. Horwitz (Charlottesville: University Press of Virginia, 1979).

[9] As quoted in Joseph P. Lash, "The Roosevelt 'Rendezvous with Destiny'," Remarks at the ADA/FDR Centennial Conference, March 5, 1982.

[10] Michael Walzer, "The Agenda After Reagan: The Community," *The New Republic*, March 31, 1982, p. 14.

[11] Herbert Croly, *The Promise of American Life* (Cambridge, Mass.: Harvard University Press, 1965), p. 23.

[12] Ibid., p. 22.

[13] Ibid., p. 406.

[14] Ibid., p. 185.

[15] Ibid., pp. 409–54.

[16] Ibid., p. 453.

[17] Samuel Rosenman, ed., *The Public Papers and Addresses of Franklin D. Roosevelt*, vol. 2 (New York: Random House, 1938), p. 12.

[18] Ibid., vol. 6, p. 3.

[19] Ibid., vol. 4, p. 449.

[20] Ibid., vol. 2, p. 14.

[21] Ibid., pp. 340–42.

[22] "Energy and National Goals," *Public Papers of the Presidents of the United States: Jimmy Carter (1979)*, 2 vols. (Washington, D.C.: U.S. Government Printing Office, 1980), II, pp. 1235–41.

[23] Walzer, "The Agenda After Reagan: The Community," p. 12.

24 Quoted in John McLaughry, "Where Is the Mob? I Am Its Leader," *Vital Speeches of the Day*, vol. 48, no. 2, p. 38.

25 Cf. note 1.

26 Alexis de Tocqueville, *Democracy in America*, ed. J. P. Mayer (Garden City, N.Y.: Doubleday, 1969), pp. 506–8.

27 Ibid., p. 511.

28 Ibid.

29 Ibid., p. 510.

30 Ibid., p. 512.

31 Ibid., p. 513.

32 Ibid., p. 191.

33 Ibid., p. 515.

34 Marvin Zetterbaum, *Tocqueville and the Problem of Democracy* (Stanford, Calif.: Stanford University Press, 1967), p. 89.

35 Tocqueville, *Democracy in America*, pp. 525–28.

PART TWO

The Role of Business, Labor, and Neighborhood Groups

Business Initiatives
in the Private Sector

V. Ruth McKinnon, Patricia W. Samors, and Sean Sullivan

Introduction

One way to illustrate both the breadth and the depth of business
involvement in social problem solving is to highlight a number of
interesting, varied examples of business initiatives in this area. Instead
of developing an exhaustive list of business initiatives, however—a
task that could fill volumes—this chapter contains short case histories
of ten such experiments and presents detailed case studies of how
two companies developed their particular programs.

It is worth reemphasizing a point stressed in the first chapter in
part 1—that an analysis of attempts by business to solve social problems should not be misconstrued as a campaign to exhort firms to
meet guidelines for charitable contributions. We applaud corporate
financial contributions to nonprofit organizations, but we reject arbitrary guidelines or publicly announced targets that prescribe a certain
percentage of profits for such purposes.

Rather, we believe that businesses can help and are helping those
in need in a variety of ways. Some contribute primarily by donating
a portion of pretax earnings. Others make smaller financial contributions, but lend their talent and expertise to nonprofit groups
in the local communities where they conduct business. These actions,
of course, cost a company money in the same sense that a donation
costs money. By "lending" the services of a technician, instructor,
or manager, for example, a company forgoes the opportunity to use
that person's skills directly in its regular business operations. We
found these kinds of involvement illustrated again and again, as seen
in the case studies that follow.

In the two detailed case studies especially, we try to show the
evolution of business initiatives such as creating job opportunities

for handicapped or disadvantaged workers or using a company's retired work force in a variety of community agencies. At the same time, we mention some problems confronting such efforts and cite the basic underlying principles or criteria these companies use as they initiate such programs. We take care not to engage in unwarranted generalizations, but we try to go beyond a simple description of company activities to highlight the themes running through a single company's programs.

Our purpose is not to stress one kind of activity or concern over another, but rather to provide an array of examples that, taken together, suggest *some* of the many kinds of efforts being made by business firms. We hope that the spectrum of business activities described here will be useful to others who would help address social problems through private initiative.

Amalgamated Clothing Workers of America

Patricia W. Samors

In the late 1960s, there were growing complaints from the men's clothing manufacturers in the Maryland area about employee absenteeism. Members of the Amalgamated Clothing Workers of America (ACWA) said that the lack of adequate day care for workers' children was causing the problem. The Baltimore regional joint board of the ACWA, which serves Maryland, Virginia, Delaware, the District of Columbia, and the southern tip of Pennsylvania, decided to seek a solution.

Members of the union and several manufacturers had, at various times, toured the garment centers of Europe to observe the industry. In Italy, in particular, they noted that the factories themselves provided child-care facilities for their employees' children. Sam Nocella, manager of the Baltimore board, proposed a similar idea to the manufacturers in his five-state area—a solution agreed to by seventy of the area employers.

In 1966 the Amalgamated Clothing Workers of America, together with several men's clothing manufacturers, initiated the first union-management day-care service program in the United States. Thus, under Nocella's leadership, a day-care program, to be funded from the union's Health and Welfare Fund, was created for children two to six years of age. Participating employers agreed to contribute 1 percent of their gross hourly payrolls to the fund to establish and maintain the child-care program, in addition to the 1 percent that manufacturers were already paying to cover other employee health-related services. This fund is administered by a board of trustees, which includes five union officials and five manufacturing representatives.

In September 1968 the first center was opened in Verona, Virginia. Five other centers were opened over the next ten years, costing a total of $5 million. The actual operating costs for each child are approximately $85 per week. Union parents pay $15 per week for each child, and community children are charged $45. The difference is covered by the union's Health and Welfare Fund, whose total contributions for operating expenses were approximately $14.4 million in 1981.

Each of the centers is staffed with specialists in teaching, health care, and dietary planning and preparation. The two teachers in each classroom provide a developmental educational program to foster the physical, mental, emotional, and social progress of each child. Medical care is also an integral part of the day-care program. The children receive a preenrollment physical examination and periodic immunizations that fulfill state requirements. Each child also receives a daily health check by the center's full-time nurse.

There are many advantages to this program. A working mother is able to obtain care for her child at a fraction of the cost of care available elsewhere. In addition, the manufacturers gain a more stable and dependable work force. Also, because the joint union-management program is unique to the Baltimore board of the ACWA, the participating employers find it easier to recruit women employees, who make up the majority of the work force.

Unfortunately, the program has met with severe obstacles in the past few years. Since 1978, three of the six centers have been closed and enrollment at the remaining centers is only 50 percent of capacity. The drop in enrollment and the closing of the centers are the results of several factors: (1) the average size of families has decreased; (2) there is little turnover of the union members, and as the work force ages, there are fewer employees of childbearing age; and (3) the textile industry itself has been weakened by foreign competition and shifts in demand. One of the day-care centers was closed because the manufacturers it served went out of business. The factories using the other two centers have not closed, but the number of employees has declined to such a degree that child care is no longer feasible.

Despite the obstacles faced by the ACWA, the Baltimore board still receives numerous inquiries from colleges, businesses, and non-profit organizations about the child-care program. The board feels that even though it is experiencing some difficulties at the present time, the program has been successful in several ways. It has provided union members with a badly needed service, and it has set an example that may be imitated by others.

Campbell Bosworth Machinery Company

V. Ruth McKinnon

The Campbell Bosworth Machinery Company is a small leather-goods machinery manufacturing company located in New York City. In response to a request by the Queens Chamber of Commerce, Campbell Bosworth joined with the Vocational Foundation, Inc. (VFI), in 1981 to develop an on-the-job training program for hard-to-employ youths.

Barry Schiller, a partner in the small forty-five-employee firm, decided that, instead of designing a more traditional in-depth skills training program, he would create a short-term program to teach young people the skills necessary to operate equipment used in the leather-goods industry. Schiller felt that in this way young people could enter the job market as operator trainees having already learned through "hands-on" experience from employees of the industry itself.

Schiller initially set up a four-week four-session program, enlisting the help of several mechanics who agreed to volunteer several hours a week on a rotating basis to train groups of three or four trainees at the factory location. The VFI, meanwhile, screened potential trainees—many of them high school dropouts—through counseling and aptitude testing. (The VFI receives referrals from approximately 300 agencies city-wide.) Many trainees came to the VFI having little or no prior job experience and few skills. Schiller's only request was that the VFI send him motivated trainees with manual dexterity.

Commitment, attentiveness, competence, and, of course, consistent attendance were stressed from the very beginning. Trainees were assured job placement, particularly if they met these criteria. If no job was available at the time of graduation, they would be given temporary work assignments to continue developing their skills until a permanent position became available.

In a cooperative effort, two other companies, also manufacturers of leather-goods machinery, made their equipment available to Campbell Bosworth for use during the training sessions. This gave trainees the opportunity to broaden their knowledge of the industry by learning about other manufacturers' machinery.

The first training program ended in October 1981, with five women and four men graduates, all high school dropouts. Graduation exercises were held at the Campbell Bosworth plant site, and the graduates were awarded a certificate for successfully completing training, and a pair of scissors, symbolizing their entrance into the leather-working machinery trade. Seven of the trainees were hired immediately. One returned to school. Another remained at Campbell Bosworth for additional specialized training before taking a job with another company.

Since completion of that first training program, eighteen trainees have joined the ranks of Campbell Bosworth graduates. It is hoped that in the near future other small firms will establish similar training programs at their own facilities. Both Schiller and the VFI are working toward this end.

Schiller believes there are several reasons for the success and continuation of the program. First, he believes that the role played by the VFI is vital and necessary. By the time a trainee arrives at Campbell Bosworth to begin training, the individual has already been thoroughly screened, tested, and informed as to the various facets of the program. Thus Campbell Bosworth personnel are free to concentrate on the logistics of the program, and on the trainees themselves once they become involved in the program. In addition, the fact that students are not paid for their time and work during training tends to draw more highly motivated and committed students into the program.

It should be noted that Campbell Bosworth has not designated any funds for the program. Employees volunteer their own time, plant machinery is used for training, and students receive no stipend.

By establishing such a program the company hoped that other equipment manufacturers would recognize the benefits of having their own employees train youth. In a sense, Campbell Bosworth is preparing young people to perpetuate the craft and skills of a particular industry—all without great effort and with payoffs that can benefit trainers and trainees alike.

At this writing, a second training program has been completed, and Schiller is hopeful that he can launch a third one. Because of economic conditions, however, placement of graduates from the previous session has been slow, and Schiller's first commitment is to these newly graduated trainees.

Control Data Corporation (City Venture Corporation)

V. Ruth McKinnon

Control Data Corporation (CDC), a computer-manufacturing company located in Minneapolis, Minnesota, is considered an innovator and leader in the area of corporate social responsibility. Under the guiding hand of its founder, chairman, and chief executive officer, William Norris, the company has been addressing major societal needs as profitable business opportunities. Control Data applies its technical, financial, and human resources, as well as its professional services, to meeting societal needs that are selected on the basis of a number of criteria. They include (1) the importance of the problem to society; (2) Control Data's ability to address the problem; and (3) the likelihood that the methods developed will result in a business opportunity. The first major effort to address societal needs was that of locating plants in depressed urban areas.

In 1968, Control Data built the Northside Manufacturing Plant in a depressed area of Minneapolis. The plant manufactures peripheral controllers for CDC. Despite the usual start-up setbacks and problems, the plant now employs over 250 individuals, many of whom live in the neighborhood. The company was committed to making the plant a success in more than meeting its own need for the manufactured goods produced by the plant. In the beginning, for example, counselors from Control Data made themselves available to work with employees in a variety of areas of need. Assistance was provided on financial, legal, and personal problems. Realizing the relationship between the lack of adequate day care and employee tardiness and absenteeism, Control Data used the facilities of a local church to set up the Northside Child Development Center, which now enrolls many of the plant employees' children as well as those of the neighborhood.

Control Data's commitment to inner-city facilities led the company to establish the Selby Bindery on the site of an old bowling alley in a poverty-ridden area of nearby St. Paul. Upon opening, the plant introduced "flex time," whereby employees work a twenty-five hour workweek—a system more convenient for the area's residents. Mothers of school-aged children make up the majority of the morning-shift workers, and high school students make up the rest of the work force during afterschool hours.

Another service Control Data provides for its employees is the Employee Advisory Resource (EAR) twenty-four-hour "hotline" service to help employees solve personal and work-related problems.

If necessary, cases are referred to outside sources for help. The program has been marketed to outside businesses.

Control Data's Fair Break program was created to help prepare young, disadvantaged, unemployed persons to find jobs. By means of Control Data's PLATO computer-based education system, individuals can improve basic skills and learn job training skills that will better equip them for entry into the job market.

In 1979, CDC and other professional businesses, church-related organizations, and individuals joined together to form the City Venture Corporation (CVC). The goal is a self-reliant community that can respond from within to its changing needs without continually depending on government programs or corporate philanthropy. The City Venture Corporation attempts to use a holistic approach in solving many different kinds of problems related to life in urban areas, such as problems related to health care, education, housing, and employment.

Start-up money for the venture came from area businesses that came together as shareholders in the new project. Its present income is derived from CVC's work in designing job creation and revitalization strategies and then helping to implement those strategies.

The capabilities of City Venture's stockholders and staff are substantial and varied. Management and technical personnel from stockholder organizations, as well as nationally recognized experts, have been organized into resource groups to address areas of prime importance to inner-city revitalization.

City Venture Corporation's five working city projects (in Toledo, Ohio, Baltimore, Philadelphia, Benton Harbor, Michigan, and Charleston, South Carolina) sprang from original Control Data models. One objective of the Toledo project, for example, is to create approximately 1,500 new jobs over a five-year period by building a new industrial park, a shopping center, and a Control Data Business and Technology Center. Other objectives include the creation of a Fair Break program and a job bank to match applicants to available jobs. The Toledo housing industry is scheduled to receive help through a combination of rehabilitation and new construction projects, especially from the provision of $1 million in interest subsidies for home purchases and home improvements, and the use of solar-energy demonstration houses. Another project objective is to create several community support systems such as a health care center to focus on primary health care delivery to mothers and small children, and a neighborhood antiarson conference/program.

CVC's confidence in the Toledo project's success hinges on two key factors: (1) the interest of the city itself in laying the ground-

59

work for effective public-private partnerships and (2) the presence of seven large corporations in the Toledo area, which allows critical corporate decision makers to provide the needed job opportunities in the areas of development. It will be a while before a final evaluation can be made of the long-range effects of the Toledo venture. Much will depend on the city's own response to the needs of its citizens.

Levi Strauss & Co.

V. Ruth McKinnon

Levi Strauss & Co. established a Community Affairs Department in 1968 to develop and coordinate community-related activities for the company. Located at Levi Strauss's headquarters in San Francisco, the department works in cooperation with the Levi Strauss Foundation, which provides financial assistance to many needy areas. Levi Strauss & Co. is involved in a variety of community-related activities, including programs that provide incentives for charitable contributions by employees, training programs to help disadvantaged youths, and projects that encourage employee involvement with community agencies and groups.

Employee Social Benefits Program. The foundation's Employee Social Benefits Program helps to encourage the involvement of Levi Strauss employees, both personally and monetarily, in community activities and educational institutions. This program is a three-pronged effort. First, the Matching Gifts Program invites company employees and retirees to apply to the foundation for gifts that match their own charitable contributions. Second, the Board Service Program channels contributions from the foundation to community organizations that include Levi Strauss employees and retirees in leadership roles on boards and advisory councils. Third, the Local Employee Action Program (LEAP) channels foundation contributions to community groups and programs that actively involve Levi Strauss employees.

Opportunities Training Program. The Opportunities Training Program was established about ten years ago as a hiring program for economically disadvantaged young people of all ethnic backgrounds—including those who are unemployed, hard-to-employ, handicapped, and ex-offenders. The program is also open to Vietnam-era veterans. The program teaches skills, provides on-the-job training, and guarantees job placement at the session's end. Hirees are employed on a full-time basis at the home office. Approximately twelve individuals are hired and placed annually.

Summer Training Programs. Levi Strauss & Co. sponsors two programs that concentrate on training disadvantaged youths during the summer months. The young people participate in these programs on a volunteer basis. To enter these programs, students must be high achievers, with academic grades averaging better than B+.

The first of these programs, the Office of Minority Business Enterprise Program (OMBE), trains graduating high school seniors who, once admitted to the program, continue in it for the duration of their college careers. The program concentrates on training students in areas that best facilitate their academic pursuits and career goals. Students are not guaranteed full-time employment after graduation.

The second program, the Career Cadet Program, trains high school juniors and/or seniors, who must reapply to join the program each summer. A student who successfully completes this program is eligible to apply for the OMBE program.

Community Involvement Teams. Each Levi Strauss plant coordinates its employee involvement in the local community through Community Involvement Teams (CITs). These teams are organized by interested plant employees who are granted one hour per month during regular working hours to meet together to identify the needs of their particular communities and to develop projects to meet those needs. The projects might be short-term—such as sponsorship of a community clean-up day or visits to a nearby prison facility. Other projects might involve a long-term commitment by team members—for example, weekly visits to a nearby nursing home and planned recreational activities for the residents throughout the year.

Individual teams often sponsor fund-raising activities to pay for various projects. One CIT, for example, prepares a hot lunch for fellow employees on a designated day each week. Team members share the cooking and clean-up duties. The monthly profits of $200 help finance new and existing CIT projects. CITs may also apply for grant aid from the Levi Strauss Foundation to help defray the costs of larger projects.

Many CIT-sponsored activities are geared to the interests and concerns of the individual employees and the communities where they live and work. The CIT of Levi Strauss's plant in Little Rock, Arkansas, for example, helped raise money to purchase new playground equipment for a nearby day-care center. In addition, team members frequently sponsor parties for the center's abused children during holidays.

In San Angelo, Texas, CIT members have focused their attention on the town's facility for battered women. The team has raised money for a variety of projects to benefit the home—for example, to produce an informational brochure about the center and to help renovate the building. The Levi Strauss Foundation granted funds to help with basic operating expenses. In addition, team members donate their time to the facility's residents.

Special Programs. Levi Strauss & Co. helps supplement the efforts of various CITs that identify needs they cannot meet for one reason or another. Problems related to domestic violence and to senior citizens, for example, have recently come to the attention of many CITs throughout the country. The Levi Strauss Foundation recognizes the efforts of the Mid-America Institute on Family Violence, located in Little Rock, Arkansas, to tackle this problem. The foundation recently awarded a sizable grant to the institute to encourage its work.

In addition to the foundation's numerous contributions to projects related to the problems of the aging—problems concerning medical services and the quality of care for the elderly, for example—the foundation has awarded grants to the National Council on Aging and the Southern California Andrus School of Gerontology, organizations that are active in this area. New York's Vera-Easyride program, whereby ex-offenders provide transportation services for the elderly and handicapped, has received funding from the Levi Strauss Foundation as well. These are just a few examples of Levi Strauss's growing interest in meeting a variety of special needs within the community.

Project Partnership

V. Ruth McKinnon

In July 1981 Project Partnership was set up by members of the Reagan administration staff and individuals from the private sector for the purpose of providing more job opportunities for disabled individuals.

In 1976 there were 16.4 million individuals in the United States who had a work disability—a health condition that limits the kind or amount of work a person can do. According to various studies, the prevalence of disability in the population is on the increase. Between 1966 and 1976 the number of persons permanently limited in their activities for health reasons increased 37 percent, whereas the total population increased only 10 percent.

The need for a program like Project Partnership became obvious to its initiators, Virginia H. Knauer, special assistant to President Reagan, and White House Fellow Harold E. Krents. They recognized the difficulty in finding jobs that can be modified to accommodate disabilities. In addition, they saw that one of the most serious problems in fully rehabilitating the disabled in the private sector is locating jobs once a disabled person has been trained. The objective of Project Partnership was to determine whether precommitting jobs would enable disabled individuals to train better and faster and return permanently to the work force.

One such program was inaugurated in 1981 in the New York and Connecticut area. Connecticut General Corporation agreed to be the coordinating business partner in that area's Project Partnership program. Thirteen other corporations joined with Connecticut General in committing a minimum of three jobs each (both blue- and white-collar jobs) to disabled individuals.

The participating companies begin the process by identifying appropriate jobs in advance and selecting candidates. These candidates are drawn from Connecticut General's disability insurance rolls. Connecticut General fulfills its commitment to train and place the individuals who are chosen for the program. Prospective employers then make final hiring decisions.

Project Partnership has several benefits. Disabled individuals have a greater number of job choices open to them. Companies gain access to a new pool of trained individuals. Reduced numbers of people on the disability rolls produce significant savings of both public and private money.

Two other projects have been established in California, one under the auspices of the Atlantic Richfield Company in Los Angeles, and the other under the guidance of the Kaiser Aluminum and Chemical Company in San Francisco. These programs are similar to the New York/Connecticut project in that businesses are working with local groups of disabled and the Social Security Administration to recruit and train disabled persons. The following list contains the names of participating companies in the programs in New York and Connecticut, Los Angeles, and San Francisco.

New York/Connecticut
    American Can Company
    American International Group
    Chemical New York Corporation
    Citicorp
    Connecticut General Corporation
    Consolidated Edison of New York, Inc.
    Exxon Corporation

Federal Reserve Bank of New York
Kaman Corporation
Manhattan Cable Television
New York Telephone
Paramount Pictures Corporation
Philip Morris, Inc.
Time Inc.

Los Angeles
Atlantic Richfield Company
Avery International
Carnation Company
Carter Hawley Savings and Loan
Hughes Aircraft Company
Knudsen Corporation
Lockheed Corporation
MCA Inc.
Northrop Corporation
Pacific Mutual Life Insurance Company
Southern California Edison Company
United California Bank

San Francisco
Kaiser Aluminum and Chemical Corporation
Bank of America
Bechtel Group
Clorox Company
Fireman's Fund Insurance Company
Foremost-McKesson Inc.
Kaiser Foundation
Levi Strauss & Co.
Memorex Corporation
Natomas Company
Safeway Stores

Shell Oil Company

Sean Sullivan

Shell Oil Company, based in Houston, Texas, has set up the Shell Employees and Retirees Volunteerism Effort (SERVE). This program was established in 1975 to match the skills and interests of Houston-area Shell employees and retirees and their families with volunteer opportunities in the community. As an extension of the SERVE program, Shell set up the SERVE Community Fund to provide special project funding to qualified organizations in which Shell employees and retirees are active volunteers. The fund is expected both to support their efforts and to enable them to influence the distribution of some of the money that Shell spends on local community support.

Grants can be up to $1,000 for each project. Organizations receiving funds must be involved in social welfare, health care, education, civic, or cultural activities; they must be nonprofit and tax-exempt and must provide services directly to the community rather than serving as a clearinghouse or fund-raising apparatus. Shell employees and retirees must have been involved actively as volunteers in the organizations for at least six months.

The funds must be used to purchase equipment or materials, not to pay for overhead expenses. Projects must be completed within a reasonable time, with measurable results and a positive impact on the community. They must also demonstrate a need for Shell's assistance and must not normally receive funds from the community. In 1981 there were 450 active SERVE volunteers, and thirty-four grants totaling $34,000 were made from the fund.

Stride Rite Corporation

Patricia W. Samors

The Stride Rite Children's Center, located at the company's main plant in an inner-city area of Boston, Massachusetts, provides daycare services to fifty children of both employees and community residents. Stride Rite Corporation has had a long history of responding to diversified community requests. It has supplied funds for an after-school program, for purchasing a bus for a community program, and for renovating a local building. It has also provided shoes for orphans.

Because of Stride Rite's reputation as a company concerned with community needs, a local citizen's organization approached Stride Rite in 1971 to request funding to open a community day-care center. At the same time, the KLH Corporation, another Boston-based firm, was successfully providing child-care services to its employees. In view of the success of KLH's program, Arnold Hiatt, the president of Stride Rite, also decided to link his company's social support services directly to a specific community problem. Hiatt conducted a survey of the company's employees and decided that Stride

65

Rite should offer quality day care for its employees and residents of the community. He received the backing of the company's board of directors.

The Stride Rite Children's Center was established on the factory premises in an area previously used for offices. The area was renovated by independently contracted workers at a cost to Stride Rite of $25,000. A federal program reimbursed the company for 75 percent of the cost of installing a new kitchen. Plans for the original center were developed by the center's director.

The planning, renovation, and staffing of the center were completed in three months, and the center opened in May 1971 with accommodations for thirty children. The center now has a staff of ten paid employees and several volunteers.

Although the quota of fifteen community children was quickly filled, registration of fifteen employees' children was slow. There were several reasons for the delay: the unfamiliarity of bringing children to the factory; the reluctance of some white employees to place their children in an integrated setting; and the fear that those employees whose children used the center would not receive raises or would be exploited in some way by the company.

To overcome these registration obstacles, the director implemented a plant-wide campaign in August 1971 to advertise the merits of the program. Films were produced showing activities at the center and were shown during lunch time to workers throughout the factory. The films helped acquaint Stride Rite employees with the program and its particular strengths—namely, the educational curriculum, health services, and staff and parent involvement. The information campaign slowly helped to overcome early prejudices and fears.

The center now serves fifty children (with a waiting list of twenty) ranging in age from two to six. There are no criteria for acceptance into the program. Entrance is on a first-come, first-served basis. If community residents were not served by the program, there would be more room for employees' children. Stride Rite's management believes, however, that it is important to respond to the needs of the community as well. More than half of the employees whose children use the facility are office workers, and some are middle-management personnel. It is also used, however, by the children of Stride Rite factory and warehouse workers.

When the center first opened, it was licensed by the Massachusetts State Office for Children. Because it served welfare recipients and received federal funds through the Department of Social Services, it was required to meet federal interagency day-care regulations. The latter, however, are currently in abeyance.

When the program began, it was not considered a pilot program, but rather a fully operational effort with the total moral support and financial backing of Stride Rite. As the staff developed relationships with local agencies over the years, more services were provided for the children. Today, the children receive two meals daily. Besides dental screening (with follow-up dental work if necessary), the children are tested for speech, hearing, vision, and lead levels. They also have access to psychological services. The curriculum stresses self-development and skill building through both play and learning experiences.

Incorporated as a nonprofit organization, the Stride Rite Children's Center has a board that includes three representatives from the company, three from the community, three parents, and two staff members. Parental contribution—as board members, volunteers, and participants at regular parent-staff meetings—has been important in building strong relations between the parents and the center, between the center and the community, and among parents themselves.

Weekly operating costs for the center are shared by many sources—the state Department of Social Services, the Bureau of Nutrition, the Stride Rite Foundation, and parents whose children use the facilities. The cost of running the program is approximately $65 per week per child. Tuition for the children of Stride Rite employees ranges from a minimum of $15 to a maximum of $25 weekly. The Stride Rite Foundation contributes the difference between this amount and the $65 weekly operating costs. The community parents, most of whom are eligible for state funds, pay tuition on a sliding scale. Their fees range from $1 to $65 per week; the difference is met by a contract with the Department of Social Services, which allows for such coverage for as many as twenty-three children. Families from the community who use the center, but do not receive subsidies, pay the entire $65 weekly fee.

A state Bureau of Nutrition grant provides approximately two-thirds of the annual food program allowance. Furthermore, the center receives in-kind contributions, such as the services of pediatric interns from local hospitals and student interns from local teaching colleges. Dental services are provided by the Boston University School of Dentistry. The Stride Rite Foundation pays the difference between income derived from all of these sources and actual expenses. This amounts to an annual gift of approximately $45,000.

The center's costs are less than comparable alternatives in the community because the availability of Stride Rite's telephones, maintenance crews, secretarial pool, and so on, helps reduce administrative costs. Yet the Stride Rite Children's Center is able to attract top-notch staff because it pays salaries that are among the highest in the field and offers medical and dental benefits through the company's health plan.

Although the program was not intended to reduce absenteeism or turnover among its employees, by making day care available the company has not only enjoyed the benefit of having a more stable work force, but has also found it easier to recruit personnel. In July 1981 corporate headquarters were moved to Cambridge, Massachusetts, where the company expects to open another children's center in the near future. This time, however, because of a lack of space at the new location, the center will not be located on the company's premises.

The Stride Rite company/community day-care program serves as a model for other companies. The center has responded to requests for information through its publication *How We Do It*. Workshops are offered once a month for representatives of companies interested in establishing similar programs.

West Baking Company

Patricia W. Samors

Since February 1980, Goodwill Industries of Central Indiana, a nonprofit organization, and the West Baking Company (which produces bakery products for the McDonald's hamburger food chain) have been operating an industrial training program for physically and mentally disabled people. Richard A. West, the president of West Baking and a member of Goodwill's board of directors, decided to use West Baking Company in Indianapolis as a training site to develop a more effective means of training the disabled.

Goodwill Industries' sheltered workshop could provide only limited preparation for the disabled to enter a real industrial setting. At the bakery, however, the trainees learn on the job in an actual industrial setting. They are carefully supervised (the trainee/supervisor ratio is five to one). The trainees, who make up the majority of the bakery's labor force, gain experience in monitoring complex machinery in a high-speed production process using mechanized packaging equipment. Upon completion of the training program, the disabled employees are prepared to compete for jobs in a wide variety of industrial settings that pay more than the minimum wage.

This project has been financed without any government funding or job subsidies. Instead, private funding has purposely been used to demonstrate that the private sector can offer more effective training for disabled persons than the government and, at the same time, can make a profit.

Goodwill Industries selects trainees from disabled people in Indiana who want vocational training. They are first evaluated for vocational purposes, after which they either receive adjustment training at Goodwill or proceed directly to the bakery site. The trainees remain on Goodwill's payroll. Thus, in a sense, the organization provides contract labor for which it is reimbursed by the West Baking Company. All trainees are paid wages above the federal minimum wage.

Since the project's beginning, of sixty-five participants, thirty-three have completed training—twenty-three of whom have been placed in other jobs at an average starting salary of $5.21 per hour. Presently, twelve trainees are "placement ready"—that is, they are working with Goodwill's placement department to obtain permanent jobs elsewhere.

This industrial training program has proved successful from the beginning. Although job placement has been slower than hoped because of economic conditions in Indiana, in general there have been good results.

Goodwill wishes to promote the success of the venture by informing area businesses about the program and by persuading them to participate by designating a certain number of their job openings for training disabled people. Although one other firm has joined as a participant in the program, Goodwill's goal is to make this type of training more widely available.

Xerox Corporation

Sean Sullivan

The Xerox Corporation of Stamford, Connecticut, has two major programs designed to encourage employees to participate in community affairs: the Social Service Leave Program and the Xerox Community Involvement Program.

The Social Service Leave Program was begun in 1972 when 21 Xerox employees received a one-year leave of absence with full pay to work on social projects in nonprofit agencies. Leaves now range from one to twelve months, depending on the project. Through 1981, 258 employees had participated in the program, at an average annual cost to Xerox of $450,000 in reimbursed salaries. Any employee in good standing who has been with Xerox for three years may apply for a leave. Selections are made by a committee representing a cross section of employees rather than by management—a unique feature of the Xerox program.

Projects must meet certain criteria. They must be sponsored by a functioning nonprofit organization that is not involved in political or religious activity. Xerox employees must obtain written acceptance from the organization of the work proposed. Employees must also pay their own personal expenses. Projects have included work in such areas as minority and youth counseling and training, minority-business counseling, and drug and alcohol rehabilitation. Examples of recently approved projects include instructing the blind in office skills, assisting in placing Southeast Asian children in foster homes, establishing a shelter for battered women, and teaching functional living skills to the developmentally handicapped. The Xerox Social Service Leave Program has served as a model for several other companies.

The Community Involvement Program was begun in 1974 as part of the Xerox Philanthropic Program. Xerox provides as much as $5,000 to each of its more than 100 company locations across the United States for the purpose of selecting, planning, and starting a project that will provide lasting benefits to the community. The funding is earmarked for expenditures related to implementing Xerox employee involvement.

Local Xerox branches that choose to participate in the program form Location Committees made up of at least seven volunteers, including a location manager. Activities must meet several criteria: involvement of Xerox employees and funding; innovation and creativity; focus on only two or three major projects in a given year; and noninvolvement with organizations that normally have commercial relations with Xerox. Most projects are concerned with renovation of facilities, recreation, tutoring programs, youth activities, skills training, senior citizens, and the handicapped. Xerox money is sometimes used as leverage to get greater financial support for a project. In New Orleans, for example, it was used to start a fundraising drive for a community home. As of 1981, 115 Location Committees had been formed, with an annual cost to Xerox of about $600,000 for community involvement projects. Employees do not receive time off for these projects—they must contribute their own time. In 1981, Xerox employees participating in the program numbered 6,600.

Project Pride, Inc.

V. Ruth McKinnon

In 1975, employees of New Jersey Bell, an operating company of the Bell System, formed an ad hoc committee to study the growing problem of vandalism in the city of Newark, New Jersey. Representatives from the mayor's office, the departments of public housing, parks and recreation, education, the Office of Criminal Justice Planning, and New Jersey Bell were among those who joined together to study the problem. In six months' time the committee members not only confirmed their perception of the seriousness of vandalism in Newark, but also determined that vandalism threatened the growth of the city's neighborhoods and businesses.

A New Jersey Bell employee was chosen to present the committee's findings to key public and private groups, including the city's chamber of commerce. In response to one of the committee's specific suggestions, an eighty-member Anti-Vandalism Task Force was formed in October 1976. The objective of the group, made up of volunteers from many public and private agencies throughout the city, was to encourage citizen participation in creating a safer and more desirable community in which to live.

During an initial period of planning and study, the task force studied an antivandalism program called Project Pride, which was conceived by a California educator. The success of this smaller program in California helped prepare the way for the establishment six months later of Newark's own city-wide antivandalism program—called Project Pride, Inc.

A full-time administrator was charged with coordinating the program's activities from offices at Newark's chamber of commerce. Subcommittees were formed to implement various aspects of the program: public relations, education, housing, recreation, community organizations, juvenile justice, and research and evaluation. An administration subcommittee was formed to coordinate recommendations and plans for action suggested by the other subcommittees.

During the first eighteen months of operation, Project Pride offered numerous recreational events for youths throughout Newark as a means of redirecting energy and enthusiasm away from destructive activities. Young people became involved in disco contests, decathlons, football and basketball tournaments, as well as music programs at Newark's Symphony Hall.

Another activity that became part of the Project Pride program was the use of youth patrols in public housing sites. Using citizens' band radios, young people patrolled corridors and stairwells at regular intervals and reported any signs of vandalism to security personnel. As a result, vandalism was significantly reduced in these areas. The money saved through decreased property damage costs was channeled into improving services and modernizing these public housing sites.

Since its origin, Project Pride has been supported through volunteer help. Funding comes from unsolicited contributions from both corporate and public groups. In an effort to broaden the program's outreach, however, Project Pride sponsored its first Pride Bowl Football Classic, in 1979. The game had community-wide support, and the proceeds were almost $20,000. The proceeds had doubled by the time the third game was held, in 1981. This annual community-wide event has become a primary source of financial support and a means of providing exposure for the program in the Newark area.

Project Pride became a nonprofit corporation in 1979. A twenty-member volunteer board of directors was formed, with Robert W. Reynolds of New Jersey Bell serving as its first president. At the same time, the organization was restructured, and finance, nominating, and planning committees were formed. Greater emphasis was placed on reducing incidences of vandalism by working through the city's education system.

A scholarship program was launched in 1980, for example, as Project Pride awarded ten $500 scholarships to qualified, deserving applicants from schools throughout the city. In 1981 the number of scholarship awards was increased to twelve. In addition, Project Pride contributed $5,000 over a two-year period to encourage the growth of a local high-school debate team. Project Pride hopes to continue its efforts to cut down on vandalism especially by working through the education network. By encouraging the growth and development of better-educated and ultimately more employable students, Project Pride volunteers believe that individual young people and the community as a whole can benefit.

Honeywell, Inc.

V. Ruth McKinnon

Honeywell, Inc., is an international, advanced-technology company with headquarters in Minneapolis, Minnesota. The company was founded in 1883 when a Minneapolis inventor developed an apparatus to control individual room temperature by regulating the output from home heating furnaces. Since then, Honeywell has expanded into the business of computer and control systems and today has 97,000 employees.

Honeywell's history of community involvement can be traced back to the urban riots of the 1960s. The company's president at that time, S. F. Keating, set the tone for the firm's commitment by helping to form the Minneapolis area's first urban coalition in an effort to deal with growing minority-related problems. Under Keating's leadership, the coalition, comprising several local business leaders, tried to bring area businesses and minority groups together to talk about their mutual problems. This activity eventually led to the creation of the area's first jobs programs and housing projects, and it channeled money into a troubled area.

Within the company itself, Keating asked general managers about their involvement in the communities where Honeywell factories and sales offices were located. A more visible statement of Honeywell's commitment to the community was made in the mid-1960s. When most other downtown Minneapolis businesses were moving to the suburbs, Honeywell decided to stay at its original location. The money saved by not relocating was used to renovate the neighborhood surrounding Honeywell's home office.

Throughout the 1960s, Honeywell's activity in the community was piecemeal at best. The company's community involvement was often unorganized and initiated only by various company managers who had taken a personal interest in such involvement. The company did not have a formal program, nor did it specifically encourage one. There was only the belief, and Keating's personal example, that such community involvement *should* happen within the company structure.

By 1975 Honeywell had both a new president/chief executive officer, Edsen W. Spencer, and a growing philosophy of community involvement. Spencer continued Keating's ideas by stating that involvement in the community should be a natural part of the company's overall program—and that if representing the company in the community is important, it is important in every company location. Wherever there was a Honeywell plant with fifty or more employees, Spencer felt a community relations mechanism should be in operation.

Honeywell's Corporate and Community Responsibility Department. That same year the Community Relations Department (CRD) was created, partly because of Spencer's concern for these formalized objectives and partly because of a growing pressure on the country's leading businesses to address certain societal issues and social policy questions. Although Honeywell, like other businesses, had long been interested in such issues, it was hesitant to voice an opinion on such matters because of the traditional belief that business lacked credibility on issues not directly affecting its operations. Times were changing.

To head the new CRD, Ronald Speed came to Honeywell in 1968. His first position was that of congressional researcher, developing legislative analyses for the company and, in addition, he was asked on occasion to act as a spokesman for Honeywell. He would meet with community groups, for example, to explain the company's role as a manufacturer of defense materials, particularly during the volatile years of the Vietnam war. Thus, when Speed was eventually asked to head the new CRD, he used the skills he had developed in his previous positions at Honeywell to communicate to all levels of personnel the need for the company's commitment to community involvement and the role the newly formed CRD would begin to play in that process.

One of CRD's first functions was to organize and run the National United Way Campaign. The Community Service Awards Program, which was also instituted by the CRD, was one of Honeywell's first internal means of recognizing Honeywell employees who served as volunteers in the community. It encouraged the continuation and expansion of volunteerism among employees. The award is still presented annually.

The role of the CRD was expanded as Honeywell's philosophy of community involvement took on a more definitive shape. The CRD acted as a facilitator in helping corporate offices and field locations develop community action programs. In 1979, to increase its effectiveness in community involvement, the company brought together its divisions of government relations, community relations, and philanthropy under the umbrella of the Public Affairs Department. In 1982 the Honeywell Fund joined the CRD. Under Speed's direction, both offices began to function as the Corporate and Community Responsibility Department (CCRD). Speed's staff grew to twelve, including five professionals, two consultants, and three support personnel.

Honeywell's Philosophy of Community Involvement. A business takes from its surrounding community both human and nonhuman resources, and, in Honeywell's view, it should give something in return. Honeywell's philosophy of community involvement can be summarized as follows. First, by its presence as a successful business in a community, Honeywell feels it can influence the quality of life and standard of living of a community in a variety of ways: through jobs, products, dollars, service, and leadership. Second, by fostering a healthy community environment, Honeywell can ultimately benefit business. Third, when a community is growing and healthy, the employees can benefit because they have a better place to live and work, and the community itself can enjoy new resources of energy and expertise.[1] Simply put, Honeywell feels that corporate community involvement is necessary.

Honeywell weaves its philanthropic principles into its overall tapestry of community involvement. In the 1960s Honeywell's gifts to the community were primarily "give-aways." Today, however, the company tries to "lead with people—not dollars." [2] Honeywell contributes to organizations and groups in which Honeywell employees are involved or to those related in some way to Honeywell as a corporation. Funds might flow first, for example, to a nonprofit agency that uses the services of a Honeywell employee as a volunteer or to an educational institution that fosters growth in the science and technology industries.[3]

Developing a Managerial Network. In 1975 Honeywell reorganized its divisions to decentralize operations. At the same time, Speed encouraged the managers in each division to form management (not employee) committees to address the issue of community involvement. Since then, the CCRD has learned that it can attract employees as volunteers with the help of the general managers in each division. "Community relations is best planned and implemented through a management/team approach. . . ." [4]

Speed believes that seriously capturing the attention of these general managers is crucial for employee involvement. Managers are encouraged to budget a certain amount of their operating money for community activity projects. The CCRD works with an annual budget of $1–1.5 million used as *operating* money—not for philanthropy—not only to meet its own staff expenses but also to fund other corporation-wide projects and programs. Division managers are encouraged to form a team of people from their various departments to identify key issues and community projects that could be addressed by the division—and who will eventually get such projects under way.

The prescription for community involvement in the early days of CCRD's existence, then, was simply that every division throughout the corporation should have a plan for community activity, organized through division managers and management committees. (It should be noted that no pressure is placed on employees or their managers for community involvement; but voluntarism is certainly encouraged.)

Motivating People to Get Involved. To communicate its goals, the CCRD distributes a manual entitled *Honeywell Involvement in the Community* to all division general managers. It clearly states the company's philosophy regarding community involvement and community relations, and it also identifies ways of implementing that philosophy. The manual lists specific company objectives and guidelines for community relations. It suggests ways of selecting and developing projects to help meet specific community needs, as well as methods for budgeting funds for these projects.

Another tool used by Speed's staff to encourage community involvement is Honeywell's Minnesota Management Community Relations Committee. The committee, which was begun in 1979, consists of the general managers of divisions located in Minneapolis, the employee relations directors in those divisions, the director of the Honeywell Fund, Ronald Speed, and others. This committee meets several times a year for the purpose of developing the interest of the various division managers in community activities. The committee makes contribution decisions, reviews policy issues, and coordinates several subcommittees which focus on such issues as education, health and welfare, equal opportunity, and employee services. The subcommittees are chaired by employee relations directors who work in conjunction with middle-management personnel from the various company divisions.

Criteria for Choosing Community-Related Projects. In choosing a community-related project, the CCRD staff attempts to determine whether the project meets certain guidelines. "It should be a project in which Honeywell's skills, capabilities and resources can make a special and significant contribution. . . . It should be a project which can be structured to maximize involvement. . . . Involvement or potential involvement by Honeywell management and other employees in the community should be the single most heavily weighted factor in any committee's project decision. . . . " [5] In addition, the company's management often considers expanding its association with a community organization that has attracted a significant number of Honeywell employees as volunteers.

Speed and his staff continually refine the list of possible projects and inform the committees and divisions about them, exercising care not to overstructure the process or the product.

Honeywell's Projects for Community Involvement. Honeywell's various community involvement projects—in the areas of education, health and welfare, equal opportunity, minority businesses, cultural and civic activities, energy conservation, and crime and correction programs—have had diverse beginnings. The following are examples of such projects.

Management Assistance Program. The Management Assistance Program (MAP) developed out of many discussions between Ron Speed, representatives from area businesses, and several nonprofit agencies. They discussed the possibility of using corporate people as consultants to nonprofit agencies, especially when these agencies needed such expertise to remain solvent, but could not afford to pay for it.

In the early stages of discussion, surveys were distributed to businesses and nonprofit agencies alike to try to assess the feasibility of such an arrangement. Although reaction was mostly positive, obstacles—such as nonprofit agencies' distrust of business—had to be overcome before both groups were willing to test the program.

In 1979 Honeywell joined with several other Minneapolis businesses and the United Way Voluntary Action Center to establish a program linking administratively and technically oriented employees from local corporations with nonprofit agencies requesting aid in those areas. The agencies receive the benefits of the consultants' expertise and free advice about how to increase their effectiveness and efficiency.

The volunteer consultants provide nonprofit agencies with information regarding personnel, accounting, marketing, public relations, and general administration. Specifically, assistance may be given by means of computerization, analysis of office procedures, determination of insurance needs, evaluation of personnel policies and procedures, and evaluation and development of systems and procedures manuals.

The program is made available to any nonprofit agency in the metropolitan Minneapolis area. A nonprofit agency interested in receiving assistance from MAP must first submit an application. After approval and acceptance by MAP, the groups meet to discuss the implementation of MAP assistance.

Volunteers are recruited from all levels of the corporate structure and normally function on a short-term basis only—averaging forty to eighty total hours per project. They are granted paid leave time to perform these volunteer services.

One Honeywell employee provided management guidance to the

77

Jewish Family Children's Service, a United Way member agency providing aid to Jewish immigrants, tutoring, services for the elderly, and the like. The agency benefited from the professional consultation and the MAP volunteer was given an opportunity to improve his leadership skills.

Present funding and operation of the program are provided jointly by the United Way of Minneapolis and several area corporations, among them the Bemis Company, First Bank of Minneapolis, Northern States Power Company, St. Paul Companies, the Honeywell Corporation, Northwestern National Bank, Dayton-Hudson Corporation, General Mills, and 3M.

In 1981 MAP placed approximately ninety-three volunteers in sixty-five agencies. Presently, ten agencies are on a waiting list for assistance. The number of participating agencies has doubled in the program's two years of operation.

Further spinoffs from MAP include management training sessions for nonprofit organization managers, the establishment of a management resource library, and the creation of a newsletter. It is hoped that the MAP will eventually be expanded to involve corporate retirees.

Honeywell Retiree Volunteer Project. The Honeywell Retiree Volunteer Project (HRVP), among the most progressive of Honeywell's projects, was the result of a conversation between Speed and an outside consultant as they began to explore the idea of using Honeywell retirees in community-related work. At the same time, a student in the Metro Intern Program (in which University of Minnesota students engage in semester-long research programs) had been assigned by one of Honeywell's divisions to work on the development of a project involving Honeywell retirees.

By means of a survey of 3,000 retirees, this student discovered that a significant proportion were interested in offering their time and energy to community activity. Thus, the HRVP was initiated as a pilot project, and a management committee was formed as part of the project's first phase. This fifteen-member committee included several Honeywell executives, retirees, consultants, and the CCRD staff. Over a period of six months the committee, working in conjunction with Speed's staff, determined the nature of the project. In the second stage of development, six months were spent setting guidelines, goals, and directions for the project. The third stage concluded with implementation of the project in May 1979.

More than 400 retirees, representing all levels of the corporate structure, now work an average of one or two days a week. In 115 different settings, they work in youth and educational programs, social agencies, hospitals, technical service firms, and schools. The director of the program is a retiree who works four days a week with other retirees managing the program from offices designated for HRVP use at Honeywell headquarters. The staff interviews potential program participants and helps to coordinate the activities of retirees already involved.

In HRVP's first three years, the retirees contributed an average total of 84,000 hours annually, with a dropout rate of only 8 percent over a three-year period. Honeywell contributed the initial start-up money for the program of $50,000 and continues to support the HRVP's annual budget of $35,000 to $40,000. The retirees receive no stipend.

One retiree who had worked at Honeywell as a tool and die maker devised an extra key on an electric typewriter, enabling disabled individuals to use the equipment. A former Honeywell engineer who volunteered to work in the library of a local hospital became involved instead in modernizing the hospital's heating and cooling systems for greater cost efficiency and easier maintenance. Another former Honeywell employee, with thirty years' experience as a toolmaker, works at a nonprofit trade school with students studying tool and die making, in exchange for which he receives a free lunch in the school's cafeteria.

A retired husband and wife work as a team at the Minnesota Literary Council with adults eighteen or older who want to learn to read. This couple's involvement with HRVP continues the volunteer work they began for the council while employed full-time at Honeywell. In addition to teaching reading, these retirees counsel students on other problems.

Staff members of the CCRD communicate daily with the HRVP staff in coordinating existing activities and developing new ones. The HRVP Management Committee is active in monitoring the progress of the program and in planning for expansion.

Apparently, four elements account for the success of the HRVP: (1) the interview procedure, which carefully matches a volunteer's skills and interests with suitable placements; (2) the consistency of the volunteers' commitment, along with follow-up and personal contact with the volunteers by the HRVP staff; (3) Honeywell's reputation in the community and a retiree's pride in being associated with the corporation; and (4) the satisfaction volunteers glean from such an experience.

The program has been replicated at several Honeywell locations, and other companies in the Minneapolis area have inquired about starting similar retiree programs. As a result of the success of HRVP, another of Honeywell's divisions has started exploring the concerns of the older worker. Another major Minneapolis corporation has begun to discuss with Honeywell the possibility of forming a consortium of Minneapolis businesses to review the growing needs of older workers.

Task Force on Women's Issues. In 1978 Honeywell's Equal Opportunity Committee began to look at the growing needs of women in the community. The committee at first explored fund raising and volunteer work for community organizations already in place. After a CCRD staff member brought together four women employees of Honeywell with a special interest in women's issues, however, the group began to examine women's issues with respect to Honeywell itself. They identified several significant problems, including the high number of women in lower-level jobs and the lack of women in engineering and technically oriented positions.

As the discussion grew, so did the size of the group, until as many as thirty women, from a wide range of positions within the company, were meeting together. In the first eighteen months of meetings the group established goals to promote upward mobility for women at Honeywell.

After the Task Force on Women's Issues was formed, the group organized committees to perform such duties as drawing attention to women's work-related needs and making top management aware of the need for career advancement for women within the company. Several career forums (attended by both men and women) have been held in an attempt to educate and inform women of the possibilities for career advancement. In addition, "network dinners" have been held as a means of dealing with the problem of isolation in the workplace. The task force appears to be able to communicate its goals and objectives consistently, especially to top management. This has been a key element in its forward movement and has helped keep the image of the group high.

Task Force on Working Parents. A study produced by the Women's Issues Task Force in 1980 initiated another project. When questioned about problems related to child care and other issues of importance to working parents, 25 percent of those surveyed reported serious child-care problems. In response, the CCRD appointed a full-time consultant to examine the problems of working parents at Honeywell. In March 1981 a Task Force on Working Parents was created to explore options and present recommendations to management. Many of these recommendations have already been implemented.

Others that would require policy changes are still being considered. The primary concern of the CCRD is to keep the problems of working families known and to try to anticipate related needs. An advisory committee has been established to continue reviewing the issues, and a member of Speed's staff works with this committee on day care and many other problems that affect working families.

Minneapolis Education and Recycling Center. Honeywell's involvement in education is extensive and growing. The Commercial Division at Honeywell's headquarters, for example, conceived a program to keep potential dropouts in school and to give dropouts a chance to obtain a high school equivalency degree. Honeywell contributed $30,000 and set aside some space for this facility, the Minneapolis Education and Recycling Center (MERC). Two teachers, a supervisor, and an administrator coordinate the activities of thirty students per session at the center. Students receive educational instruction for half of the day, and during the rest of the day they learn basic job skills while recycling materials donated by the community.

Regis College–Bay State training program. The state of Massachusetts recently established the Bay State Skills Corporation to help train individuals facing career changes—especially those facing layoffs or job loss. To achieve its objective, this corporation agreed to provide matching grants to businesses that would establish acceptable training programs—particularly in high-technology industries. In response to this objective and to relieve a shortage of teachers, Boston's Regis College joined Honeywell in a program to provide introductory computer programming classes for individuals (primarily women) wishing to transfer into the computer field. After the program was approved by the Bay State Skills Corporation, the first session was held in early 1981.

Regis provided classroom space and a project director to accommodate thirty students. Honeywell contributed computer equipment and employees' time to train and teach the students. The company also donated computer time at its facility. The program's budget for the first year was $66,000. Honeywell contributed $44,000; the commission, $17,000; and Regis, $5,000.

The students completed two full sessions in 1981. Honeywell hired eight graduates, and other area businesses took many of the other graduates. The success of the first year's program led the corporation to renew its matching grant to start a more extensive training program in 1982, with thirty-five students and a total operating budget of $117,000. Honeywell is contributing $77,000 of that amount.

Other educationally related programs initiated by Honeywell include its tutoring and Adopt-A-School programs and the Massachusetts Future Problem-Solving Bowl, in which Honeywell employees and some company funding are used to provide a competitive program for high achievers and creative students.

(Additional information about Honeywell's involvement in the education arena may be found in the chapter by Denis P. Doyle and Marsha Levine in part 4 of this volume.)

Problems in Developing a Program of Corporate Community Involvement. Although Honeywell ran into some obstacles in developing its program, Speed and his staff regard them as growing pains rather than real impediments. They believe that there are fewer bureaucratic obstacles to project starts today than there were ten years ago. Although the need for the CCRD was acknowledged from the very beginning, there were fears concerning the greater financial burden, the greater demands that would be placed on the corporation by outside requests, and the lost productivity as general managers were diverted toward community involvement. All of this contributed to a quiet skepticism as to the appropriate emphasis to place on community involvement. Over time, however, the CCRD staff gained the confidence of top management and built up credibility as it developed programs. As department director, Speed has attempted to make Honeywell's corporate executives more aware of the long-term significance of such community involvement.

Another problem faced by Honeywell is that of helping its program of community involvement keep pace with the growth of the company. Also, with growth comes diversity, and so the staff of the CCRD tries to avoid suggesting overgeneralized formulas for developing community programs in diverse settings. The staff and resources of the CCRD have been made available to communicate with increasing numbers of division managers interested in community involvement. Speed and his staff also try to keep the company's employees informed as to the department's existence and its goal of carrying out Honeywell's commitment to corporate responsibility in the community.

Another problem Honeywell faced in developing its community involvement program concerned community attitudes. Often, the community does not know how to respond to assistance (that is, volunteers) coming from outside its own environment. Honeywell has tried to tread softly in building its credibility in the community to avoid arousing suspicion or resentment. Refining the procedures for placing volunteers has been one means of achieving this and has led to mutual benefits for both the community agency and the volunteer. These efforts appear to be working: several recent projects have been like partnerships between public and private groups. There have even been instances in which community groups have sought Honeywell's help in beginning new projects because of the company's growing reputation for experience and expertise in areas of social concern.

Conclusion. Responsible corporate action in the community has been defined by Honeywell as a progressive activity on four levels, each level depending on the one preceding it. At the most basic level there is funding. This important step should lead naturally to the second level, involvement of individuals in helping to solve community problems. Often, however, the individual cannot fully empathize with the community and its needs, so, at a third level, individuals join forces with community groups to enlarge the resources at their disposal. Level four is perhaps the most important because the community group can begin to use the company's help, making the relationship a mutually beneficial one.

Today, Honeywell still follows the two-part strategy for community involvement that was used when the CCRD was first established. As one part of this strategy, top management is made more aware of the importance of community activity. At the same time, equal attention is given to those working at the grass-roots level of the business. The CCRD staff will continue in its role of monitoring the growth of existing projects and promoting the development of new ones. In addition, an important task in the future will be that of continuing its communication with top management and general managers and spreading that same type of dialogue to the middle-management level.

Through projects, programs, and committees, Honeywell is striving to develop and foster the growth and the interests of both the employees and the company as a whole in the area of community involvement. Speed feels that Honeywell has made significant progress since the Community Relations Department was first established in 1975. With increasing demands for human services in the community, however, corporations like Honeywell will have to be prepared to respond and act even more responsibly in the future.

IBM Corporation

Sean Sullivan

International Business Machines Corporation (IBM), headquartered in Armonk, New York, conducts various social responsibility programs to deal with social needs. IBM's heavy involvement in private sector initiatives has been chosen for special attention because of the strength of the company's commitment in this area, as evidenced by the breadth and scale of its programs.

Although IBM's concern with social problems goes back several decades, it is only in the past ten to fifteen years that the company has formalized that concern into specific programs. The company's founder, Thomas Watson, established three guiding principles for IBM: respect for the individual, the pursuit of excellence, and service to the customer. Service to the larger public—that is, the community—though not explicitly mentioned, has always been an integral part of the company's operations. IBM's work with the handicapped, for example, began in 1942 and is a natural extension of Watson's first basic principle of respect for the individual.

After assuming the leadership of IBM from his father in the 1950s, Thomas Watson, Jr., enunciated a fourth principle of service to the community. This led to the formation of the Public Responsibility Committee of the Board of Directors to see that the corporation fulfills its commitment to good corporate citizenship and active social responsibility. The committee has recently set an overall goal of greater IBM involvement in private sector initiatives which relate to the corporation's principal business and to the expertise it has developed in the course of conducting that business, and in which its actions can have an influence.

Training—in specific job skills as well as general management skills—is considered one of IBM's greatest strengths, and this has guided most decisions on what kinds of initiatives to take. Initiatives also build on the company's own management strength. Because of the decentralized way that IBM manages its public service programs—and because each program has grown out of particular circumstances—it is best to trace the programs individually to show their evolution from informal activities to more managed lines of business at IBM.

Job Training for the Disabled. The oldest of IBM's private sector initiatives, job training for the disabled was begun in 1942 at the company's Topeka, Kansas, branch office. Individuals with cerebral palsy were taught typing and key punching. The next year the company began another training program in New York City, primarily for the blind. With referrals from state rehabilitation agencies, more than 600 individuals were trained under this program.

These early activities were branch-office initiatives and not part on a formal, ongoing corporate program. Such a corporate program —Computer Programmer Training for the Severely Disabled—was begun in 1972. It grew out of IBM's experience in retraining a marketing employee who had become disabled. This employee in turn proposed that IBM help other people with severe physical disabilities who were otherwise capable of becoming computer programmers.

The Federal Systems Division of IBM was asked to determine if the company could make a unique contribution to helping the disabled. After discussions with people in the field of vocational rehabilitation, with state and federal officials, and with business and industry representatives, IBM decided to establish and fund two demonstration training projects sponsored and supported by state vocational rehabilitation agencies. The sites chosen for these projects were the Woodrow Wilson Rehabilitation Center in Fishersville, Virginia, operated by the state of Virginia, and the Center for Independent Living in Berkeley, California. The Berkeley project also involved creation of a Business Advisory Committee of data-processing managers and other interested business people who guide and monitor the training program and assist directly in evaluating and placing students.

After the first two centers had been established—completing the IBM-sponsored phase of the program—the Federal Systems Division was asked by the Rehabilitation Services Administration, then part of the U.S. Department of Health, Education, and Welfare, to continue establishing similar centers in other states under a shared-cost contract that has been renewed annually. The company has established twenty such centers, with another scheduled to open soon and others yet under consideration. Each center has a Business Advisory Committee, usually made up of the representatives of twenty or more member companies, which helps develop the training curriculum to meet local hiring needs and teaches general business skills. Committee members often hire the first class of graduates. Training is usually done by a university, a community college, or a rehabilitation center. Nationally, the program has trained 655 disabled people and placed 83 percent of them in computer-programming jobs through the end of 1981.

At each project location, IBM, through its Federal Systems Division representative and local branch office personnel, has helped to plan the program, establish the Business Advisory Committee, and act as consultant to the center as the local rehabilitation agency assumes management responsibility. The company's role changes as each project progresses—IBM is first an organizer/planner/entrepreneur, and then an adviser/consultant, until it moves on to begin the next program. The federal government's Projects With Industry program is modeled on this cooperative effort of businesses, rehabilitation agencies, and government to establish high-quality rehabilitation projects. IBM considers the Business Advisory Committees the key to the success of the program because they ensure that training will be relevant to the needs of the local job market—and that the graduates will, therefore, be hired.

The staff of the Federal Systems Division in Gaithersburg, Maryland, evaluates prospective locations for new centers, looking for a strong local rehabilitation agency, business partners, and enough disabled people who qualify for the program. IBM and other companies provide equipment and materials for the training as well as expertise and manpower. Funding has been provided by state vocational rehabilitation agencies, the Comprehensive Employment and Training Act (CETA), Governors' Discretionary Fund, CETA Private Industry Councils (PICs), private foundations, and directly by industry.

Job Training for the Disadvantaged. This public service program was begun by a local IBM manager in Los Angeles in 1968 after the Watts riots. Like the training program for the physically disabled, it developed out of an existing informal practice—in this instance, lending equipment to organizations engaged in job training. In cooperation with the Bank of America and the Los Angeles Urban League, IBM established a center to train unemployed area residents in data processing and to place them in jobs with a future. Bank of America made one of its properties available as a training site, and IBM contributed computer equipment, training materials, and instructors.

Out of this first effort has grown a program that now encompasses eight major training centers and IBM support for about 200 smaller training operations. The major centers are all operated in conjunction with local community-based organizations (CBOs) and businesses. Partners include the Urban League in Los Angeles, Chicago, Oakland, and Washington, D.C., and Opportunities Industrialization Centers in New York, Dallas, and San Antonio. As with the training program for the handicapped, IBM also insists that each center have a Business Advisory Council, made up of representatives from local businesses, to give advice, contribute money and materials, and hire some of the successful trainees. The involvement of other companies is considered crucial to the success of the program. Individual companies have made major contributions in some cities, for instance, Bank of America in Los Angeles and Sperry and Hutchinson in New York.

In these centers IBM begins as the organizer and eventually serves as an adviser. Although IBM is the initiator and the catalyst, the company does not run each center indefinitely. The size of an installation is a factor in how large a role IBM will play. The major training centers that offer courses in computer skills such as programming, computer operations, and word processing receive data-processing equipment, help in developing a curriculum, and instructors from IBM until the CBO's staff is trained to take over the teaching. The smaller centers offer basic business courses such as typing, key punching, data entry, and general office skills and generally receive only equipment on loan, although IBM will help with curriculum development if requested. Major and small centers alike work toward self-sufficiency, so that they do not remain dependent on IBM indefinitely.

The major centers have trained more than 5,000 students since the first one opened in 1968 and have placed 80 percent of them in permanent jobs. Several reasons account for this success: responsibility for projects is given to local IBM branch managers; the involvement of local businesses ensures that training is relevant to the needs of employers and improves job placement opportunities; classroom environments simulate that of the workplace as closely as possible; the instructors are professionals in their fields; rigorous standards are imposed that are keyed to business world performance requirements; and, finally, there is follow-up for a full year after placement to ensure that training remains current. The smaller centers—now more than 200 in number—have trained more than 150,000 people.

In view of the success of the program and the magnitude of the problem of preparing the disadvantaged for employment, IBM has decided to more than double the number of major training centers. In doing so, the company is renewing its emphasis on private sector initiatives as a way of meeting its commitment to responsible corporate citizenship. The first eight centers were established between 1968 and 1982, a period of about fourteen years. The company plans to bring eleven new ones into operation by the end of 1982 and is considering further expansion in 1983.

The significant expansion of IBM's program for training the disadvantaged marks a shift in the company's perception of its role in the community—that is, a shift to greater activism. Instead of waiting for CBOs to initiate proposals for new centers—which was the usual procedure after the Los Angeles center had been opened—

the company has tried to look for opportunities on its own. Starting with the thirty U.S. cities with the largest absolute numbers of unemployed, IBM went to the national CBOs to discuss their needs. Eleven of the thirty cities were selected as sites for training centers. The company gave CBOs direct help in preparing their proposals and in getting partners for their programs.

IBM's more active role was guided by its director of equal opportunity and affirmative action programs. The new approach attempts to implement a directive from the Public Responsibility Committee of the Board of Directors of IBM to increase the company's involvement in corporate social responsibility programs. The criteria for choosing new program sites remain the same: the CBO must select the trainees; it must demonstrate the ability eventually to run the program self-sufficiently; and it must show that it can place a high proportion of program graduates in jobs. Furthermore, there must be a local Business Advisory Committee to share responsibility for keeping the curriculum up to date and helping with money, materials, and management. IBM's decision to open new centers is made on a first-come, first-served basis. There are currently more proposals than can be acted on.

The programs that IBM has helped to develop for training the handicapped and the disadvantaged are similar in some important respects. They provide skills training for good jobs to people who are at a serious competitive disadvantage in the job market, and thereby demonstrate IBM's commitment to the principle of respect for the individual. The programs also draw on the company's special expertise in its own field, thereby using IBM's strengths to help fill particular social needs. Finally, they are managed in a decentralized way, allowing local people to keep the programs attuned to local circumstances.

Other public service programs sponsored by IBM might generally be called manpower loan programs. These will be discussed next.

Social Service Leave. The Social Service Leave Program has been in operation since 1971, and IBM gave leave to certain employees who worked in the community before that. The practice grew out of IBM's desire to be an active, responsible corporate citizen. The formal leave program was set up to ensure that IBM was supporting the right kinds of activities through its employees. This took place at the same time that the Public Responsibility Committee of the Board was being formed to give structure to the company's public service activities.

Social service leaves can originate in three ways: (1) on the initiative of an employee involved in a nonprofit organization; (2) when a nonprofit agency approaches IBM with a request for assistance; and (3) when IBM offers its help to a community agency. Applications are approved by the director of personnel resource planning at IBM. Most leaves are granted with full pay and can last up to a year of full-time work with a nonprofit community organization. More than five hundred employees have been granted full or partial leaves to work in the community since the program was formalized in 1971. The company is attempting to expand participation.

There are now more than sixty people on leave in a given year, at an average annual cost to the company in salary alone of $43,000 per employee. The full costs—including benefits—are charged to the operating divisions sponsoring the selected employees. Some of the organizations in which IBM people on leave are working are the Urban League, Junior Achievement, the National Alliance of Business, the Indian Center, the American Productivity Center, Disabled Programmers, Inc., the Chicano Education Project, the Center for Employment Training, and the United Way.

Faculty Loan Program. The Faculty Loan Program was established by IBM in 1971 when the company's Personnel Group discovered that many new hires under the company's affirmative action program lacked some of the skills needed to perform their jobs properly. The program is designed to help colleges and universities with large numbers of minority and disadvantaged students to improve the education of their students in fields of interest to employers like IBM. Each year, approximately fifty schools are invited to send proposals, but other schools send them as well.

The Faculty Loan Program Committee at IBM then considers the proposals and selects employees who have been nominated by their divisions for the program. More than 300 IBM employees have participated in the program, with full pay. About 40 IBM employees per academic year teach subjects in the schools, such as computer science, engineering, and business administration. Others serve as well in nonacademic roles such as planning, curriculum development, student counseling, and administrative support. IBM employees have also served the National Association for Careers for Minorities in Engineering and the United Negro College Fund. Although the Faculty Loan Program has for the most part been made available to minority schools, current assignments also include Brigham Young University (to serve Indian students) and the New York City Comprehensive Math and Science Program.

89

Community Executive Program. IBM has had considerable experience in running a major management training center for its employees. This has given birth to its most recent private sector initiative, the Community Executive Program. Designed to help urban service groups such as the Urban League, Opportunities Industrialization Centers (OIC), and SER-Jobs for Progress, Inc. manage their human and financial resources more effectively, this IBM program is offered free of charge to full-time staff managers with people and/or program responsibilities in private nonprofit urban organizations involved in providing specific social services.

An intensive one-week course is conducted by IBM management development personnel and some noncompany faculty. It focuses on planning and financial control techniques, management skills, and team process skills. IBM provides room, board, class facilities, and materials and will be able to handle about 800 students by the end of 1982.

Fund for Community Service. Any discussion of IBM's private sector initiatives must include mention of the company's fund for community service, from which it donates money to community organizations in which IBM employees and retirees are involved. Since its beginning in 1972, the fund has made grants to more than 21,000 IBM employees and retirees for more than 10,000 projects sponsored by organizations in which they are active. These grants have totaled more than $10 million, a sum that will probably grow more rapidly now that the spouses of employees and retirees are also eligible.

Conclusion. Corporate responsibility in the community has been a part of IBM's corporate ethos since the company was founded by Thomas Watson. The idea has been continued by IBM's three chief executive officers since Thomas Watson, Jr., who enunciated corporate social responsibility as an explicit operating principle of the company twenty years ago. With the creation of the Public Responsibility Committee of the Board of Directors ten years later, IBM expanded and formalized its role in this area. The committee has announced IBM's intention to do even more in the future.

The formal programs established in the late 1960s and early 1970s either grew out of existing informal practices (social service leave and training of the handicapped) or were the result of responses to new problems—some local (such as training of the disadvantaged in Watts), others national (the Faculty Loan Program). IBM has recently doubled the number of its major training centers for the disadvantaged, added several new centers for training the physically disabled, and created a management training program for executives from the nonprofit sector.

IBM has not plunged into more social service activities without regard for its own interests. The initiatives undertaken not only have built on the company's strengths in skills training and management development—enabling it to achieve demonstrable results—but have also been related to its various lines of business. One result has been to enhance IBM's reputation as a socially concerned corporation.

This combination of expertise and interest guides IBM's development of public responsibility programs. Even if the objective of the programs is not profit making in the business sense, IBM's approach is no less businesslike—the company wields enough influence on projects to produce results, such as the high placement rates of trainees.

The success of IBM's private sector initiatives depends not only on keeping them in tune with company interests and principles but also on managing them in the same decentralized way as the profit-making business operations are managed. Line managers in the districts and regions are responsible for achieving objectives such as opening new training centers for the handicapped just as they are responsible for meeting sales objectives for IBM products.

Notes

[1] In November 1977, Honeywell published its "Employee Relations Principles," which identifies the company's goals in relating to its employees.

[2] William D. Conley, Honeywell vice president, public affairs, January 1982.

[3] In addition, in its "Principles of Community Relations," Honeywell states, among other things, its preference that contributions be evaluated by those involved themselves in community work.

[4] From "Principles of Community Relations."

[5] See the section on "Guidelines for Project Selection," in *Honeywell Involvement in the Community* (manual for division managers developed by the Honeywell CCRD staff).

The Social Programs of Organized Labor

Michael P. Balzano and Marlene M. Beck

To appreciate the activities of labor unions in social programs today, they must be viewed in the context of labor's involvement with human and social problems over the past hundred years. In most unionized industries, an individual who joins a union receives a wage and benefits package equal to or better than those enjoyed by the rest of the work force. Union members share in the affluent society. Steelworkers, autoworkers, and other skilled and nonskilled blue-collar workers own homes, campers, and boats, as well as other luxury items enjoyed only by the wealthy of forty years ago.

This high standard of living is reflected in the issues debated in collective bargaining agreements. Contemporary labor negotiations tend to focus on wages and benefits; with the exception of the coal industry and a few others, health, safety, and working conditions are not as highly contested. Unions over the past twenty years have demanded more paid holidays and vacations and extensions of medical coverage and dental care. In short, the stress has been on economic rather than social advances.

Before unions won recognition as members of the trinity of business, labor, and government, the situation was quite different. Historical accounts of the Haymarket riot, the Pullman strike, and the coal mine strike of 1922 testify to the violence of labor's struggle to achieve its present status. In decades past, labor's demands reflected the social conditions of the workers. Unions have come far since the days when they demanded the forty-hour week and the right of collective bargaining.

The poor economic and social conditions of American workers gave union organizers a fertile field. Union organizers rallied members around the central theme of a higher standard of living—decent housing, adequate food, and other necessities of life. Although they had no academic degrees in social work, union organizers acquired a profound understanding of the sociological problems faced by the wage earner. Their intimate knowledge of those problems gave them the credibility with workers to lead the movement for reform. The labor movement was a social movement. The goal of union organizers was to champion the cause of those who had no spokesman. Union organizers offered social services to potential members.

Union concern for the social problems of workers stemmed from first-hand knowledge of the plight of individuals at the grass roots level. In many areas, unions operated an intelligence network similar to the precinct and ward structure of the big-city political machines. Services and social outreach were essential to both. No birth, death, illness, or hardship went unnoticed by the union hierarchy: no member faced a hardship alone. The goal was to meet the social needs of the membership. As labor unions became both accepted and more established, union officials maintained a constant vigil over the social concerns and problems of their members. The cohesiveness of a union could often be measured by its sensitivity and responsiveness to the social problems of its members. It was this cohesiveness that often provided nonmembers with the incentive to belong, the feeling of oneness that gave meaning to the union term "brother and sister."

Before the 1950s, union officials could easily address the social needs of union members, such as the rising cost of housing, food, and medical care. The more established unions, especially the industrial unions, sought to embellish previously obtained benefits. The hard core needs that had been the rallying cry of organizers had by and large been met.

Pensioners lived out their years in the neighborhoods in which they had lived and worked, often in sight of the mills and factories in which they spent their lives. They enjoyed the company of their children and grandchildren, without becoming a burden on them. For mothers who worked, child care was not a problem: many a grandmother functioned as a day care center both for relatives and for nonrelatives.

In the 1950s and 1960s, everything changed. As the children of the first-generation immigrant factory workers fled the urban centers for their dream home in the suburbs, they left their parents behind. As America's antiquated industrial facilities fell victim to foreign competition and plants closed, economic and social deprivation could be measured by the number of abandoned buildings, churches, and schoolyards. Social life also began to change. Neighborhood streets, once safe and pleasant, became combat zones where neither young nor old could safely venture. Suddenly, social problems, eclipsed in earlier years, emerged everywhere.

All of these problems were brought in one way or another to the union halls and labor locals. Retirees, active members, and union officials came together to assist needy members of communities throughout the country. In some cases, one-to-one service was rendered to a family or person in distress, and that service led to a vast array of others, including meals for the homebound, help for alcoholics, transportation for the physically disabled, rehabilitation for stroke victims, home maintenance and repair, and day care. Over the past twenty years, there has been a vast expansion of union social programs aimed at providing such services. At about the same time the Great Society and the War on Poverty were pouring billions of dollars into the Job Corps, the Office of Economic Opportunity, and the Model Cities program, unions at the local level were quietly establishing social programs aimed at the social problems of community residents—members and nonmembers alike. These programs were not ostentatious, the offices were not plush, and the staff possessed no degrees in social work, and sometimes no degree at all. The funds might be raised through members' contributions, local drives, bazaars, raffles, Wednesday night bingo, or a variety of other ways. The programs might operate from a small corner of the office of the business agent. And the vehicles used might be the personal cars, trucks, and vans of the members. Nevertheless, the social programs run by these unions meet the perceived needs in a manner every bit as sophisticated as programs designed and operated by sociologists, and other credentialed professionals funded by the public treasury. By providing low cost social services to people in need, free of bureaucratic red tape, these union programs constitute a vital community resource at a time when communities are desperately trying to cope with rising demand and shrinking revenues.

In this study, which is by no means exhaustive, we will attempt to trace the development of union-operated social programs. We will describe union social programs operating today and the social needs they address, as well as the techniques and the systems they employ to meet those needs. Our goal is to provide public policy makers and the general public with information on these programs, so that they may be incorporated into any plan for increasing the role of the private sector in providing social services.

Approach and Methods. The central theme connecting the sections of this review is that unions, working through neighborhood, church, and other local organizations, design and operate social service delivery systems that are as sophisticated as publicly funded programs.

Many questions cannot be answered, however, because the data are unavailable.

The researcher attempting to understand union-operated social programs will initially be struck by the paucity of data. There is no Washington program data base as there is for federally funded programs. There is no Department of Health and Human Services or Community Services Administration from which to obtain budget justifications presented to congressional appropriations committees. There is no national program directory containing even a rough description of programs or sponsors.

The chief reason for the absence of even a partial program anthology is that union social programs are generally local programs. Turning attention to the local community, the researcher is confronted with an enormous amount of information, but it is generally unassembled. Unlike federal programs, which generate massive paperwork, local programs have a far less formalized reporting structure. The researcher must seek out the functions being performed and describe the structures performing them.

For many social programs written historical records are nonexistent. One must rely on the recollections of those operating the program, since earlier organizational charts never existed. The same gaps are evident in the financing and budgeting of programs at the early stages. In many of the examples presented in this chapter, people were served by groups without established budget procedures or ceilings. The immediacy of the problems often called for an attitude of a "Brothers, let's pass the hat and help this person out," rather than "Wait for the scheduled authorization hearings, and hope for adequate funding for this yet-unauthorized program." The attitude of labor unions toward local problem solving is, Don't talk about it, and don't salute it or build a monument to it, but rather, Let's do it!

Finally, one must make allowances for the difficulties encountered in obtaining program information from grass-roots organizations. The appearance of researchers from "Washington" wandering through neighborhood projects can be unsettling. Many routine questions about needs assessment and eligibility are considered personal. Questions about the size of the budget or the salaries of program personnel—all public information in federal programs—arouse suspicion and must be raised with sensitivity. In many of the programs, we were allowed to examine financial data and were given copies of records. In other programs, the atmosphere was not conducive to requests for such information. In all cases, however, the data obtained, both objective and subjective, are sufficient for a fair appreciation of the low-cost, high-impact social services rendered by these community programs.

The method used in our inquiry is *structural functional* analysis. We examined social programs from three perspectives. We asked:

1. What kinds of union activities are being employed to alleviate social problems? That is, *who* is rendering a specific service to someone in need?
2. Is there a systematic approach to social service delivery? That is, is there a program?
3. How is this effort financed?

Of the twenty-two programs we analyzed, we selected for detailed case studies examples that present different aspects of programming. The case studies are a cross section of union programs in Sunbelt, Midwest, Northwest, Northeast, and Great Lakes industrial centers. Though by no means exhaustive, they constitute a comprehensive sample of the program models operating in communities where unions are present.

Case Studies

The Brown Baggers of Iowa: A Program Operated by a Local Union. Roger Bleeker served as a volunteer on the community service committee of United Auto Workers [UAW] Local 838 in Waterloo, Iowa. From this vantage point, he noted the diet deficiencies of elderly, low-income area residents. Like many union members raised in this farm belt community, Bleeker planted a small garden each year to meet his own needs. In 1979 his garden produced far more than he could use or store, and he learned that many of his union neighbors had similar harvests. He then began to think about how the surplus food could be used to help feed families in need.

He marshaled several members from his union contacts on the community service committee and sent out a call to area farmers to donate whatever food they could. The response was so great that it overwhelmed the service capacity of the simple effort almost before it began. When one farmer donated 1,500 pounds of pears and another 1,200 pounds of sweet corn, Bleeker and his fellow members realized that a one-to-one service approach would not be adequate to handle the volume.

The program began to take shape with the combined effort of the union and the community. A local Catholic church offered a vacant house on its property for use in storing and distributing the food to the adjacent neighborhoods. Others in the spiritual community then became involved. A nun organized what has come to be called the Crisis Pantry.

When food brought to the union labor temple immediately outstripped the facility's ability to store the surplus, the UAW local authorized the installation of a walk-in cooler in its labor hall to accommodate the rapidly expanding supply of perishable foods. Soon busloads of senior citizens were going to nearby farms to help gather food for the program.

Today all the activities one would expect to find in a well-run social program are present in the Iowa program, known as the Brown Baggers. Fresh produce, canned goods, and other surplus food, including live chickens, are collected and then distributed to older residents through several sites operated by senior citizens. Brown Bagger volunteers, who are both active and retired workers from Local 838, collect the food donations from community growers, pick produce from gardens and orchards, bag food, plant and harvest gardens, and assist with fund raising. In the program's first year they distributed 10,000 pounds of fresh produce to senior citizens and in 1981 more than 68,000 pounds.

The food is delivered in a number of ways to those who cannot come to the distribution centers: by volunteers using their own vehicles and gasoline as in a Meals-on-Wheels program, by vans used by the local area agency on aging to transport elderly persons from place to place, and by a truck donated to the program by a local Ford dealer.

The Brown Baggers work closely with the local Salvation Army, the Jesse Cosby Neighborhood Center, and the Hawkeye Valley Agency on Aging. Chris Harshberger, director of the Area Agency on Aging, said it is the attitude of these union volunteers that made this program go. The Area Agency on Aging (AAA) is using the Brown Baggers to help distribute surplus government cheese and butter. They anticipate 1,500 new volunteers in nine neighboring towns, using a kind of pony express system of delivery. The AAA receives the surplus, the unions contact agencies in neighboring towns and meet them at a drop-off point, and the town enlists its residents to get the surplus to the needy.

Bleeker never worries about finding additional volunteers for the expanded services. "Ninety percent have had hard times and are having good times now," he says. "Most of us haven't forgotten the bad times; so we are trying to help people where we can." Bleeker wants no government money. He "wants none of the hassle" and wants to keep the program as "cost free" as possible.

This program is significant for at least three reasons. First, it is an excellent example of a program run under the auspices of a labor union local. The local is the smallest unit of analysis in this study, and is the matrix that has potential for growth. Second, it is a program that has flourished in a rural community. Most of the programs we analyzed were in urban areas with greater concentrations of people needing service. Third, this program demonstrates how the efforts of one man and one union local can be a catalyst for a community-wide effort.

The Steelworkers Oldtimers Foundation: Fontana, California. One of the oldest and most diversified union social programs is the Steelworkers Oldtimers Foundation in Fontana, California. The impetus for this program, as for most of the programs in this study, came from one person seeking to help another.

Early in 1963 Dino Papavero, now president of United Steelworkers of America Local 2869, watched his uncle grow more and more restless in retirement. Concerned over his isolation, depression, and generally low morale, Papavero noticed others in the same emotional state and thought of a way the union could help alleviate their isolation.

Twelve percent of the population of Fontana is over the age of sixty-five. Many of these people came to southern California in the 1940s to work in defense plants or in the Kaiser steel mills, leaving family ties behind in the industrial Northeast and Great Lakes areas. When they retired, they felt a deep sense of loss. Realizing that retirees feel a common identification as steelworkers, Papavero took the nucleus of his idea first to his local and then, with Hugh Moore, a fellow worker at the Kaiser steel mill in Fontana, to other area locals. They sought a way to promote fellowship and a renewed sense of purpose among retired workers. From their meeting with retired and active union members, they set out to establish a union outreach to serve retired members just as the union served those in the active work force.

In the early days, the program consisted of an array of one-to-one services, with program records divided between Papavero and Moore and "filed" in the trunks of their cars. When a more established setting and structure became necessary, an office was acquired through donations from members and the union. This soon became inadequate as larger and larger numbers of older persons and other members and nonmembers overflowed the small space. Once again the union modified its approach and increased its commitment. A nonprofit entity was established with funds donated by the workers themselves. In 1964 Papavero's idea for improving the quality of life for those in retirement was realized in the creation of the Steelworkers Oldtimers Foundation.

The programs of the foundation seem to have evolved logically from one service to another. As in most of the programs we analyzed, the first service rendered was information and referral. At the outset, up to thirty elderly persons were being referred each week to the appropriate state and federal offices for problems ranging from receipt of the wrong social security checks to errors in hospital bills. Many of the problems stemmed from clerical errors that were quickly corrected. Others required the assistance of an ombudsman to renegotiate a payment schedule or other arrangement to alleviate pressure upon the elderly person.

As the phone calls requesting services increased, it became apparent that some were motivated by loneliness rather than by a need for an ombudsman. Older persons living in isolation exhibit even greater uneasiness when homebound with an illness or recuperating from an operation. Believing that much of this isolation could be temporarily alleviated by a phone call, the foundation began a twenty-four-hour-a-day Phone Alert League (PAL), through which volunteers call homebound persons daily to inquire about their needs. The call alone, often the only human contact of the day, is sometimes enough to comfort the recipient. The knowledge that there were homebound persons unable to care for themselves led to the creation of a homebound meal service. The foundation applied for and received a grant for fifty home-delivered meals in the Fontana area—its first government grant.

It was through the delivery of meals to the homebound that one of the most innovative programs took shape. Volunteers carrying meals to shut-ins saw homes badly in need of maintenance: a worn step tread, a loose railing, a dimly lit stairwell, locks that were not secure—small things that most of us take for granted but that make life hazardous to the elderly. John Piazza, director of the foundation and a steelworker himself, knew that workers within the community were capable of solving this problem. He envisioned a home maintenance program that would match skilled workers with those in need. In 1976 the foundation received a nonrenewable grant from the governor's discretionary fund, with which it bought four vans and equipped them with tools to be used for minor home repair.

The home maintenance service assigns workers in four categories: carpentry, plumbing, electrical repair, and general repair. They rehang doors, frame and glaze windows, repair water heaters, sinks, and faucets, install light plugs and fixtures, install safety rails, repair roofs, do replastering and concrete work, repair lawn sprinklers—the list is nearly endless.

The service has one coordinator in an office at the foundation headquarters. With the use of a two-way radio, she is in constant touch with the eight retired craftsmen who, in teams of two, are the core of this operation. Their workload is scheduled according to requests, but a truck can be quickly dispatched in emergencies.

The participant is asked to pay the wholesale cost of the parts involved if he can. There is no charge for the labor or the visit. Printed on each side of the van, in bold letters, are "Steelworkers Oldtimers Foundation," the address and phone number, and "Home Maintenance for the Elderly." This is a traveling announcement for the service.

Often the work crew will perform several tasks. An example is the work done for an elderly woman who had been robbed twice. New deadbolt locks were installed, outside lights were connected, and the overgrown shrubbery surrounding the doorway was trimmed so that another intruder could not surprise the woman as she entered the house.

A primary reason for initiating the maintenance program was that it would reduce the risk of accidents for the program participants. Inquiring about the husband of a woman visiting the center, Piazza learned that the man had fallen from a ladder while attempting to fix a window shutter. It became apparent that many of the center's program recipients sustained injuries in similar ways. "It's the little things that get these people," Piazza said.

> An elderly person stands on a chair to change a lightbulb. They get dizzy, the chair slips. Who knows what happened? All of a sudden, they are lying on the floor with a bad fracture. Then you've got the pain and suffering on top of the problem of care during convalescence. You know, where does it stop? All for what? Because no one was there to change the bulb. You see, now we send out a van. The guys change the bulb, look around, tighten a stair rail, tack down a rug near a stairway. You know, preventive maintenance. The wife makes them coffee. She's had some company. Five or six needs have been served in one visit.

Piazza concludes, "It's good for the maintenance crew as well. It gives them the feeling that they are needed." Since 1976 the program has employed thirty maintenance men. Joe Gonzalez, a former steelworker at the Kaiser plant who has been with the program since its inception, has been helpful in giving each one on-the-job training.

This program keeps Gonzalez and others like him productive, contributing members of society.

The center also operates a program to help stroke victims begin dealing with others again. Stroke victims released from the hospital are given a series of exercises designed to help them regain the use of damaged limbs. They are monitored by their doctors and physical therapists. The Stroke Resocialization Program does not compete with or take the place of these specialists. It provides a group where those recovering from strokes can test strengths and skills and vocal cords without fear of ostracism or stares from the outside world.

The program began in the spring of 1977 with a direct donation from the Fontana Lions Club of $2,000. Two volunteer nurses were sent to a seminar on stroke victims, and Caffey College provided an instructor to coordinate the program. The city of Fontana allows the use of its community center for the minimal cost of five dollars a week. The group operates on a budget of approximately $750 a year, which is used for arts and crafts material, exercise equipment, and field trips.

Along with the programs we have outlined above, the foundation also offers: hot lunches five days a week; nutrition information; welfare and food commodities for those without means; the Retired Senior Volunteer Program; consumer assistance; advice on wills and insurance; a free library service; transportation to appointments with doctors, dentists, clinics, and meal sites; and voter registration.

In addition to these many services, the foundation administers a modern high-rise apartment complex housing 170 senior citizens. The complex contains game rooms and recreation areas as well as a nonprofit grocery store. It was financed through a grant from the Department of Housing and Urban Development in a funding formula that used foundation resources.

The Steelworkers Oldtimers Foundation tries to meet human and social needs in a multifunctional way. The foundation has skillfully combined government grants, community donations, and proceeds from the steelworkers' weekly bingo games to meet these needs.

Perhaps the greatest service rendered to the community is a spiritual one. To the more than 30,000 residents of the southern California area who have been touched in one way or another by it, the Steelworkers Oldtimers Foundation offers the assurance that someone cares and understands and is readily available to listen and to help.

The National Steelworkers Oldtimers Foundation. The success of the Steelworkers Oldtimers Foundation of Fontana had a profound impact on the national officers of the United Steelworkers of America. Frank

McKee, now the union's international treasurer, had been both an officer of Kaiser Steel's Local 2869 and the director of District 38. Thoroughly familiar with the Fontana program and its widely recognized success, McKee set about creating a national program modeled after the California foundation. His goal was realized in 1978 when the Nineteenth Constitutional Convention of the United Steelworkers of America (USWA) established the National Steelworkers Oldtimers Foundation (NSOF), a nonprofit entity whose purpose is "to serve the educational and community needs of the elderly residing in steelmaking towns."

Working out of the USWA headquarters in Pittsburgh, the NSOF established a service network that covers the Mon-Youth valley. Ten community centers, each operated by a site coordinator, are the focus of the program activity. The centers fall into three territorial divisions, each served by an area manager who provides various kinds of program and management help to the site coordinators. The three area managers report to a project manager on the staff of the NSOF at the Pittsburgh headquarters. Funding for the field operation is derived from grants and contracts with Allegheny County's Area Agency on Aging.

The centers teem with activity. Educational and social events are regularly scheduled. Legal aid, senior counseling, and other needed services are channeled through an information and referral system. Senior citizens may also participate in a congregate meal service, similar to that operated in Fontana.

Outside the centers, a variety of in-home services are also provided. The manager of each center coordinates services provided by the Comprehensive Employment and Training Act (CETA), the Senior Aide Program, and the Senior Companion Program. In addition to the more elaborate, federally supported services, the NSOF has initiated other efforts with resources generated from within the local community. The David McDonald Labor Lyceum of Montgomery County, Pennsylvania, is one example.

Today, the labor lyceum is the rallying point for retired steelworkers in this depressed area. The union hall formerly belonged to steelworker Local 1392, which was dissolved when the Allenwood Steel Company closed its doors in 1977. The NSOF has provided funds for maintenance of the building and has thus made it possible for the 900-member steelworkers' retiree club to continue to meet at the hall. Dominic Soletta, who was treasurer of the local union, is now employed by the NSOF to direct operations and activities at the center.

The community has rallied behind this union effort. A local attorney gives one day a week to counsel members. A local businessman has organized a dinner dance to benefit the center, with the entire event paid for by donations. Through fund-raising efforts such as this, Soletta wants to expand the center's meager kitchen facilities, so as to increase the number of days and meals served.

Another self-supporting NSOF venture is the Sam Camen Center in Youngstown, Ohio. Youngstown was virtually a city in decay after the closing of the U.S. Steel Ohio Works. Sitting as a constant reminder of this closing was the former union hall that housed USWA Local 1330. This facility was once the hub around which all their union activity revolved. Four thousand steelworkers once met there regularly. They not only held union meetings, but also sponsored blood pressure tests for the community, a Babe Ruth Little League team, and many other events that benefited members and the rest of the community.

When the plant closed, the headquarters was abandoned. Time and vandalism took their toll. The unused building became not only an eyesore but a constant reminder of how life had been. Bob Vasquez was president of this local when the mill closed. He saw a resurrected union center as a means of lifting the spirits of the workers and their families. Harry Mayfield, director of District 27, worked with Vasquez and former members of the local in getting help from the NSOF.

Vasquez, along with Al Battafarano, Joe Gavini, and a score of former union members, worked to renovate the old union hall. Their original intention was to fix it up as a meeting place. But as it took shape, they saw the possibility of bringing back the commitment, the sense of purpose, the pride of accomplishment, and the feeling of family to the entire community. Former members of Local 1330 renovated and restored the battered structure inside and out. Laid-off bricklayers, carpenters, and steelworkers replaced windows and paneled and painted walls.

The center is constantly seeking funds for small projects. It received a grant from the National Council of Senior Citizens to help the elderly weatherize their homes to make them energy efficient. The program was very successful, but the grant money was soon depleted. The center has been sponsoring bingo games and using the profits to continue energy care at least part-time.

There are plans for housing senior citizens near the center with funds from the U.S. Department of Housing and Urban Development. The NSOF staff is working with city officials in looking into the possibilities. The center owns nine and a half acres adjacent to its building and would like to construct a high-rise apartment building there using its own tradesmen to do the work.

Sam Camen (the steelworker for whom the center is named) said the abandoned building had symbolized the hopelessness and frustration of members who had been abandoned when the mill closed. The new center, he said, should be a rallying point for the entire community and an example of what can be done.

In addition to the programs we analyzed for this study, we learned of other steel communities seeking to emulate the program efforts of the NSOF. The foundation is contemplating other projects in the Canton, Ohio, area. One steel producer in California offered the NSOF a 188-acre tract of land in return for a plan to develop a complex capable of providing a full range of services to the elderly.

Although these programs may seem geographically fragmented, there is a link that ties them all together. The United Steelworkers of America sponsors the popular periodical *The Oldtimer*, a quarterly that is sent to over 300,000 retired steelworkers nationwide. The mailing list is kept up to date on the United Steelworkers' computer in Indiana. Thousands of extra issues are sent to all the centers run by the NSOF. It is an important link that ties the programs, the projects, and the people of the NSOF together with steelworkers everywhere. It gives them information on activities of retirees and retiree clubs, on foundation projects, on legislation affecting older workers and older people generally, and on all items critical to the lives of senior citizens. It is this link with fellow unionists throughout the country that the National Steelworkers Oldtimers Foundation has fostered.

The activity of the NSOF has proved inspirational to steel communities in the tristate area of Pennsylvania, Ohio, and West Virginia. The foundation attracts proposals for assistance similar to that rendered to the labor lyceum and the Sam Camen Center. These are excellent examples of communities taking the initiative and using the foundation to launch their efforts. They are truly grass-roots programs.

Camp Variety: A Coalition of Unions. Many of the social programs we observed in our research were sponsored by one labor local or a national union. This case study of the work done by the Building and Construction Trades Council of Pittsburgh to aid the Variety Club is an excellent example of trade unions uniting to perform a community service. It also demonstrates how one labor-sponsored social service, the Variety Club, can call on other unions to serve.

The Variety Club, founded by eleven theatrical performers in Pittsburgh in the fall of 1927, is one of the largest international children's charities in the world. In 1927 the club decided to adopt a foundling baby and act, in effect, as her godparent, underwriting her support and education. They received national publicity for this endeavor, and Pittsburgh was recognized as the "mother tent" of the charitable Variety Club. The club is now embraced by all phases of the amusement business and has "tents" in most cities of the United States and in eight other countries. It has dedicated itself over the years to meeting the needs of underprivileged and handicapped children.

From its first modest efforts of raising $3,737.99 by putting on a circus in Pittsburgh, the Variety Club, which has become international in scope, raises millions of dollars for children each year. America's first cancer hospital for children came from Variety Club funds, along with a score of schools for crippled, retarded, and blind children and clinics and hospitals open to all children, regardless of race, creed, or color.

There is a natural affinity between trade unionists and the show business community, as union members, actors, electricians, and stage-hands are all "brothers."

One way that Variety Clubs raise money is through an annual telethon. One of the goals of the 1980 fund-raising campaign was to refurbish the Camp for Handicapped Children in the northern corner of Allegheny County. The camp had been given to the Variety Club twenty years earlier and had received no intensive improvement in that time. Over the years, the building and construction trades in Pittsburgh have manned the phones for the telethon, taking pledges and encouraging their members to contribute. Nick Stipanovich, the business representative of the Pittsburgh Building and Construction Trades Council, was manning the phones the night the chief barker for Variety appealed to the audience for funds. Stinpanovich, moved by the appeal, contacted all the various trade unions and organized a major reconstruction effort.

When Ray Thompson, business manager of International Electrical Workers Local 5, and the local's vice-president, John McIntyre, visited Camp Variety, they found rows of frayed electrical wiring strung through trees, creating a danger of fire everywhere. Twelve camp buildings required a great deal of attention—many of them were unsafe. As trade unionists, they were appalled at the conditions. But they also knew that their members could make the needed repairs and renovations.

The union leaders went directly to the locals to appeal to the members, who were already committed to helping the Variety Club. But now they were being asked for their tools, their talents, and their time—not just money. They worked together on a project that required ironworkers, painters, carpenters, cement workers, electricians, and landscapers working together in a project that would benefit an entire community. They persuaded local building suppliers to donate needed materials. Heavy equipment for digging ditches and improving the road into the camp was lent by construction firms. Firemen from nearby communities provided transportation and food. The local brewery provided liquid refreshments. In eight weekends, more than 350 tradesmen contributed more than $200,000 in goods and services to renovate this camp.

The Building and Construction Trades Council subsequently decided to make this an annual event. Each year they will designate weekends to inspect the camp and keep it up to standard. Through their efforts, 500 handicapped children can safely use Camp Variety for summer recreation they could enjoy nowhere else.

A similar effort has been conducted in the Philadelphia area. The building trades unions there constructed a building for the Philadelphia Variety Club. The members raised money to hire a supervisor to manage the volunteer workers. They are now rehabilitating a building to house veterans. Stinpanovich argues that any building trades council that has a leader committed to meeting community needs can rally such a team effort. It requires commitment from the top and a worthwhile cause.

Unionists receive little credit in the media for this kind of giving. More camps, more buildings, and more sites would probably be built, renovated, and cared for if their efforts were recognized.

President Ronald Reagan is quoted in "This Is Variety" as saying, "I am very proud to applaud the members of Variety Clubs International for your heartfelt and living concern for those who are least able to help themselves: handicapped and underprivileged children throughout the world."

Carrier Watch: St. Louis, Missouri. This case study illustrates the first of three relationships we found between organized labor and the United Way of America.

Like most major American cities, the greater St. Louis area is served by a large United Way office, with a labor liaison office. Its purpose is to deal with social problems that affect the labor force in general and union workers in particular. The three staff representatives come from different union backgrounds: an auto worker, a meat cutter, and a letter carrier. The men are paid by the United Way, are housed in the United Way office complex, and are responsible to the United Way hierarchy in St. Louis. Although they deal with union and nonunion members, their labor backgrounds give them the credibility needed to serve a sensitive constituency.

In many respects, the services offered to a union member experiencing a social problem may be no different from those offered to any other person in trouble: a laid-off union member may require the same information and referral services as the owner of a small business that has failed. Because of the number of layoffs among union members, however, the labor staff must work with the unions. It conducts training for many of the locals for dealing with both the emotional impact and the economic consequences of unemployment:

- How long does one wait before registering for unemployment compensation?
- Should one notify creditors, utilities, and mortgage holders of one's unemployment?
- Is there a minimum income requirement for food stamps?

These are some of the questions the labor staff answers as it assists the individual.

The activities of the St. Louis labor staff are similar to those performed by their counterparts in other cities. What is unique to St. Louis is the program operated by the letter carriers. It is a form of outreach that has both a local and a national dimension.

Harold Wright, a member of the United Way labor staff, coordinates Carrier Watch, a program operated by the National Association of Letter Carriers, one of two unions representing the nation's postal workers. The program consists of an informal verbal agreement between a letter carrier and residents along the route. A red-and-white sticker marked "Carrier Watch" is affixed to the mailboxes of participants in the program. While delivering mail, the letter carrier looks out for any changes that appear out of the ordinary at the home of a participant. The accumulation of mail in the box for more than one day is cause for the carrier to see if illness or accident has incapacitated the occupant. If so, the mailman calls for an emergency unit.

One postman was recently honored by the mayor of St. Louis for saving the life of an elderly handicapped St. Louis woman. Noticing that mail from the previous day had not been collected, he inquired at the apartment door and he heard a faint voice calling: "Help me. I can't walk." Finding the door locked, he summoned the building supervisor and the mayor's Office on Aging. The police were notified and entered the apartment. The woman had injured herself in a fall and was unable to move. She had been lying there for almost twenty-four hours.

Harold Wright's experience in social service is extensive. For ten years he was national director of community services for the National Association of Letter Carriers, serving in the unpaid position in addition to his regular duties as a letter carrier. Under the last three presidents of the national association, he coordinated several of the union community service drives. Each year the union endorsed and sponsored a national blood donor program, assisted the diabetes association in conducting diabetes detection, information, and fund-raising drives, and took a leading role in the muscular dystrophy telethon.

It was the union's interest in developing the Carrier Watch program, however, that resulted in Wright's joining the labor staff of the United Way in St. Louis to institute the program, which has the full endorsement of the national association and Local 343.

From either the St. Louis branch of the United Way or another office in nearby Belleville, Illinois, Wright assists those seeking to participate in the program in St. Louis and the surrounding area. He also answers program inquiries from around the nation. Anyone seeking information about the Carrier Watch program is sent the Carrier Watch Manual, which contains a description of the three "logical" steps one must take to initiate a Carrier Watch program: First, obtain the endorsement of the letter carriers' local (a sample resolution is attached for submission to the membership). Second, secure the services of an umbrella coordinating agency such as the United Way or local area agency on aging. Third, establish a coordinating committee of representatives of local organizations, such as the letter carriers, the U.S. Postal Service, the police department, the umbrella coordinating group, the area agency on aging, the highest elected local official (the mayor or the county executive, for example), the local United Way, or other representatives as determined by the committee.

Finally, the manual lists programmatic considerations that should be addressed by the committee, such as the geographic program boundaries, the materials to be used in the program (samples are attached), the method of distributing materials, the program cost (specifically, for publication of materials), and the method of informing the elderly of the program (agencies on aging alone should not be expected to do this task). Questions to be decided include the following: Who will be responsible for training workers dealing with the elderly? Whom will the letter carrier call in an emergency? Who will be responsible for checking on residents if trouble is expected? Who will be responsible for calling the police in emergency situations? And who will be responsible for handling any problems that occur? As simple as they appear, these checklists present the components of a good program.

The Carrier Watch program provides a systematic check on older persons living alone, which could help to keep some of them out of an institution. Many elderly people are alone for weeks at a time. Often the mere lack of monitoring whether or not they are all right leads to institutionalization.

Another potential benefit of the Carrier Watch program lies in the prevention of neighborhood crime. Insurance rates even for suburban areas have risen dramatically over the last decade, primarily because of the increase in home burglaries. There is hardly a suburban resident who has not been affected by the crime problem. Letter carriers can work as another neighborhood surveillance system. Unlike the policeman who controls a neighborhood in a squad car, the postman knows the people who live in the houses. Harold Wright tells of a letter carrier who notified police when he saw a moving van emptying the house of a family he knew was away on vacation. The carrier can prevent burglaries by reporting strange cars or vans in the area.

The Carrier Watch has two great assets as a national program. First, it costs almost nothing to design and install and nothing at all to operate once installed. Second, it can be replicated anywhere.

The Emergency Assistance Program: Phoenix, Arizona. A variation of the United Way–labor union relationship is found in the United Way Labor Agency of Phoenix, Arizona. In this arrangement, the labor liaison staff is not located in the United Way office complex, but operates what is called the United Labor Agency. Program and support funds are a combination of United Way revenues raised by the labor agency itself.

Labor's involvement in community services in the Phoenix area dates from the late 1940s. Soon after the United Way in Phoenix was established as the central private sector charity, a labor liaison function similar to that in St. Louis emerged. The labor staff performed one-to-one services as the labor staff does in other United Way offices. Robert Connolly, president of the AFL-CIO Central Labor Council of Greater Phoenix, was the United Way labor liaison early in the 1970s. In time he favored placing liaison outside the United Way structure to identify it more closely with labor, in part because of the less-than-friendly union climate there. In 1976 labor liaison was moved out of the United Way complex and established in a separate office, where it is closely connected to the AFL-CIO structure. From his position as president of the labor council, Connolly maintains a close working relationship with Joseph Marto, the labor agency's present director.

One of labor's many kinds of outreach is to senior citizens. For ten years, it has conducted an influenza inoculation program. Flu vaccine is purchased by the agency, and inoculations are administered by licensed nurses and physicians in accordance with Arizona laws. The fee charged for the service is five dollars, considerably lower than the twelve- to twenty-dollar fee charged for the same vaccine administered by their own physicians. The injections are administered in shopping centers and other public areas, which offers convenience and avoids the trauma often associated with an office appointment. Each flu season from 10,000 to 13,000 people take advantage of this service, many of whom would not otherwise receive them. No one is refused vaccine for want of money.

Through its close links with the trade unions, a union-operated program can marshal building materials and skilled craftsmen and use them instead of financial resources. When the budget for housing for victims of domestic violence was cut, for example, the labor agency assembled the materials and workmen to complete the roof repairs, which cost $4,000. The labor agency also generated some $10,000 in materials and skills of carpenters, electricians, bricklayers, and plumbers needed to construct an extension of a facility for the blind.

Perhaps the most interesting service offered by the agency is its emergency assistance program. Over the years, the agency has encountered people who need more than services: they need money to meet bills accumulated because of some temporary hardship. To provide for such hardship, the emergency assistance fund was created.

The fund is used to address a variety of problems. One man who had been out of work for a long period was given a few tankfuls of gasoline to drive to a new job in the next county; a car is a necessity for most construction workers because the work area is often not served by public transportation. One man was given funds to obtain tools that would enable him to work. Another was given funds for the books needed for the last semester of course work for a college degree. Often the funds are for prescription drugs for people too hard pressed to purchase them. Many times the fund has been used to pay the rent or utility bills for a head of household who for those few months had nowhere else to turn.

Marto, the program's director, screens the potential recipients carefully, consulting references to confirm their need, but he concedes that judgment calls are often made in lieu of a formal assessment of needs. As in most of the other programs we surveyed, empathy plays a significant role in the assessment of clients. "When you eyeball a guy, you get a feeling about where he is. I've been in the street; I've had cardboard in my shoes," says Marto, who has been in the labor movement for twenty years.

Cash is seldom given to recipients of emergency assistance. The gas or the prescription drugs are purchased with a card filled out by the program director. The rent, utility, and other bills are paid by the agency. "It's not that we are afraid that the person is trying to beat the agency for the money, but rather that circumstances might cause the person to use the money for some other purpose and still wind up having his electricity turned off or having his family evicted from the house. We made the determination that to help this person the agency would pay his rent, utilities, doctor bill, whatever. We pay that bill."

On the other hand, there are times when a head of household is given ten or fifteen dollars with the suggestion that "since the wolf is away from the door at least for this month, take the family to McDonald's or to a movie and forget it for one day." Marto argues, "You have to deal with the morale of the person; a person that has been up against it needs something for the soul, too."

Marto recognizes that misconceptions abound concerning the purpose of the fund. Occasionally someone will apply for funds to make a payment on an automobile or a camper, assuming that the fund is a union-oriented short-term loan program. Such misconceptions are soon cleared up.

Money for the emergency assistance program comes from the flu inoculation program and from bingo games. Arizona state law allows the operation of games of chance only if the proceeds are to be used for charities and only for two nights a week. The games, held in the agency auditorium every Thursday and Sunday, produce annual revenues of $10,000 to $12,000.

In one case, a government regulation prevented a union social program from performing a needed service. Each year since 1975 the Central Labor Council has participated in a drive to collect non-perishable foods for the Phoenix food bank program, which is stored in six food banks and distributed to needy families. Many people willing to donate food were, however, reluctant to deliver it to the food banks; they wanted someone to collect it.

In 1975 the labor agency enlisted the letter carriers. The president of the local letter carriers' union and the local postmaster were delighted to participate. On appointed days publicized in advance, the letter carriers would collect food contributions from the residents along their route. Even the one or two cans of food donated from each family collectively produced tons of food. Then their mail trucks and jeeps brought the food to a point where food bank trucks would pick it up.

111

Everything went well until a similar program in California met with the disapproval of the local postmaster. When a definitive ruling was requested, the office of the postmaster general denied approval because of regulations on the use of government vehicles and the questionable appropriateness of their use in a social program.

Robert Connolly, the president of the Central Labor Council, appealed unsuccessfully. He commented: "A few years ago we had a run of bad weather. Herds of deer were starving in the countryside. The army used helicopters to drop hay to the starving wild animals. Nobody said anything about using government property then. So it is all right to feed the animals, but not the people." Since no one has taken the place of the letter carriers, tons of free food for the needy are no longer available to them.

Union Retirees Resources: Seattle, Washington. Jim Bender is president of the King County AFL-CIO Central Labor Council in Seattle, Washington, where unions wield immense power. The Central Labor Council there represents almost 150 unions, ranging from maritime unions to those dealing with the lumber and forest industry. Bender and Red Victor, a labor staff representative for the Seattle United Way, shared the hope of using the skills of the estimated 48,000 union retirees in a union social service program. Victor outlined a home maintenance program for area needy senior citizens operated by senior citizen union craftsmen. In 1975 a $38,000 nonrenewable mini-grant from the Action Agency, which was seeking ideas for programs involving labor unions, established the Union Retirees Resources program at the King County central labor headquarters.

The program initially dealt with light home repairs—broken windows, door knobs, leaky sinks and faucets, and roof repairs. Sixty-seven volunteer craftsmen were soon working in a wide area. They received no compensation beyond reimbursement for mileage, though the program carries accident and liability insurance on them while they are working on service calls.

The Muscular Dystrophy Association requested help for a person confined to a wheelchair who could not leave the house because it had no ramp. Within a few days, Victor assembled some retired carpenters, who built a ramp in one afternoon for $138, the cost of materials alone.

Union Retirees Resources then added ramp building to its growing list of services. The labor agency receives requests for ramps from persons working for the Red Cross, Easter Seals, the Veterans Hospital, and Muscular Dystrophy.

For major repairs and installations, the program offers to engage a licensed and bonded contractor and to inspect the completed work for compliance with building codes. The charge for work contracted in this fashion is scaled to what the person can afford. For more than 90 percent of the calls, no charge is made.

The construction trade unions support this program; they assure their members that the work done by the retired union volunteers for low-income elderly persons takes no jobs away from union members.

As in the other case histories presented in this study, the home repair service stimulated a modification of the program—in this case, the development of a unique service. A volunteer making a house call to repair a broken lock found an elderly woman sitting before a pictureless television set listening to the audio portion of the show. Within two days, Victor found a retired television repairman to repair the set for the cost of the parts alone. The sight of a woman happily watching her favorite program provided the final justification for making the repair service a permanent part of the program.

The program took still another turn when a woman asked if someone could repair a washing machine. A volunteer appliance repairman went to the home and repaired the machine. Unlike a television set, however, a washing machine could scarcely be brought to the home of a volunteer for repair. Victor therefore established an entirely new service. Old appliances, functional or broken, were collected and brought to a warehouse, where they were repaired and recycled at cost for needy senior citizens. Bender authorized the purchase of a truck with a tailgate lift and two paid staff for pickups and deliveries. The program took all sorts of appliances, using the parts of those beyond repair. No calls for service wait more than three days, and emergency cases are usually handled immediately. Because of the heavy use of volunteers, emergency repairs are often made on weekends.

Service recipients sometimes ask incredulously, "You mean a union man is coming to fix my water heater, and it won't cost me anything?" Ironically, these retired union volunteers most often work for nonunion families; more than 90 percent of their service calls have been for families without any union affiliation.

Union Retirees Resources is supported by all local agencies. The Seattle police contributed $1,000 from its charity committee, commending the organization's "exemplary human care services." The Board of Realtors awarded the program its People Making Things Happen award, stating, "Your all-union volunteer project has contributed greatly to the community by providing transportation, home maintenance, and other services and also has aided union retirees by allowing them to continue to utilize their skills. Union Retirees

Resources has made this community a better place for both those receiving and giving these services."

This innovative program, which began with the one-time mini-grant, has continued through the years with grants from Retired Senior Volunteer Program (RSVP) and CETA. In 1981 the agency served 4,018 clients with funds from the Community Services Administration and the Private Industry Council, private donations, and, of course, the support of the United Way of Seattle. With a paid staff of five, it also provides information and referral, operates a food bank, runs an alcohol abuse program, and coordinates union counseling courses.

The United Labor Agency: Cleveland, Ohio. The United Labor Agency of Cleveland exemplifiies one of the three arrangements between the United Way and the AFL-CIO. As in Phoenix, the labor function is located not in the United Way office complex but in a separate facility more clearly identified with labor.

The Pittsburgh case study of Camp Variety showed many unions cooperating in the delivery of services to a specific cause. Those unions, however, were all building trades unions. In Cleveland the labor agency has gone beyond the AFL-CIO unions. In addition to the AFL-CIO labor council, which in most areas is the core of the United Way–AFL-CIO relationship, the Cleveland program enjoys the cooperation of the United Auto Workers and the Brotherhood of Teamsters Joint Council No. 41. Program operators point out that a multi-union approach is a necessity in Cleveland: the variety of strong unions there prevents any one industry from dominating union public affairs, as the United Auto Workers do in Detroit and the United Steelworkers do in Pittsburgh.

The scope of the Cleveland agency is extensive. Its staff of seventy coordinates fifteen social and cultural program services throughout the Cleveland area with a budget of $1.5 million. Although its programs deal with many aspects of community service, this case study focuses on one of its programs.

Looking at the range of programs offered today by the United Labor Agency (ULA), one would scarcely suspect that they began from a response to one person in neeed. In 1970 a steelworker confided to his fellow union members that he was under tremendous financial and emotional pressure: his wife required the help of a kidney dialysis machine to sustain her life. After officers of the brewery workers and the auto workers met with Sebastian Lupia, of the Cleveland AFL-CIO, an ad hoc, pass-the-hat campaign among the locals raised the funds for a dialysis machine. As word of the effort spread through the community, the union learned that two more members needed kidney machines. Rather than asking members for money, this time they conducted a fund-raising drive.

As calls for assistance began to accumulate, the union leaders realized that they could never raise sufficient funds to pay for all the required medical treatment. The unions therefore established a program to buy, store, and lend medical equipment. Requests for equipment must be accompanied by a doctor's prescription, stating the equipment needed and the approximate length of treatment. The medical equipment is delivered to the patient's home in an agency van. As other calls for the same equipment arrive, priorities are established on the basis of medical need. The equipment is examined by a medical supply house or a union worker before it is taken to the next patient.

The program circulates more than 170 types of reusable medical equipment—kidney machines, hospital beds, wheelchairs, crutches, walkers, portable commodes, breathing machines. Because of this constant moving of equipment, the program has been called the Hospital on Wheels.

Referrals come to the agency from doctors, hospitals, union members, and others. In 1980, 601 families were served by the durable medical equipment program at little or no cost to the recipients.

Three years ago the agency staff arranged with Nationwide Insurance to be listed as a third-party provider for the Cleveland area. This program is totally financed by the direct donations of the union members (fifty cents per year per member), the third-party payments, and community donations.

The Career Exploration Program: Wilmington, Delaware. The United Way Labor Outreach of Wilmington, Delaware, exhibits a number of features that set it apart from the models we have analyzed. First is the relationship of labor to the United Way structure. In St. Louis the local union people serve directly on the United Way staff. In Seattle and Cleveland, a united labor agency has program personnel and operations set apart from the United Way offices. In these two relationships, the United Way pays the labor personnel out of funds raised in its annual drives. In Delaware we find still another arrangement, the United Way Community Services (AFL-CIO) Partnership, under which the Labor Outreach staff can receive contributions to its own account with United Way.

The Delaware program also differs from the others in its focus on problems of disadvantaged young people, chiefly through the Career Exploration Program (CEP). In 1975 the Wilmington chapter of the National Alliance of Business (NAB) offered a $60,000 grant to the partnership to develop a program to help sixty disadvantaged teen-agers. Working with both the AFL-CIO and community businessmen, Felix Rapposelli, director of the program, organized an eight-week summer jobs program. This effort was so successful that after three weeks the NAB returned to Rapposelli with another challenge. It had $15,000 to be used for children of migrant workers. In one week Rapposelli, working through the Chamber of Commerce and the Small Business Administration of Kane and Delaware counties, found transportation and employment for children of migrant workers. Out of these efforts came the Career Exploration Program, which seeks career opportunities for disadvantaged young people.

The CEP attempts to bridge the transition from school to the work environment. Many young people engaged in this program have never developed the work habits necessary to find and keep a job. The program works to develop positive attitudes and behavioral patterns conducive to gainful employment. Dress, personal grooming, language, and punctuality are all emphasized as elements of success. The program screens participants through one-to-one counseling to eliminate those who are not serious about participating. Discipline is necessary because, in addition to working a twenty-hour week, participants must continue to attend school during the school year. This prepares them for forty-hour-a-week summer employment. The counselors direct participants to jobs that will maintain their interest. From businessmen the young people learn the employer's views and expectations. From union counselors they learn about labor's role in the process.

Rapposelli relies heavily on the AFL-CIO's offices for support. Each training cycle uses a host of volunteers supplied by the area's unions. It is not uncommon for the presidents of local unions to work in training sessions or to be involved in counseling. Other union officials, such as business agents, lecture on the responsibilities of the work force. The young person learns that a union is more than an organization geared to obtaining wages and benefits. The union contract also places responsibility on the union to deliver a product: a fair day's work for a fair day's pay. The teen-agers quickly learn that neither management nor the union will tolerate a worker who does not fulfill his or her responsibility under the contract. These are some of the intangible benefits derived from such counseling. In addition, the unions provide volunteers to work in the skilled-trades training programs.

Employers in the summer job and other programs are subsidized by CETA and other Labor Department grants, but the goal of the

CEP is unsubsidized permanent employment. Former CEP graduates are working as court secretaries, journalists, file clerks, child-care assistants, salesclerks, and computer operators.

The success of the CEP has attracted the attention of people working in criminal justice. A local judge worked with Rapposelli in developing a CEP model to deal with the troubled as well as the disadvantaged young people who come before the courts. Rapposelli obtained a $250,000 grant from the Law Enforcement Assistance Administration to operate a program that assumes responsibility for released offenders if they enroll in the CEP. This program has operated for two years. It combines all the activities of the CEP with an added dimension: the element of restitution. Part of the money earned by the participants must be paid to the victims of crimes committed by them. The same union and business volunteers staff the program.

In addition to the CEP, the Community Services (AFL-CIO) Partnership is involved in many other activities throughout the year. These include counselor training, information and referral, retirement programs for senior citizens, programs on alcoholism and drug abuse, and a Minor Home Repair Program for senior citizens. The home repair program makes the same minor repairs as other programs we have analyzed, but it uses young people trained in skilled-trades learning programs taught by union volunteers.

Rapposelli started the CEP program ten years ago. Today it has a staff of eleven professional and clerical workers. The community has also contributed to the effort. National Vulcanized Fiber lent a building with 30,000 square feet of rent-free space to conduct training sessions, and the University of Delaware lent a computer terminal for one year to tie into a job-listing service.

The Union Club of Sun City, Arizona. The principal difference between the Sun City program and the others we have examined is that the Union Club focuses solely on senior citizens. I. W. Abel, Walter Burke, and Lawrence Spitz are former officials of the United Steelworkers of America; Abel was the president of the 1,400,000 member union for twelve years. The three men all retired at about the same time and moved from Pittsburgh to Sun City, Arizona, and started the Union Club of Sun City.

Soon after they settled in Sun City, the three began receiving calls from other retired steelworkers facing new and different problems. Requests for advice included calls regarding pensions or promised benefits that had not materialized, questions about state legislation that could affect retirees, and the like. The volume of requests for assistance grew until the three men were operating an extensive ad hoc information and referral system. Their experience in serving a membership was an invaluable asset to their ability to help the new constituency they represented. They knew exactly whom to call in the union and the management system to get the answers their constituents needed. Social needs were identified that were common to the pool of retired union workers.

The three gathered those interested in maintaining some sort of union identification even though they were retired. The only stated criterion for attendance was "membership in a union at some time in your working career, or to have been the spouse of a union member."

On March 29, 1979, eighty-five retirees met for the first time and decided to incorporate as a Union Club. They drafted by-laws, elected officers, and appointed an advisory committee composed of retired international union officers representing five different unions. By April 1980, the club membership had risen to 934, representing fifty-one unions. Club services are open to all senior citizens, union and nonunion alike.

The Union Club consists of a series of standing committees—the telephone, welfare, consumer advisory, price watch, legislation and tax, social security, pension and insurance, and environmental committees—each performing a specific task. The committees attempted to meet specific social needs as they became apparent to the leadership. The first committee formed was the telephone committee, which periodically calls members to remind them of meeting dates and other club functions. During these calls, the needs of the membership were discovered and the committee became counselors dealing with illness, death, depression, and other stresses facing the members.

Members of the welfare committee assist the retirees by arranging transportation and providing shopping services. They also visit and help their "brothers and sisters" through periods of crisis in a variety of ways. Quite often, they simply listen to lonely older persons who are in desperate need of human companionship.

A retiree living in a new environment faces a serious problem when he needs a major household repair. Prior to retirement, such repairs were usually made by repairmen known to the union member. Trust and confidence are generally built over long periods of time. Once the retirees are on fixed incomes, however, the fear of incurring a heavy legitimate expense is compounded by the fear of being duped into making unneeded repairs or of being overcharged. Helping to alleviate this fear is the Consumer Advisory Committee, which consists of two divisions: a Repair Consultants Division and a Repair and Service Listing Division.

The Repair Consultants Division consists of retired former skilled repairmen who act as unpaid consultants to members confronted with large repair bills for home, auto, and appliance repair. Members are constantly giving testimonials to them. Mrs. Brown, a retiree who had a problem with a sewer, did not know whom to turn to or what to do. Because of her lack of knowledge in this area, she was fearful of being cheated. At an open committee meeting, which we attended, she praised a member of the committee, Mr. Mitchell. "He told me what to look for in the contract; he checked out all the materials used, and he even came and checked the finished job before I paid a cent." Only trusted peers can offer this kind of service.

The Repair and Services Listing Division maintains a list of persons who are highly recommended by members of the club who have used the service and approved the prices and the quality of workmanship. Also included are recommended professional people, such as doctors, lawyers, and dentists.

Perhaps the most controversial activity is that of the legislative committee. The Silver-Haired Legislation Steering Committee seeks to give retirees a voice in the legislative process of the state of Arizona. Originally a small but determined group, the club made a successful effort to repeal Arizona's state sales tax on food. Although repeal of the state sales tax on food had been suggested from time to time by others, it was the Union Club that mobilized the state's senior citizens and persuaded the legislature to repeal the tax in 1980. This demonstrated that the club had become a strong political force in a short time.

Lloyd McBride, president of the International Steelworkers, in addressing an April 1981 gathering of the Union Club in Sun City said, "You are one group that knows the economics of politics and the politics of economics."

Larry Spitz, the charter president of the club (which he calls "the flagship"), has watched its growth from a cluster of activities for retired union members to an effective and powerful organization. Seven other clubs are now functioning in Arizona, and four more are in the process of formation. Total membership in Union Clubs around the state is about 2,700. Of the more than half-million retirees in Arizona, 390,000 are listed in the computer at the National AFL-CIO Headquarters. All of them have been or will be approached by a member of the club.

The rapid growth and strength of the Union Club suggest trends in American industrial society that sociologists should note.

First, the shift of population from the northeastern and Great Lakes states will give a union perspective to the Sunbelt, an area that has held a different view of union activity.

Second, as this study indicates, unions are quick to help the less fortunate through organized efforts. They could influence the design and delivery of social services in Sunbelt states.

Third, retired workers, especially union workers who are skilled and disciplined in organizational action, are likely to employ a similar approach in addressing the problems of the elderly and in formulating their demands on public policy makers.

National Trends and Potentials. As we stated at the outset of this report, our goal was to provide the reader with an overview of union operated social programs. Obviously all of the programs we encountered in the course of our research cannot be included, and for each one we analyzed, there were dozens we could not study. In concluding this narrative, we will briefly touch on two program efforts that are likely to influence future union social programming. They are the Pipefitters of St. Louis and the Illinois AFL-CIO Plant Closing Project.

The Pipefitters Local 562. The pipefitters' program differs sharply from all other programs in our study in that the social services are exclusively for the members of its own Local 562. All of the services are dispensed at the 350-acre pipefitters complex. The complex is an elaborate health, social, and recreational facility that provides a multitude of services to the members and their dependents.

The health center employs full-time doctors, nurses, and medical technicians who conduct highly complicated diagnostic tests as well as routine physical examinations. The center also employs a psychiatrist to deal with emotional problems. One cannot overestimate the importance of this service for a blue collar union. Many blue collar workers are uncomfortable dealing with emotional problems and the stigma attached to psychiatric treatment. Psychiatric services at the pipefitters' complex provide treatment for members who trust the "confidentiality" of this "union service" and would not otherwise risk the social embarrassment of going to an outside psychiatrist. Nor do they risk discovery by applying for reimbursement on an insurance form. At the center, psychiatric consultation is both confidential and free.

120

In addition to the health services, the complex offers a wide variety of services for its retirees. These include housing, nutrition and social services.

Finally, the complex has many of the features that one would expect to find at a vacation resort. These features include a fishing lake, an olympic-sized pool, health spas, and picnic areas with baseball diamonds.

A unique aspect of this program is its financing. Through the collective bargaining process, the union and the contractors arrive at negotiated agreements whereby the contractor makes a contribution into the Pipefitters' Health and Welfare Fund. This is a form of deferred compensation, which the worker does not receive in cash but as a benefit, and this is why the services are for members only. Harold (Bud) Foley, business manager for Local 562, argues that unions have a responsibility to serve the social needs of their members. "We care for our own" says Foley. "If every union did for its members what we do for ours, more people would be breaking down the doors to join unions. Furthermore, you wouldn't need the massive federal programs."

From a public policy standpoint, the St. Louis pipefitters' program is a model well worth noting. It is good for the union, good for the members, and good for the public policy maker, because it offers social services at no cost to the taxpayer. This model could be attractive for unions with declining membership that seek to expand their numbers. The model should also be attractive to taxpayers, because the private rather than the public sector assumes responsibility for underwriting social expenditures.

The Illinois Plant Closing Project. Plant closures have become commonplace in many older industrial communities, causing extreme social and economic hardships to the work force. Unions have thought long and hard about this trend, but have yet to produce a unified program to deal with the problems. Seeking to minimize the human hardships arising from plant closings, the Illinois State AFL-CIO established a plant closure specialization unit within its manpower assistance program. Melva Meacham, herself a victim of a plant closing, directs this effort.

The program seeks to provide technical assistance to workers displaced by a plant closing. Project Outreach offers adjustment assistance workshops designed to acquaint the workers with income maintenance programs, retraining opportunities, social services, and job seeking techniques.

Although limited in scope, the program is the only one that currently provides systematic assistance to workers suffering this kind of unemployment. One significant development has been the linkage between the plant closing program and the community service representatives networks discussed in the preceding case studies. Community service representatives, who are already familiar with the various social services available at the state, local, and federal levels, have a firm foundation for helping workers who have never before needed social assistance. Given the likelihood of increased plant closings in the 1980s, this program seems destined to receive serious attention from the national headquarters of the AFL-CIO, as well as from its member unions.

Analysis and Preliminary Conclusions

The Phases of Program Development. Most of the case studies show a common sequence of events.

Phase I: Identification of a specific problem. In almost all the studies, it was the plight of one person that triggered a union response. In Fontana that person was the uncle of a union official; in the Hospital on Wheels example, it was the wife of a union member. The key ingredient appears to be not only the observation of an individual good Samaritan, but also the reporting of that observation to others in the union local to obtain help. This point is significant. Many Americans provide similar humanitarian or neighborly services to others as one-time events that are appreciated by the recipient and end there. They do not result in a continuing pattern of services beyond the original recipient. When the problem is taken to the union local, even in the most informal way, it is brought before individuals who share the bond of an organizational membership. This tends to lighten the burden on the person who identified the problem and to give a broader perspective on it.

It is in this phase that the plight of the person is recognized as being common to others. The group of union members establishes a data-gathering function and a loose information and referral system to report similar cases. At this stage, the system exists only in the from of person-to-person referral. This could be called a pre-program stage because no structured response has yet emerged. As referrals increase, the responses must be made on a more regular basis. At this point, a response mechanism begins to emerge.

Phase II: The early program response—the ad hoc stage. The key element in identifying an early or simple program is that the individuals who render the service do so in addition to other duties they perform for the union. In our case studies the district director, business agents, and shop stewards established a time for dealing with persons in distress. In some cases, the prime movers recruited retirees to relay requests for aid. A retiree known to be at home receives calls and at appointed times relays the messages to the business agent's secretary. The business agent in turn relays the message to a union member who will give assistance.

If there is space available, the volunteers work out of the local union office. This, of course, places the union in a leadership position; people in need no longer call an individual who happens to be a union member, but the union itself—a subtle but vital difference.

It is at this stage that not only the volume of needs but also the variety of needs begins to increase. The volunteer referral system soon becomes inadequate. The original core group must then seek assistance from other members, the union officers, the community, or all three.

At this stage also there is an apparent need for some formal structure to contain the pattern of responses that are clearly programmatic. There is a need to organize and manage volunteer shifts. There is a need for office space and a telephone. There is a need for equipment and supplies. All this, of course, begins to interrupt the normal flow of business in the union office and creates a need for a program identity apart from the day-to-day operations of the local.

In this stage, the program is supported mainly by in-kind rather than cash contributions. The office space and the phones are donated. Volunteers donate their time, with no stipend or reimbursement for out-of-pocket expenses. If vehicles are needed, they are provided by union members or the volunteers without reimbursement for fuel costs. The small amounts of money required to operate the program, as well as money to help persons in need, are contributed by members, the union, and the volunteers themselves.

At this stage of development, in our view, a program does exist. All the rudiments of social programming are present. Social needs being addressed by volunteers are managed and organized in a manner consistent with providing assistance. In fact, this is the stage where we find the real essence of voluntarism as described by Tocqueville. Further, according to some public policy makers, it is this form of neighborhood self-help that is needed to restore America's sense of self-reliance. Therefore, such terms as "loose," "ad hoc," or even "primitive" are not pejorative when applied to these programs. Quite the contrary. These efforts should be replicated in all areas where there is a social need. At this stage a social program has the greatest potential for obtaining local sponsorship and for growth.

Phase III: Program sophistication. At a point that varies from case to case, the loose program structure of phase I and phase II evolves into a full-blown program effort complete with full-time paid staff, program budget, office space, and vehicles. We have identified four conditions that either alone or in combination account for the change:

• *Volume of caseload.* The sheer weight of the demand for a service exceeds the ability of a part-time effort to satisfy it. Growing demand also requires the mobilization of larger numbers of volunteers and vehicles.

• *An increased variety of needs.* As more and more people bring their problems to the union, a greater variety of responses is necessary. This necessitates new kinds of expertise by the program operators and a greater effort to find volunteers with the time and skill required to perform the tasks involved in the service.

• *Community recognition.* As noted in some of the case studies, when the community recognizes the uniqueness of some services, public and private quarters may request that they be made a permanent part of the community's arsenal of social services.

• *Altruism.* In all the cases we saw, there was a desire to help those in need. In some cases the locals assumed the responsibility for spinning off programs they initiated. In other cases they increased their commitment.

The first two conditions alone provide the most compelling reasons for the early program to expand. This expansion obviously begins to tax the office facility, which is often no more than a desk with a telephone. Volunteers coming and going and phones constantly ringing, especially when the volunteers are out, make it necessary to move the program operation so as not to disrupt union operations. And the other two factors also encourage the union to relocate and expand the program.

Alone or in combination, these four factors move the union to transform a loose effort into a full-time social program. There now arises a need for staff (both professional and clerical), office space, telephones, and vehicles, tools, and other equipment. The need for salaries, rent, and vehicles requires budgeting, accounting, insurance, and other essentials of management. Hence the decision to move from an ad hoc, quasi-program operation must be put before the union membership.

Program sponsorship—affiliation. Our case studies display a wide range of program models that appear directly related to a particular phase of program development. Several sets of relationships are apparent:

1. one-to-one service (person-to-person rather than organization-to-person outreach in the pre-program phase)
2. programs run by a local
3. programs run by a district of one union, such as the Steelworkers Oldtimers Foundation of Fontana, California
4. programs by coalitions of various unions, such as the Pittsburgh building trades support of Camp Variety
5. programs run by a national union, such as the National Steelworkers Oldtimers Foundation
6. programs partially funded or subsidized by nonprofit community fund drives or national drives, such as the United Way; three kinds of United Way–AFL-CIO affiliations have emerged —the United Way labor liaison staff model as in St. Louis; the united labor agency model as in Seattle, Phoenix, and Cleveland; and the United Way partnership exhibited by the Delaware example

Funding. Funding for the programs is obtained in a variety of ways: from the individual members themselves; from the locals or coalition members; from bingo, raffles, and bazaars; from state and federal sources; from community fund drives, either local or national.

Program potential. Thus far our analysis has centered on the motives for union programming as well as the phases of program evolution. For readers seeking to replicate any of the program models in their geographic areas, other variables should be taken into consideration, including the programming environment.

The juxtaposition of the labor agencies in our Seattle and Phoenix case studies demonstrates that labor unions can perform needed human services regardless of their strength in a particular area. Nonetheless, the ability of programs to flourish will depend heavily on the number of labor unions in an area and the degree of their acceptance in that area. In St. Louis, Cleveland, and Seattle, unions are as much an integral part of the community as the Chamber of Commerce, the church, or the boys' club. In areas like Pittsburgh, these categories overlap considerably. In the ethnic neighborhoods that punctuate most of the urban industrial areas of the country, blue-collar union members are heavily involved in both the spiritual and the temporal communities. In some Sunbelt areas, the situation is different. Unions are not only *not* a part of the local scene, but they are also frowned upon. It is far easier to use the potential force of a labor union if labor is viewed as a necessary partner in community action.

The strength and number of other civic, professional, neighborhood, and religious organizations will also augment or diminish program potential. Many of the people operating programs in our case studies serve as the links between those needing services and organzations within the community that offer such services. In less urban communities, there are fewer community organizations to mobilize.

Finally, one cannot understate the need for energetic, talented, and creative program personnel. Advanced degrees in social work are not required to produce a social service delivery system of high quality. Rather, what is needed is at least one human catalyst capable of envisioning a dream and selling it to a host of other actors. Unlike government-sponsored social programs with captive clienteles and appropriated resources, community programming requires a mendicant approach. The programmer must often be not only the writer of the show but its producer, director, and financier as well.

Public Policy Implications of Union-operated Social Programs. One of our goals in describing these community-based programs operated by unions is to give policy makers an opportunity to assess their potential as low-cost remedies for social problems. Cuts in federal categorical programs and attempts by state and local governments to compensate for diminishing federal funds make these programs especially timely. In this section we examine programs that address *some* social needs at a cost most communities can afford.

Two preliminary observations should be made. First, these programs alone, even if vastly expanded, can scarcely make up for the budget cuts of 1981 and those contemplated through fiscal year 1984 in food stamps, housing, school lunches, Medicare, and social security. These cuts have reduced both categorical cash and in-kind transfer programs that distribute billions of dollars in aid to the program recipients and in payments to federal, state, and local public service employees. These cuts will cause dislocations that no single private sector initiative can prevent. Public policy makers should recognize the limitations of the community programs in this study and be wary of any suggestions that they are an alternative to many federally subsidized programs.

Second, these programs do nevertheless constitute an effective and affordable mechanism for providing needed social services at the grass-roots community level. This dynamic community force has not entered into the formulation of public policies aimed at meeting human and social needs.

126

The federal level. With respect to federal policy, one positive theme should be stated at the outset. Unlike some other initiatives presented in this book, these community efforts by labor have never been undermined by the establishment of competitive federal programs or by a government takeover. Many of the programs we analyzed provided services for individuals ineligible for federal assistance because their incomes were greater than those stipulated by government regulations. Other services were rendered to individuals who might have been eligible but refused to accept public assistance. Participants in programs we observed saw no stigma in receiving help from the labor programs because they were an integral part of the community. Some come to the program for assistance because they are comfortable with their fellow union members. Others come simply because it is a neighborhood program.

There has been no federal strategy for using this community-generated momentum from the private sector, though federal funds find their way into labor programs. The AFL-CIO Central Labor Council in Seattle received an Action mini-grant—that is, the one-time nonrenewable seed funding designed to test a program concept. Once the program was launched, it looked to other federal agencies to continue and broaden its activities. The Steelworkers Oldtimers Foundation of Fontana began with private funding and has since obtained considerable support from several federal agencies. Still other programs relied almost exclusively on federal funds, both to start and to continue operation. In all cases, labor programmers applied to a particular government agency dispensing the funds for a categorical program. Thus a labor agency became an indirect federal grantee. There was no public policy mandate to make use of the labor programs. Our study suggests a public policy strategy that would make labor programs the recipients of direct rather than indirect grants. This approach would eliminate the costs of an entire layer of administrative overhead, which could be spent on program recipients.

The second public policy implication concerns cost. A common characteristic of the programs we analyzed was their cost effectiveness. The overhead and operational costs were very small, especially in comparison with the costs of federal programs. The union programs pay salaries well below those of federal employees and use volunteers and private vehicles to reduce operational overhead.

One of the chief criticisms of government-sponsored programs is that they are designed by civil servants who neither live in nor understand the communities in which those programs operate. By contrast, the union programs are community efforts. Local people define the problems and select the particular program mechanism. As we have seen in the case studies, the unions obtained most of the resources needed to operate their programs through the generosity of the community, because it is the community's program. Public policy aimed at assisting communities through social programs might be more successful if it moved with the momentum of the community, rather than trying to create momentum from outside.

By and large, federal regulations have not stood in the way of delivery of services by unions. The services rendered are so much a part of the community that they may be invisible to the regulatory process. The only government interference with a union's social activity we encountered was in our Phoenix case study (where letter carriers helped the local food bank program by picking up donated canned goods from residents along their routes and delivering them to a central location). The letter carriers' food bank participation was halted when it spread to another state. Phoenix postal authorities saw no harm in the letter carriers' effort, but the Postal Service refused to sanction the activity nationally. We recommend that the federal government review its policy to allow postal workers to participate in food drives.

State and local implications. Unquestionably, the cutbacks in federal programs are going to produce massive gaps in social services at the state and local levels. Enormous pressure will be placed on state governments to continue these services. Since there will be a scramble for available funds, the states will have to extract the maximum service from each dollar spent. This will be even more important if a block grant mechanism is adopted. Interest groups of social service recipients competing for scarce resources will step up their demands that the states continue their services. The only reasonable and equitable solution would be for the states to decide which services to fund on the basis of their cost effectiveness.

A more aggressive and competitive approach to the allocation of resources can yield more services from the same resources. A union-operated program, for example, requested and received $44,952 from a county board of supervisors to operate four vans under its FY 1981–1982 budget—an average of about $11,200 per van—to cover the cost of gasoline, maintenance, and a combination of paid and volunteer drivers. At the same hearing, a community service department, a former OEO/CAP agency, requested and received, without challenge, $197,000 to operate ten vehicles, mostly vans—an average cost per van of $19,700, 76 percent higher than in the union program. At a savings of about $8,500 per van, the ten vans could have been operated for $85,000 less if the union costs had applied to the government program, and further services could have been purchased with the $85,000.

State and local policy makers might also increase private sector involvement in social services by allowing programs to operate games of chance for charitable purposes. Games such as bingo seem well within the local mores of populations in the areas we studied and would not be viewed as a loophole capable of transforming any of them into a Monte Carlo.

Private sector opportunities. In the wake of federal cutbacks in social programs, there have been rising expectations that private sector initiatives can replace federal services. We believe that the social programs of labor, business, and other private sector groups cannot replace those services. Many human and social needs can be addressed, however, by expanding the outreach of the labor programs. We do not believe that such needs can be met simply by the recent changes in tax codes boosting from 5 percent to 10 percent the amount of pretax profits that can be deducted for charitable contributions. In the past, only a small percentage of American corporations contributed as much as 5 percent. Corporations, foundations, and others able to underwrite the cost of social services must realize that there are activities they can support that will not inexorably pull them into deeper financial relationships.

In social programming, programs such as those operated by the unions are sometimes called "milk and apple pie" efforts—that is, they do not require the outlay of billions of dollars in open-ended relationships in which the program constituency becomes permanently dependent. Our case studies dealt with short-term needs. The emergency assistance program run by the Phoenix labor agency is truly an "emergency" program; it will help someone through a difficult period, but it was not designed to replace social security. Providing a rehabilitated television set or washing machine will greatly improve the quality of life for a family in need. Those requiring services in the programs we studied had needs that could be met with a minimum of assistance. They needed only a helping hand, not a new electrical household.

Labor unions are usually an integral part of the community, and are recognized by government and civic leaders as wielding significant power. Unfortunately, labor-corporate relations have often been adversarial. Corporations, either labor or capital intensive, could develop a broader dialogue with the community by participating in programs run by the unions. Corporations can build friendships by supporting community programs and working closely with unions.

Finally, an attractive feature of contributing to labor community service programs is the array of programs. From one-to-one ad hoc services to sophisticated health delivery systems, labor programs offer the contributor a clear view of the program activities at each level, as well as an accurate assessment of what financial participation would entail. State and local governments, corporations, foundations, and individuals can choose the programs they want to support. A participant might begin with a program at an earlier stage of development and assist in making the transition to the next stage. The participant could then shape program content as well as improve management efficiency.

Union Social Programs: A National Secret. We began our research with the hypothesis that union programs were a more common phenomenon than is generally recognized by the public. Our research tends to support that hypothesis. Unions are helping to meet social needs wherever they are found. Yet, as we stated in our section on methods, there is such a scarcity of data on these programs that union members call union social programming the country's best-kept secret. Why this paradox of ubiquity and scarcity? We can cite several reasons.

First, union social programs are a local phenomenon. Our case studies demonstrated time and again that these programs were not imported into the community like a fast-food restaurant to serve a ready market, but grew from informal acts of altruism into structured programs. The local union officers and members offered their help to people in need, not for recognition but because of a desire to help others. They have tended to keep their eyes on that central goal rather than to seek praise for doing so.

Second, national union leaders have neither assumed credit for the social activities of their districts and locals nor chosen to boast of their benevolence through public relations campaigns. Most of the leaders we interviewed contended that commitment to community involvement is an integral part of unionism. Indeed, they point to the constitutions of the unions and the resolutions of the AFL-CIO executive councils supporting and encouraging these efforts.

Third, unions are uneasy in the public spotlight because they have so often been accused of placing their own interests above the well-being of the rest of the nation. Union wage demands are often depicted as unreasonable and harmful to the consumer. For decades the media have reported misappropriations of union pension funds, criminal activity by some union elected officials, and strikes by fire-fighters, police, and other public service unions. Racism and discrimination have been alleged in union apprenticeship programs. In more than one community, union social programs have been accused of discriminating against those outside the union, even when the record clearly demonstrated that union membership was not a requirement for service. The overwhelming number of those served by the programs we sampled were not from union households. Perhaps it has been the negative atmosphere that has caused the unions to keep their social program accomplishments to themselves.

Finally, the most important conclusion we have drawn from this study is that the services unions provide are vital to their communities and can be of immense value in helping to fill a national need.

The Importance of
Neighborhood Organizations
in Meeting Human Needs

Robert L. Woodson

Over the past three decades, hundreds of billions of dollars have been poured into government programs intended to rebuild American cities and to improve the quality of life for the underprivileged. In 1950, local governments received $2 billion in federal aid. This assistance increased to $7 billion in 1960. In fiscal 1979, total federal aid to state and local governments approached $80 billion. Massive funds, both public and private, have been expended in a sincere and humane effort to revitalize urban neighborhoods and to improve the social and economic well-being of those who live there. Yet crime rates spiral, business and industry relocate, urban unemployment escalates, and the quality of life for disadvantaged families continues to deteriorate.

It would not be fair to say that public and private programs and initiatives have had no positive social or economic impact. It is fair to say, however, that the benefits delivered have, in many instances, differed from the benefits intended and that unforeseen adverse results have accompanied the positive effects. Social, health, and welfare programs alleviate the day-to-day problems of low-income families and individuals, but in doing so these programs create a vast constituency of clients wholly dependent on the services provided.

Many government social programs have been counterproductive by discouraging work and fostering dependency on public assistance and by herding lower-income families into high-rise buildings that breed crime and frustration. In the process, we have developed a "dependency class" that is "governed" by an army of professionals, social scientists, and bureaucrats who are usually out of touch with the true needs—and potential for self-help—of their "client" population.

132

The counterproductive nature of government social policy can be illustrated by such government programs as Aid to Families with Dependent Children (AFDC) that penalize work effort and deny assistance to two-parent, working, low-income families (see chapter 1 for further discussion). Urban renewal projects intended to revitalize decaying areas within our cities by the development of shopping malls or light industrial zones are another example of misguided government efforts. Such projects have often hastened, rather than halted, the destruction of neighborhoods because the jobs, goods, and services they provide are not the jobs, goods, and services community residents need. Similarly, the publicly funded construction of high-rise apartment buildings in low-income areas has, more often than not, failed to improve the life of residents in those communities. All too often, these buildings are filled with residents whose socioeconomic status is higher than that of the surrounding population. Even when the new units are filled by families displaced during construction or by families of similar means, the problems afflicting the community do not disappear. Instead, blocks of substandard housing are replaced by a vertical ghetto that meets the building codes, but not the needs of its residents. In either case, construction of high-rise apartment buildings in low-income areas leaves the fabric of the community irreparably torn, and the area continues to decay.

This chapter describes the cycle of dependency and provides the conceptual framework for an alternative approach. Selected examples of successful strategies are included along with the barriers facing neighborhood groups as they strive to meet the needs of their community.

A Solution in Search of a Problem

Historically, families and local groups have been the primary helping agents in many societies, and this was true in the United States until the Great Depression. The broad array of government social policies that today offer help directly to individuals meeting certain standards of need derive from the public policy responses to economic conditions in America during the early 1930s.

In 1930 6.5 million people were over age sixty-five, and most of them were supported by relatives. No more than 100,000 persons had any sort of pension, and no more than 100,000 were cared for in poorhouses.[1] The depression of the 1930s broke down the ability of families to provide for their needy (particularly their elderly) and opened the way for the New Deal.

With millions of people unemployed for lengthy spells during the depression, the prior system of caring for the elderly and other needy groups was severely strained. New Deal social programs supplemented, and in some cases supplanted, smaller, more indigenous helping networks, and, it must be said, did help to alleviate the widespread deprivation of the times. It is important to recognize, however, that the growth of these government programs brought with it a professional class of social policy bureaucrats and a corps of sociologists, psychologists, and social workers whose purpose was to help the individual adjust to modern society. Thus, an adjustment process formerly worked out by people in their own communities with the help of their own families was now directed from above by a new group of professionals.

This burgeoning class of social service/social science professionals has become a powerful force in American life. As Peter Berger points out in his article "Ethics and the New Class," the group that he calls the "New Class" has its own social status, goals, interests, and set of moral ethics; and it rivals the business community in its effect on the public.

> Indeed, the New Class is marked by a strong hostility to the capitalist system and to the business community. This animus ranges from the left-liberal orientation of the majority to more pronounced socialist views of a vocal minority. The reasons for this New Class *gauchisme* are, in all probability, more complex than their rootage in class interest, but it is very important that the latter be perceived too. The greater part of the New Class derives its livelihood in expanding this type of employment. Thus, the vested interest of this group in replacing market forces with government intervention is, at the very least, as important in explaining the statistical inclinations of the New Class as more idealistic aspirations.[2]

Although members of the New Class may be sincere and conscientious, the way these professionals perceive a problem and the solutions they propose are not necessarily in the best interest of the population they serve. Nor are their recommendations the best basis for public policy. Policy sponsored by this group tends to favor a continuous expansion of government regulatory powers, welfare dependency, and economic programs.

In addition to their appetite for government expansion, New Class professionals and experts are wary of nonaccredited persons who are able to provide the same services and who, by their very presence, challenge the professionals' authority as the sole providers of services. Thus, professionals have responded to the increasing number of nonprofessionals taking an active part in social, legal, educational, and health programs by requiring that these paraprofessionals be in some way registered or certified. A variation on "if you can't beat them, join them," their slogan in this instance seems to be "if you can't beat them, make them join you." By trying to co-opt a group that threatens the professionals' hold on society's problems, the New Class has defended its turf, but has, perhaps, done so at the cost of scaring away or isolating from power the very individuals who have demonstrated their ability to solve social or economic problems successfully.

Regardless of whether the professional favors one policy over another because of a conviction that it is in the best interest of those he or she is trying to help or because of a vested interest in maintaining the status quo, the New Class has a stake in the success or failure of the programs it espouses. Therefore, in order to ensure the success of a particular solution, professionals habitually practice a type of selective vision when defining the problem to be "solved." As Mark Twain once said, "When the only tool you have is a hammer, every problem looks like a nail."

The consequences of the New Class's tunnel vision and policies based on enlightened self-interest, though grave, are not as serious as the seemingly inevitable "professionalization of the client" that is part of every successful interaction between professional and client. Thomas Dewar defines this professionalization of the client as a process whereby persons being helped take on some of their helpers' theories, assumptions, and explanations about their problems and what will reduce them.[3] In this process, the professional's role is active—identifying and defining the problem, choosing the way the problem will be solved, and directing the process of recovery. The client's role is passive. The client not only accepts a subordinate status, but also believes that it is in his or her best interest to cooperate fully with the helper's plans. "Good" clients are those who never question the helper's wisdom or challenge his authority by trying to take a more active part in solving the problem.

Through exposure to the "ideology of service," clients learn that whatever their helpers do is for their own good. They also learn that, relative to their helper, they are incompetent. While their helpers seek to know and to act, clients must learn to trust and to obey. Unfortunately, the very qualities that make a client good may interfere with that person's competence as parent, friend, employee, or, simply, adult human being. The more the clients accept the view that "they have or are the problem, and that their professional helpers have or are the solution,"[4] the less they are able to act in a confident, competent manner. When adult independence is replaced by childlike dependency, the client's ability to function as a fully competent adult is diminished.

The Impact of Public Policy on Mediating Structures

Throughout history, people have relied upon what Peter Berger and Richard John Neuhaus call "mediating structures" to define the relationship between the individual and the state.[5] Mediating structures are those institutions standing between the private lives of individuals and the large institutions of public life. Mediating structures may be churches, ethnic groups, neighborhood associations, families, or voluntary organizations within the community. Modern society forces individuals to balance the demands of their private lives and the realities of such megastructures as the modern state, big business, organized labor, and the public and private bureaucracies that administer wide sectors of society.

People vary in their ability to cope with the dichotomy between their public and private lives. Berger and Neuhaus note that

> Many who handle it more successfully than most have access to institutions that *mediate* between the two spheres. Such institutions have a private face, giving private life a measure of stability, and they have a public face, transferring meaning and value to the megastructures. Thus, mediating structures alleviate each facet of the double crisis of modern society.[6]

Studies have shown that most people in lower-income areas turn in times of trouble to someone or some group in their neighborhood for advice and help. Donald and Rachel Warren of Oakland University in Rochester, Michigan, found that 80 percent of low-income residents in Detroit, when faced with a crisis, turned to individuals or institutions within their neighborhood for help.[7] These findings were confirmed by a study conducted by the University of Southern California. When asked to list those they turned to first in times of crisis, persons who had been in distress indicated they went most frequently to someone within the neighborhood. In fact, the top seven choices were sources within the neighborhood (ministers, friends, hairdressers, and so forth). Yet, federal, state, and local governments spend enormous sums of money to staff, operate, or otherwise fund professional service agencies—sources of help that people typically choose to avoid, according to these studies.

Not only is much of this money wasted since the services rendered tend to foster dependence on the system rather than promote reliance on self, but government emphasis on professional services also frequently undermines the strengths and effectiveness of local mediating structures. It does so at great cost: to the public coffers, which must pay for services that could have been more cheaply and more successfully provided by local institutions and organizations; to the community as a whole, which suffers when the institutions that define it and give meaning to the lives of its residents are stripped of legitimacy by government's refusal to recognize their capability; and to the individuals themselves, who pay for the help they receive with the coin of dependency.

It need not be this way. Studies conducted by the American Enterprise Institute indicate a huge potential for assisting rather than hampering neighborhood mediating structures and for adopting public policies that encourage their good work. Some changes are major and require restructuring the way public policy is developed and programs are funded. Many changes are minor, but still important, and require eliminating barriers imposed, often unwittingly, by regulatory and funding agencies.

Mediating Structures and Their Response to Community Problems

In countless communities, urban and rural, throughout the United States, individuals, churches, and neighborhood organizations have succeeded where large-scale programs have failed to solve, or even to address, a specific community problem. In places as diverse as the Bronx, Appalachia, and the Mississippi Delta, community groups have rehabilitated scores of housing units, established cooperatives, fed the elderly, attracted new businesses, set up security patrols, and provided job training programs and day-care services for their youth.[8] Working with only their determination and their willingness to volunteer hours of their time to solve a community problem, these groups have managed to revive their neighborhoods and improve the lives of residents. The track record of neighborhood groups is, perhaps, most clearly exemplified by the success of individuals, churches, and community organizations in reducing youth crime.

In Philadelphia, "The City of Brotherly Love," David and Falaka Fattah in 1969 opened their home and their hearts to fifteen members of a street gang called Clymer Street. At that time, the youth gang problem was so acute that the *Philadelphia Inquirer* dubbed 1969 "The Year of the Gun." With unorthodox ideas and no formal training in social work, the Fattahs have since taken in more than 500 of Philadelphia's toughest gang members in a new concept of peace. Their efforts have been rewarded as the number of gang deaths in the city declined from an average of thirty-nine deaths per year to six in 1976 and to just one in 1977. Furthermore, the West Philadelphia community, home to the Fattahs' House of Umoja, is coming back to life: the crime rate is slowly abating, and plans for restoration are being made.

La Playa, the port section of Ponce, the second largest city in Puerto Rico, has a population of more than 17,500, or 10 percent of Ponce itself. La Playa has always been a distinctive area, adjacent to but separate from Ponce and notorious as the "bad" section of town. It was generally avoided by outsiders, who considered it too dangerous to walk through. Rates of juvenile delinquency and crime ran twice as high in La Playa as in Ponce itself, and politicians had written off La Playa as too problem-ridden for effective programs of social reconstruction. In 1968, however, Sister M. Isolina Ferré, of the Order of Missionary Sisters of the Blessed Trinity, with five sisters of her order, one social worker, and one employee of the Agricultural Extension Agency began a community and human development program in La Playa. The program now provides education and vocational training, cultural and recreational activities, a foster grandparents program, and well-attended monthly community meetings at which any topic of special concern to the community is discussed.

Sister Isolina was able to obtain a Family Health Comprehensive Services Grant for a health care center on the condition that the community itself organize and supervise its administration. The community rose to the challenge, and the result is the Cento de Diagnostic y Tretamiento, a comprehensive family health center with a board of directors comprising mainly people with little or no formal education elected from a neighborhood that had never before had any community organization. Equally impressive has been Sister Isolina's success in rehabilitating "bad" children who had been rejected or abandoned to live in the streets. She has been able to parlay these young people's interest in horses into an interest in an equestrian club and other center activities. Significantly, all categories of juvenile offenses recorded by the police have shown a marked reduction in La Playa since the program went into effect.

The success of these individuals or organizations has been recognized by community residents, documented by statistics collected by the police, and given official sanction when city agencies contract with these groups for services. Community programs and projects are studied by experts. Their leaders are interviewed by local and national media. Yet when a major social crisis erupts, like the riots in Miami or the racial violence at the federal prison in Albuquerque, New Mexico, rarely if ever are these leaders included in the task forces and conferences following the disruption. Nor are these leaders asked to help formulate research agendas and develop public policy. Grants for major policy research on crime, racial violence, gang warfare, and drug abuse usually go to universities and large white-controlled research firms and not to qualified black or other minority firms and organizations. Of the forty participants in the conference following the violence in the Albuquerque prison, only one was a member of a minority group. Instead of turning to community leaders after the Miami riots of 1981, the authorities retained a white-controlled Washington-based research firm to help the Miami police determine the cause of the riots and then to advise other municipalities how to avert such disturbances. The U.S. Justice Department's Office of Juvenile Justice and Delinquency Prevention awarded $55 million in research grants over a five-year period, but not one minority individual was asked to write a background paper and not one minority-controlled institution or research firm was ever consulted. It should surprise no one that the programs and policies designed by professional planners in consultation only with equally accredited experts should falter and frequently fail when they meet the realities of life on ghetto streets.

Toward a New Public Policy

Regardless of how one feels about the cuts in government spending proposed by the Reagan administration, the cuts provide an unparalleled opportunity for rethinking the presuppositions, program designs, and implementation mechanisms of social policy in this country. If one looks at the huge sums of money expended by government since the 1960s on the solution of social problems, especially those related to poverty, it is clear that there have been some positive outcomes. Indeed, some progress has been made in reducing the most acute deprivation; but the most vexing and potentially most explosive problems, such as youth unemployment and street violence, continue to plague society. Furthermore, even the positive results of social policy in the last two decades have come at a high price. Although some argue that government programs designed to help the poor are inefficient, incurring huge program costs without commensurate benefits, the dollar amounts of money "wasted" is not the key issue here. What is of concern is the high price society pays for the creation of a dependent class of poor people who have, in effect, become permanent clients of the state.

139

This long-run societal cost may be greater than the size of the current outlays that taxpayers must finance. There is no sign of relief for taxpayers or of a break in the cycle of dependency for the beneficiaries themselves. Moreover, the way social programs have been developed and administered has resulted, albeit unintentionally, in the merging of racial and class categories, with large numbers of blacks and Hispanics gradually forming an underclass permanently dependent on government largess. Both cost considerations and human dignity would be well served by wholesale reforms in our public policy.

What is needed is not the continuation of a public policy framework that virtually guarantees maximum frustration for everyone, but a radical new approach that places at the center of public policy those groups and structures essential to the life of a neighborhood. As discussed earlier in this paper, in poor neighborhoods throughout the country, there exist both formal and informal groups and structures that hold neighborhoods together in times of crisis and work to improve the quality of daily life. The purpose of social policy should be to recognize the existence of these structures, to remove barriers that hinder them, and to use these same structures more creatively. The examples in this chapter and in the chapters on child welfare and youth crime illustrate the effectiveness of these grass-roots organizations in alleviating our most stubborn social problems.

A new social policy should be based on the conviction that the best interests of people cannot be determined by outside experts, however benevolent in intention. Benevolence, or compassion, is an insufficient premise for public policy. What matters is not what people feel, but the real consequences of what they do. The poor should not serve the purpose of providing therapeutic outlets for the compassionate aspirations of other classes; nor should they serve as the power base for those who profess to represent their interests or as the subjects of social experiments. Social policy must be founded on trust among people and in their innate capacity to help themselves.

This does not mean that government has no role in helping the poor, and it certainly should not abandon them. It does mean, however, that a new balance between government and smaller institutions must be found. Crucial to the success of a new social policy is the reduction of dependency, the recognition of people's capacity to help themselves, and the opening of institutional means of empowerment.

Over the past six years, the AEI Mediating Structures Project has been studying the role of churches, ethnic subcultures, families, and neighborhood associations in relieving social problems concentrated in the urban inner city. The papers and books from this study reveal the way mediating structures are impeded in their work and point to ways of enhancing this work. Although the project has not been completed, the results of research completed to date strongly indicate that a new social policy should focus on removing regulatory and economic barriers encountered by small enterprises, on creating incentives for economic development, and on establishing mechanisms by which those served by social programs can have greater influence on the way services are provided and a greater role in making the policies that affect their lives.

Barriers to Neighborhood Development

Ad hoc neighborhood organizations often coalesce around a particular community problem, develop creative strategies for attacking and resolving the problem, and disband when the problem has been alleviated. Some groups, however, do not dissolve when their initial concern has been resolved, but continue to provide important community leadership in the solution of other problems. They frequently attempt to solidify the gains they have made for their community by establishing a small business enterprise—a day-care center, a job-training facility, a security protection service, a housing rehabilitation program, or other endeavor to benefit their community. When neighborhood groups move from strictly voluntary intervention and advocacy and try to formalize their efforts by forming a business or by providing social services, they often come up against economic and regulatory barriers that seriously affect their ability to continue revitalizing their community.

The economic barriers encountered by neighborhood organizations and other local institutions will be discussed later in this chapter. Financing notwithstanding, the maze of regulatory barriers to be surmounted before an enterprise has a "license to operate" is frequently so formidable that some groups give up and their project dies aborning. Other groups innocently persist in their efforts to provide needed community services only to discover that the costs of complying with various regulations put the fees they must charge for their services beyond the reach of community residents. Still others do not anticipate the lengthy delays and high transaction costs encountered when applying for small business loans.

A study of the regulatory and administrative barriers encountered by would-be providers of day-care services was undertaken as part of the AEI Neighborhood Revitalization Project. Day care was chosen for examination for two reasons: (1) day care is regarded as a relatively basic business enterprise for which neighborhood indi-

141

viduals and organizations have skills, and (2) an adequate supply of day care within a neighborhood contributes substantially to the economic and social well-being of a community because it allows parents to work or to receive job training while assuring them that their children are safe and well cared for.[9]

It was found that, for the most part, the barriers faced by day-care providers came not from laws and regulations governing day care per se but from building, fire, and zoning codes and from inconsistencies in the way the codes and regulations were applied. Zoning codes, not unexpectedly, had the greatest effect on the amount of day care available within a neighborhood. In the city studied, any form of day care is considered to be a small business and is therefore prohibited in residential zones unless a waiver is granted. No distinction is made between day care offered to six or fewer children by women in their own homes or day-care centers serving a larger number of children. Nor does it matter if the day-care program is located in a church or in excess classrooms belonging to an elementary school. Under this city's zoning code, churches and schools are viewed as providing essential community services and are therefore permitted to locate in any area of the city, however zoned. Yet these same churches and schools are not allowed to use their buildings to provide day-care services to community residents if the church or school is located in a residential zone. Similarly, zoning codes do not prohibit a woman from caring for six (or more) children in her home if the children are all hers, but she is prohibited from taking care of two or three unrelated children if her house is located in a strictly residential area.

It is unclear why zoning codes designate day care as a small business instead of an essential community service. The designation leads to some odd situations, one of which is described by an irate director of a day-care center who testified at a zoning board hearing:

> You're telling us that we cannot operate a day-care facility in a residentially zoned middle-class neighborhood with a large number of working mothers, but we can operate a center in a commercial zone between two topless bars because day-care centers are classified as small businesses.[10]

Zoning codes were written to protect communities from possible "negative environmental impact," but this quirk in the zoning codes protects no one. Day care in already existing homes, churches, and schools would have no negative environmental effect other than that already "suffered" from the existence of these homes and buildings.

Also, zoning codes do not take into account the problems caused by "latch key" children roaming unsupervised through the neighborhood, nor do they consider the economic loss to the community that results when parents with young children cannot prepare for or hold jobs that would make them financially self-sufficient. Moreover, classifying day care as a small business does not ensure that children are adequately cared for and protected.

Standards set by building and fire codes and, in some cases, by day-care regulations governing a day-care center's physical plant also pose problems. A residence that otherwise satisfies fire, building, and safety codes of the city studied must comply with a host of additional standards when it is used as a family day-care home. A case in point involves the requirement that family day-care homes install fire escapes if the second story is used by the children in care. As one day-care mother noted, this means that her own four children can use the the second floor for napping, playing, and doing homework, but the day-care children cannot. Not only could this day-care mother not afford the $2,000 cost of installing a fire escape, but, as she pointed out, her neighbors would object to the so-called negative environmental impact of a fire escape.

The barriers that interfere with the supply of ample, affordable day-care services are only the tip of the iceberg. Building, fire, and safety codes assume that the facilities to be inspected have been newly constructed for the express purpose of providing day care; they fail to realize that urban day-care centers are almost uniformly located in previously existing structures. Therefore, in order to comply fully with these codes, day-care center directors must spend thousands of dollars renovating their facilities. None of the day-care directors or family day-care home providers interviewed for this study objected to meeting standards and regulations clearly linked to children's safety, but they questioned the necessity of meeting standards designed for schools serving far larger numbers of children or for hospitals and orphanages providing round-the-clock care. They felt not only that these codes and regulations were irrelevant to the protection and safety of small numbers of children in care for only part of the day, but also that they added unnecessarily to the fees they had to charge parents of the children in their care.

The regulatory and administrative barriers to obtaining a license for day-care services are not unique. Unfortunately, other small business enterprises face obstacles in addition to those cited above before they, too, can take their place in the business market. Chief among them is the requirement that staff members in social service and similar organizations meet accrediting standards before they can receive pay for the same services they rendered free as volunteers. Furthermore, small entrepreneurs pay the same fixed licensing application fees as do enterprises ten, twenty, or one hundred times their size. It is no wonder that many grass-roots organizations retreat in the face of such barriers and give up their plans for establishing a small business enterprise in their community. Public policy must address the issue of whether the legal protections and quality controls contained in various regulations and codes are effective, logical, and cost-efficient. It must also determine whether the cost of protection is greater than the potential harm to children and adults were the regulations and other protections to be modified.

Incentives to Economic Development

The removal of barriers alone will not suffice to produce social and economic development, nor would the healthy functioning of mediating institutions alone guarantee their survival. The well-being of any community is dependent upon a sound economic framework that functions within a proper system. John McKnight and his colleagues at Northwestern University addressed this point:

> The social and political institutions may be the heart and soul of a community, but these economic resources supply the essential blood. Income represents the basic plasma while capital and credit act like the iron, without which the whole body becomes anemic and loses its resistance to disease.[11]

According to economist Charles Kindleberger and others, economic development means more than economic growth. It implies changes in "the technical and institutional arrangements by which output is produced." If it is true that development is largely the process of adjustment to change, then the goal of development policy should not be to help people resist change but to enable them and their enterprises to respond successfully to it. As to employment, such policy should help people cope with national and regional shifts "in *levels* of employment, *locations* of employment, *who* gets jobs, and the *types of jobs created*."[12]

In the complex American economic system, this essential process of development is often hindered by inefficiencies or barriers in markets that allocate factors of production—especially capital and labor. A major purpose of markets is to send signals, which people and enterprises use to change their behavior in response to events. Markets that give wrong or distorted signals—that is, inefficient markets —make it difficult for an economy to adapt properly to change and thus to develop. Artificially low government-controlled petroleum prices, for example, may have seemed like a bargain before the recent enactment of decontrol measures, but those ceilings led to greater dependence on higher-priced foreign oil, and postponed energy conservation measures, and this ultimately cost consumers more than they would have spent under a market-determined price system.

While public policy needs to be redesigned to encourage economic development in distressed areas, the way both the private and the public sectors view nonprofit organizations and their associated economic enterprises also needs to be changed. Probably the most frequently mentioned barrier to neighborhood development organizations and community enterprises is the lack of access to capital and credit. In his chapter on economic development, Paul Pryde has noted that a "tiny shift" in the four-trillion-dollar private capital market "could make more of an impact on the problem of poverty than could even a doubling of the charitable giving of major corporations and foundations."

Efforts to revitalize neighborhoods have been hampered not only because neighborhood organizations start with very little, but also because they are unable to hold on to what they have. Systematic disinvestment in inner city neighborhoods by financial institutions and insurance companies has been particularly damaging. In addition to a lack of capital, marginal or disinvested communities also lack reliable information about themselves that might allow potential investors to make an informed decision. Models of risk-worthiness are routinely applied to groups with whom an investor has no firsthand experience, yet both public and private investment circles lack an investment rationale appropriate to the inner city, especially when inclined to raise their "standards" before dealing with any "unusual" project.

Research has shown that community groups pass through six distinct stages as they evolve from an ad hoc, loosely organized group to a self-sustaining community institution. These are:

1. The Ad Hoc Stage. Concerned citizens come together to decide what needs to be done about a community problem; they take action and disband when the problem has been resolved.
2. The Volunteer Stage. Community members do not disband but continue to address other community issues and concerns. Individual roles and responsibilities are identified, and contribu-

tions of time, in-kind services, and materials are made. Since virtually all grass-roots efforts start with no money, the effort is purely voluntary.

3. The Tax-Exempt Certification Stage. As the movement or organization takes on a life of its own, it soon attracts donations of materials and administrative support and assumes the responsibilities of maintaining records and meeting basic administrative overhead. At this point the organization usually recognizes the advantages of a tax-exempt status that both benefits contributors and volunteers and confers legitimacy on the organization itself. Incorporation, the development of by-laws, the selection of a board, and the application for tax-exempt status with the Internal Revenue Service characterize this stage of development. Many grass-roots organizations never get beyond this stage, nor do they have any intentions of developing anything other than a purely or predominantly voluntary effort. Many operate effectively as voluntary organizations with budgets that range from a few hundred to a few thousand dollars.

4. The Administrative Stage. At this stage, enough money has been contributed to justify a core administrative staff (usually an executive director and an administrative assistant, often part-time). Once an organization has reached this level of development, fund raising, planning, and maintaining the core program support become the central activities and driving force.

5. The Professional Stage. Fund raising is systematized, and the organization develops specialists to carry on programs as well as development activities. It is no longer the charismatic leadership that opens doors; rather, the organization's reputation, competence, and service delivery ensure its continuity as an institution. Information and financial management systems have been implemented and refined, and the organization usually includes a comptroller as part of its administrative arm.

6. The Equity Stage. This equivalent of institutional status is achieved when the organization has developed a self-sufficient equity base that ensures future activities independent of gifts and contributions. Most organizations that reach this level of development are constituent-based (that is, they have an established membership that provides funds from dues, fees, subscriptions, and so forth) and receive income from a professionalized, self-supporting enterprise, such as real estate income from property and subscription and advertising revenue from

publications. Other organizations achieve equity through development partnerships, capital improvements, or the development of unique services or products. These enterprises often take the form of for-profit subsidiaries whose utility frequently outlives and overshadows the usefulness of the nonprofit parent organization in pure economic terms.

As more is learned about the way successful groups function in any of the stages outlined above, potential investors will be able to evaluate more wisely the risks involved in funding a group's activities.

Pluralistic Decision Making and Freedom of Choice

Social policy is usually designed by government bureaucrats and professional experts, all of whom are members of what has been called the "New Class," the "knowledge class," or the "social welfare–poverty complex." If the putative beneficiaries of social policy are asked their opinion at all, it is usually after the fact—that is, they are invited to "participate" in programs that have already been formulated and organized by the above-named experts. Quite apart from the undemocratic and elitist character of this process, this type of thinking is responsible for many of the failures of social policy. Categories, labels, values, and reformist schemes are irrelevant in certain situations, but are nonetheless enforced by people who are strangers to these situations and who are ignorant of the needs and dreams of those they profess to serve. America takes pride in being a pluralistic society. Yet the primary vehicles of social policy have been antithetical to pluralistic notions of American life and, in fact, monopolistic in reflecting the values and perspectives of only one group—the group that can be called the "knowledge class."

Procedures must be established by which the perspectives and values of those intended to benefit from social policy become an integral part of both the design and the implementation of programs. Social policy thus conceived must not only include technical assistance and resources from all sectors, classes, and ethnic groups that make up our nation but also recognize the diverse norms and cultural patterns of the people involved. Only a social policy based on the consensus of all concerned can ensure that programs derived from that policy will succeed.

Social policy forged through a consensus of those governed and those governing would have, as a key component, a mechanism for strengthening its recipients' independence and freedom of choice. To say that a particular social need is a governmental responsibility is *not* to say that every program designed to meet this need must be developed and implemented by government. Upper-income people in our society already have a wide range of choices in the securing of services. The purpose of social policy should be to extend these choices to lower-income people as well. This result cannot be achieved, however, by simply devolving responsibility from one level of government to another—state and local governments can be as monopolistic as the federal government in limiting people's choices. Public policy should expand citizens' choices beyond government, and one way to accomplish this is to force the government to compete in the marketplace as a supplier of services.

The voucher concept is admirably suited to meet this purpose. Originally conceived in the area of education, it can be applied to a full spectrum of social programs. The concept essentially means that government funds are channeled directly to eligible individuals who can then assign these funds to programs and institutions that best meet their particular needs. A voucher system does not automatically ensure that the services and providers selected will alleviate the problem at hand. It does promise, however, that low-income families will have the opportunity to shop for services as do more affluent families in our society. The voucher system thereby makes the market more competitive and increases the chances that one or another innovative program, public or private, will meet their particular needs.

Americans today must either agree to the continuation of current social programs and policies as they are or accept the opportunity to modify and redirect those programs and policies to empower beneficiaries more fully. The outcome of either approach is uncertain; but, given the documented failures of current social policies, the creation of a class of citizens permanently dependent on social programs, and the economic realities of current budget cuts, the time seems ripe for adopting a new social policy. A new policy could maximize the freedom of choice and the independence of those receiving government-funded services while not excluding the need for government-funded maintenance programs like AFDC and food stamps. The shift in government emphasis proposed in this chapter in no way condones the abandonment of programs that alleviate the problems of the poor. Arguments made in favor of a policy shift do, however, emphasize the need to empower the people "protected" by social programs and support the necessity of removing inherent barriers that inhibit individuals, indigenous groups, institutions, and other mediating structures from providing the services needed.

Notes

1 Robert L. Woodson, *A Summons to Life: Mediating Structures and the Prevention of Youth Crime* (Washington, D.C.: American Enterprise Institute; Cambridge, Mass.: Ballinger, 1981).

2 Peter L. Berger, "Ethics and the New Class," *Ethics and Public Policy*, Reprint no. 9 (Washington, D.C.: Ethics and Public Policy Center, Georgetown University, September 1978).

3 Thomas R. Dewar, "The Professionalization of the Client," *Social Policy*, January-February 1978.

4 Ibid.

5 Peter L. Berger and Richard John Neuhaus, *To Empower People: The Role of Mediating Structures in Public Policy* (Washington, D.C.: American Enterprise Institute, 1977).

6 Ibid., p. 3.

7 Donald and Rachel Warren, "Helping Networks: How People Cope with Problems in the Metropolitan Community, Final Report," monograph project 3-ROI-MH-2498 (Bethesda, Md.: National Institutes of Health, December 31, 1976).

8 U.S. Department of Housing and Urban Development, Office of Neighborhoods, Voluntary Associations, and Consumer Protection, *Neighborhoods: A Self-Help Sampler*, October 1979.

9 Sean Scott, "Regulatory Barriers to Neighborhood Development: The Regulation of Day Care," mimeographed (Washington, D.C.: American Enterprise Institute, May 1982). The study examined day care in a large eastern city, and the research information is based on the regulatory processes particular to that city. The issues pertaining to these regulations, however, are relevant to many localities.

10 Ibid.

11 Bradford, Finney, Hallet, and McKnight, "Community Development Policy Paper: Structural Disinvestment—A Problem in Search of a Policy" (Evanston, Ill.: Northwestern University Center for Public Affairs, 1978).

12 Robert L. Woodson and Brigitte Berger, "Toward a New Social Policy," mimeographed (Washington, D.C.: American Enterprise Institute, February 1982).

PART THREE

Components and Economics of the Private Sector

Private Sector Components, Activities, and Policies: An Overview

Landrum Bolling

The Private Philanthropists: Numerous and Diverse

The private sector is a vast universe. Everybody is familiar with bits and pieces of it from daily experience. We are all, in various ways, part of it. Yet few ever try to describe the private sector in its entirety or to analyze its overall role or to propose comprehensive public policies that might increase its effectiveness in serving the general good. Is the "private sector" the same as the "nonprofit sector"? Is it synonymous with "private business"? Or does it include each of them? For a time, many people spoke of the "third sector," contrasting it with government and business as the two other sectors. Yet, in truth, profit-making and nonprofit organizations share many duties, responsibilities, and concerns in serving the public good and have many of the same ambivalent relations with government. Recently, "independent sector" has emerged as the label preferred by many. Indeed, Independent Sector, Inc., was adopted in 1980 as the name of a national organization comprising representatives from several hundred foundations, corporations, and associations: both grant-making and grant-receiving groups, both for-profit and not-for-profit corporate entities—the broadest coalition ever attempted in the philanthropic field.

The authors of this study examine an exceedingly wide range of public service activities and organizations—a huge, multifaceted, and very loose network known as the private sector. The main similarity among these organizations is their independence: none is controlled by government. Most are supported wholly or partly by earnings and private contributions; a great many use volunteers; and most have defined their goals in response to a private initiative rather than a government directive. To be sure, many are heavily involved with government through overlapping, cooperative, or competitive activities. Some are primarily financed by government grants or hold contracts to help carry out a government-sponsored program. Many, both profit-making and nonprofit organizations, have extensive partnerships with government agencies. Yet others, from all points along the spectrum, operate in clear opposition to government policies, programs, and actions.

This chapter examines the diverse, nongovernmental efforts of the private sector to serve the public good through churches, clubs, associations, foundations, schools and colleges, corporations, labor unions, and ethnic groups related to every religious, social, and cultural tradition of America's richly pluralistic society. These mediating structures function alongside individuals and between the individuals and an overpowering government bureaucracy. This chapter also examines philanthropy in the private sector, which involves both nonprofit and profit-making organizations. These organizations function at the grass roots, in rural communities and urban neighborhoods. They operate on state, regional, and national levels as well as on the local level. Some even engage in private and volunteer activities beyond the national boundaries. The myriad ways in which profit-making business serves society in the course of normal commercial activities is discussed in the chapter on business initiatives by McKinnon, Samors, and Sullivan.

A Long-evolving History. Many and varied motivations have drawn settlers to these shores. Some come to reestablish closely knit communities, most notably those who shared a strong religious commitment that had been threatened in their homeland. Some came out of a sense of adventure, some to escape persecution. Most came in the hope of a better life. The people who came to build America and to share in its promise and its riches have been enormously varied and enterprising individuals. Yet they joined together here in voluntary associations to serve shared needs and interests to an extent far beyond anything experienced in their home countries.

Americans are the world's greatest joiners. They have demonstrated that characteristic in countless ways since the earliest colonial days. Benjamin Franklin was, throughout his life, a kind of one-man volunteer conglomerate in establishing, and in getting people to join, private organizations to serve public needs in education, health care, fire protection, library service, and other fields. Many other citizens followed his lead. Voluntarism was, however, well established in America before he was born.

The first settlers quickly found that the New World demanded cooperation. Only by working together could they construct churches and schools and establish community services. With so much to be done, with so many needs to be met, and with government weak, remote, or unpopular, voluntary associations and informal patterns of mutual assistance flourished.

Alexis de Tocqueville, the French historian and sociologist who studied this country intensively in the 1830s, saw in that pattern of voluntary cooperation one of the most distinctive and valuable features of American life. After many months of traveling across the land and talking with people of every station, he wrote in his classic *Democracy in America* about the operations both of the government and of "those associations in civil life which have no political object."[1]

He wrote admiringly about the spirit and pattern of volunteer, neighborly service he found in frontier communities and in the growing cities:

> I have often seen Americans make really great sacrifices for the common good, and I have noticed a hundred cases in which, when help was needed, they hardly ever failed to give each other trusty support.
>
> The free institutions of the United States and the political rights enjoyed there provide a thousand continual reminders to every citizen that he lives in society. At every moment they bring his mind back to this idea, that it is the duty as well as the interest of men to be useful to their fellows.[2]

That concern, he found, had been organized and institutionalized in all sorts of ways. The associations Americans formed, according to Tocqueville,

> are not only commercial and industrial in which all take part, but others of a thousand different types—religious, moral, serious, futile, very general and very limited, immensely large and very minute. Americans combine to give fetes, found seminaries, build churches, distribute books, and send missionaries to the antipodes. Hospitals, prisons and schools take shape in that way. Finally, if they want to proclaim a truth or propagate some feeling by the encouragement of a great example, they form an association. In every case, at the head of any new undertaking, where in France you would find the government or in England some territorial magnate, in the United States you are sure to find an association.[3]

After his stay in America Tocqueville traveled extensively in England and made fresh comparisons on this issue. He concluded that "the principle of association was not used nearly so constantly or so adroitly [as in America]."[4]

Tocqueville warned that in democratic societies some people would tend to see the weakness and the needs of the individual citizens as evidence that "the government must become proportionately more skillful and more active, so that society [that is, the government] should do what is no longer possible for individuals." He thought that judgment "mistaken."[5]

> A government could take the place of some of the largest associations in America, and some particular states of the Union have already attempted that. But what political power could ever carry on the vast multitude of lesser undertakings which associations daily enable American citizens to control?
>
> It is easy to see the time coming in which men will be less and less able to produce, by each alone, the commonest bare necessities of life. The tasks of government must therefore perpetually increase, and its efforts to cope with them must spread its net ever wider. The more government takes the place of associations, the more will individuals lose the idea of forming associations and need the government to come to their help. . . .
>
> The morals and intelligence of a democratic people would be in as much danger as its commerce and industry if ever a government wholly usurped the place of the private associations.[6]

The Current Scale of Private Sector Activity. The prophetic nature of Tocqueville's analysis is startling. The powers of government have grown enormously. Many people, crowded into urban slums and cut off from the land and from family support systems, have indeed seemed incapable of providing "by each alone, the commonest bare necessities of life." Moreover, as government has expanded its powers and the scope of its activities, many of the kinds of private associations that caught Tocqueville's attention have suffered a diminution of their roles and influence, and some have disappeared altogether. Yet, a century and a half later, despite the phenomenal growth of government, the number and variety of private associations have continued to expand, millions of Americans volunteer their time to help their fellow citizens and neighbors, and the use of private groups to "proclaim a truth" or to provide "encouragement of a great example" has never been greater.

The development of trade unions, public policy advocacy groups, and ethnic minority organizations has brought powerful new forces into play in the broad field of private sector initiatives that were scarcely dreamed of when Tocqueville was writing. New forms of private service for the common good—grant-making foundations and corporate contribution programs, for example—have also come on the scene since his day. Religious organizations, which he noted had a powerful influence upon American life in his time, have declined in authority, though the human service roles they play are perhaps more extensive and varied than ever before.

Today, in numbers of people, scope of activities, and dollars expended, private philanthropy is one of the largest and most diversified American industries. U.S. foundations, corporations, and individuals donated in 1980 a total of at least $48 billion in cash gifts for charitable purposes. In addition, individual volunteers contributed their labor to assist charitable causes in amounts estimated by Independent Sector to have a value of $65 billion.[7] About 85 percent of all charitable gifts come from living donors, another 5 percent from bequests, and the remaining 10 percent is almost equally divided between business corporations and foundations.

Although it is generally overlooked in calculating the dimensions of philanthropic activities and the resources that support them, considerable income is generated by fees for services, government contracts, and endowment earnings. That "other income" for private nonprofit organizations amounted in 1980 to approximately $80 billion. The total income from all sources of support for private sector activities serving the public good, including a conservative dollar value placed on contributions of time, is estimated to be at least $190 billion and may, in fact, be more than $200 billion per year.

Besides the quantitative calculations of dollars given, hours of labor volunteered, and other income generated, the most significant contributions of the private sector are the broad concern that it both reflects and stimulates, the personal attention it provides the poor and the distressed, and the encouragement it gives to try new, more creative ways of dealing with human problems and social and cultural needs in informal as well as institutional ways.

In writing about private sector initiatives, the contributors to this volume intended not merely to compile more historical materials or economic data on an important but inadequately understood sector of American society. Their chief purpose is to call attention to the private sector options for dealing with many of our national needs, interests, and problems, to raise questions about public policies that relate to those options, and to provide illustrative case studies of some of the ways the private sector functions for the common good. As new responsibilities fall to the private sector and as it continues to expand its activities, there is greater need for more documentation of how it works and improved understanding of ways to help it work better.

To understand the true scope and significance of the private sector, one must examine several of its major components.

THE HUMAN SERVICE ORGANIZATIONS

The Church. Churches, synagogues, and other religious organizations have played an important role in developing this country, in shaping its policies, and in delivering many vital human services. Some of the original colonies were rooted in agreements between the British Crown and individuals or groups committed to creating a physical environment in which a particular religious movement could flourish. Many pioneer settlements were essentially religious communities. Religious language, symbolism, and values were mingled with the patterns and concepts of secular government. In the long period before the Revolution, there was certainly no "wall of separation" between church and state.

Contemporary scholars are debating anew whether any such wall as we know today was visualized by the framers of the Constitution or the authors of the *Federalist Papers,* or even by Thomas Jefferson, who coined the phrase. For the first hundred years of our history as an independent nation, the doctrine of separation of church and state seems to have had the more limited meaning of forbidding the creation of an established church and preventing the denial to any individual of the right to the "free exercise" of religion. Throughout that first century religious institutions performed many of the services, particularly in education and social welfare, that only in the twentieth century came to be dominated by agencies of government. Not until the last quarter of the nineteenth century was there a concerted move to forbid the use of tax funds to support schools related to religious organizations.

Since 1900, and particularly since the 1930s, the United States has moved more and more to involve government in activities once primarily related to religious and other private groups. Nonetheless, religious organizations continue to run a great many educational institutions from preschools to universities, to operate hospitals, orphanages, and homes for the elderly, to distribute relief assistance to the poor and the victims of calamity, to provide counseling and rehabilitation for drug abusers, juvenile delinquents, and ex-offenders, and even to implement government policies for delivering foreign aid or caring for refugees who flee to the United States.

Of all the dollars given each year to charity, about one-half go to churches and church-related organizations. Such groups and the people they serve are also the beneficiaries of a large portion of the contributed volunteer labor. Volunteer givers and workers, not just the paid clergy, keep approximately 500,000 churches and synagogues alive in this country. Beyond the many local congregations, state, regional, and national networks of denominational groups and ecumenical associations, at all levels, work together both to provide human services, spiritual and temporal, and to try to influence public policy.

Whether liberal or conservative, orthodox or heterodox, social activist or not, religious groups in America continue to influence public policy. They are involved in much discussion, challenge, and debate, and at times, one religious group may attack the goals and tactics of other groups. It would undermine our free, pluralistic society to suppress that debate, to try to silence those who speak to matters of public policy out of religious concern, or to ignore, restrict, or prohibit church-related initiatives for coping with many of our educational, social welfare, and cultural problems.

A comprehensive list of the social service activities carried on today by American religious groups would be endless, but a few examples of these activities follow:

• The Crystal Cathedral, Garden Grove, California, whose pastor is the television minister Dr. Robert Schuller, gives books and gift packages to prison inmates at the Chino Men's Facility, has donated beds and other equipment to a hospital, operates a kindergarten and school through the eighth grade, and provides the hall for concerts by the Long Beach Symphony and other performing groups.

• Hundreds of U.S. churches raised money, collected clothing and furniture, and provided initial rent money to help the "boat people" —refugees from Indochina—resettle in this country. The Church of the Savior, a small ecumenical group in Washington, D.C., sent a delegation to the Thai-Cambodian border to provide direct services to the hungry and suffering. This small church has also launched a major housing rehabilitation project in Washington, called Jubilee Housing, for the benefit of the poor. The Church of the Savior also operates a summer camp for children from inner-city neighborhoods.

• St. Luke's Episcopal Church in downtown Atlanta has for several years operated a noon meal program for the poor. Many other

159

churches throughout the country have started "soup kitchens" as unemployment has grown, reminiscent of similar church relief stations during the Great Depression. In Washington, D.C., sixty-three religious congregations provide meals for 500 people a day through the organization So Others May Eat.

• A Southern Baptist church in Americus, Georgia, and other church groups, support Habitat for Humanity, a project that helps poor people in dilapidated housing build their own inexpensive but sound homes.

• Jewish teen-agers in Rockville, Maryland, in what they call a "Friend-to-Friend" program, spend several hours each week with isolated and lonely handicapped children, taking them to movies, playing games, and just visiting.

• The Washington Hebrew Congregation, from its temple among the embassies on Massachusetts Avenue, operates a foreign settlers program to help refugees from various countries—Jews from the Soviet Union and Iran, Indochinese from Vietnam and Cambodia—set up new homes in this country. Members of the congregation contribute clothing, furniture, and initial funds for housing and offer tutoring in English. As do many other religious groups, they also provide food and clothing for the inner-city poor, conduct a meals-on-wheels program for the shut-in elderly, and operate counseling services for families struggling with adolescent stress, marital conflict, and problems with the care of elderly parents.

Neighborhood Groups and Extended Families. Despite ongoing social change, the neighborhood continues to evoke and channel many constructive private initiatives for the public good. Its potential seems far greater than most communities have realized.

In controlling crime, improving garbage collection, and strengthening public schools, neighborhood organizations have shown that they can play an important role. Neighborhood councils have been widely adopted as adjuncts to the traditional administrative bodies of city government. They often give individuals a sense of direct contact with authorities that otherwise seem distant, untouchable, and unmovable. Perhaps of greatest importance, neighborhood endeavors inspire hope that certain grass-roots, human problems can be dealt with and that the efforts of an individual or a few individuals can make a difference.

The work and the potential of neighborhoods, however, involve more than formal new organizations. The chief significance of the neighborhood is its informal support system for an infinite variety of personal and family needs. Even in deprived neighborhoods of the minority poor, loose networks of human relationships develop and are drawn upon in times of tragedy—illness, assault, fire, robbery. These extended families provide emergency or longer-term baby-sitting services, assistance with births and weddings, and foster care for the shut-in and the elderly. Such informal neighbor-hood self-help is a little-known underground economy. It is a form of social service outside the social service agencies. According to research sponsored by the American Enterprise Institute, the urban poor turn first to these informal neighborhood networks for help. We must recognize that in most neighborhoods the human resources for dealing with human problems far exceed our official calculations, and we must take these grass-roots resources into account when formulating public policies for helping even the poorest of the poor.

Changes in zoning regulations, building codes, and accrediting rules and rechanneling of some of the public funds spent on day care centers and foster homes could make possible a much broader use of neighborhood extended-family services. Freer use of these resources could provide needed human services for more people for less money.

Voluntary Associations. Tocqueville's observations about voluntary associations still hold. Americans form associations for virtually every purpose man can imagine. Those clubs, societies, committees, councils, associations, and federations perform an enormous amount of good work and stimulate much essential (if at times, tedious) public policy debate.

Social welfare. Countless local volunteer agencies are involved in caring for unwed mothers, rehabilitating alcoholics, offering voca-tional training for the physically handicapped, sheltering the home-less, and providing many other services to the needy. Hundreds of thousands of Americans give most of the money and contribute much of the labor required to operate these agencies. Even with the develop-ment of numerous government social welfare agencies, private asso-ciations provide a major part of all social services—sometimes with and sometimes without financial assistance from government.

Youth. Youth activities to develop skills, a sense of civic respon-sibility, and constructive outlets for the surplus energies of young people are the purposes of local branches of the Boy Scouts, the Girl Scouts, the "Y," and numerous other youth-oriented volunteer organ-izations. They are thoroughly private.

Health. Volunteer groups participate in the broad field of pre-ventive health care, promote medical research, and provide early diagnoses of certain major diseases. The American Cancer Society, the National Easter Seal Society, the United Cerebral Palsy Association, the American Heart Association, the Muscular Dystrophy Association, the National Foundation–March of Dimes, and other associations play major roles in promoting public education, in influencing public policies, and in raising private funds to support health care. All are privately financed.

Education. Alumni associations, to name only one kind of volunteer organization concerned with education, raise hundreds of millions of dollars each year to provide student scholarships, to buy library books, and to help cover the operating costs of the nation's colleges and universities. They also, in many cases, assist in recruiting students and finding jobs for graduates. Although alumni associations have been most active in providing support for private, church-related, and independent colleges, they are increasingly important sources of funds for tax-supported institutions as well.

The program of school volunteers is another good example of private initiatives in education. Thousands of interested, concerned, and competent volunteers—parents, grandparents, college students— in public school systems throughout the country assist paid teachers in many of the daily chores of educating the young. Paralleling the program of individual volunteers, an "Adopt a School" movement is developing among a growing number of corporations that have undertaken to provide special services to schools near their plants or offices.

Private Schools and Colleges. The approximately 1,500 private colleges and universities constitute the majority of the institutions of higher learning in the United States, and as recently as 1950 they enrolled approximately 50 percent of all undergraduate students. With the great expansion of state universities and their satellite campuses and the explosive growth of community colleges, coupled with the inflation-fueled rise in tuition, private colleges serve today only about one quarter of the nation's undergraduates. Nonetheless, as of 1981–1982 they enrolled 2.4 million graduate, professional, and undergraduate students—considerably more than all the college students of Great Britain, France, and Germany combined.

Although most private institutions of higher learning receive some form of federal assistance—research contracts and grants, student loans and scholarships, and so forth—the overwhelming bulk of their income consists of student tuition and fees, earnings on endowments, and gifts from alumni, parents, foundations, corporations, and friends. Their survival, despite many decades of dire predictions of coming extinction, is a clear manifestation of a multi-faceted private initiative of extraordinary staying power.

Private schools at the elementary and secondary levels also continue to function. Although some are hardly accessible to any but the affluent, others barely make it from one year to the next, and some of the newer ones have become objects of political controversy with racial overtones. Unlike private colleges, the private elementary and secondary schools receive no significant support from tax funds, although some states have attempted to give assistance through textbook and other subsidies.

The Arts. Funding for art, natural science, and history museums, symphony orchestras, opera and ballet companies, and many other cultural activities in America comes primarily from private sources. In addition to box office returns and admission charges, grants from foundations and corporations and gifts from individuals make possible the flourishing of the arts in this country. Although government funding became a significant factor with the establishment of the National Endowment for the Arts and the National Endowment for the Humanities, this nation's rich cultural life is essentially the creation of private initiatives—independent, nonprofit organizations governed by volunteer boards and supported by literally millions of private donors.

Broadcasting. In the diversified world of broadcast media, the nonprofit radio and television stations and networks are a remarkable phenomenon. Even in the very early days of broadcasting, some churches and a few universities secured licenses and began to send out programs over the airwaves. With new developments in technology, these not-for-profit broadcast services have proliferated.

National Public Radio and the Public Broadcast Service are nationwide networks with hundreds of affiliates. Some stations are associated with colleges and universities, but most are independent nonprofit corporations committed to educational, cultural, and public service programming markedly different from that of commercial stations. Most affiliates related to institutions of higher education receive state funds; some connected to local school systems receive local tax support. In recent years they have all benefited from federal government support, but that is now declining. Private grants and gifts from corporations, foundations, and individuals are basic to their financing and are becoming increasingly important. A few of these stations are beginning to experiment with straight commercial advertising. It might be called an untidy arrangement, but it works; and in the total mix of funding, as well as in management and governance, private initiatives are decisive.

PUBLIC POLICY ADVOCACY GROUPS

In the protection of human rights, in the advancement of justice, in the struggle against manifest social evils, in the advocacy of countless "good causes"—the abolition of slavery, the reform of prisons and insane asylums, the extension of voting rights to women, the abolition of child labor, the establishing of civil rights for minorities, the protection of the environment, the preservation of historic buildings, the encouragement of arms control—private volunteer organizations have taken the lead.

Ironically, government reforms are seldom initiated by the government. Major new public policies are rarely the ideas of public officials. Social change, whether from the left, the right, or the middle, is almost always the result of long preparatory work by private committees, associations, and voluntary organizations of concerned citizens. Their work is often, in the initial stage, lonely and unpopular. Their efforts have, at times, brought them verbal abuse, threats, and physical attack. Nonetheless, on one major social issue after another, private volunteer organizations, through contributions of money and labor, have changed the course of the nation.

Ethnic Organizations. Of all the associations active in American life, few have been so persistent or, in the long run, so effective as those rooted in an ethnic community. The Irish, the Germans, the Italians, the Poles, the Swedes, the Greeks, and countless other nationalities have formed thousands of local clubs and regional and national associations to serve a great variety of their members' needs. The Scots' Charitable Society of Boston, established in 1657, may have been the first of these private organizations to care for the interests of an ethnic minority in the New World. Its purpose was to provide assistance to Scotsmen who fell ill or became indigent in a colony dominated by settlers who called the area New England. Emergency help of this kind has been the concern of a great many of the ethnic organizations, including recent ones set up to serve Cuban, Cambodian, Haitian, or other refugees.

Religious institutions have been powerful carriers of those ethnic traditions—whether Polish Catholic, Greek Orthodox, Swedish Lutheran, or Hasidic Jew. Growing out of those religious bodies, or developing parallel to them, have been numerous ethnic organizations to serve special purposes—German gymnastic clubs, Russian choral societies, Finnish consumer cooperatives, Scottish bagpipers and Highland dancers, retirement homes for German Jewish refugees, and so on.

Since World War II, the ethnic minorities having the greatest effect on American life have been blacks, Jews, and Hispanics. The civil rights movement made the rest of the American population more conscious of the needs, rights, and interests of black Americans than it had been at any other time in our national history. The Holocaust and the postwar creation of the state of Israel made other Americans more sensitive than ever before to the concerns of Jewish Americans. The growing number of immigrants, legal and illegal, from Spanish-speaking countries in the Western Hemisphere—now the largest single ethnic minority in the United States—has produced an unparalleled awareness of Hispanic Americans and their problems.

In none of these cases, however, did that heightened general consciousness of a particular minority arise on its own. Most Americans, no matter how compassionate and ecumenical in spirit, did not spontaneously reach out to these minorities and offer to adopt their concerns. Each ethnic group, determined to do what it could for its own members, undertook comprehensive programs of education and public information, lobbying, and other pressure group activities to reach the broadest possible audience. In the process, public attitudes have been profoundly affected, societal norms have been changed, and public policies have been reshaped.

The churches and the private voluntary associations, including the ethnic and other special affinity organizations, do the day-to-day work of private philanthropy. Foundations, corporations, and millions of individual donors provide the necessary money and volunteer labor. It would be a mistake, however, to try to draw a clear line between givers and receivers within the vast and complex network of philanthropic activities in the United States. All givers, in a variety of ways, are receivers. And, even among the very poor, a high percentage of the beneficiaries of philanthropy also make charitable gifts, primarily to their churches.

The functioning of private nonprofit service-providing institutions and agencies depends on the contributions of large sums of money, in the aggregate, and the labor of millions of volunteers. The next section deals specifically with these assorted givers, the dimensions of their giving, and some of the factors that influence their contributions of money, goods, and labor.

The Givers: Foundations, Corporations, and Individuals

Millions of private donors, large and small, institutional and individual, support education, health, social welfare, and scientific, religious, and cultural activities. They have many motivations for their giving.

All the world's great religions have taught their followers to give aid to those in need and to support religious institutions and their activities. This is still a powerful motivation. Beyond that, however, people give to please friends and neighbors, to "look good" in the community, to secure favor or advantage, or simply to avoid the risk of criticism for nonconformity. The income tax laws offer incentives for charitable gifts by allowing individuals and corporations to deduct a portion of the value of such gifts from their taxes. Corporations and wealthy individuals give increasingly from the conviction that if private initiatives, backed by private contributions, do not deal adequately with certain social needs and problems, government spending and government controls will grow. Although some gifts may be made for other than purely altruistic reasons, the importance of charitable giving in American life is not diminished.

Little information or understanding exists about the extent of private philanthropy, the role it plays in relation to government activities in various fields, and the effect of public policies and popular attitudes on private giving. To examine those questions, we must look at the three chief categories of givers and how they function.

Foundations. Benjamin Franklin, whose achievements in voluntarism are legendary, founded in 1743 the American Philosophical Society, which assumed in time many of the characteristics of present-day foundations, with an endowment fund devoted to grants for research and scholarly purposes. Franklin also established by bequest two funds of one thousand pounds sterling (then the equivalent of less than $5,000) for the benefit of his two favorite cities, Boston and Philadelphia. Philadelphia collected $1.5 million, in 1929, to help build the Franklin Institute. Boston received more than $400,000 to assist in the construction of the Franklin Institute of Boston. The final portions of Franklin's two bequests, with their accumulated earnings, will be available in 1990 and now have a value of several million dollars.

The Peabody Education Fund is usually regarded as the first modern grant-making foundation. Established in 1867 by George Peabody, who had earlier provided the initial endowment for the Peabody Conservatory of Music in Baltimore, the education fund was directed to use its assets of approximately $2 million for postwar school rehabilitation and development projects in the defeated states of the Confederacy. Although authorized to liquidate its holdings and go out of business within thirty years of its founding, it continued to operate until 1914 and then transferred its remaining assets to the John F. Slater Fund.

In the history of U.S. philanthropy, two landmark events were the founding of the Carnegie Corporation, by Andrew Carnegie, in 1911, and the chartering of the Rockefeller Foundation, by John D. Rockefeller, Sr., in 1913. Those were the first general-purpose professionally managed foundations established in the United States, and they operated, nationally and internationally, on a scale never approached before by any American philanthropic agency.

Since World War I, and particularly after 1940, private and family foundations have been created by the thousands. By the 1960s, at least 25,000 legal entities called foundations, chartered by state governments, had been established. Because of the increased federal government controls over foundations in the Tax Reform Act of 1969, a considerable number of small foundations have dissolved, and their assets have been distributed to colleges, churches, and other nonprofit charitable organizations. Some merged with other foundations.

Today, according to the best available estimates, there are about 22,500 foundations, though many of these are relatively inactive. Most of them have assets of less than a quarter of a million dollars. *The Foundation Directory*, published biennially by the Foundation Center, listed in its 1981 edition 3,363 U.S. foundations.[8] Constituting only about 15 percent of the total number of foundations on record, they held 93 percent of all foundation assets ($38.6 billion in 1979) and distributed 89 percent ($2.5 billion) of all grant dollars paid out within that year. These grant-making organizations were selected on the basis of having assets of $1 million or more or making grants of at least $100,000 within a given year.

The grant makers listed by the Foundation Center conduct most of the grant programs identified with foundation work and are often important in the support of major local and national institutions. Nonetheless, it must still be recognized that the almost 20,000 foundations not listed held assets of $2.8 billion in 1979 and made grants of $300 million. In the total mix, the very small foundations also have useful roles.

In the present universe of U.S. grant-making organizations there are four categories of foundations: independent, community, operating, and corporate. Each type has its own peculiar characteristics of structure and style of operation; they all, however, share many common program interests, are subject to similar appeals and pressures, and are partners on many public policy issues.

Independent foundations. These are sometimes called family or private foundations, for their initial capital assets commonly come from a single family—often from an individual originally, and added to later by other members of the family. Final authority over administration and grant decisions rests with a self-perpetuating board of directors or trustees. In many cases, at least in the initial stages, these boards are made up of members of the family, plus, sometimes, close business associates of the founder and trusted bankers and lawyers. Over time, a number of these family-dominated foundations have been transformed into independent entities unrelated to any family or its business interests.

Independent foundations vary widely in size, range of program interests, geographical spread of grants, and political and social orientation. They are a heterogeneous representation of the pluralism of U.S. society. Some have long had major commitments to research, public policy development, and direct service activities related to broad national and international issues. A large majority of them, however, concentrate on educational, cultural, and social welfare institutions and programs in their home communities. The 2,618 independent foundations listed in *The Foundation Directory* reported assets of $33.8 billion at the end of 1979, the last year for which complete information was available. During that year they made grants totaling $1.9 billion.

Community foundations. A new type of grant-making agency, the community foundation, was established in 1914 in Cleveland, Ohio. The Cleveland Foundation, designed by a local banker, was intended to draw gifts and bequests from many sources into a common pool. Contributors could designate the purposes they wanted their money to serve but be relieved of the burden of administration. A committee of bankers managed the investments; other local citizens, aided by professional staff, acquired responsibility for the grant-making decisions. Projects to be supported were selected from among the activities of local institutions and agencies.

About 250 American cities have copied the community foundation model; and Arkansas, Rhode Island, Oregon, and North Dakota have created community foundations to function on a statewide basis. Foundations in New York, San Francisco, Chicago, Charlotte (N.C.), and Indianapolis, for example, have grown into major philanthropic institutions. In some places, however, they have had only modest success. A major element in determining their effectiveness has been the degree of enthusiasm and practical cooperation of the local banks. If bankers can see themselves and their banks continuing in their roles as fund managers for the community foundation, they are usually quite willing to recognize that the specialized staff and committees of the foundation manage grant programs better and more flexibly than would bank employees.

As a social invention, the community foundation is one of the most creative developments in the history of private philanthropy. It offers a permanent vehicle by which many people, regardless of the scale of their giving, can have an ongoing role in philanthropy. It involves a broad cross section of the community in making decisions about the needs of the community and in securing and distributing the necessary support funds. The community foundation could and should be used much more extensively to serve the public good. A few foundations—the Charles Stewart Mott Foundation of Flint, Michigan, for one—have made "seed money" grants to help start community foundations.

A major appeal of the community foundation is that it enables a donor to make a gift for a specific purpose and to have that intention carried out by independent and responsible people, with minimal administrative costs. It also provides continuity of recognition—a named scholarship fund, for example—if that is desired. Moreover, gifts to community foundations are fully tax deductible, a greater tax incentive than the provision under the Tax Reform Act of 1969 for gifts to independent or family foundations.

The ninety-five community foundations listed in *The Foundation Directory* reported assets in 1979 of $1.7 billion and grants for the year of $102 million.

Operating foundations. As with the independent foundations, operating foundations may be the creation of an individual or a family. They are, however, dedicated to carrying out specified charitable, educational, cultural, or scientific purposes through institutions, agencies, or programs operated directly by the foundation. They sometimes make grants for related purposes, but these are usually limited to less than 15 percent of total expenditures.

Operating foundations own and administer hospitals, research laboratories, museums, and other institutions. For example:

- The Carnegie Endowment for International Peace, of Washington, D.C., "conducts its own programs of research, discussion, publication, and education in international affairs and American foreign policy." It publishes the quarterly journal *Foreign Policy*.

- The Kettering Foundation, of Dayton, Ohio, conducts extensive programs in science, education, and government affairs, using both its own staff and outside agencies.
- The Stanley W. Hayes Research Foundation, of Richmond, Indiana, operates a regional arboretum, sponsors ecological research, and conducts a popular teaching center for biological sciences.

Among the 3,363 foundations large enough to be included in *The Foundation Directory*, 48 are listed as operating foundations; their combined assets totaled slightly over $1 billion.

For the donor the operating foundation has the advantages over the more common independent foundation of fully tax-deductible contributions, exemption from the minimum pay-out requirements mandated in the Tax Reform Act of 1969 and subsequent revisions, and the enjoyment of greater direct involvement with the chosen field of activity.

Corporate foundations. The philanthropic activities of U.S. business firms are far more extensive than the grants made by legal entities called corporate or company-sponsored foundations. The next section of this chapter, "Corporate Philanthropy," contains an overview of those diverse activities. *The Foundation Directory* lists a total of 602 "company-sponsored foundations," each of which made grants in 1979 of at least $100,000. Their combined grants for the year came to $438 million. That sum constitutes, however, less than 20 percent of all corporate charitable contributions of record made that year.

Company-sponsored foundations are separate not-for-profit corporations governed by a separate board of directors or trustees. Both board members and staff, however, are generally drawn from the parent company; policies are unlikely to run counter to company policies and interests.

Sometimes the company-sponsored foundation receives capital funds, usually in the form of company stock, to provide a permanent endowment. More commonly, however, the foundation receives its funds as annual gifts from the company, varying, usually, with the size of company profits.

CORPORATE PHILANTHROPY

Corporate giving is today the fastest-growing segment of private philanthropy in the United States, having outstripped the combined expenditures of independent, community, and operating foundations in dollar amount of giving and other charitable activities. In 1980, through both corporate foundation grants and the much larger charitable contributions made directly as corporate expenditures, American business firms gave to educational, scientific, cultural, and welfare programs more than $2.8 billion, up from an estimated $2.45 billion in 1979.

These monetary gifts, however, are only a portion of the philanthropic activities carried on by U.S. profit-making enterprises. A comprehensive look at these activities reveals additional business initiatives that serve the general good—or, as is often said, that discharge "corporate social responsibilities":

- contributions of goods and services to charitable organizations: discontinued models, used or damaged products, surplus office equipment; outright gifts of currently salable products out of regular inventory; professional services, such as accounting or legal counsel, provided without cost by firms in these fields
- contributions of managerial assistance by business executives working with nonprofit organizations to improve their fund-raising, public relations, fiscal planning and controls, personnel policies, and overall administration. Such management services range from a few hours or an occasional day to a full year of sabbatical leave with pay by the company. Many high-level corporate executives make such personal contributions themselves, with the agreement of their boards. One major corporate chief executive officer estimates, for example, that he devotes more than 30 percent of his working week to philanthropic services
- time for employees to engage in charitable work as volunteers, for example, soliciting charitable funds on company time; employee meetings during working hours to plan support for charitable activities; time off, with pay, for volunteer works of social service
- loan of facilities and equipment to charitable organizations, for example, use of photocopying machines and computers; making rooms and, at times, meals available for meetings of groups associated with charities; loan of special equipment for maintenance of buildings and grounds
- use of regular business operation expenditures (notably advertising) to provide income or fund-raising assistance for charitable or cultural organizations
- training programs for employees, prospective employees, and other individuals interested in the fields related to the principal work of the firm

171

- investments and purchases directed toward charitable organizations or needy communities, without strict regard for the most immediate advantage of the company
- provision of special services or products to charitable organizations at special discount rates, sometimes at less than cost

Charitable donations by U.S. firms have a long history. Traditionally, business charitable giving was tied to the firm's self-interest. A gift of company funds was supposed to produce some direct benefit to the company. In less than a century after the Civil War, however, American business had moved by stages into far broader involvement in philanthropy. The three factors most important in that shift were the building of the railroads across this continent, the vast human needs related to World War I, and the development of the Community Chest movement, now called the United Way.

According to Marion R. Fremont-Smith, writing in *Philanthropy and the Business Corporation*, "It was the railroads, looking for housing of their employees, who first supported a charitable organization on a large scale."[9] That organization was the Young Men's Christian Association (YMCA)—with its railway Y's scattered across the country at division points and terminal cities. The railroad companies put up more than half of the capital costs of these buildings and often contributed as much as 60 percent of the operating costs to supplement the low daily charges paid by their employees.

Building upon its relationship with the railroads, the YMCA broadened its community-wide fund raising among business corporations. Having made initial contributions in their own self-interest, the railroad companies and, later, other businesses were able to rationalize continued and expanding contributions to the local YMCA without serious challenge.

With the onset of World War I, the YMCA and the American Red Cross became the major agencies to provide large-scale services to this country's vast military forces. To support these activities, the YMCA and the Red Cross undertook massive and continuous solicitation for charitable gifts and gained extensive support from business firms. Wartime patriotism silenced most doubts expressed by opponents of corporate philanthropy, at least for the duration.

By the end of the war, the Red Cross and the YMCA had been joined by the Salvation Army, the Young Women's Christian Association (YWCA), and several other national human service agencies in making coordinated appeals for business contributions. From this experience the idea of the Community Chest developed in Detroit and other major industrial centers and soon became a nationwide movement. Now known as the United Way, or United Fund, its annual federated campaigns for financial support of national and community social service agencies have become a major feature of U.S. philanthropy. There is great appeal in a system that stresses "one asking" for many charitable causes. Active business participation has been the key to the success of these endeavors. The United Way, in turn, has become the major charitable interest of many corporations.

Along the way, corporate thinking has shifted concerning both the range and the amount of charitable contributions. Let us first look at how the legal and philosophical justifications for corporate philanthropy have evolved.

Official approval of corporate giving. The "direct benefit" concept as the sole basis for charitable contributions by business firms began to fade legally, as well as psychologically, during World War I. Texas, in 1917, was the first state government to adopt legislation explicitly stating that corporations chartered by or doing business within their boundaries were *not* prohibited from contributing to any "bona fide association . . . actively engaged in purely religious, charitable or eleemosynary activities."[10]

In 1949, the Committee on Business Corporations of the American Bar Association proposed language for a Model Business Corporation Act, which, as now adopted in nearly all states, has spelled out clear powers of corporations "to make donations for the public welfare or for charitable, scientific or educational purposes."[11]

In 1953, the Supreme Court of New Jersey handed down a landmark judgment in the case of *A. P. Smith Mfg. Co. v. Barlow,* ruling that corporate management has the legal right to make charitable contributions without claiming any direct benefit for the corporation.

Similar decisions have been made by the courts in other states, so that legal constraints against corporate giving have long since disappeared. The lack of legal barriers, however, has not persuaded all businesses to give and has not ended all differences of opinion among businessmen, economists, and social philosophers. Vigorous arguments are still made that the direct-benefit test is the only truly valid justification for charitable gifts by a corporation. Some argue that business firms have no generalized social responsibility to the community or the nation. Others express the fear that charitable activities by corporations may give business excessive influence in social policy making and interfere with the human service role of government.

This is a debate without any resolution. Honest persons, widely divergent in their political philosophies, are on each side of the argument. The evolution of American business, however, with respect to philanthropic activity is instructive. The evolving practice shows strong, steady, increasingly imaginative growth in wide-ranging corporate giving—justified for a variety of reasons by the donors. Moreover, a number of associations and working groups representing the business community have attempted to formulate policy statements to stimulate and guide business leaders in developing their own guidelines for corporate social responsibility and philanthropy.

From rhetoric to action? Given the growing affirmation by business leaders of the importance of, even the necessity for, corporate philanthropic giving, inevitable questions arise about how such sentiments should be translated into action. Many of the larger corporations, beyond any doubt, are expanding their commitments to charitable giving. *The Foundation Directory* takes note of the trend with this encouraging comment:

> Company-sponsored foundations show a record of remarkable growth compared with independent and community foundations. During the four-year period, company-sponsored foundations have registered a 65.8 percent increase in assets measured in current dollars, and 23 percent in constant dollars. Gifts for endowment or for current grant-making comparing 1979 with 1975 figures have gone up 192 percent in current dollars and 116.4 percent in constant dollars. Grants are up 79.5 percent in current dollars and 33.2 percent in constant dollars. Corporations are spending much more today than previously for charitable purposes through their foundations. If figures were available for the corporate contributions of this group outside their foundations, the total might be several times the figure for the company-sponsored foundations alone.[12]

The American Association of Fund-Raising Counsel observes in *Giving USA-1981*, its 1980 annual report on facts and trends in American philanthropy, that despite a decline of nearly 6 percent in business profits in 1980, corporate giving increased by about 4 percent. The total amount of those corporate contributions was estimated by the association's researchers to be $2.55 billion, or 1.05 percent of overall pretax net income. This was a record high for the decade, both in dollar amount and in percentage of profits.

Yet within the corporate community there is limited rejoicing over this achievement. Many business leaders have pointed out that only a minority of business firms make any charitable contributions at all and have expressed the view that those that do give do not give as much as they could and should.

Willard C. Butcher, chairman, the Chase Manhattan Bank, speaking at the University of North Carolina on October 16, 1981, said:

> In this area of corporate philanthropy . . . we in American industry have not been doing enough and simply must do more. The low level of overall corporate giving is frankly appalling. Fewer than 30 percent of all corporations in America today make any charitable contributions at all. And only 6 percent give more than $500 a year. That means 94 percent . . . cannot dig up a dollar and a half a day for charity in their own self-interest. Unless we in business do a good deal better, we will have no right to complain . . . when the chickens come home to roost.

How much is enough? No comment about corporate philanthropy stirs more debate these days than suggestions of how much business firms should give to charity. Although "target goals" are commonplace in United Way and other campaigns, many business leaders insist they do not want to be told how much to give—not even by their peers in the business community. Despite that reaction, however, a growing number of philanthropic activists, within and outside the business world, are urging that higher levels of giving than those already reached should be set. One goal commonly put forth is 5 percent of pretax net income. The Cummins Engine Company, of Columbus, Indiana, has been making its charitable contributions on that basis for about twenty-five years. The Dayton-Hudson Corporation, of Minneapolis, has a similar record. Within the state of Minnesota, it is reported, more than forty business firms have now reached or committed themselves to attain the 5 percent goal. In Seattle and Louisville, groups of business leaders have agreed to push local corporations to give at least 2 percent of pretax profits.

The 5 percent figure comes from the Internal Revenue Code and dates back to 1936. Despite some opposition from the critics of business in those New Deal days, the Congress decided to allow tax deductions from corporate tax bills for charitable contributions up to 5 percent of pretax net income. It is a goal still far distant. In the Tax Reform Act of 1981, Congress voted to raise the allowable tax-deductible ceiling to 10 percent of profits, though some have expressed the suspicion that this was not a serious proposal but a way for the liberal sponsors of the provision to needle business and the

Reagan administration. Lyndon B. Johnson, after he left the White House, is reported to have challenged a group of business leaders with this comment:

> In spite of the fact that your federal government has seen fit to allow a charitable deduction of 5 percent of your profits, the record is quite clear that your business leaders still feel that the federal government can spend this money more wisely than you can.

The record also seems clear that jaw-boning the business community on this issue is not effective. Many businessmen who genuinely support the cause of increased corporate giving believe that the 5 percent goal is unrealistic for most business firms. They point out that such a scale of giving is easiest in firms where there is still strong family-owner involvement. Kenneth N. Dayton, of Dayton-Hudson, and J. Irwin Miller, of Cummins, for example, are the two leading supporters of the "5 percent club." Moreover, approximately 50,000 business firms already make charitable gifts equal to 5 percent of pretax profits; most of these, however, are very small "mom and pop" firms, which the owners draw upon to do some, if not all, of their personal charitable giving.

One of the arguments against the 5 percent goal, as expressed by representatives of giant firms like General Motors and American Telephone and Telegraph, is that with the amount of profits they normally make from their vast operations, they would find themselves running "philanthropic businesses" bigger than any existing foundation if they adopted the 5 percent formula. This would give them influence in the philanthropic world far beyond what they believe they are prepared to manage, or what the nonprofit world would accept. They do not want to contemplate the political and public relations implications of such a situation.

A common argument against increasing corporate contributions used to be that the stockholders would never stand for it. The point is still made, and, no doubt, is of concern. Yet experience has shown, again and again, that corporations have enlarged their giving for charitable purposes with no challenge whatever from shareholders; and when, on occasion, objections are raised, they draw very little support. Without question, the climate of public opinion, including opinion within the ranks of stockholders, has never been more favorable to corporate philanthropy. The management of each firm, however, will still have to decide for itself how much it ought to give.

How to give and for what? Although the direct-benefit concept no longer dominates the patterns of corporate giving, many responsible people active in the field believe that much can still be said for a healthy component of self-interest in planning grant-making programs and procedures. But what kind of self-interest? What sorts of grants express an appropriate and acceptable self-interest? Here are some of the answers exemplified in the giving patterns of a variety of U.S. business firms:

• *Programs that benefit employees and their families.* Direct training programs for improving the competency of workers are, of course, chargeable to the cost of doing business and are not charitable contributions. College scholarships for members of the employee's family, however, if awarded on an open competitive basis, are considered charitable contributions, as are matching gifts added to an employee's contribution to a college alumni fund.

• *Projects that enhance or support community facilities where the company operates.* Hospitals, swimming pools, libraries, mental health clinics used by, or available to, company employees also benefit the whole community. In some isolated or depressed communities, such self-interested philanthropy may make possible facilities and services the community would not otherwise be able to acquire.

• *Programs that increase the pool of potential personnel for business.* Firms heavily involved in the sciences and engineering tend to support educational programs that train scientists and engineers. Moreover, during the past forty years corporate support for higher education in general has grown remarkably. Joint fund-raising associations of private colleges now cover the entire country. Some firms, however, prefer to target their gifts to particular schools of business and engineering or programs in economics and the physical sciences. In any case, higher education is a high-priority interest of most corporate philanthropists, whether the self-interest is remote or not.

• *Programs that create new knowledge in a given field.* Research is the lifeblood of many modern industries. Most of them invest heavily in research and development directly related to their products and services. Beyond that, however, they also have a stake in the expansion of knowledge in related fields. Support of research institutes, laboratories, and individual scientists may well be a long-term, highly important investment.

• *Projects that help create a positive image of the company.* Advertising and public relations are legitimate business expenses. Some philanthropic gifts could be handled as a business expense or as a tax-deductible contribution. In the sponsorship of concerts, art exhibits, special documentary films, or plays on television, from which the corporation expects a public relations benefit, there is usually an option. Some companies treat the expenditure as a regular business expense. Others make a tax-deductible contribution to some non-profit organization associated with the production. The costs and benefits are virtually the same either way. The broadcast of the Metropolitan Opera on Saturday afternoons via both commercial and noncommercial radio, for example, has been an advertising project of Texaco for half a century. Other companies have found it rewarding to contribute to such major institutions as the Lincoln Center in New York, the Kennedy Center in Washington, and the Metropolitan Museum of Art in New York.

• *Projects and programs that help create a climate favorable to the stability and growth of our economic system.* Propaganda and lobbying for the enactment of legislation are not an appropriate use of tax-deductible contributions. Research on public policy issues by independent scholars, however, can make an important contribution to formulating national goals and to exploring avenues for reaching them. Therefore corporations have increased their charitable support of "think tanks" that study the problems of the economy, the government, and society in general and that develop analytical reports on the alternatives before the nation.

Although many corporate gifts may reflect some measure of self-interest, there are also many corporate giving programs that even the most cynical critics could not identify with any benefit to the company. As business firms have enlarged their commitments to philanthropic activities, as they have developed professional staffs to administer their charitable giving, as their boards and chief executives take more seriously this important segment of their total operations, they have increasingly become concerned about the same social, educational, and cultural issues that engage leaders in government, church, education, and the media and thoughtful citizens generally. Corporations, also, are concerned with what their contributions can do that will be most significant. Inevitably, those who make decisions about corporate philanthropic activity, like their counterparts in foundations, discover that it is easy to "get rid" of charitable dollars, but it is often hard to determine how to make a truly creative gift of long-term significance.

Individual Givers. Despite all the attention fixed on foundations and corporate philanthropic activities, private individuals give the great bulk of charitable contributions. Individuals go far beyond their gifts of money to give enormous outpourings of time and energy as volunteer workers in activities for the public good.

How much do individuals give? Nobody knows how much individuals give. Millions of gifts are made from one person to another, often with no record of the gift and no claim to the IRS (or to anyone else) of a charitable contribution having been made. People also make countless gifts to churches, schools, welfare agencies, and other charities without obtaining a receipt or record of the donation. Many nonprofit organizations, including many churches, keep very poor records, or no records at all.

Useful calculations can still be made, however, on the basis of determinable giving to United Way and to certain church groups, projections of itemized deductions recorded by federal income tax returns, and sampling and polling exercises carried out by various organizations.

The most credible estimates appear in *Giving USA*. The American Association of Fund-Raising Counsel calculated in its 1980 report that individual giving in 1980 came to $39.93 billion. It estimates in its report for 1981 a jump to $44.5 billion, an increase of 11.9 percent, compared with a 9.7 percent increase from 1979 to 1980.

In relation to the total of all philanthropic giving in 1980, individual contributions from living donors accounted for 83.7 percent, individual bequests 6 percent, corporations 5.3 percent, and foundations 5 percent. Thus, living or deceased, individuals accounted for almost 90 percent of all charitable giving. Roughly the same percentage held true for 1981.

Although the rate of increase in individual giving has not kept up with inflation in recent years, there is remarkable evidence of growing individual responsiveness to the increasing need for charitable contributions. United Way reported that in 1980, with an inflation rate of 12.4 percent, contributions increased by 11.1 percent in Louisville, Kentucky (despite a loss of 10,000 jobs in that city in that one year), by 10 percent in Indianapolis, by 10.1 percent in Dallas, by 14.2 percent in Seattle, by 19 percent in Winston-Salem, North Carolina, by 18.6 percent in Houston, and by 13.3 percent in Madison, Wisconsin.

Even before the Tax Reform Act of 1981 allowed all taxpayers to claim itemized charitable deductions, the number of taxpayers who record their tax-deductible contributions had started to increase. A survey directed by Professor Martin Feldstein, of Harvard, calculated that those who itemize their charitable contributions on their tax returns give more than twice as much to charities as those in the same tax brackets who use the short form and do not itemize. Some people, therefore, see great hope in a return to general itemizing of charitable gifts.

Volunteering. A major part of the individual contributions to the public good comes not in money or goods but in personal labor. Nobody knows for certain how many people work as volunteers in a given year, or in a given week. The total, however, is in the millions. Nobody can put a precise dollar value on the labor contributed, yet as previously stated, at least one study has estimated the total to be $65 billion a year.

A number of surveys have been conducted during the past decade to try to establish the extent of volunteering and the age and other categories into which volunteers might be grouped. In 1974 the Bureau of the Census undertook an in-depth study of the question. In 1981, the Gallup Organization conducted a survey under the sponsorship of Independent Sector, Inc. A few months later the Harris polling group made a related investigation of volunteering. All of these scientific, cross-sectional studies reveal an enormous outpouring of individual efforts in service to neighbors, the community, the nation, and the world. The most recent data seem, also, to indicate a rising trend among several population groups in the percentages that volunteer.

A Census Bureau study of 1974 reported that 24 percent of the adult population participates in volunteer activities; the Gallup figure for 1981 was 40 percent. Gallup calculated that 84 million Americans do some volunteer work, contributing more than 8 billion hours of free labor each year. Both the Census Bureau and Gallup agree that the most active volunteers are to be found among employed people who have had college education and earn more than $20,000 per year, yet there are dedicated volunteers in all categories. Gallup reports a marked increase in volunteering by teen-agers, the "not employed," and minorities.

How much time must a person put in to be called a volunteer? The frequency with which people contribute their time and the number of hours they give in total vary greatly. One estimate suggests that about one-fourth of the country's adults contribute at least two hours of volunteer work per week.

The Westinghouse Corporation, which actively encourages volunteer activities by its employees, did a survey of thirty-one work locations. It found that 44 percent of the people surveyed do volunteer service activities, and of these more than half say they contribute more than eight hours per month.

Two simple conclusions may be drawn from these data. A great many Americans—about half of the population from teenage onward —do some volunteer work in the course of a year, with at least a quarter volunteering on a regular and substantial basis. A great many other Americans are still not yet motivated or do not find it possible to give their time as volunteers. The present contribution is enormous. It could be greater.

Problems and Policy Options

Private sector initiatives for the public good are an important part of our national life. They are needed now, and they will be needed in the future. The institutions that carry out those initiatives are essential national resources. Their responsibilities already strain and often exceed their capabilities, and they are being asked to do still more. A serious challenge to American society is to find the best and most appropriate ways to strengthen those private public-serving programs and institutions and to expand the giving and volunteering that sustain them.

At the outset, it should be made clear that the private sector does not need an expansion of government regulations and controls. Nor does it require any supervisory "supportive" agency of government to stimulate its activities and advance its causes. The genius of private sector initiatives is that they draw upon the interests and concerns of an enormous number and wide range of individuals and groups and summon their diverse and creative energies. Their success cannot be guaranteed by government patronage, or wholly prevented by government indifference. Nor can they be neatly programmed. What will most assist them is a social environment in which their significance is recognized and their roles accepted as alternatives to or partners with government programs. Except in emergencies when they have to assume temporary functions that should more appropriately be performed by government, they should not be treated as poor substitutes to be brushed aside as soon as some government agency can take over.

Also needed is a thorough, comprehensive, and objective examination of the impediments to private sector initiatives, of the weaknesses and strengths of the institutions involved, and of the strategies that might be adopted to make them more effective.

There are numerous ways to define the problems that affect private sector institutions and organizations. Some involve public perceptions and attitudes, some have to do with internal management, and some relate to governmental policies and activities.

Public Attitudes. What people feel about things is very much influenced by what they know and how well they understand what they know. The truth is that the American public does not know very much about the private sector—absurd as that sounds.

When Independent Sector, Inc., was formed in 1980 as the long-hoped-for national service agency to the vast assortment of organizations, associations, and federations that have grown up within the private sector, an extensive survey was made to find out what the membership most wanted done. The clear first choice was a major program of nationwide information and education to promote better understanding and appreciation of what these organizations are doing. Even though practically all the constituent groups—United Way, National School Volunteer Program, the Junior League, the United Negro College Fund, and more than 300 other major national groups—have their own public information offices, they all felt that more information for the general citizenry about the work of the private sector was a matter of highest priority.

The Need to Communicate. All who are concerned about this information and communication issue appear to agree that more than a traditional public relations campaign is needed: a varied and sustained education and information program is called for. Some of the suggested components are:

• *Research.* The scarcity of hard data on the activities of the private sector is striking—and regrettable. The bare statistics about private giving, especially from individuals and corporations, are very difficult to come by. The records of foundations are more complete, up-to-date, and accessible. Government record keeping, although voluminous, is not comprehensive, and its reports are far out of date.

The collection of case histories of successful (and unsuccessful) private sector programs is of high importance, and a vast amount of that kind of information needs to be gathered. Analyses of the factors that seem to influence their performance and studies of the cost effectiveness of comparable private and public programs could be very useful for the institutions involved and for society in general.

The development of both scholarly and popular literature ought to be encouraged, for, as John Gardner, former secretary of health, education, and welfare, has frequently said, "Most of the worthwhile books we have on the subject could be fitted into a schoolboy's knapsack."

• *Formal academic study.* At no level in our educational system, from elementary school through graduate school, is adequate attention given to this field. Programs of study, individual courses, textbooks, and bibliographies are conspicuous by their absence. History, sociology, economics, and religion are some of the disciplines in which formal academic studies could be appropriately developed. Units of study on voluntarism and the role of nonprofit human service organizations would be natural components for social science programs in high schools and the lower grades.

The academic community has almost uniformly overlooked this whole area of our life. There are some signs, however, that this may be changing, as indicated by the Yale University Program on Nonprofit Organizations and by occasional Ph.D. dissertations on topics concerning nonprofit organizations and assorted private initiatives to serve the public good. The public schools of Connecticut have been exploring the possibility of taking on this subject for regular classroom instruction. Individual scholars and writers are becoming increasingly interested in this as a legitimate field for study and teaching.

• *Media coverage.* News, as has been observed, is what an editor says it is. The day-by-day activities of human service agencies that care for handicapped children, the lonely elderly, pregnant teenage girls, drug addicts, and alcoholics do not normally make the news columns or appear on television news shows. Murders, car wrecks, and fires do. Many newspapers and producers of local television news programs, however, appear to be expanding their space for "community bulletin board" coverage of voluntary organizations and cultural institutions. More deliberate in-depth interpretive reporting on the working of the private sector and its numerous components could be of enormous public benefit. Fresh and extensive efforts are being made to encourage the popular media to provide more thorough coverage. As this is written, Independent Sector, Inc., through one of its committee members, has persuaded a local television station in Columbia, Missouri, to develop pilot vignettes, short case reports on voluntary human service organizations and programs in various parts of the state.

• *Recognition and awards.* Public perceptions and attitudes are in part shaped by highly visible recognition of individuals and institutions and their achievements: hence, the great attention to the Motion Picture Academy "Oscar" Awards and to the Nobel Prizes.

While Outstanding Citizen, Volunteer of the Year, and All-American City awards have been made from time to time on a local basis, with occasional national attention, there has never been a systematic, sustained, and large-scale effort to provide national recognition to individual volunteers and private human service programs and institutions. A number of possibilities are now being put forward to provide suitable awards to both individuals and organizations that exemplify outstanding achievements in these service capacities. It is even proposed that the president of the United States might preside over such an awards celebration each year. In any case, high-level sponsorship and high-visibility recognition events could, with nationwide coverage on television, greatly help to enhance public awareness of the importance of private initiatives for the public good and build supportive public attitudes.

Internal Management. In a world of all-pervading bureaucracies, virtually every institution—governmental, business, religious, educational, or voluntary human service—ought to be better run. The real problem is usually not gross corruption, though that can happen in any segment of human society, nor is it a matter of public relations manipulation of the media.

The real problem is that most voluntary, nonprofit organizations have substantial difficulties with administration. The classic comment of college presidents and executives of voluntary organizations is, "I don't have any problems a million dollars wouldn't solve"—the implication being that securing more income, primarily gifts, is the most urgent, and maybe the only, issue. Although the available funds are usually inadequate, the lack of funds is often a symptom of deeper troubles: poor planning, fuzzy goals, incompetent staff, underutilized boards of trustees, faulty financial controls, or the failure to design and carry out a consistent, sustained, and sophisticated program of fund raising. At times, sadly, the idealistic, charismatic person who inspired people to give and to join in working for some evident need is simply an unsuitable administrator—and yet has great difficulty turning over the managerial reins to someone who could do that part of the work better. Whatever the problem, donors who take their giving seriously are increasingly raising tough questions about how their money is spent. They should.

Some foundation and corporation donors have come to believe that they should attach to their grants requirements for the adoption of certain kinds of fiscal controls. Some corporations lend their executives for just such advisory work. Sometimes grant makers earmark part of a grant for administrative expenditures they feel should be made for the organization to fulfill its program objectives more effectively: outside consultant services, more modern office equipment, periodic evaluation of programs, additional training for key personnel, expanded fund-raising activities. One foundation keeps on its staff a full-time fund-raising specialist as an adviser to organizations that receive grants but need to improve their overall fund-raising capabilities and strategies. Another foundation makes its grants primarily for improvements in the management of nonprofit organizations, not for their programs or projects.

More than 100 private voluntary organizations have had contracts or grants from the U.S. Agency for International Development (AID) to assist development projects in the third world. Some voluntary organizations, however, refuse to enter into these partnership agreements, and at times there are complaints from those that do. Others say that the detailed procedures and expectations set down by the government as conditions for receiving funds have, on occasion, compelled them to make administrative improvements they might not otherwise have made.

Many national associations have undertaken management training programs and advisory services for their member organizations. Independent Sector, Inc., has made this kind of support program one of its objectives. Improving internal management is now a lively issue within the private sector.

Public Policy. Government and private sector organizations that serve the public good are inextricably interwined. Government laws and regulations affect the daily decisions of individual volunteers, foundations, corporations, and nonprofit agencies. Government support for their activities and reliance upon them can be seen in a variety of their relationships.

Government tax policies at the federal, state, and local levels provide extensive indirect assistance to nonprofit organizations: they are tax exempt. They pay no taxes on their income, their property, or their purchases, within the bounds of certain rules and procedures. They also receive preferential postal rates.

Government regulations and reporting requirements, however, have increased the operating costs of private nonprofit organizations. The federal government, since the Tax Reform Act of 1969, has imposed a so-called excise tax on the investment income of private foundations. Moreover, numerous technical regulations issued by the IRS place constraints on grant making both by corporations and by foundations. Some of the aspects of the government–private sector relationship that need to be examined are discussed in the following sections.

Official recognition and liaison. Symbols are important in most aspects of life; they are especially important in government. Individual officials, government committees, and administrative agencies are both symbolic and substantive. Consideration should be given to the possibility of such official instruments for recognition of and liaison with the private sector as these: (1) an officer on the White House staff; (2) a standing committee in the House and the Senate; (3) appropriate liasion offices in the executive branch—specifically in the Departments of Health and Human Services, Housing and Urban Development, Education, Interior, Agriculture, Justice, Treasury, and State and in special agencies such as Action, the Peace Corps, AID, the National Science Foundation, the National Endowment for the Arts, and the National Endowment for the Humanities. Although these agencies already conduct liaison activities on a substantial scale, they are at times directed at negotiating grants or contracts with particular private organizations or at co-opting them into public support of government programs. Instead, we need mechanisms that keep the government well informed about private initiatives to serve the public and that focus on ways to improve those services. There should be a continuous study of what government activities inhibit or enhance private initiatives and of how government and private agencies might cooperate more effectively in areas of common interest.

The president, cabinet members, and members of Congress can contribute signficantly to the strengthening of private sector initiatives by calling attention to them through their speeches and writings. A national awards program for honoring outstanding volunteers and their organizations would more likely succeed with the direct backing of the president.

Tax policy. Incentives for individual and corporate charitable giving have been built into the Internal Revenue Code for many years. The Tax Act of 1981 provides renewed encouragement for individual gifts from lower- and medium-income taxpayers who use the standardized short form by allowing them to claim itemized deductions for charitable gifts. It raises the ceiling on corporate tax-deductible gifts from 5 percent to 10 percent of pretax income. Nevertheless, the whole question of how best to use tax incentives to increase charitable giving needs to be reexamined thoroughly.

The so-called excise tax on private foundations, adopted in 1969, was, in effect, a punitive measure that expressed the annoyance of Congress with foundations. Set at 4 percent of net investment income, the tax ostensibly was to cover the cost of expanded IRS auditing of the accounts of all nonprofit organizations. When it became clear that this tax was producing several times as much revenue as was being used for the greatly expanded auditing program—and was, in essence, a tax on the charitable agencies since it reduced the grants available to them—Congress voted to reduce the tax from 4 percent to 2 percent. This tax directly takes away from charitable agencies at least $30 million per year that would otherwise go to support their programs. It should be abolished.

Another tax problem for private foundations is that since 1969 they have been put into a special "disfavored" category of nonprofit organizations. Donors who wish to create new foundations or add to the capital of existing private foundations may still receive tax deductions for their gifts, but on a markedly less advantageous basis than if they gave the money directly to "public charities" to which the foundation's grant money would go anyway. To maintain the private foundation sector within the philanthropic system, the "birthrate" of foundations must be stimulated, not retarded. Existing foundations also should enlarge their capital base. Sound public policy seems to indicate that private foundations and other nonprofit, charitable agencies should be allowed to retain on a nondiscriminatory basis their legal attractiveness as beneficiaries of charitable contributions.

Program controls. IRS regulations that interfere with the autonomy of grant makers in distributing their funds should be reviewed. For instance:

• Community foundations are subjected to constraints on the percentage of their total gifts they must receive in a given year from a broad public—that is, community foundations must meet a "public support" test. They are not allowed to accept a very large gift that would throw their percentages off balance.

• Corporations are subjected to arbitrary restrictions as to what percentage of the scholarship funds they supply may be received by children of their employees, even though the selections are made by an objective, outside selection panel.

• If a foundation makes a single grant providing more than 25 percent of the budget of any new charitable organization, it thus places the recipient in a category outside the approved "public charity" classification as defined by the IRS, to the disadvantage of the grant receiver and with severe penalties to the grant maker.

These are some of the regulations that hamper the effective operation of foundations. They serve no useful purpose and should be abolished.

Government contracts and grants. For many years and through many administrations, the federal government has pursued a considerable number of its purposes through private institutions and organizations. Contracts often define in detail the work to be accomplished on a given project. In other situations, the government agency makes an outright grant to the private organization, allowing it some latitude to carry out its purpose.

As in all human arrangements, there are opportunities for mistakes in judgment and misuse of funds. Not all contracts with private agencies have worked out successfully, but neither have all comparable projects done directly by government. Not all grants to private institutions have been well advised, but the same can be said for many expenditures for direct government activity.

The use of private agencies, either through contracts or grants, offers many advantages. It is a means for increasing flexibility, encouraging the exploration of options, limiting the risks of experimentation, and evoking fresh thinking. Sometimes, as AID has found with its multifaceted programs of contracts and grants for organizations working in international development, private agencies can bring about better results for less money.

Although much has been learned through long experience about what works and what does not work in government–private agency relationships, the whole subject needs more intense study than it has yet received. It should be possible to document the ways these contract and grant agreements can be carried out most effectively and what kinds of common mistakes to avoid.

Special government subventions and services. From its inception the Postal Service has had certain social purposes, such as dissemination of knowledge through low rates for news and other publications. With the growth of voluntary, private human service institutions and the rise of direct-mail appeals for funds, the U.S. government has encouraged these organizations and their programs through subsidized postal rates. Pressure has developed within successive administrations to make the Postal Service self-supporting and to eliminate all subsidies, except for mail to isolated homes in rural areas. This pressure has caused jumps in postage charges of several hundred percent within a few years to publications and to nonprofit organizations for their fund-raising appeals. As the nonprofit charitable organizations are being asked to expand their services and raise more and more private funding, the recent and projected increases in postal costs place heavy burdens on all of them and will likely be enough to force the demise of some of them. This is not the place to argue the controversial issue of postal subsidies for nonprofit organizations, though the whole question deserves thorough, sustained study and the exploration of policy options.

One major service the government already provides for nonprofit organizations—and could perform much better—is the collection and dissemination of basic data. The Census Bureau and the Internal Revenue Service are but two government agencies that gather vast amounts of information of concern to the private sector. With modern high-speed computers, the government could gather, process, and release data that the private sector needs to target its activities, to assess the needs of society, and to evaluate its performance in addressing those needs. Unfortunately, the wheels of the government data-gathering agencies turn slowly, and the government information available is generally so far out of date that it provides much less help than is needed. Careful attention ought to be given to solving this basic information problem. Out of frustration and growing need, many private agencies are gearing up to do research that they cannot afford on the scale on which it should be done and that government, with all its available data, should be able to do much better.

There are many other problems in government relationships with the private sector that need to be addressed. It is a fertile field of inquiry for all serious centers of public policy study.

Notes

[1] Alexis de Tocqueville, *Democracy in America,* trans. George Lawrence (Garden City, N.Y.: Doubleday, Anchor edition, 1969), p. 513.

[2] Ibid., p. 512.

[3] Ibid., p. 513.

[4] Ibid., p. 514.

[5] Ibid., p. 515.

[6] Ibid.

[7] Estimate in unpublished report by Independent Sector, Inc.

[8] *The Foundation Directory,* 8th ed. (New York: Foundation Center, 1981), p. vii. Subsequent citations of *The Foundation Directory* refer to this edition.

[9] Marion R. Fremont-Smith, *Philanthropy and the Business Corporation* (New York: Russell Sage Foundation, 1972), p. 6.

[10] Ibid., p. 7.

[11] Ibid., p. 8.

[12] *Foundation Directory,* pp. xvii, xviii.

Macroeconomic and Tax Policy Environment for Private Sector Initiatives

Rudolph G. Penner

The Macroeconomic Environment

Economic historians may refer to 1982 as the "year of the jitters." Businessmen and investors are nervous about the timing and durability of the recovery from the recession and about the future course of monetary and fiscal policy. Federal politicians are anxious about the election, and thus policy making may become more volatile. Political and economic uncertainty feed on each other, and the result is not conducive to charitable giving or other private sector initiatives.

The extent of such activities, however, is not determined solely by economic conditions. Community leadership and the perception of increased need can counteract the effects of considerable economic adversity on donors.

Moreover, in assessing the environment for private sector initiatives, it would be a mistake to concentrate on the short term. Conditions seem bleakest near the trough of a recession. It is important, then, to look ahead to the mid-1980s, and to ask what factors will be important in shaping the macroeconomic environment.

Over the long run, policies that enhance economic growth can have a profound impact on charitable donations and other private sector initiatives. People become more generous when their own income is rising. Although one year of enhanced growth may not have much impact, the effect compounds year after year and in the long run has great significance.

The Reagan Strategy. Like all preceding U.S. administrations, the Reagan administration wishes to lower inflation and enhance economic growth. Unlike most other U.S. administrations, however, the current administration entered office with a comprehensive plan to achieve its goals. The plan covered all aspects of monetary, spending, tax, and regulatory policy.

There was to be a gradual slowing down of the growth rates of monetary aggregates such as currency, bank reserves, and checking and time deposits. The growth rate of federal spending was to be brought down below the growth rate of the gross national product (GNP). Marginal tax rates on personal income and the disincentives facing investors and savers were to be cut significantly to help undo the damage done by combined legislative action and inflation since the late 1960s. The regulatory activities of federal agencies were to be reformed to bring regulatory burdens more in line with regulatory benefits.

Thus far the administration has had a mixed record in implementing these policies. The most important monetary aggregates grew slowly in 1981, below the targets set by the administration. The shift from a pro-inflation to an anti-inflation monetary policy created significant adjustment problems for the economy and was the main cause of the 1981–1982 recession. The policy change, however, has already helped to reduce inflation rates significantly. Unfortunately, the growth of the monetary aggregates has been erratic, and this, along with other factors to be discussed later, has left financial markets skeptical. Businessmen and investors are not confident that the anti-inflation policy will continue, and, as of early April 1982, interest rates have failed to fall as fast as the inflation rate. More generally, inflationary expectations have failed to react fully to falling short-term inflation rates, and the feeling of inertia afflicting financial and other market participants intensified the recesson of 1981–1982.

Nevertheless, it must be emphasized that the decline in the inflation rate represents a major success for the administration. If the monetary authorities continue the strategy outlined by the executive branch, inflationary expectations are bound to respond eventually and the foundation will have been laid for healthy, long-term non-inflationary growth.

I believe that the negative impact of inflation on economic growth is often underestimated. When the real value of the fundamental measuring rod of the economy—the monetary unit—becomes highly uncertain, efficient decision making is bound to suffer. Investors, savers, and consumers have difficulty in planning future activities. This alone would be enough to reduce the efficient allocation of real resources, but the situation is exacerbated by the effects of inflation in distorting real tax burdens and regulated prices and interest rates.

The administration has been less successful in controlling the growth of federal spending. It is true that the growth rate of some programs was slowed as a result of legislative action taken in the summer and fall of 1981, and this must be considered something of a triumph. Cuts in nondefense programs have seldom occurred in past U.S. history. The extent of the cuts, however, was much less than the administration desired. Cuts in nondefense programs were outweighed by increased spending for defense and social security and by an exploding interest bill on the federal debt. Unless there are radical new cuts in spending, the ratio of federal outlays to GNP is very likely to be higher in fiscal 1985 than it was in fiscal 1980. Moreover, it is difficult to believe that the rate of growth of total spending can be slowed significantly without also slowing the growth of spending for defense and social security. Those two categories already constitute about one-half of the budget and with current policies will grow very much faster than other types of spending and GNP. As of early April 1982, the administration showed little willingness to cut either program.

The administration was much more successful in getting Congress to cut taxes than it was in getting Congress to cut spending. Theoretically, the tax system is now more conducive to economic growth than it was previously. Marginal tax rates have been reduced, and tax impediments to savings and investment have been lowered. Under the Economic Recovery Tax Act of 1981, the aggregate tax burden for FY 1980–FY 1985 will definitely show a decrease. It has already been pointed out, however, that the spending burden will not decrease over the same period unless policies are changed significantly. Consequently, the prospect is for a growing deficit relative to GNP even if we assume a substantial economic recovery. Because the period began in fiscal 1980 with a substantial deficit equal to 2.3 percent of GNP, future deficits relative to GNP will probably be larger than any experienced since World War II.[1]

It cannot be said that growth is impossible in the presence of such deficits. Indeed, little can be said with certainty about their impact because we have not seen anything like them under anything approaching current economic conditions. It is foolish to accept the risks posed by large deficits. Deficits relative to GNP can be lowered by relatively small changes in future spending and tax policies.

The prospect of huge deficits is exacerbating the current economic uncertainty and together with unstable monetary growth is helping to keep interest rates high despite falling inflation. Many doubt that the monetary authorities can continue anti-inflationary policies while the Treasury is flooding the marketplace with an unprecedented volume of debt.

The problem of achieving a better balance between future tax and spending burdens represents the greatest challenge facing the administration in the spring of 1982. Unless the deficits are decreased, the administration's substantial accomplishments in lowering inflation rates and rationalizing the tax system could be negated in the long run. It is not easy to believe that private capital formation and economic growth can proceed satisfactorily while the federal deficit is absorbing a large and growing proportion of national saving.

The administration's record in lowering regulatory costs is also mixed. The deregulation of oil prices—which was a triumph for the administraton—as well as the more significant slowdown of economic growth in the developed world has greatly weakened the Organization of Petroleum Exporting Countries (OPEC). This, in turn, has enhanced the prospects for long-run American economic growth. Progress in reforming other areas of regulation has been sporadic, but it is too soon to judge the administration's success or lack of it in regulatory reform.[2]

In summary, the administration need not abandon its long-run strategy of reducing spending and tax burdens. It must simply put those reductions in line with each other. Unfortunately, at this writing, the administration seems to believe that minor changes in its defense, social security, and tax policies represent a major change in its overall strategy. As a result, the economy faces major risks ranging from a worsening recession to accelerating inflation.

If this uncertainty could be reduced, the prospects for healthy economic growth in the mid-1980s would be extremely optimistic. A number of exogenous variables are working in our favor.

Exogenous Forces. In the 1970s the United States faced a serious demographic problem. Large numbers of teenagers born during the baby boom of the 1950s were searching for jobs. At the same time, the long-term upward trend in female labor force participation continued, but it was no longer offset by the earlier retirement of and longer time spent in school by adult males. The result was an extraordinary surge in the size of the labor force. Still more extraordinary, most people found jobs, and this was the one great economic accomplishment of the 1970s.

Indeed, had anyone predicted beforehand that during the 1970s employment would have to increase by 27 percent or at an annual rate of 2.5 percent, most economists would have said that that was impossible—but this was what happened. Yet the achievement was costly. The labor force became less experienced on average, and lagging investment meant that the net capital stock per worker declined. The result of these two factors was a significant slowdown in the growth of labor productivity.

The problem, however, is now largely behind us. The population aged sixteen to nineteen peaked in 1977 and is now falling rapidly. Although the labor force participation rate for females is still showing a strong upward trend, the society and the economy have adjusted relatively well to this social revolution.

Thus, demographic changes should enhance productivity growth. It probably will not be possible to achieve the productivity levels of the 1960s because the shift of labor from low-productivity agriculture to higher-productivity sectors—a shift that contributed greatly to the growth in productivity throughout our history—has now come to an end, but it certainly should be possible for the country to improve on the record of the 1970s.

Demographic developments will undoubtedly change the supply of and the demand for private sector initiatives in a variety of fields. The relative reduction in the teenage population will reduce the social problems associated with that age group. All else being equal, crime rates should fall, and there will be less of a need for job training. The aging of the population, however, creates a growing need for social services associated with improving the status of the elderly.

The growing labor force participation of females will have complex effects that, to my knowledge, have never been clarified in the literature. It will be more difficult for some nonprofit institutions to attract volunteers. There will be a growing need for nonprofit child care facilities for the children of low-income mothers. The growing number of multi-earner families, however, will enhance incomes and add to economic security. This in turn should enhance money donations and make up for part or perhaps all of the negative impact of the reduced supply of volunteers.

Future economic growth will also be affected greatly by the pace of technological change. One can only speculate about the future of technological change, but it is my strong impression that gene splicing, microchip technology, and a revolution in the communications industry are only now being exploited. Such forces may have a dramatic impact on economic growth that rivals the effect of some of the major technological innovations of the past.

Thus I believe that exogenous forces will be conducive to economic growth in the long run. If government policies can be reordered, the middle and late 1980s are likely to see a return to the growing levels of prosperity that Americans have experienced throughout most of their economic history. With higher living standards, there will be less of a need for social services, but those services that remain should find it much easier to attract private support.

Microtax Policies and Private Sector Initiatives

Ironically, tax policies that are conducive to economic growth are not conducive to charitable giving and other private sector activities. The achievement of higher levels of economic efficiency requires that marginal tax rates be reduced. That is to say, it is necessary to reduce the individual and business tax burden on the reward to additional units of work effort and on the return to additional units of saving and investment. If marginal tax rates are reduced, however, the after-tax cost of donations and other deductions from taxable income rises. The cost of donating an extra dollar, for example, is only thirty cents for an individual being taxed at a 70 percent marginal tax rate. When the tax rate is lowered to 50 percent, the private cost of donating a dollar rises to fifty cents. In the jargon of economists, it is said that lower marginal tax rates raise the price of giving.

Of course, lower tax rates also mean that potential donors have more after-tax income, and when people have more income, they become more generous. Consequently, marginal tax rate cuts have two opposite effects on donations—a negative price effect and a positive income effect.

The preponderance of empirical evidence suggests that the negative price effect outweighs the positive income effect.[3] The net negative impact may be very powerful. While a cut in marginal tax rates raises the cost to the taxpayer of giving, it lowers the cost to the Treasury of the charitable deduction in that a lower revenue loss is associated with the deduction. But some research suggests that charitable giving actually falls by more than the reduction in the revenue loss.[4]

The tax policy changes enacted in the summer of 1981 will have a large number of effects on charitable giving. The price of giving has been lowered for taxpayers now utilizing the zero-bracket amount (formerly called the standard deduction). These nonitemizers will be able to deduct an amount equal to 25 percent of contributions up to $100 in 1982 and 1983, rising to $300 in 1984. The cap on the total eligible deduction is removed in 1985 and 1986. The percentage of charitable donations that can be deducted rises to 50 percent in 1985 and to 100 percent in 1986. The provision expires in 1987.

The provision's cap on eligible deductions will not provide an extra incentive for giving by taxpayers who typically give more

195

than the cap amount. The special deduction for nonitemizers will also have its largest impact on religious charities. This is because most nonitemizers are found in the lower half of the distribution of taxable income, and empirical studies suggest that the donations of lower-income taxpayers are heavily concentrated on religious organizations. Upper-income taxpayers concentrate more heavily on giving to the arts and educational institutions.[5]

Although the new charitable deduction for nonitemizers will have a small positive impact on total giving, its economic impact will be overwhelmed by the effect of the scheduled 23 percent reduction applied to all individual tax rates. This cut is scheduled to take place in four installments. Compared with the old law, tax rates will be 1¼ percent lower for all of 1981, 10 percent lower in 1982, about 20 percent lower in 1983, and 23 percent lower in 1984. The cuts in calendar year liabilities are associated with three cuts in tax withholding: 5 percent on October 1, 1981; a further cut of 10 percent on July 1, 1982; and another 10 percent cut on July 1, 1983. High-income individuals who previously faced marginal tax rates as high as 70 percent on so-called unearned income will see the highest rate fall to 50 percent in 1982.

Until 1985 the cuts in marginal tax rates will be offset by inflation and real growth pushing taxpayers into higher brackets. The effects of inflation are scheduled to be neutralized in 1985, however, and in subsequent years by the indexing of tax brackets and exemptions for price increases.

Charles T. Clotfelter and Lester M. Salamon have carefully examined the net impact through 1984 of the price and income effects on charitable giving created by the changes in the personal income tax.[6] Their assumed income effect investigates the effects both of the rise in after-tax incomes for any level of before-tax income and of the rise in before-tax income that the administration assumed would follow from the new economic policy. Because the economy has not lived up to the administration's expectations, the Clotfelter and Salamon analysis clearly understates the negative impact of the tax changes on charitable donations.

Their results indicate that charitable donations will be about $10 billion lower in 1980 dollars, a more than 7 percent decrease, over the 1981–1984 period than they would have been under the old law. Aggregate donations will still rise over the period but at a slower rate than they would have under the old law. Because the marginal rate reductions have their most signficant impact on the donations of upper-income groups and because lower-income nonitemizers now have a special deduction, the impact on religious institutions is much less than on hospitals and educational institutions. According to the Clotfelter-Salamon estimates, hospitals and educational institutions will actually experience a decline in real donations between 1980 and 1984.

It should be emphasized that the Clotfelter and Salamon estimates examine only the economic effect of changes in the tax law. These factors may be offset to some degree by more vigorous solicitations inspired by budget cuts and by moral suasion on the part of local and national political leadership. It should also be noted that the estimates examine the effects of all personal tax changes scheduled for the future. Pressures created by large deficits may bring about changes in the law prior to 1984, and marginal tax rates may again be increased.

Further, the Clotfelter-Salamon analysis focuses only on the impact of changes in the personal income tax. Tax laws governing estates, corporations, and foundations were also changed in 1981, and all of these changes are likely to have a negative impact on charitable giving in the short run.

High marginal estate tax rates have encouraged charitable bequests in the past. Michael J. Boskin investigated this factor prior to 1976 and found that the revenue cost of allowing charitable deductions for estates was exceeded by the increase in gifts that ensued.[7] Estate tax law was changed radically in 1976, and this may have altered its impact on donations. Nonetheless, it is safe to say that the existence of an estate tax still increases charitable bequests significantly. Consequently, we may infer that the drastic reduction in estate taxes occurring in 1981 will lower charitable bequests significantly. To my knowledge, however, there has been no detailed study of this problem.

The 1981 act raised the maximum allowable corporate charitable deductions from 5 to 10 percent of taxable income. This is unlikely to have a major positive effect on donations, however, because few corporations donate as much as 5 percent of total taxable income. A more important negative impact on donations will come from the new enhanced depreciation deductions that will wipe out all tax liabilities for many corporations. This implies that the after-tax price of giving will rise for many corporations, producing an impact similar to that caused by the reduction in marginal personal tax rates. Still, the negative effect will be reduced to the extent that the new "safe-harbor" leasing rules allow the sale of excess depreciation deductions. Unfortunately, safe-harbor leasing is in considerable trouble politically and is quite likely to be eliminated in the near future.

Under prior law, foundations were required to pay out the

greater of their adjusted net income after certain taxes or an amount equal to 5 percent of net investment assets. The new law requires only that the 5 percent rule be followed. This will probably reduce donations by foundations in the short run, but will strengthen donations in the long run because the old law often forced foundations to pay out interest income that only compensated them for inflation's negative impact on the real value of their assets.

Clearly, the tax changes of 1981 will have a powerful negative impact on charities and other private sector initiatives. This could obviously be countered by creating new tax incentives for donations. I shall not take a position on this possibility, but will instead attempt to enumerate the advantages and disadvantages of such policies.

Two possible options are discussed most frequently. First, a deduction of more than 100 percent could be allowed for contributions to charitable activities. Second, and alternatively, a new tax credit could be created. For a given revenue loss, a tax deduction is, of course, more valuable for high-bracket taxpayers. A credit would subsidize the gifts of all taxpayers equally. As has already been noted, empirical work suggests strongly that different income groups allocate their gifts very differently. Support for the arts, hospitals, and higher education would be helped more by a deduction exceeding 100 percent, whereas religious institutions would be helped relatively more by a credit.

The advantages and disadvantages of new tax initiatives are quite obvious. The benefits of increased private charitable contributions do not need elaboration. The disadvantages of new tax subsidies are twofold. First, there is the revenue loss. For the reasons discussed earlier, there will be a desperate search for new revenues over the next few years. Proposals that reduce revenues are unlikely to gain favor in either the administration or Congress. Second and less important, any new tax initiative makes the tax system and tax returns more complex. Given the current extraordinary complexity of tax law, however, it must be admitted that a new deduction or credit would add only marginally to the problems of tax administration and compliance.

Robert Sproull, president of the University of Rochester, proposed an ingenious way of increasing donations financed by dividends.[8] He suggested allowing shareholders in corporations to dedicate, say, one quarter per year of dividends to their favorite charity. The dividend would be deductible from corporate taxable income, and the corporation would also forward its tax saving, thus increasing the donation. Universities and other eligible institutions holding shares would, of course, designate themselves as their favorite charities, thus enhancing their income from equity investments.

In effect, the plan allows shareholders to draw directly from the Treasury to augment donations. Some may object to giving the limited population of equity owners this privilege. As with all plans to enhance tax subsidies for giving, the revenue losses and equity impacts must be compared with the benefits derived from the enhanced income of eligible participants.

Overview

The tax changes of 1981 have drastically reduced incentives for giving, while increasing incentives for work, saving, and investment. In the long run, charities and other private sector activities can most benefit from enhanced economic growth. Rapidly rising living standards lead to more generous giving, an effect that compounds over the years. As this analysis has pointed out, the Reagan administration has given enhanced economic growth highest priority, and it is only the means toward that end that are in question. If uncertainty about the economy can be reduced and if markets can be convinced that policy will remain firmly committed to reducing inflation, the prospects for healthy economic growth in the mid-1980s are very bright because of favorable and significant demographic and technological changes. At present the major barrier to exploiting these opportunities is a huge and growing deficit. More vigorous attempts to control spending, along with some tax increases, should allow us to breach this barrier. If healthy growth can be restored, the effects will eventually compensate for the negative impact of changes in the tax law. This will take more than a few years, however, and in the interim it will take political and community leadership to mitigate the negative effects of tax changes and a temporarily weak economy on charities and other private sector initiatives.

Notes

[1] Rudolph G. Penner, "The 1983 Budget," *The AEI Economist* (March 1982), p. 7.

[2] For the most up-to-date assessment of the Reagan administration's regulatory reform policies, see Marvin H. Kosters and Jeffrey A. Eisenach, "Is Regulatory Relief Enough?" *Regulation* (March/April 1982), pp. 20-27.

[3] Martin S. Feldstein and Charles Clotfelter, "Tax Incentives and Charitable Contributions in the United States: A Microeconomic Analysis," and Martin S. Feldstein and Amy Taylor, "The Income Tax and Charitable Contributions: Estimates and Simulations with the Treasury Tax Files," in volume 3 of *Research*

Papers, sponsored by the Commission on Private Philanthropy and Public Needs (Washington, D.C.: Department of the Treasury, 1977), pp. 1393-1440.

4 Ibid.

5 Feldstein and Taylor, "Income Tax and Charitable Contributions," pp. 1431-33.

6 Charles T. Clotfelter and Lester M. Salamon, *The Federal Government and the Nonprofit Sector: The Impact of the 1981 Tax Act on Individual Charitable Giving* (Washington, D.C.: The Urban Institute, 1981).

7 Michael J. Boskin, "Estate Taxation and Charitable Bequests," in volume 3 of *Research Papers,* sponsored by the Commission on Private Philanthrophy and Public Needs (Washington, D.C.: Department of the Treasury, 1977), pp. 1453-84.

8 Robert L. Sproull, "Cost-effective Way to Spur Private Giving," *Harvard Business Review,* vol. 60, no. 2 (March/April 1982), pp. 62-67.

Incentives to Economic Development

Paul L. Pryde, Jr.

Overview

The administration's recently enacted Economic Recovery Program has dramatically reduced federal assistance programs for poor people and distressed areas. Of the $38 billion in cuts from the 1982 budget, approximately two-thirds have been made in social, human service, and job programs. To those who oppose these budget reductions as harmful to the poor, the Reagan administration has responded with two main arguments. The first is that government programs designed to help the poor are largely inefficient; as a result, huge program costs are incurred without commensurate benefits accruing to those in need. The second is that the best answer to poverty and unemployment is a strong national economy that generates new private sector jobs. According to this view, public job creation and support efforts merely produce subsidized make-work.

Despite its distaste for federal aid programs, the administration recognizes that improvements in the national economy will not automatically improve the lot of poor people and distressed areas. Consequently, it has stressed the importance of finding creative means of encouraging the private sector to assume some of the responsibilities that the federal government is no longer able, or willing, to shoulder.

As yet, however, the administration has set forth no coherent set of policies or strategies for achieving that end. The apparent reason is that it has not yet formulated answers to two fundamental questions. First, *What should be the principal aims of private-sector-oriented policies designed to address social and economic problems?* Public efforts to help the poor have usually been of two types—those designed to help disadvantaged individuals raise themselves out of poverty (development policies) and those designed to alleviate the distress of being poor (income maintenance policies). Minority business development and job training programs are good examples of the first category, food stamps and aid to families with dependent children (AFDC) of the second.

Both philosophy and arithmetic suggest that policy initiatives aimed at mobilizing the private sector to help the poor should center on development rather than charity or maintenance. With regard to philosophy, the administration clearly prefers federal programs that help people become self-reliant rather than more comfortably dependent. While the administration appears to understand the importance of maintenance and social service programs, it has a clear bias toward programs designed to make the disadvantaged full and productive members of society. The poor and their advocates also see the goal of self-reliance as important to their future; increasingly, they express a desire for independence from what many view as a bungling social service establishment.

The arithmetic is equally clear. In 1982 total federal spending on social and other programs that support nonprofit human and social service organizations will be reduced by about $20 billion from the baseline growth projection for federal spending in this area. By 1984 this "public service gap" will reach an estimated $90 billion. Even in the unlikely event that corporations and foundations, which together contribute about $5 billion to social and human service programs, were to double their giving, the increase would make barely a dent in a shortfall of this magnitude. The estimates for a development-oriented alternative look substantially better. A principal obstacle to the revitalization of depressed communities is their inability to attract the investment they need to finance development and growth. This nation now has a $4 trillion private capital market. Policies successful in shifting only one-half of 1 percent of this amount into distressed neighborhoods and communities could produce $20 billion in new investment for (1) new small firms of the sort that create most new jobs, (2) infrastructure improvement and rehabilitation, and (3) a variety of needed local services. This calculation is admittedly simplistic, but it is useful in making the central point: a tiny shift in the private investment resources of the nation could make a greater impact on poverty than even a doubling of the charitable giving of major corporations and foundations could.

Second, *What policies should be employed in pursuit of these aims?* Theoretically, government can influence the flow of investment in three ways. First, it can use tax revenues or borrowing to create or support public agencies that provide direct funding for specified purposes. The Carter administration, for example, at one time proposed to expand the Economic Development Administration as a means of attacking the unemployment and economic growth problems of distressed areas. Second, government can use its regulatory powers to encourage or retard certain types of investment activity. An illustration is the effect of regulations promulgated by the Labor Department pursuant to the Employee Retirement Income Security Act (ERISA); for a long period of time they effectively prevented pension funds from investing in small young firms. Finally, the government can use the tax system to influence investment. The current administration, for example, has supported the use of tax incentives to encourage business expansion and investment in depressed areas.

Designing an Effective Development Policy for Distressed Communities

Principles. The correct choice of policy tools—direct spending, regulation, or taxation—is important to the success of any development policy. Policy makers should therefore weigh alternatives in terms of the following tests:

• *Will it increase the capacity of people and places to adjust to economic change?* In a dynamic economy, the process of growth causes continuing change in the value, location, and character of jobs and economic activity. Old products and resources lose worth, while new ones gain in demand. Houston becomes prosperous, while Gary declines. One neighborhood is "gentrified," while another becomes a wasteland. This process of "creative destruction" is always more painful for some than for others but, nonetheless, is essential to a nation's, or even a community's, vitality. Accordingly, development policy should not encourage people and places to resist change, but enable them to adapt successfully to it. For a city like Houston it means finding ways of relieving pressure on infrastructure and services caused by its population influx. For Gary it means aid in creating new firms and jobs to replace those it has lost.

• *Will it reduce barriers?* In the complex American economy, the process of development is often hindered by inefficiencies or barriers in capital and labor markets. Markets allocate production resources inefficiently and make development difficult if they are constrained by poor internal organization, poor communication, monopolistic control, and other problems. These market barriers have any number of underlying causes, ranging from the absence of good information for workers and investors, to regulations that promote risk-averse behavior by financial institutions, to policies that favor investments in new suburban areas over similar investments in older cities. Sound development policy should aim not to replace the private market, but to remove barriers to market efficiency.

• *Will it cost less than the cost of the problem addressed?* Attacking a problem through changes in public policy makes sense only if the cost of the solution is less than the price imposed by the continuation of the problem. It makes no sense, for example, to establish a subminimum wage for teen-agers if the benefit is a few lower-paying jobs but the cost is an expensive new bureaucracy to regulate a two-tiered labor market, coupled with the loss of jobs by older workers.

• *Will it include adequate means for ensuring equity?* Even under conditions of greatly improved efficiency, private markets will not ensure that the cost of the adjustment process will be allocated fairly. Unemployment is a case in point. Few would argue that an inventive computer firm should be required to provide unemployment benefits to all the file clerks whose jobs its technology makes unnecessary. To do so would be to discourage the very sort of innovation on which development and growth depend. Yet it would be equally unfair to impose the entire cost of joblessness on people who, through no fault of their own, find themselves unemployed. Good development policy must, therefore, be designed to distribute the costs and benefits of adjustments equitably among people and places.

• *Is it properly targeted?* Development policy will fail if the intervention employed fails to affect the people and places desired in the manner required. For example, tax incentives designed to encourage investment in new young firms in distressed areas may produce poor results if speculative investments in real estate are also made eligible for the same tax treatment.

Taxes and Development. The administration prefers the use of tax and regulatory relief to direct spending. Consequently, it has supported—at least at the conceptual level—the creation of enterprise zones to increase business activity in distressed areas. It has, however, not yet endorsed any specific bill.

The available evidence strongly suggests that a development strategy based on the use of federal tax reductions cannot be expected to overcome all the barriers to development that exist in poor communities in a country as diverse as ours. We know, for example, that providing tax relief to business firms will do little to upgrade the streets, water systems, and public facilities that localities maintain in order to support increased private investment. Nevertheless, well-designed tax incentives can be useful in overcoming some of the barriers to development faced by so many communities.

The tax provisions regarded as useful in changing or improving rates or levels of investment include corporate tax rate reductions, accelerated recovery of fixed-asset expenditures, and investment tax credits. Clearly, these tools increase the attractiveness of capital investment. There is some question, however, whether they really influence business behavior. The investment tax credit, for example, is available to the firm that happens to invest in a capital asset whether or not it influences the investment decision. In other words, a tax credit adopted to encourage investment goes to firms that would have made the investment without the credit as well as those for whom the availability of this incentive is decisive. In the former situation, the tax credit is wasteful; in the latter, useful. Accelerated cost recovery systems and corporate tax rate reductions are intended to increase cash flow, thereby encouraging new investment. Yet economic research has shown that decisions to invest are based as much on factors like plant capacity, technology, productivity, expected sales, cost of capital, and before-tax profitability as on changes in the tax code. It has thus been postulated that tax incentives may influence the timing of investment decisions more than the decision to invest. Finally, since small young businesses have relatively small tax liabilities, they are less likely to be influenced by these tax reductions than larger companies, a problem discussed later.

The use of local tax abatements to influence business location is also limited. Numerous surveys of corporate managers reveal that state and local taxes rank relatively low on the list of factors determining the locations of branch plants. This is not a surprising finding in view of the fact that such taxes compose a small portion of business expenses—about 4.4 percent of total costs, according to the Federal Reserve Bank of Boston.

Although tax policies are unlikely to be influential in attracting industry, relatively high taxes can deter business expansion. If taxes in one state or region are substantially higher than those in a neighboring state or region, the first area's attractiveness to industry may be diminished by comparison. In other words, taxes may not significantly enhance a region's attractiveness, but a relatively heavy tax burden can reduce it.

The New Firm and the Development Process

Though economic recovery and development programs have historically been designed to influence the investment decisions of established firms, a society's new enterprises provide the means of adjustment to changing economic circumstances. Development programs should therefore not be designed principally to shift economic activity from one place to another. Some redistribution of economic activity may be necessary, but, in the final analysis, the revitalization of America's distressed inner cities will depend largely on their becoming, once again, centers of entrepreneurial activity. One need not look terribly far for evidence to support this proposition.

In his recent analysis of Dun and Bradstreet data, David Birch of the Massachusetts Institute of Technology found that the creation and disappearance of firms explain most changes in employment. He discovered the rate of job loss to be roughly equal throughout the country, with faster growing and dynamic areas actually losing jobs at a slightly more rapid rate than declining areas. Houston, for example, loses jobs more rapidly than Buffalo or New Haven. Moreover, this high rate of job loss is consistent among regions and within metropolitan areas. Communities, on the average, lose 50 percent of their employment base every five years.

Birch concluded that the key to economic development and job creation is the rate at which businesses are formed and expanded to replace those that are lost. Houston grows faster than New Haven because its business replacement ratio is higher, not because its rate of job loss is lower. These findings call into question the popular, but misleading, notion that job loss is largely attributable to declining manufacturing industries in the Snow Belt. While occasional episodes of industrial trauma can be associated with real hardship in particular industries or regions, a more general national perspective reveals that such isolated cases are not central to the problem of job loss.

Birch also found that most new jobs are created by new young firms, not by large established corporations. Specifically, his study found that between 1969 and 1976, 86 percent of new employment came from the creation and expansion of businesses with fewer than 500 employees and that independent businesses accounted for half of all employment. Birch's work has been criticized on the grounds that a shift from manufacturing to service industries may show the period of study (1969–1975) to be atypical; his conclusions, however, are not disputed.

Studies by the National Federation of Independent Businesses (NFIB) and the American Electronics Association (AEA) support the proposition that small young businesses have generated significant employment. NFIB found that the number of businesses employing fewer than 100 people increased 13.2 percent between 1967 and 1972, compared with an 8.9 percent increase for firms with more than 1,000 employees—a reversal from the previous decade. In 1976 AEA surveyed its member corporations to measure growth rates.

It found that employment growth rates were twenty to forty times greater among teen-age firms (ten to twenty years old) than among mature firms (more than twenty years old).

There is also substantial evidence that small young firms are a major source of technological innovation in the American economy. Research by the National Science Foundation (NSF) concluded that small business is responsible for half of the "most significant new industrial products and processes." NSF has also found that small young companies produce twenty-four times as many innovations per dollar of research and development investment as large companies.

In addition to job creation and product innovation, the creation and expansion of new enterprises is, in the view of many development economists, the means by which communities can best meet the challenge of changing economic conditions. According to Albert Shapero, former professor of management at the University of Texas, development strategies designed to support the process of business formation have four advantages not usually derived from other approaches to development, such as branch plant recruitment:

• *An increased ability of the community to respond appropriately to changes in the marketplace.* Effective programs for enterprise formation provide a "response capability" to predicted and unpredicted events. This allows new firms to be created or expanded faster than changes can be made in major corporations.

• *An actuarial approach to events.* A large number of independent companies (as contrasted with a small number of corporate plants) provide a community with a variety of independent decision-making units, each appraising the environment from its own vantage point. There is an extremely low probability that all these independent units will make the same, perhaps incorrect, response to the same event. The corporate monolith must, however, unify all views into one, perhaps erroneous, action.

• *Greater innovation.* Almost all the available evidence shows that small firms are more innovative than large, mature companies.

• *Low political and economic risks.* The potential benefits of the successful formation of an enterprise are huge. Another Xerox could be created. The potential negative consequences of failure are not nearly as dramatic. At the very worst, the failure will be disastrous for the founders and backers of the enterprise. But it will rarely represent a new loss for the community at large.

Despite their importance to the development process, small new firms have difficulty attracting the capital that they need to grow and expand. And the capital that is available from institutional sources is often provided in an inappropriate form—short-term loans. Equity capital and long-term loans—the "patient money" crucial to the success and growth of these enterprises—are perilously short in supply from such sources. The new firm, therefore, has had to rely on the entrepreneur's savings and investments from his friends and associates for start-up capital.

The reasons that young firms can look neither to institutions nor to government as sources of risk and equity capital are well known. It is very costly to acquire information on, and complete transactions with, small young firms. Evaluating a transaction is time consuming. On-site inspections, analysis of financial statements, and discussions with the management team are required. Since such costs are usually fixed and do not vary with the size of the project, small financial transactions are relatively expensive. Similarly, information about small young firms is not readily available. Major corporations publish annual reports and make other data easily accessible; information about closely held young firms is almost impossible to obtain. Institutional investors prefer to invest in firms that offer easily accessible information and entail low transaction costs. And financial institutions tend to be cautious in negotiating with firms having unconventional structures and innovative, unfamiliar products. Serious problems are often encountered by minorities and women and by firms located in economically distressed communities. Their ventures may go unfinanced unless there is a strong probability of a significant return for perceived risk.

The difficulty young firms have in attracting risk capital from investors is exacerbated by federal regulations governing financial markets. Despite their obvious benefits, many of these regulations have had the unintended effect of increasing the cost and decreasing the availability of seed money and venture capital for such firms. The Securities and Exchange Commission, for example, requires a registration fee, an annual report, and multiple copies of several financial statements, making the cost of marketing a small issue prohibitive. These expenses have been calculated to be as high as 15 percent of the capital raised for public offerings of less than $1 million. By contrast, the cost of offerings of $100–500 million were calculated to be less than 4 percent.

The regulation of financial institutions encourages conservatism and restricts competition by creating barriers to market entry. The Glass-Steagall Act, for example, prohibits commercial banks from providing investment banking services in competition with brokerage houses, thus decreasing the availability of equity capital for young firms. Banks, which are usually required to lend at fixed rates and therefore unable to share in the profits of the growing business, have little incentive to invest in risky new ventures. Likewise, bank examinations, concerned with "safety and soundness," tend to reward conservative behavior at the expense of new and innovative firms.

Recommendations

Tax Incentives. These tax proposals are designed to compensate investors for incurring the risks and costs just described and thus to encourage investment in the new young firms responsible for creating most new jobs.

• Allow investments—in the form of common stock or unsecured term loans—in new firms in distressed areas to be written off by investors in the year in which the investment is made. This incentive would substantially improve after-tax rates of return on equity and near-equity investments in young small firms and should therefore increase the number of such investments. Among other things, it is likely to encourage investment houses to organize seed capital funds that pool the savings of many individual taxpayers and invest them in enterprise zone firms. This incentive would result in little revenue loss to the Treasury since the encouraged investments would largely compete with less-productive tax shelters elsewhere in the economy, rather than with taxable investments.

• Allow capital gains taxes on such investments to be deferred for as long as the proceeds are reinvested in similar firms. Taxpayers should be allowed to defer taxes on successful investment gains from qualified companies as long as the proceeds are reinvested in other qualified companies. This proposal is analogous to allowing homeowners to defer capital gains taxes on the sale of their homes as long as they reinvest the proceeds in housing of approximately equal value.

• Target industrial development bonds to designated distressed areas. The administration and the Congress have shown interest in reducing revenue losses attributable to so-called abuses in the use of industrial development bonds, especially the issuance of tax-exempt obligations by large profitable companies having easy access to the nation's capital markets. Rather than being eliminated entirely, such bonds should be more carefully directed toward firms creating jobs in distressed areas.

• Establish a loss reserve for small and young business suppliers. Next to family, friends, and business associates, suppliers are a principal source of credit to young firms. Risk, however, discourages suppliers from extending credit. Allowing suppliers to establish a loss reserve of, say, 10 percent of credit extended to young small enterprises would encourage them to offer needed credit.

Other Incentives. Obviously, business tax incentives cannot solve the need of the nation's "social entrepreneurs" for operating and capital funds. And community-based organizations can rarely make a profit dealing with social barriers to development. Alternative tax incentives are needed to encourage corporations to support local groups in alleviating problems that businesses cannot or will not address.

• Remove the requirement that state neighborhood tax credits be treated as income for federal tax purposes. The importance of entrepreneurship is not limited to commerce, industry, and trade. In almost any community there are individuals and groups of individuals who have successfully taken new and risky approaches to complex problems or new opportunities. In this sense, Sister Falaka Fattah of the House of Umoja, whose work with gangs has reduced both crime and unemployment among youth in her Philadelphia neighborhood, is an entrepreneur just as much as the engineer who starts a new business in her neighborhood.

Several states encourage such local activity by giving tax credits for corporate contributions to and investments in specified neighborhood development projects. Unfortunately, these credits are taxed at the federal level, which decreases their value to corporations and provides the federal government with a windfall. Eliminating this inequity would bring the federal government into fuller partnership with the states and encourage greater giving by corporations.

In addition to encouraging the adoption of neighborhood tax credit programs by more states, this proposal would encourage corporate support of desirable development activities in states with no income tax. Consideration should therefore be given to a federal credit of 25 percent of any qualifying corporate contributions or investments in local development activities.

• Permit the liberalized leasing rules established under the Economic Recovery Tax Act to be applied to all property within designated distressed areas. The recently enacted Economic Recovery Tax Act creates new rules to ensure that transactions meeting certain conditions will be treated as leases entitling the lessor to tax benefits not permitted by the previous rules. Unfortunately, the new rules apply only to certain equipment and exclude individuals and closely held companies as lessors. Extending the new leasing provisions to all property and to all firms and individuals within designated distressed areas should greatly increase the financing options for local governments and businesses.

• Provide employers in distressed areas a 10 percent wage credit for all new employees hired in distressed areas and a 50 percent tax credit against wages paid to employees from specially targeted groups during their first five years of employment. The success of almost any development program is measured in employment terms—how many jobs are created, what types of jobs are created, and who gets them. And the availability of an adequate labor force is, of course, an important factor in any firm's location decision. If local residents, especially disadvantaged and minority workers, are to receive the jobs generated by increased local business formation and expansion rates, job training is essential.

Since most training occurs on the job rather than in classrooms, employers should be given incentives to hire and train the people whom development programs are intended to benefit. The credits proposed above would reward all new job creation and would provide a greater subsidy to employers who hire and train disadvantaged workers. To make the credits most useful to employers, payroll deductions should not be reduced by the amount of the credit. Finally, since young firms in particular may be unable to use all credits to which they are entitled, companies should be allowed to sell and trade their unused employment credits in a free market.

Managing the Development Process. The tax measures outlined above should go a long way toward helping declining communities overcome barriers to new economic activity, but they alone cannot do the job. The development process must be managed. This requires, as economist Albert Hirschman has argued in *The Strategy of Economic Development*, a "binding agent," the initiative-taking organization capable of organizing and facilitating the development process. In a country as diverse as ours, a universal management formula cannot, of course, be prescribed. But a few principles can be offered to guide public and private decision makers in organizing and implementing development plans. Four are worth considering.

1. The partnership should be built on local strengths and skills. Managing the development process is a job that places a premium on scarce entrepreneurial skills, creativity, risk taking, and team building. Few communities are likely to have any organization with all the skills, reputation, and resources required to tackle deeply embedded problems or long-ignored opportunities in an effective way. In most places development success will demand a development partnership, a collaboration involving important public, private, and neighborhood interests. We now know that development programs cannot be

"parachuted" into a community; a program that does not involve all of those with a stake in the outcome is likely to fail.

2. The partnership should mobilize resources equal to the problems to be addressed. Any strategy aimed at creating employment opportunities or economic activity in distressed communities will lack credibility if it cannot summon resources equal to the variety and size of the barriers to be overcome. Development problems are interconnected, separable only for purposes of analysis. Newly employed workers may have no prospect of obtaining, for example, affordable housing or transportation. A sound development program must therefore be designed to respond to a number of problems of job creation.

3. Program rules and regulations should be kept simple and easily enforceable. No government program aimed at stimulating development can be entirely free of risk. Regulations, no matter how well crafted, can never anticipate all the ways in which a particular incentive will be employed. Public officials should therefore approach the problem of program administration mindful that beyond certain limits each additional rule costs more in lost creativity than it buys in abuse prevention. Many studies have pointed out the flaws in HUD's Urban Development Action Grant program, but critics and proponents alike agree that despite its deficiencies the UDAG program is admirable for its simplicity.

4. The partnership's strategy should create conditions conducive to private risk taking and investment. Government will never have the means to finance the development of distressed communities. Nor is government equipped to take the risks upon which development depends. Thus, the principal role of the partnership should be to create conditions favorable to private investment and entrepreneurship. On this point, the importance of an attractive and safe physical environment cannot be overemphasized. Tax incentives by themselves will never induce businesses to locate in a derelict area that lacks basic amenities and offers no prospect of improvement.

Conclusion. The Reagan administration's plan for a national economic recovery is now largely in place. Only time will tell whether it will work as promised to increase overall levels of output, employment, and income. What is clear, however, is that a sound economic *growth* policy requires good economic *development* policy. It is hoped that the ideas offered in this chapter will be useful in framing national strategies to help distressed communities adapt to shifting economic activities.

PART FOUR

Private Initiatives and Public Policy Reform in Selected Sectors

Youth Employment

Sean Sullivan

The purpose of this chapter is to describe the dimensions of the youth employment problem, to review the public and private responses to this problem, and to suggest the most hopeful directions for public policy and private initiative to alleviate it.

The chapter begins by looking at measures of youth employment and unemployment to identify the chronically unemployed. It also considers whether high youth unemployment is more a structural or a cyclical phenomenon, that is, whether it results primarily from particular labor market disadvantages that young people suffer or from the condition of the economy.

The next part of the chapter reviews federal policies that have tried to reduce youth unemployment, particularly the Comprehensive Employment and Training Act (CETA). In discussing federal policies aimed at increasing job opportunities for youth, it is necessary also to evaluate policies that may decrease job opportunities, particularly the federally mandated minimum wage.

After reviewing federal initiatives, the chapter considers examples of efforts by the private sector to prepare young people for the labor market. These efforts are private in the sense that the initiative for them comes from private parties, even though much of the funding comes from public programs, especially CETA. Their origin distinguishes them from traditional public sector initiatives, many of which have consisted largely of creating temporary public sector employment rather than training youths for permanent employment in the private sector, where the great majority of jobs are created.

From the experience with both public and private approaches to the youth employment problem, the chapter cites lessons that have been learned and discusses policy options and preferences.

I would like to give special thanks to Richard H. deLone, Harry T. Martin, Marvin H. Kosters, and Jack A. Meyer for reviewing this chapter in its entirety and providing many helpful suggestions.

Measuring the Problem

The customary way to begin describing the youth employment problem is to point to the high unemployment rate for young people. This gets attention because the numbers are high, but it fails to create a perspective from which to view the numbers.

A better way to start is to consider how many teen-agers are still in school. Employment and education should be looked at together, for they are often either alternatives to or complements of each other. Table 1 shows the proportion of youths of each age within the sixteen- to nineteen-year-old group that was enrolled in school in October 1979. Two-thirds of all sixteen- to nineteen-year-olds were enrolled in school, and nearly 90 percent of sixteen- and seventeen-year-olds combined. Unemployment for these youths does not typically have the same meaning as it has for an older head of household. The great majority of them live at home and typically do not suffer as much economic hardship when unemployed because they are not primary wage earners. Much of their unemployment is of a casual kind, especially since most of them seek only part-time work. Teen-age unemployment rates that fail to consider school as an alternative to, or even as a kind of, work overstate the problem—although there are economically disadvantaged youths who must work to remain in school.

Measures of Unemployment. The traditional measure of unemployment published by the Bureau of Labor Statistics (BLS) counts a teen-ager in school as unemployed if he or she is looking for a job.

TABLE 1

SIXTEEN- TO NINETEEN-YEAR-OLDS ENROLLED IN SCHOOL, OCTOBER 1979

Age	Total (thousands)	Number in School (thousands)	Percentage in School
16	4,142	3,890	93.9
17	4,015	3,389	84.4
18	4,177	2,163	51.8
19	4,037	1,530	37.9
Total	16,371	10,972	67.0

SOURCE: U.S. Department of Commerce, Bureau of the Census, *Current Population Reports.*

TABLE 2

UNEMPLOYMENT RATES BY AGE AND SEX, 1978–1981

(percent)

	1978	1979	1980	1981
Males				
16–19	16.9	15.9	19.2	23.4
20–24	8.7	9.6	12.1	14.6
25–54	3.5	3.5	5.2	6.9
Females				
16–19	14.6	14.6	14.2	17.5
20–24	8.4	9.2	9.8	11.2
25–54	5.0	4.7	5.8	6.5

NOTE: Figures are for December of each year.
SOURCE: U.S. Department of Labor, Bureau of Labor Statistics, *Employment and Earnings.*

Youth unemployment rates measured this way have been much higher than comparable rates for older workers, as table 2 shows. The rates have worsened for all groups during the current recession, but the pattern of large differences holds. There are also large racial differences within the youth population, as shown in table 3. Unemployment rates for nonwhites have been two to two and one-half times as high as rates for whites. Even though the official numbers are high for youths generally, they indicate the relatively greater seriousness of the problem for nonwhite youths.

Michael Wachter of the University of Pennsylvania has constructed an alternative measure of youth unemployment that takes into account the availability of alternatives to market work, such as schooling and military service. Because the military is not a large employer of the labor force generally, its exclusion in measuring aggregate unemployment rates is not important. It is a very large employer of youths, however, and using the total labor force (which includes the military) instead of the civilian labor force lowers the calculated unemployment rate for youths since everyone in the military is counted as employed. Similarly, many youths who are in school are not looking for work. If the number of unemployed sixteen- to nineteen-year-olds is divided by the total of the civilian labor force, the school population, and the military population instead of the civilian labor force alone (with double counting of youths who

TABLE 3

UNEMPLOYMENT RATES BY RACE FOR SIXTEEN- TO NINETEEN-YEAR-OLDS,
1978–1981
(percent)

	1978	1979	1980	1981
Males				
White	15.0	14.3	16.7	21.5
Nonwhite	32.1	31.6	39.6	38.9
Females				
White	12.4	12.5	12.2	15.0
Nonwhite	32.4	32.0	31.7	37.9

NOTE: Figures are for December of each year.
SOURCE: U.S. Department of Labor, Bureau of Labor Statistics, *Employment and Earnings*.

are both in the labor force and in school eliminated), unemployment rates drop dramatically for all subgroups by age, race, and sex.

Wachter further refines his measure by not counting youths who are enrolled in school as unemployed even if they are looking for work, thereby removing them from the numerator of the calculation. He argues that time in school will generally pay off in better jobs and that students seeking part-time work generally have only a marginal attachment to the labor force and do not suffer greatly from occasional spells of unemployment. The unemployment rate derived by eliminating unemployed students from the numerator of the unemployment calculation while counting the school and the military populations in the denominator is, of course, even lower. Table 4 shows the rates calculated by Wachter for 1978.

It is not suggested that these measures should supplant the traditional BLS measure, but rather that they add perspective on the problem. They suggest several conclusions: (1) youth "unemployment" is not so serious as official measures indicate when school and military service are regarded as forms of "employment"; (2) the problem is actually more serious for older than for younger teenagers, reversing the conclusions from the official measure; and (3) the problem group of youths not in school who are looking for jobs but cannot find them—the Wachter 2 group—is disproportionately black.

Labor Force Participation. Unemployment rates measure the proportion of the labor force that is actively seeking work but is not em-

TABLE 4
ALTERNATIVE UNEMPLOYMENT RATES FOR SIXTEEN- TO NINETEEN-
YEAR-OLDS, 1978
(percent)

	BLS Rate	Wachter Rate 1	Wachter Rate 2
White males			
16–17	17.1	10.1	4.8
18–19	10.9	8.0	6.1
Black males			
16–17	40.7	15.4	7.8
18–19	30.9	18.5	14.2
White females			
16–17	17.1	9.8	4.8
18–19	12.3	9.5	7.6
Black females			
16–17	41.9	14.8	8.7
18–19	36.8	23.8	18.4

NOTE: Wachter rate 1 includes the student and military populations in the denominator; Wachter rate 2 removes students from the numerator.
SOURCE: Michael L. Wachter, "Dimensions and Complexities of the Youth Unemployment Problem," in Bernard E. Anderson and Isabel V. Sawhill, eds., *Youth Employment and Public Policy*, American Assembly, Columbia University, p. 50.

ployed. People who are not looking for work are not included in the labor force. Labor force participation rates measure the proportion of the civilian population that is either working or seeking work and is, therefore, in the labor force. This measurement may reflect expectations, since some people drop out of the labor force during less buoyant times because they do not expect to find work. Presumably one cannot find a job unless he or she is looking for one, and "discouraged" workers are counted by some economists as unemployed even if they are not in the labor force.

Labor force participation rates are thus a measure of "potential" employment as well as a basis for determining the rate of unemployment. Not surprisingly, participation rates are much lower for youths than for older groups. Between 50 and 60 percent of sixteen- to nineteen-year-olds are in the labor force, either holding jobs or looking for them. Participation rates range from 85 to 95 percent for older men, but only from 60 to 70 percent for older women. There is nothing particularly disturbing about this pattern, since many young people are still in high school or college whereas older people have usually completed their education and become part of the work force. The differences in participation rates reveal a natural progression from school to labor force; if there is a problem, it is not the fact of such differences but their size. Young people might participate at a higher rate if they had a greater expectation of finding jobs and were less discouraged by the high unemployment rates they perceive.

Participation rates show the same striking disparity by race as unemployment rates—they average about twenty percentage points higher for whites than for nonwhites. There may be a Catch-22 operating here: nonwhites cannot get jobs if they are not looking for them, but they are less apt to be looking because their higher unemployment rates discourage them. Other explanations are also advanced to help explain the great difference in participation rates: nonwhites are more likely to have dropped out of school, they are more likely to be from families that are on welfare and so have a diminished work ethic, or the "street" economy may hold the allure of easier and better money than they can expect to earn in the "straight" economy. Whatever the complex of causes, the effect is a much smaller proportion of nonwhites seeking to enter American life through the traditional door of a job.

Wachter has also calculated what he calls a "residual rate," measuring the percentage of the population that is not in the labor force, not in school, and not in the military. These are the youths who are not participating or ostensibly even trying to participate in the economic life of the nation (unless they are part of the extralegal economy) and the youths about whom we need to be most concerned. Table 5 shows Wachter's residual rate and the official unemployment rate for 1978. Residual rates are much higher for females than for males, presumably because some of them are "keeping house," to use the BLS classification. Again, rates are higher for blacks than for whites.

Employment Rates. The employment-to-population ratio is a gauge of how well a group is actually finding rather than just seeking entrance into the nation's economic life. Because this ratio compares the number of employed with the total population whereas the unemployment rate compares the number of unemployed with the labor force, both can be increasing at the same time.

The ratio of employment to population for sixteen- to nineteen-year-olds has ranged from 40 to 50 percent. Ratios for older men run from 70 to 90 percent, with cyclical variations much like those of

TABLE 5
ALTERNATIVE UNEMPLOYMENT RATES FOR SIXTEEN- TO NINETEEN-YEAR-OLDS, 1978
(percent)

	BLS Unemployment Rate	Residual Rate
White males		
16–17	17.1	8.2
18–19	10.9	4.5
Black males		
16–17	40.7	11.7
18–19	30.9	10.4
White females		
16–17	17.1	13.6
18–19	12.3	16.1
Black females		
16–17	41.9	16.6
18–19	36.8	24.9

NOTE: The residual rate is the percentage of the population that is not in the labor force, not in school, and not in the military.
SOURCE: Wachter, "Dimensions and Complexities," p. 54.

unemployment rates; ratios for older women run from 55 to 65 percent. Again the differences are not surprising, given that more than 80 percent of the youths not in the labor force are still in school.

Employment-to-population ratios for whites are about twice those for nonwhites, and the disparity has been growing—in part because the ratio for nonwhite males has been falling since the 1950s. The economy has created a considerable number of jobs for youths, but nonwhite, principally black, males have not shared equally in getting them.

Studies show that school enrollment rates have risen sharply for blacks over the past fifteen years and now equal or exceed those for whites. This helps to explain some of the decline in black male employment-to-population ratios, since many young black males are choosing to remain in school rather than seek jobs. Wachter has estimated that the increase in school enrollment accounted for all of the decline between 1965 and 1978 in the employment-population ratio for sixteen- and seventeen-year-old black males and nearly half the decline for eighteen- and nineteen-year-olds. Because there is a positive correlation between years of schooling and later income, the increase in black male school enrollment may be more important in the long run than the decline in their employment-population ratio.

Duration and Concentration of Unemployment. Another "measurement" of the problem is the duration of unemployment for youths who suffer it. Teen-agers' periods of unemployment are shorter than those of older workers, apparently because youths are more apt to drop out of the labor force when they are unemployed. Adding time spent out of the labor force to time spent unemployed results in longer periods of *non*employment for youths. Conversely, their periods of employment are typically much shorter than those of older workers, as many of them undergo a period of labor market experimentation.

Within the youth group, the incidence of joblessness is highest among blacks, dropouts, and teen-agers from low-income families. This high concentration means that much youth joblessness is accounted for by a relatively small number of youths who go many weeks without working; Robert Lerman estimates that 10 percent of youths account for 75 percent of youth unemployment. It is estimated that half or more of the unemployed male teen-agers who are out of school have been unemployed for more than six months while many teen-agers shift jobs frequently and move into and out of the labor force while experiencing only short bouts of unemployment. Bernard Anderson and Isabel Sawhill have suggested that the largely low-income minority youths of the inner cities who account for so much of the problem may number about 500,000 nationwide. While this is a large number, it represents only about 6 percent of the teen-age labor force.

Curiously, while black joblessness has grown worse both absolutely and in relation to that of whites, wages of black youths who are employed have risen continuously in relation to those of whites over the past decade. Indeed, studies of youth in the 1970s show that—when other factors are corrected for—white and black youths now earn essentially the same wages. This may be due in part to the uniformity of rates for those who work for the legally mandated federal minimum wage, as many youths in unskilled jobs do. Whatever the reasons, it appears that, although racial discrimination may still be a factor in some hiring decisions, it typically does not prevent those black youths who do get jobs from earning the same wages as their white counterparts.

Demographic factors are working in favor of lower unemployment rates for teen-agers in the 1980s, with an expected reversal of the relative rise in teen-age unemployment from the 1950s through the 1970s. The great postwar baby boom sent a bulge of teen-agers through the labor force, but lower birthrates since will mean fewer teen-agers and lower youth unemployment rates in the years ahead. Other factors that probably contributed to higher youth unemployment after the late 1960s were the extension of the minimum wage to a much larger proportion of civilian employment and increases in public assistance payments to low-income families; the former tends to restrict demand for unskilled labor, while the latter reduces incentives to accept low-wage jobs. The minimum wage is discussed later. Public assistance policies are beyond the scope of this chapter.

There is one storm cloud on the brighter demographic horizon: while the proportion of teen-agers in the labor force will decline in the years ahead, the proportion of black teen-agers will increase. The ratio of teen-age unemployment among blacks to that among whites has risen from 1.3 to 2.2 over the past two decades and may continue to rise over the next decade.

Cyclical and Structural Factors. Unemployment rates for all age groups respond to changes in economic conditions, and a growing economy is a prerequisite to reducing youth unemployment. Young people will not find their job opportunities increasing in a stagnant economy. Job creation is clearly an important part of the solution to the problem of joblessness, and it depends on a host of macroeconomic government policies and microeconomic decisions by individual business firms.

Our focus is not on these questions of economic growth and development, because they concern employment generally rather than youth employment in particular. Cyclical swings in economic activity raise and lower unemployment rates for all groups, with youth rates perhaps a little more volatile, but these cycles do little to affect the structure of rates among groups. The youth "differential" has changed over time principally for reasons that have little to do with the level of economic output (although changes in the structure of the economy, such as the shift from a manufacturing-based to a more service-based economy, do have some effect). Demographic factors and government regulatory policies clearly do influence this differential, and this chapter discusses the minimum wage and tax credits, which can both affect the availability of jobs for youths.

The focus, however, is more on the structural factors, which concern the readiness of young people for the jobs that are available. These should be the object of effective training programs to prepare youths to meet the demands of the labor market. Most young people

TABLE 6

RATES OF LABOR FORCE PARTICIPATION AND UNEMPLOYMENT,
SIXTEEN- TO TWENTY-FOUR-YEAR-OLDS, OCTOBER 1979

Educational Attainment	Population (millions)	Labor Force Participation Rate (percent)	Unemployment Rate (percent)
Total	20.9	81.5	10.8
Dropouts	5.3	66.7	19.0
Eight years of school or less	1.2	59.9	18.0
One to three years of high school	4.1	68.7	19.3
High-school graduates	15.6	86.4	8.7
Four years of high school only	11.1	84.6	9.8
One to three years of college	3.0	88.9	6.5
Four or more years of college	1.5	95.2	4.9

SOURCE: U.S. Department of Labor, Bureau of Labor Statistics, *October Employment Report.*

make the transition from school to work successfully on their own, but some are reaching adulthood without having become employable. The problem is better characterized as one of "employability development" for this population, rather than as one of youth unemployment generally.

Education and Employment

Intertwined with employment and training is the subject of the appropriate role of the educational system in enabling youths to make the transition from school to work. For our purposes the youth population can be divided into three groups: (1) those who complete high school and go on to college; (2) those who complete high school but do not go on to college; and (3) those who do not complete high school. This paper is concerned with the second and the third groups. Table 6 shows the labor force participation rates and unemployment rates for subgroups of the sixteen- to twenty-four-year-old population by educational attainment.

The table makes plain the reason for directing our greatest concern to dropouts, whose unemployment rate was more than twice that of high-school graduates even while their labor force participa-

TABLE 7

RATES OF LABOR FORCE PARTICIPATION AND UNEMPLOYMENT, SCHOOL
DROPOUTS AGED SIXTEEN TO TWENTY-FOUR, BY RACE, OCTOBER 1979
(percent)

	Labor Force Participation Rate	Unemployment Rate
Whites	69.0	16.4
Blacks	57.3	31.6

SOURCE: U.S. Department of Labor, Bureau of Labor Statistics, *October Employment Report.*

tion rate was twenty percentage points lower. More years of school-ing are clearly associated with better employment prospects.

Table 7 compares labor force participation rates and unemploy-ment rates for white and black dropouts aged sixteen to twenty-four. Clearly, the problem is much worse for black than for white dropouts.

Staying in school may improve employment prospects, but it is still not a guarantee of finding employment. Table 6 shows high-school graduates with an unemployment rate of nearly 10 percent—twice that of college graduates. A high-school diploma is still worth something in the job market, but it has lost some of its value for at least one reason that concerns us: it no longer means that its holder is able to read, write, or compute well enough to meet the basic demands of even many relatively unskilled entry-level jobs. Much discussion of skills revolves around vocational education, but inade-quate basic education may be a more serious drawback to the employability of minority and poor youths.

The Elementary and Secondary Education Act of 1965 provides funds to school districts for compensatory education. Title I of the act, which gives money to help educationally disadvantaged children, serves millions of children annually, almost all of them in elementary schools. Recent evaluations of Title I programs show some progress toward closing the gap in basic skills—as measured by test scores—between disadvantaged and other students. At the secondary level, the "back to basics" movement has led most states to require students to pass minimum competency tests before graduating from high school. A renewed emphasis on academic subjects together with compensatory programs for the disadvantaged may gradually increase their employability, but many youths need remedial education right now.

225

The Vocational Education Act of 1963 targeted some federal vocational education money toward disadvantaged groups. Amendments in 1976 included new provisions targeting money for the disadvantaged. U.S. Department of Education statistics for 1978 showed nearly 19.6 million enrollments in vocational education programs, more than 12.7 million of these—or about two-thirds—at the secondary level.

Support for vocational education is based on a model according to which people acquire certain skills that they then sell in the labor market to employers with jobs that require those particular skills. But the labor market often fails to conform to this model. Most job-specific skills are gained not through formal education or training but on the job from employers, and getting hired, especially for many entry-level jobs, may depend as much or more on basic aptitudes and attitudes. Vocational education programs enroll millions of youths and may help some of them find jobs, but there is little evidence that they result in greater labor market success for most of those enrolled. They are not the way to get youths who lack basic competencies into the job stream. Giving youngsters the skills and attitudes needed for getting and holding a job and making them aware of the requirements and opportunities for different kinds of jobs—these are the tasks of prevocational and career education programs.

The public schools are the largest and most significant part of the overall training and employment system. What goes on in them has far more impact on total youth employment than CETA programs that account for less than a dime of each dollar spent on developing human resources in the United States (as estimated by the National Commission on Employment Policy). The federal policies and private sector initiatives described in the next sections should not be considered apart from the question of what the schools should be doing to improve the employability of teen-agers. Indeed, some of the initiatives make use of the public school system or work in cooperation with it to provide the prevocational or preemployment training many youths need to enter the job market.

While reading about the programs described, it is important to consider which youths are being served. Our concern here is with noncollege youths generally and their preparation for the world of work. Within this large group, however, are subgroups that experience different degrees of difficulty in getting started at working. High-school graduates and nongraduates are two obvious subgroups, but there are also potential dropouts who are still in school and youths who never made it to high school at all. Our chief concern is what is being done to make youths employable who otherwise would not be.

Federal Employment and Training Policies

Federal responses to youth unemployment have been of two kinds: programs of job creation and training programs. The former have included various subsidized work experience and public service employment programs as well as the recent targeted jobs tax credit, while the latter encompass the array of training programs under CETA and its predecessors. The federal minimum wage is a policy that cuts the other way, restricting demand for unskilled workers by eliminating jobs that are not worth the minimum to employers. Of course, the intended purpose of the minimum wage was to guarantee all workers a wage level that some might not command in the market. It has benefited some, mostly older, workers who have jobs, but at the expense of others, mostly younger, whom it has deprived of jobs.

Under the Manpower Development and Training Act of 1962, training was provided for the economically disadvantaged regardless of age; nothing is definitively known about the results for youths. Training took place both in institutional classroom settings and on the job. Classroom training involved more people, but on-the-job training was likelier to help participants to get jobs, although the programs may have subsidized some behavior that would have occurred without them. Both kinds of training have continued under CETA, along with work experience programs.

Public Employment Programs. Although federal job creation programs have served large numbers of youths, few assessments of their impact specifically on youths have been made. Approximately 20 percent of the participants in public service employment (PSE) programs under CETA and its predecessors have been under twenty-two years old, but most PSE jobs have been short-term work experience programs designed to give economically disadvantaged youths income and actual work experience with public or nonprofit employers. In-school, out-of-school, and summer youth programs originally authorized under the Economic Opportunity Act of 1964 and continued under CETA provided minimum-wage jobs to hundreds of thousands of youths each year, but have had little if any lasting impact on the youth employment problem. It may be in the nature of these programs that the goal of income transfer largely eclipsed the goal of making disadvantaged youths more employable at permanent jobs with improved earning prospects. The kinds of temporary, often make-work jobs created under various PSE and work experience programs did not give the young people who filled them much more than paychecks. If temporary employment is to be meaningful, it ·

227

should help to develop the skills and attitudes necessary for getting and holding permanent jobs. If work experience is to accomplish this, it must give participants tasks from which they can learn, provide close supervision, and establish performance measures. The PSE programs largely failed to do these things and thus ended up almost wholly as programs of income transfer. Income redistribution may be a defensible goal in some circumstances, but CETA programs should develop employability while they transfer income.

The PSE programs administered under Title II of CETA have been eliminated, but the Summer Youth Employment Program (SYEP) survives. Summer employment grew to include a million youths at a cost of $750 million in the last years of the Carter administration, but has been cut back substantially. It is probably unrealistic to expect a nine-week program—aimed chiefly at keeping inner-city youths out of trouble by keeping them busy and putting a little money in their pockets—to improve employability as well, although summer jobs can be designed as part of a twelve-month training and work experience program.

Later "enriched" versions of SYEP, such as the Career Exploration Program operated by the Opportunities Industrialization Centers of America (OIC), provide career education and counseling, motivational training, and job referral and placement assistance. These programs seek to help SYEP participants prepare themselves better for longer-term employment later. Evaluations so far indicate that the enriched programs may increase both employment and school enrollment rates but do not measurably change job-related attitudes.

The Job Corps. The federal job training program that is generally acknowledged as the most successful is the Job Corps. It was established under the Economic Opportunity Act of 1964 to help some of the most disadvantaged youths—those at the opposite end of the spectrum from college-bound youths. Few of them have completed high school, most come from low-income backgrounds, and some have been convicted of crimes. The Job Corps gives them an intensive and comprehensive program that includes basic education, skills training, health care, and counseling, generally in a residential setting. Its purpose is to break them out of the poverty and welfare dependency cycle by improving their employability and long-term earnings prospects. Because it deals with some of the most disadvantaged and is a residential program that keeps the average trainee for nearly six months, the Job Corps is expensive. There is a high dropout rate in the first ninety days—especially among younger teen-agers—because of the intense, very structured nature of the program; but those who stick it out have been shown to have higher employment rates and higher starting pay the longer they stay: in 1978 employment rates varied from about 60 percent for trainees who stayed less than three months to about 80 percent for those who remained a year or longer. And corps members were more likely to be in further training or work experience programs than youths in the comparison group, indicating a potential for higher future earnings.

Appraisals of the Job Corps have generally agreed that it has improved trainees' employability and potential earnings and reduced the likelihood that they will engage in crime. The Job Corps is designed to meet the specific needs of a defined "target" population, and in this sense it is better conceived than scattershot programs that shoot resources at unemployed youths and hope to hit some of them. One of the reasons suggested for the effectiveness of the Job Corps is that many of its centers are operated by private contractors, such as RCA, Singer, Teledyne, and AVCO.

New Youth Programs. A new batch of youth initiatives was created in 1977 under the Youth Employment and Demonstration Projects Act (YEDPA), which is now Title IV—the youth programs title—of CETA. The purpose of YEDPA was to test a variety of approaches to dealing with the "structural" problem of youth unemployment in different local contexts. New Title IV programs were Youth Community Conservation and Improvement Projects (YCCIP), Youth Incentive Entitlement Pilot Projects (YIEPP), and Youth Employment and Training Programs (YETP).

The YCCIP, a successor of sorts to the Neighborhood Youth Corps of the 1960s, was designed to avoid the drawbacks of earlier work experience programs by giving primarily out-of-school youths useful work such as community rehabilitation projects and supervising them properly. The participants could also receive academic credit for their work experience through coordination between the school system and the employment service on job placement. The YCCIP thus had some of the marks of a cooperative vocational educational program.

The YIEPP was designed to test whether job guarantees would induce youths to complete high school. Participants were provided part-time jobs during the school year and full-time jobs in the summer as long as they met performance standards both in school and on the job. They could remain in the program until they were twenty or

I am indebted to Andrew Hahn for many of the points made about YEDPA. They were taken from Andrew Hahn and Robert Lerman, *Representative Findings from YEDPA* (1982), forthcoming report to the Department of Labor, Washington, D.C.

229

had graduated. The YIEPP was not a "quick fix" program but rather a sustained effort to link the worlds of education and work in a way that would improve employability by combining a high-school diploma with work experience.

The YETP offers a mix of training and support services designed to improve employability. These include institutional classroom and on-the-job training, apprenticeship, general education development (GED) certification, labor market information, and placement. Youths are still eligible under Title II of CETA as well (about 45 percent of those served under Title II are less than twenty-two years old), and the YETP is intended to supplement but not to replace Title II programs. A 22 percent set-aside of YETP funds for in-school youths is an attempt to forge links between CETA prime sponsors and local education agencies.

In addition to the Title IV programs, another youth initiative was added under a new Title VIII of CETA—the Young Adult Conservation Corps (YACC), modeled on the Civilian Conservation Corps of depression days and the more recent Youth Conservation Corps, which was a summer program. The YACC, administered by the Departments of Agriculture and Interior under an interagency agreement with the Labor Department, provided employment in conservation work on public lands. It was not aimed only at the disadvantaged, but was open to unemployed youths regardless of family income.

The YEDPA programs taken together constituted the largest collection of social experiments the federal government has undertaken on a single public policy issue. Assessments of YEDPA yield mixed conclusions. Its programs served hundreds of thousands of disadvantaged minority youths, before all but YETP were discontinued, but underserved school dropouts—although YIEPP did draw some back to school. Work experience seems to have been more productive than under earlier programs—there has been less makework—but still seems to have had little effect on initial employability. Finally, despite the 22 percent set-aside under YETP for in-school youth and the stay-in-school incentives under YIEPP, there is still little effective collaboration between schools and training institutions.

Private Sector Programs. In 1978 Title VII was added to CETA to increase business involvement in employment and training and to expand job opportunities in the private sector for the disadvantaged clientele served by CETA. Until the passage of Title VII, the private sector had played no oversight role in federal efforts. Part of the explanation for CETA's failure to have much lasting impact on youth unemployment lies in its substantial failure to relate employment and training efforts to the private economy, where most permanent jobs are created. Many private employers have criticized CETA programs as unrelated to the requirements of the workplace, although those who have had some experience with CETA graduates have generally expressed satisfaction with them.

The mechanism for involving private business more deeply in the employment and training effort is the private industry council (PIC), which must be established for any prime sponsor to receive funds under Title VII. The PIC must include representatives of industry and business (including small and minority business), organized labor, community-based organizations, and educational agencies and institutions; industry representatives must constitute a majority. The role of the PICs is to participate with the prime sponsors in developing and implementing "private sector initiatives" under Title VII and to confer with them about other CETA programs such as activities related to the private sector under Title II. Title VII private sector initiatives can include small business internships, cooperative education programs combining secondary or postsecondary schooling with private sector work, on-the-job training on a declining subsidy basis, follow-up services for people placed in private sector jobs, direct contracting with private organizations to provide training, and apprenticeship and other skills training programs.

The Title VII programs are not aimed exclusively or even primarily at youth, although more than a third of their enrollees have been under twenty-two years old and it is hoped that youths will benefit as much as others from private sector participation. Prime sponsors have generally sought such participation only at the placement end of the process; Title VII is a new attempt to involve the private sector in the total training and placement effort.

PICs are seen as the institutional intermediary between CETA and the private sector, seeking to establish links between trainees and the business community, and they figure prominently in legislative proposals for the renewal of CETA. It is too early to judge their effectiveness; many are still getting established, defining their roles and their relationships with prime sponsors. But the percentage of private sector placements is a little higher under Title VII than under the other CETA titles, and the very existence of PICs may be raising the level of consciousness of the need for private sector involvement in training as well as placement. Among youths, however, PICs have tended to deal primarily with high-school graduates rather than dropouts. This is not surprising, since private employers are likely to pay attention to youths who are easier to prepare for employment.

Summary. In retrospect it seems that CETA has evolved through several phases during its ten-year existence. It had multiple or alternative goals at the outset: training the structurally unemployed, creating jobs in the cities, transferring income to the poor. When it became increasingly evident that it was not well targeted to youths, YEDPA was added. It also became clear that PSE programs often deteriorated into make-work while little was done to link with the private sector, where most jobs are created; the answer to this was the private sector initiatives program featuring the PICs. Now the PICs are assuming greater importance in the legislative debates over the renewal of CETA, as reformers try to give it a more private sector look while targeting its diminished funds more than ever for the poor.

Targeted Jobs Tax Credit. Another kind of federal job-creation initiative is the targeted jobs tax credit (TJTC), which is a tax expenditure rather than a direct spending program. The TJTC was passed in 1978 to encourage for-profit employers to hire disadvantaged youths by giving them a tax credit equal to 50 percent of first-year wages and 25 percent of second-year wages (up to $6,000 per year). Although the response from employers was slow at first, hires reached an annual rate of 400,000 by early 1981. Fewer than half of these were low-income youths, however, because the law also allowed the credit for students from cooperative education programs. Still, the annual hire rate of low-income youths reached 170,000, which is as large as the total under all CETA youth programs except summer employment. And the law was changed in 1981 to limit eligibility of cooperative education students to those from low-income families and at the same time to extend coverage to CETA workers terminated from public service employment jobs, both of which changes could increase the hiring of disadvantaged youths.

During its first two and one-half years, the TJTC provided employers with tax subsidies for more than 600,000 hires. There are no studies to tell how many of these were induced by the TJTC, since employers have obtained certification for many youths in the target group whom they would have hired in any case. Nor are there any data on job duration: the credit is good for only two years. Program data on certifications and informal surveys of employers suggest that most employers do not use the TJTC, that many certifications are for workers hired independently of it, and that only a few employers use it to increase employment either of the target group or overall. It seems clear that the TJTC has failed to make a visible impact on either the unemployment rate or the employment/population ratio of low-income youths. Tax subsidies may yet have some potential as a job creation mechanism, however, if they are carefully designed.

The Minimum Wage. One issue that generates considerable debate in discussions of youth unemployment is the effect of the minimum wage on jobs for relatively unskilled teen-agers. The idea of a youth subminimum has been around for many years. Since 1961 the student certification program has allowed employers in the retail service, agriculture, and higher education sectors to hire full-time students for part-time jobs during the school year and full-time jobs during the summer at 85 percent of the minimum wage (subject to restrictions on the numbers exempted for each employer). In 1981, nearly 325,000 students were exempted under this program—somewhat fewer than in past years because of a change in the rules governing federal subsidies for students in work-study programs under the Aid to Higher Education Act.

Other exemptions for entry-level workers in specific occupations in the textile and garment trade, for student learners, for messengers, and for apprentices are so restrictive as to be little used; wages must typically be 95 percent or more of the minimum, exemptions apply for short periods and to a small portion of the work force, and employers must get prior approval from the Labor Department. No certificates have been issued since 1967 under one program, and the apprentice exemption has not been applied for since 1977 because of a nice Catch-22 in the rules that requires all exemptions to be approved by the Bureau of Apprenticeship Training, which has its own rule that apprenticeship rates must *exceed* the minimum wage. The student learner exemption for students in vocational education programs allows payment of 75 percent of the minimum wage for part-time employment for one school year; it covered 17,000 students in 1975, but covers only 3,000 now.

Studies generally agree that the minimum wage has some adverse effect on youth employment, but they do not agree on how much. A study for the Minimum Wage Study Commission appointed by Congress in 1977 concluded that a 25 percent youth differential would increase teen-age employment by about 3 percent, or by 250,000 jobs. The commission staff estimated a larger effect from the same differential, an increase of 4 to 5 percent. The commission's review of previous studies found their estimates of the effect of a 10 percent increase in the minimum wage to range from a 1.0 percent to a 2.5 percent reduction in teen-age employment—a loss of between 80,000 and 200,000 jobs. The commission's own estimate was lower—from

TABLE 8

MEAN RESERVATION WAGE AND EARNED WAGE OF HIGH-SCHOOL SENIORS,
SPRING 1980

(dollars per hour)

	Male		Female	
	Reservation wage	Earned wage	Reservation wage	Earned wage
Black				
Employed	3.11	3.35	3.05	3.20
Unemployed	2.97	—	2.98	—
Out of labor force	2.93	—	2.88	—
White				
Employed	3.08	3.43	2.86	3.12
Unemployed	2.97	—	2.79	—
Out of labor force	3.01	—	2.71	—

NOTE: The minimum wage in the spring of 1980 was $3.10 per hour. The reservation wage is defined as the lowest hourly wage that students would accept.
SOURCE: U.S. Department of Education, National Center for Education Statistics.

0.5 percent to 1.5 percent. The impact of minimum-wage increases may be relatively greater, however, on minority and disadvantaged youths, who already suffer the greatest unemployment.

The commission found that 44 percent of all sixteen- to nineteen-year-olds were working at or below the minimum wage in the spring of 1980—38 percent of males and 51 percent of females. That age group constituted 9 percent of all employed workers and 31 percent of all minimum-wage workers. Table 8 shows the results of a survey of high-school seniors carried out at the same time by the National Center for Education Statistics.

The table shows that all groups of seniors who were employed—black and white, male and female—earned a mean wage that exceeded the minimum wage by two cents to thirty-three cents per hour. It also shows that all groups of seniors who were either unemployed or not in the labor force had a mean reservation wage (the lowest wage they would have accepted) that was below the minimum wage by nine cents to thirty-nine cents per hour.

The fact that many unemployed or discouraged teen-agers would be willing to work for less than the minimum wage is not persuasive for opponents of a youth differential. Some argue that much of the gain in youth employment would be at the expense of older workers, and the commission did find that 14 percent of workers twenty to twenty-four years old and 38 percent of those sixty-five years and over were working at or below the minimum in the spring of 1980. Others claim that the minimum wage defines a level below which no one should be paid regardless of the kind of work performed.

Private Sector Initiatives

The initiatives discussed in this section are private in the sense that the approaches they take originated outside the federal training establishment and differ in various respects from the more or less standardized CETA programs, even though some of them receive CETA funds.

It is important to recall how CETA operates. Most funds are allocated to prime sponsors: states, local governments, or consortia of local governments. This relatively decentralized system allows prime sponsors to use their funds with some imagination within the program guidelines set out under each title of the act. Some of the initiatives described in this section are funded by CETA prime sponsors and others by private foundations and corporations. The important point is not the source of funds but the private origin of the initiative.

Jobs for America's Graduates. Jobs for America's Graduates (JAG) began in 1979 as Jobs for Delaware Graduates (JDG), a program to prepare high-school seniors for employment in the private sector. Started in eight of the state's twenty-five high schools, the program has become part of the curriculum in twenty-four schools because of the favorable results of the pilot program. Nearly 60 percent of all students desired to participate, and more than 85 percent of participants who graduated from the pilot schools in 1980 had been placed in jobs, in military service, or in higher education three months later. Comparisons with control groups showed that those in the program were nearly 50 percent more likely to get jobs by the end of three months and earned nearly $1,000 more in the first year after graduation. Funding for JDG comes from local companies such as du Pont, Hercules, and ICI as well as from CETA, the U.S. Labor Department, and the state of Delaware.

Using the Delaware program as a model, JAG intends to test the basic approach of preemployment or prevocational training in varied geographic and socioeconomic settings over the next three years to see if it can serve as the basis for a national program to reduce youth unemployment. Programs are now operating in four locations outside Delaware. The First National Bank of Boston was instrumental in getting a program started in six Massachusetts high schools. The Arizona program is active in all high schools in the state that have 500 or more senior students, which covers half of all the seniors in Arizona. The program in Memphis involves nine high schools, and the Missouri program is operating in three high schools in Kansas City and four in St. Louis with support from such major companies as Hallmark, Monsanto, and Ralston Purina. A program will open next year in Virginia, and another is being considered for Kalamazoo, Michigan. Most of these programs, like the original one in Delaware, have substantial private funding, but the bulk of the money comes from CETA and from state governors' and legislatures' budgets.

Each JAG program is a joint public-private venture, governed by a board of community leaders from business, labor, education, and government who take personal responsibility for it. Their involvement is felt to be critical to a program's chances of success. Indeed, much of the success of the Delaware program is attributed to the leadership of Governor Pete du Pont; Governors Kit Bond of Missouri, Lamar Alexander of Tennessee, and Charles Robb of Virginia are trying to play similar roles in their states.

The local JAG enterprises are operated like other nonprofit corporations. Their staffs work with schools to identify seniors who need help in finding and getting jobs. A job specialist is responsible for training, counseling, placing, and following up on about forty students; this personal responsibility for results is cited as one reason for JAG's apparent success. Training concentrates on developing the basic employment skills and attitudes identified by employers as necessary in making the transition from school to entry-level jobs. Remedial education is sometimes required to give students the reading, writing, and computational abilities they must have to be employable. Staff members identify job opportunities in the local community, making special efforts to find openings with small businesses. After being counseled on how to present themselves, students go for job interviews, although some choose to join the military service or to attend college. Staff members follow up all job placements for nine months, to help with any problems experienced by either the youths or their employers, and they encourage the youths to stay on the job and earn pay raises and promotions. The motivation of JAG participants is reinforced by involving them in an organization patterned after Junior Achievement.

The average cost per placement, including nine months of follow-up, is less than $1,500, compared with an average of $6,000 under Title II of CETA.

70001 Ltd., the Youth Employment Company. 70001 Ltd. is a national nonprofit youth employment company. Springing from a 1969 pilot project in Wilmington, Delaware, that was funded by the Thom McAn Company and run through the Distributive Education Clubs of America, 70001 has grown into a network of programs located in forty-five communities.

The programs are aimed at a particularly difficult-to-place group of youths—high-school dropouts sixteen to twenty-one years old. Applicants are screened to discover their interests, academic levels, aptitudes, and attitudes. Those willing to accept the ground rules of 70001—which, unlike typical CETA programs, does not pay stipends— are assigned to individual coordinators after they sign an agreement that specifies their responsibility for meeting agreed-upon goals. A two- to five-week period of intensive preemployment training follows, during which they learn how to dress, how to fill out job applications, and how to conduct themselves in job interviews. They are also taught the basic responsibilities of a job, including the need to avoid tardiness and absenteeism and to develop positive attitudes toward work. Local training programs are usually operated by community-based organizations, with guidance and support from the 70001 national office.

During their preemployment training, enrollees can also begin working toward the general education development (GED) high-school equivalency certificate, which they are encouraged to earn if they want to get good jobs. A continuum of educational upgrading programs is offered, from GED to basic competencies.

Staff coordinators arrange job interviews as soon as they decide that trainees have developed the proper attitude and skills. Once youths are on the job, their coordinators work with them and with their employers for ninety days to improve their job performance so that they can earn raises or promotions that will build their confidence and increase their attachment to the workplace. During off-hours they can continue work toward GED certificates.

An important part of 70001 is its national youth organization, Seventy Thousand One Career Association (SEVCA), where associates learn skills of organization and leadership, develop a sense of responsibility to the community, and gain recognition for their achievements. SEVCA serves to maintain the important motivational aspect of 70001 for associates who participate in its activities. Described by one evaluator as a cross between a social club and a service organization, SEVCA provides peer support for 70001 youths while increasing both career and community awareness.

The 70001 programs are generally funded with CETA money, chiefly through prime sponsors but also under a contract with the

U.S. Labor Department. Support and advice come also from forty-four major companies and sixty-four members of Congress who are business and congressional associates of 70001. A recent grant from the Charles Stewart Mott Foundation is being used to reach some 2,000 corporations and encourage them to become involved in tackling the youth employment problem. Given the year-to-year uncertainty about CETA funding, 70001 is also seeking private financial support.

Since it became a private nonprofit corporation in 1976, 70001 has placed 15,000 trainees in jobs, at an average cost of about $2,000 per placement, or one-third that of Title II CETA programs—largely because it pays no stipends. Roughly three of four enrollees complete the program, and three-quarters of those who do are placed in jobs. A major independent evaluation by Public/Private Ventures found that 70001 trainees retain their jobs longer and have higher earnings than members of a comparison group.

The model developed by 70001 has been refined, but the basic elements remain unchanged. Youths are drawn not by the payment of stipends but by the desire to develop such qualities as self-confidence and self-respect, which will contribute to long-term success in the job market. They are placed in unsubsidized private sector jobs because 70001 would rather offer employers good workers who are ready to go to work than lure them with subsidies.

In addition to its principal model for prevocational training and placement of dropouts, 70001 started the Detroit Pre-Employment Training Center. The center prepares youths who are still in school as well as dropouts for manufacturing jobs with specific skills instead of the service jobs that are the entry point into the labor market for most 70001 youths. Now in its fourth year of operation, the center receives some private funding under a partnership with General Motors, Ford, Burroughs, and the Budd Company; other partners include the city of Detroit, the Detroit Board of Education, and the state of Michigan. It graduates 1,200 trainees a year and has had only fourteen dropouts of 3,800 total enrollees. Placement rates are not as high as for other 70001 programs because of the depressed local economy in Detroit, but 40 percent of the graduates are placed. The center is run in cooperation with the public school system, which releases students for four weeks of eight-hour daily shifts during which they learn the dynamics of the workplace—such as labor-management relations—as well as general occupational skills in on-the-job training.

The 70001 model has been adapted to training youths who are former offenders at a center in Prince George's County, Maryland.

Work-Education Program/Youthwork, Inc. In June 1980 Youthwork, Inc., a national intermediary organization working with the public and the private sectors, was given a grant by the Edna McConnell Clark Foundation to test nationally a private sector/education partnership program for disadvantaged high-school students. The Clark grant is being used as leverage to raise funds for demonstration projects in ten cities, to supplement local or state CETA funds, and to provide more flexibility in working with the private sector. The projects are being administered by PICs, chambers of commerce, and other organizations representing local business. The sites and programs vary—from New York City and Westinghouse High School's Partners for the Advancement of Electronics to Blanding, Utah, and Naalnish Nizhoni (Navajo for "good work") to help Native American high-school students compete for jobs off the reservation.

The idea began in Oakland in the summer of 1979, when Kaiser Aluminum and Chemical Corporation worked with Oakland high schools and the University of California to create a program called Summer on the Move. The objective was to improve the basic academic skills of disadvantaged youths while giving them work experience during the summer in some fifty local businesses.

A Youthwork grant from the Edna McConnell Clark Foundation helped the program expand to a year-round operation that became Success on the Move. Employers were interviewed to discover what deficiencies in attitudes and skills limit the employability of youths, and a modified high-school curriculum was developed to correct the students' general lack of preparedness for employment. The curriculum, developed in cooperation with the University of California, stresses improvement of basic communication, computational, and problem-solving skills related to work. In-service training prepares teachers to teach the curriculum. Planning involves school officials, university faculty, business representatives, state and federal officials, and foundation staff.

The link between the worlds of school and work is reinforced by paid work experience. This part of the program depends on the agreement of local employers to give students part-time and summer jobs. Work experience is intended to expose students to the demands and disciplines of a job, to help them develop a work ethic, and to acquaint them with the kinds of entry-level jobs available and the skills needed to fill them. Students in the summer program get six weeks of morning classroom instruction and afternoon on-the-job experience. The in-school program requires an extra hour of daily classroom study plus an average of ten hours of paid work experience

239

for fifteen weeks. Students are selected for participation through interviews and recommendations, and their parents are involved in orientation sessions and activities. In 1979-1980 about a hundred students were placed in regular part-time jobs, and participants showed improved school behavior and higher achievement in graduation competency tests.

The experience in Oakland led Youthwork to help develop and support a similar project called New Horizons in Richmond. It was a collaborative effort of Virginia Commonwealth University, the local school system, and thirty-one major companies, including Reynolds Metal and Philip Morris. Integrated into the regular curriculum in 1981-1982, it served seventy-five students.

An interim evaluation of the program concluded that incentives can be created or already exist to get employers involved with the targeted group but that there are significant obstacles to developing successful private sector initiatives. The greatest difficulties encountered have been generating enough private sector jobs; maintaining adequate links between the educational and employment parts of the program and, concomitantly, bringing about enough contact between educators and employers; and involving employers in planning, curriculum development, instruction, job training, and evaluation —in all phases of the program, rather than solely as providers of jobs.

Given widespread misgivings of employers about any program with a CETA label, the outside funding from the Clark Foundation was helpful. These funds also give managers more flexibility by allowing them to do things that cannot be done with CETA money— such as subsidizing private sector jobs (which is allowed in only one small CETA demonstration program under the youth entitlements projects), recruiting youths who may not strictly meet CETA eligibility requirements, and engaging in support activities outside the permissible scope of CETA regulations.

Career Intern Program. The Career Intern Program (CIP) grew out of the Urban Career Education Center, begun in 1971 by Dr. Leon Sullivan, founder of the Opportunities Industrialization Centers of America (OIC). With the cooperation of the Philadelphia Board of Education and funding from the National Institute of Education, CIP was born in 1972 as an alternative high-school program for dropouts and potential dropouts, to help them integrate their education with their career goals.

Courses were coordinated with the regular public school system and stressed basic academic skills and improvement of attitudes, but they were conducted at alternative sites because of the conviction that the youths being served learn better outside traditional classrooms. Subjects were career oriented, and classroom studies were supplemented by visits to work sites. Instruction was accompanied by intensive counseling to help prepare interns for the attitudinal and behavioral adjustments required in the world of work.

As interns completed more terms and accrued more credits toward graduation, more advanced course work, with more specialized career-oriented subject matter, was introduced. As they focused on particular careers, they spent more time at work sites observing the work routines and discovering the educational requirements of those careers. Where company and union regulations allowed, they also performed some tasks. When they approached graduation, they were taught how to find jobs if they sought employment, were helped to enroll in postsecondary institutions if they sought advanced skills or technical training, or were helped to get information on scholarships if they became interested in college. The CIP tried to aid their transition into whatever situations were commensurate with their training, abilities, and goals.

After the Philadelphia program was evaluated by Richard A. Gibboney Associates, Inc., for 1973 through 1976, the CIP approach was tried at four additional sites—Detroit, New York City, Poughkeepsie, New York, and Seattle. The Philadelphia evaluation showed that the program participants were much likelier to stay in school than members of the control group. Studies by RMC Research Corporation of the additional sites concluded that CIP could be replicated. OIC has a design for implementing CIP nationally, but the funding from the National Institute of Education has run out, and new sources—either of Department of Education or of Labor Department funds—have not been found.

OIC has run comprehensive employment training centers for the disadvantaged since 1964, training more than 640,000 people and placing nearly 80 percent of them in jobs. There are now 144 OIC affiliates in forty-two states and sixty organized interest groups that could become affiliates. Most of the funding comes from CETA prime sponsors, although some has come from the U.S. Commerce and Education departments and from local governments. OIC is not specifically a youth training organization; it serves mainly disadvantaged people of all ages, but 40 percent of those it has served have been less than twenty-two years old. It does provide so-called feeder training, its name for prevocational programs that emphasize basic education, motivation, and the development of character and positive work values before trainees are fed into more traditional training courses in occupational skills. Thus OIC offers an integrated program of prevocational and vocational training, with the aim of turning out trainees who have not just functional skills but the motivation to stay with a job after getting it. Some evaluators believe that OIC training is better suited to older youths—twenty years old and older—than to the teen-agers who are specifically targeted by programs such as JAG, 70001 Ltd., and OIC's own Career Intern Program.

Project Opportunity. Project Opportunity was developed by Public/Private Ventures, a private nonprofit research and demonstration firm, in cooperation with ADVOCAP, a community action agency serving two largely rural counties in Wisconsin. It places unemployed, disadvantaged, and out-of-school youths in jobs with small businesses for up to six months, after giving them preemployment counseling on personal appearance, interviewing, and attitudes and behavior expected on the job. Youths entering Project Opportunity are often dropouts with little or no work experience, lacking business contacts to enable them to approach employers, and generally not readily employable. The program's staff finds the youths, screens and counsels them, and helps to place them in appropriate jobs. They are paid the federal minimum wage, the project paying the full cost for the first half of the training period and splitting it with the employer for the remaining half. The youths were originally fully subsidized for six months, but employers later agreed to share the expense after three months.

Employers interview the youths before taking them on and then train them on the job. Most of the firms have fewer than twenty employees and offer the youths a close, personal working relationship as well as opportunities to learn a variety of skills. Since Project Opportunity began in May 1974, some 120 small businesses have employed about 190 young people, three-quarters of whom are either still working or continuing their education. Most new jobs created in the United States are in small businesses (a recent study by David Birch estimated that two-thirds are in businesses with fewer than twenty employees), and the experience of Project Opportunity shows that they can be given incentives to hire young people whom they could not otherwise afford to hire.

Ventures in Community Improvement. Ventures in Community Improvement (VICI) was established to give out-of-work, disadvantaged youths on-the-job training in construction skills by putting them to work improving deteriorating inner-city buildings. Public/Private Ventures developed and managed the VICI demonstration project for the U.S. Labor Department.

Eight sites were selected for demonstrations—Atlanta, Chicago, Milwaukee, Newark, New Haven, Philadelphia, the South Bronx, and Broward County, Florida. The principal features of the VICI "model" were (1) a local management agency able to operate training programs in construction skills, (2) provision of journeyman instructors by local building trades unions, (3) a ratio of six youths to each instructor and a total of sixty youths in each program, (4) an agency to find work sites for VICI crews, and (5) local community development funds for materials and supplies. During the training period youths received stipends equal to the minimum wage plus small increases for superior performance.

Of 1,346 participants through the first eighteen months, 601 were graduated—about the norm for a program serving this population. But 61 percent of the graduates—a high number for such programs—found unsubsidized jobs, chiefly in the building trades or in union apprenticeship programs at an average wage of $4.47 per hour. A follow-up study found VICI graduates more likely to be working eight months later than a control group of similar youths or former enrollees of similar CETA programs. The VICI graduates also had significantly higher earnings, largely because they were more likely to be in construction jobs, which pay well. One reason for these results has been the involvement of union journeymen as instructors. They are demanding teachers, serve as effective role models for youths, and refer graduates to jobs.

The work done by VICI crews on more than 1,300 housing units has helped to improve local neighborhoods as well as train young workers. Despite reduced funding for all such ventures, five of the VICI projects have made the transition from outside to local funding sources and continue in operation. A large portion of these local funds has come not from traditional training sources but from communities that have benefited from VICI work products.

Vocational Foundation, Inc. Vocational Foundation, Inc. (VFI), is a private, nonprofit job placement agency created in New York City in 1936 to help youths in trouble with the law to find jobs. It continues to serve those aged sixteen to nineteen who are most difficult to place. Most of its funding now comes from the federal government, although it also receives private foundation and business support.

Half of VFI's clients have drug or correctional backgrounds, three-fourths are dropouts, and more than a third lack previous work experience. A remedial education program works to improve their reading and math skills and to prepare them for the high-school equivalency certificate. The curriculum is designed to conform to the specifications of the state Education Department's Bureau of Continuing Education.

VFI must find nearly four job openings for each placement that it makes. It prefers to work with small employers because they have the most jobs to offer, are easier to follow up on, and give youths better settings in which to learn a wider variety of skills. VFI's job bank contains more than 1,500 companies.

In its forty-five years, VFI has placed more than 15,000 youths. It attributes its success to rapport with employers, continuing counseling after youths are placed, and the performance of its graduates—three-quarters of whom complete their on-the-job training.

Work-Study Programs. *Continental-Illinois Bank* has employed more than 1,000 students in part-time jobs since 1972 in a work-study program that enables it to train potential employees internally to meet its employment needs while assessing them before they are hired full-time. Continental has found that work-study students are better motivated and better adjusted to the work world when they become full-time employees.

The program is administered by a recruitment coordinator who informs Chicago public high schools of job opportunities, helps them to screen and place applicants, and serves as liaison with the divisional staff that supervises them. Applicants are chosen on the basis of school attendance records, abilities, attitude, appearance, and desire for a business career. The students chosen may begin working in the summer before their senior year and typically continue working twenty hours per week during the school year, chiefly as clerks and typists. They are evaluated periodically by their supervisors. The program enables some who need money to stay in school.

Continental has found that the students lack basic communication and computational skills at first. Most of their training is on the job, although a typing and secretarial training class is being tried.

In 1980 Continental hired 80 percent of the students as full-time employees after they graduated, in jobs as typists, clerks, secretaries, and tellers. Work-study employees compared favorably with other employees in a 1977 evaluation: they had a higher retention rate, a better attendance record, and somewhat superior performance ratings.

The program has also improved teachers' understanding of the working world. Observing the students at work and reading performance appraisals from their supervisors give the teachers a better sense of business needs and employers' expectations. This can stimulate the schools to teach students more about career opportunities and job training requirements. By enabling students to see more clearly the link between school and work, work-study can help them make the transition.

Security Pacific National Bank has a program in California that trains 2,000 high-school students and adults annually in entry-level job skills. Security's state-wide Project STEP (Skills Training Educational Program) runs classes in seventeen subjects, taught in the evening and on Saturdays by bank employees in bank facilities.

The St. Louis Work-Study Program has been in operation for twelve years, with an annual enrollment of about 200 students. The program is a partnership between the St. Louis public schools and seventeen companies. Students spend their mornings studying academic subjects and have paid work experience each afternoon. School and work sessions both take place at business locations. Teachers on site can adjust the curriculum to the needs of individual students and employers. Students are able to explore careers, learn business skills and behavior, and gain work experience while using the up-to-date equipment available in large companies. Conducting the classes at the business sites provides a good study atmosphere, and class size is kept small.

The program now involves such companies as McGraw-Hill, Standard Oil, and Shell Oil as well as a consortium of banks, but it started small with a grant from the Danforth Foundation to help establish the first partnership between the schools and the Ralston Purina Company. Ralston Purina's is still the largest program, with as many as forty high-school seniors from inner-city schools participating each year.

Ralston Purina provides classroom space as well as the latest office equipment for an intensive business education program. Two teachers are assigned—and paid—by the Board of Education, one to teach academic and the other business courses. Students receive the minimum wage from Ralston Purina for a twenty-hour workweek and earn high-school credit for both the course work and the training.

The curriculum is designed to relate to the work assignments as closely as possible. Training and supervision are primarily the responsibility of Ralston Purina people, although the teachers remain on the site to coordinate work experience with classroom instruction

245

and to monitor students' work performance. The company is committed to training the students rather than just giving them part-time employment. Students are screened by the schools before being matched with training stations, which include all kinds of clerical jobs, the data processing unit, and jobs as laboratory technician assistants. Department supervisors are recruited on a voluntary basis, although the company says that it always has more requests than available students. Supervisors rate the students after each of four ten-week periods on attendance, punctuality, work habits, skills and knowledge, attitudes, and personal characteristics. Ratings help the teachers to work with students on individual needs as well as to refine the curriculum.

An average of 75 to 80 percent of the students have been placed annually, and another 15 to 20 percent have continued their education. The annual attrition rate is less than 5 percent.

Ralston Purina Summer Employment Program. Since 1970 Ralston Purina has invited about 300 community nonprofit organizations each year to send proposals for summer job programs. Organizations submitting proposals must certify their tax-exempt status and give details about the jobs and about the amount and quality of supervision to be given the youths.

Ralston Purina evaluates the proposed jobs on the basis of their potential for developing and using skills. The company wants jobs that will give youths "hands-on" experience, rather than those that simply introduce them to a particular occupation or that try to provide long-term training. Unless the youths are handicapped, housekeeping or custodial jobs are not acceptable.

Last year the company provided funding for 467 jobs, selected from ninety-four proposals for about 1,500 jobs. The grants funded programs in thirty-three cities in twenty-one states in which Ralston Purina has operations. Organizations selected for funding must submit interim and final evaluations of their programs and must return unspent funds to Ralston Purina.

The program is directed to low-income youths who have completed their junior year of high school and who might drop out of school for financial reasons but for the opportunity to earn summer money. Ralston Purina pays for their wages at the minimum wage rate and for any mandated withholding taxes, for twenty hours per week for ten weeks. In some instances the company also funds a portion of supervisory costs, but no general administrative costs. The primary purpose is to provide wages for the youths.

246

South Central Connecticut Regional Council on Education for Employment. In 1973 the Olin Corporation began providing high-school vocational students in New Haven with direct exposure to the workplace by allowing them to spend time in the factory learning how workers with various skills do their jobs. This experience spawned other cooperative arrangements with the Central Labor Council and with Southern Connecticut State College and led eventually to formation of the Connecticut Foundation for School/Community Relations.

The foundation brought together manufacturing companies, banks, public utilities, colleges, and city agencies with schools throughout the city—with support from Olin and the state Department of Education. A good example of its efforts is the school/bank program, which has nine banks working directly with nine inner-city classes of primary-school students and their teachers. The curriculum, developed jointly by teachers and bank staff, gives each class the chance to spend several hours a week in the bank putting its classroom training in arithmetic to work while learning about bank operations and using calculators and computer terminals. A three-year evaluation of this program indicates that student participants had significantly higher math achievement levels than the control group.

Last year the foundation began linking schools and business resources in the neighboring towns to New Haven. The IBM Corporation, for example, gave an areawide workshop on computer literacy for educators, and a series of eight workshops is being organized for guidance counselors to familiarize them with the range of local employment opportunities through meetings with industry personnel directors. And the foundation has worked with the Greater New Haven Chamber of Commerce to publish the area's first *Directory of Employment and Training Resources* for all schools and employers.

To emphasize the expanded scope of its activities, the foundation changed its name to the South Central Connecticut Regional Council on Education for Employment (RCEE) and added area school superintendents, presidents of local technical and community colleges, and officers from the region's large corporations to its membership. Its stated purposes remain the same: to give schools the opportunity to use local business and community resources to increase students' awareness of the world of work; to help teachers to enhance their students' learning; and to encourage local businesses to help prepare students for the transition from school to employment.

Most recently, the New Haven foundation has commissioned the RCEE to create a top-level business task force and to hire staff to

247

investigate the existing education/training/employment system and recommend structural and institutional changes.

Philadelphia High School Academy Program. In 1970, the Philadelphia Urban Coalition, on behalf of the Board of Education, started a prototype industrial academy for inner-city youths who could not qualify for vocational schools. The prototype became the Academy of Applied Electrical Science, Inc., a model three-year educational program that has given rise to similar academies—a Business Academy with three units, an Academy for Applied Automotive and Mechanical Science, and a Health Care Academy. These academies are schools within the Philadelphia school system. They can handle 520 students now and will be expanded to handle twice that number within two years.

The electrical academy was put together by a project team with representatives from business and industry, labor, and education. The curriculum was designed to relate basic skills such as reading and math to vocational skills in order to motivate the students, whose approximately fifth-grade basic skills were insufficient to qualify for entrance to vocational schools. The curriculum is kept current with changes in requirements for employment. There is also an in-school "factory" to provide after-school and summer work experience as well as some income for the youths. An evaluation by Temple University shows that the academy has improved the employability of the great majority of students and that its graduates have been able to retain jobs after getting them.

The other academies were modeled after the electrical academy, and the incremental costs of adding them to the existing school system were borne by industry. Each academy has a full-time director either on loan from or paid by a major company. The academies use part-time instructors from industry and regular teachers from the schools as a team. They seek to improve employability by developing better work attitudes and basic skills and have reduced the dropout rate. The four academies are forming an association to coordinate their programs and to expand into other fields.

A key element in the program's approach is the linkage between basic skills and vocational skills; when students can see the need to improve their English and math ability to gain more specific occupational skills, they become motivated, and the results are good. Another key element is finding work slots after school and during the summer; the director of the academies believes that work experience is critical to developing a work ethic.

The private sector seems to have been accepted as a full partner in the educational process as a result of this joint venture, and the feasibility of further expansion of the program is being studied.

Peninsula Academies. The Philadelphia academies' approach of involving private business in public education is now being tried in California. The Stanford Mid-Peninsula Urban Coalition studied the employment situation on the San Francisco peninsula and found that many entry-level jobs were unfilled because the local public school system concentrates on college-bound students and fails to prepare potential semiskilled workers for the labor market. Traditional vocational and career education programs have not effectively served many students with deficiencies in basic academic skills. In cooperation with private industry and local school districts, the coalition is forming the Peninsula Academies to provide disadvantaged students with programs that will upgrade their basic skills while motivating them to complete high school by combining basic academic and vocational career education with job training.

The first two programs have been established in the Sequoia Union High School District. Executives on loan from private industry helped develop the curriculum and also serve as instructors. Each academy is serving 30 students in each of three grades, a total of 180 students, with a curriculum in electronics and computer technology matched to the predominant kinds of entry-level jobs in the area. The funds to implement the model plan were contributed by the David and Lucile Packard Foundation, the San Francisco Foundation, the Edna McConnell Clark Foundation, and private corporations. Local companies also provide summer and after-school jobs for the youths.

Comparison with European Experience

Unemployment rates for youth—and for other age groups—have historically been lower in Europe than in the United States, although the difference has narrowed in recent years. The Europeans' rates are lower in part because they do not count in-school youths in their labor force or unemployment statistics. Michael Wachter's adjusted rates, which omit students, might be more comparable to European figures than the published BLS rates for youths. Youth unemployment as a proportion of all unemployment has varied from year to year

I am indebted to Beatrice J. Reubens of the Conservation of Human Resources Program at Columbia University for much of the information on European experience.

in the United States, but has not risen over the past decade. By contrast, youth unemployment in the European Economic Community has risen sharply over the same period and has become a more serious problem than it was, though still not so serious as in the United States.

Most European countries put less emphasis than the United States on keeping youths in academic education. While there is less concern over dropouts, there is more interest in specific occupational skill training as a worthwhile employment policy. Europeans also have a significant employment problem with minority youths similar to that of the United States (though involving foreign workers), with unemployment rates at least twice as high as for youths as a whole. European countries, however, have not typically undertaken targeted labor market programs of the American variety on behalf of their minorities.

A major difference between European and American employment policies concerns the statutory minimum wage. Some European countries have no legal minimum, and those that have provide for youth differentials, generally on a graduated basis. In France, for instance, the legal minimum is reduced 10 percent for seventeen- to eighteen-year-olds and 20 percent for those under seventeen, and in the Netherlands the reductions are even larger. It is difficult to tell whether such differentials account for any of the difference in youth unemployment rates between the United States and Europe.

A review of youth unemployment programs in Europe and the United States reveals two significant differences. The greatest is the emphasis in some European countries on creating a network of programs to ensure that every unemployed youth has either a job or a place in a training or an educational program. Such a commitment has been made explicit in the Scandinavian countries, Great Britain, and the Netherlands, and Germany tries to provide occupational training—either on or off the job—to all youths.

The other major difference is the greater use of the private sector in European youth programs. Through either wage subsidies or government allowances, private sector involvement is on the whole greater than in the United States, where CETA rules have almost entirely barred subsidies to private employers, leaving the targeted jobs tax credit as the only such measure.

Finally, European countries have recently been working toward closer ties between employment and educational authorities in striving to provide all out-of-school teen-agers with a useful activity—a job, an educational experience, or a training opportunity. Consequently, there has been much cooperation in improving the entire educational process to prepare young people for the transition from school to work.

Youth unemployment, then, is becoming a serious concern in Europe. European countries are trying to meet the problem with a mix of policies that we might give some attention to: overall commitments to employment or training opportunities for out-of-school youths, with cooperation between the educational and the employment systems; subsidization of private sector employment; and youth differentials where there are legal minimum wages.

Conclusions and Policy Options

Youth unemployment has always been higher than unemployment generally, but the ratio increased from the mid-1960s through the early 1970s as the postwar baby bulge passed through the economy. Youth unemployment has remained high, but this is now more attributable to higher general unemployment, the youth-adult ratio having returned to its historical level with the passing of the postwar generation of teen-agers into adulthood. As the teen-age population continues to decline in the 1980s, youth unemployment may also decrease. But if past patterns continue, the decline will occur chiefly among white males. Unless present trends or policies change, the situation is unlikely to improve for young blacks, whose numbers will grow proportionally, or for young women, whose labor force participation rates will continue to increase.

Since unemployment rates decrease with age, the problem is self-correcting over time for most youths. The school-to-work transition is a gradual maturation process rather than a springing forth full grown like Athena from the head of Zeus. A high incidence of unemployment is part of it, as young people find their places in the labor market through trial and exploration, gaining beneficial information and contacts. Many teen-agers combine school and work before completing the transition: more than half the teen-agers working or seeking work are in school, and youths who stay in school are more likely to be working than those who do not.

But the many youths who do not stay in school—more than 25 percent do not complete high school, and the percentage is double that in many inner cities—are less likely to find jobs. Although most of them are eventually assimilated into the labor market, unfavorable early experience can lower their aspirations and weaken their self-confidence, which in turn can have negative long-term effects on their

251

occupational status and earnings. Marketable work skills can be learned either in school or on the job, but youths who are in neither place lose experience and skills that would increase their employability.

The most important question may be not whether a teen-ager is employed but whether whatever he is doing is improving his long-term employability. Years of schooling correlate well with long-term employment success, but lead to a longer period of movement between school and work in the short term. Although blacks have made dramatic gains in educational attainment, these have not led to commensurate gains in the labor market—indicating that their academic credentials do not translate as readily into jobs. Black youths who have found jobs now earn wages equal to those of white youths, but even well-qualified black youths may be handicapped in the job search by their race. And increases in the coverage and level of the legal minimum wage have—in the judgment of nearly all economists—eliminated unskilled jobs that they might otherwise have held.

All groups of workers depend ultimately on a growing economy to create jobs, and youth unemployment declines as the economy grows. But while economic growth may reduce unemployment for all groups, it will not solve the structural problems of youths who lack the basic equipment to enter the permanent work force. The clear need is to ameliorate these structural problems.

History has shown that it is relatively easy to provide employment for the disadvantaged but more difficult and expensive, at least in the short term, to improve their employability. Most subsidized job creation programs, such as PSE, have increased employment of needy youths—especially black youths—temporarily, but they may also have substituted for unsubsidized employment in the regular labor market and have done little to prepare their participants for permanent jobs. These programs have generally emphasized income transfer to the detriment of developing employability.

The CETA approach has been diffuse rather than concentrated, delivering a large variety of services to a broad target population. Generalized funding practices based on broad formulas and tied to unemployment statistics have resulted in allocations of funds and choices of programs that have had little effect on the labor market problems of youths. Only a few of the programs under YEDPA, the youth addition to CETA, had explicit targets and treatments, such as youth entitlements.

The first step toward solving the youth employment problem is to identify which youths need help. Given the natural relationship between education and employability, better coordination is needed among general education, vocational education, job training, work experience, and job placement.

We can start by classifying youths according to the kinds of aid they need to gain entry to permanent jobs in the labor market and by targeting assistance not only by need but also by the willingness of those being helped to meet explicit performance standards. We must also determine the appropriate roles for the public and private sectors. Our examples of private sector initiatives show clearly that better targeting of resources is related to selecting program operators who can reach target groups with effective services. There must be a large public sector role in dealing with youth unemployment because of the responsibility of the educational system, broadly conceived, to prepare young people for the world of work. But there must also be a larger private sector role, because most permanent jobs are created in the private sector and private employers know their own needs best.

College-bound high-school graduates have the fewest labor market problems. One-third or more of the youths who complete high school go on to some form of higher education, which enhances their later employment prospects. High schools give most of their attention to those students, often to the neglect of students who will enter the job market full-time after graduation. College-bound youths often seek part-time and summer work, but they generally have the advantages of better basic skills and job contacts. They are not a target group for special youth employment policies (some may find their higher academic credentials mismatched with the needs of the labor market, but that is a somewhat different problem outside the scope of this chapter).

The next group along the spectrum consists of high-school graduates who are not going on to college. These students have traditionally been served by various vocational programs, but the schools need to offer them curricula better related to the labor market. Their greatest needs may be awareness of the demands of the workplace and information on job opportunities and requirements. The existing educational and employment systems remain largely separate, hindering the gradual transition from developing employability to finding employment. Promising initiatives in this regard are Jobs for America's Graduates (JAG) and the Youthwork demonstrations like Success on the Move. JAG is aimed at seniors who may have trouble entering the job market successfully. It gives them remedial education in basic academic skills, attitudinal and behavioral training for the responsibilities of a job, help in getting placed in jobs, and counseling after they are placed. The Success on the Move program in Oakland, New Horizons in Richmond, and similar programs overseen by Youthwork emphasize the same kind of prevocational or preemployment training and depend on contacts with local employers to place students in part-time and summer jobs.

Youthwork and JAG programs work to create the cooperation between the education and business sectors that can do the most to prepare students for employment after graduation. The National Association for Industry-Education Cooperation (NAIEC) also seeks to promote such cooperation through the creation of local industry-education councils. These councils bring together business, labor, local government, and community-based organizations. They can link education and industry by developing curricula related to the labor market, training teachers to teach work-related subjects, and offering work experience opportunities for youths who are not college bound. Councils are being established around the United States; for example, there are statewide networks in New York and California.

This is not to rule out any useful role for the existing vocational education system, whether in-school cooperative or postsecondary programs. But specific skills training is most effective when given to youths who have already gained the competencies and motivations that prevocational training emphasizes. Linking the two kinds of training to add job-specific skills to basic labor market preparation is the kind of task that an industry-education council could perform. Indeed, the tasks of coordinating employment and training with academic education and developing curricula to prepare students for the world of work should be done through just such local initiatives, without any need for federally sponsored programs. Efforts to relate school to work can begin much earlier than high school, as shown by the Regional Council on Education for Employment in New Haven. The federal funds that do go to support secondary and vocational education can be better used to help finance some of these local programs, but the initiative must come from local and state governments, which are responsible for public education, and from local business, which has a large stake in the products of the educational system.

Given the correlation between educational attainment and labor market success, it is worth trying to keep potential dropouts in school. There is little evidence that work opportunities alone will accomplish this. The Career Intern Program (CIP) developed by OIC has had some success in keeping youths in school. Career education seeks to develop realistic expectations about work, to give students knowledge of how labor markets function, and to help them explore career alternatives. Together with prevocational training to relate basic academic skills to work situations, it can form part of a curriculum that makes young people ready for the labor market. Keeping youths in school may have little value if they are not being prepared for work. The Philadelphia Academies and the Peninsula Academies go even further to ensure that they are by offering curricula that prepare students for particular kinds of skilled jobs in, for example, electronics, automotive mechanics, and computer science.

Policies to improve educational competencies can focus on increasing basic skills (the thrust of the "back to basics" movement in public education), on increasing years of schooling (dropout prevention), or on offering a second chance to those who have dropped out. The dropouts present the most difficult challenge.

They are not a monolithic group, of course. Some dropouts are no more "disadvantaged" than youths who are still in school and need only the same kind of help to enter the labor market—perhaps in an alternative setting. Others need more help if they are ever to be assimilated into the work force and leave a state of dependency or the criminal economy.

One successful program for dealing with dropouts is 70001 Ltd., the national youth employment company. The 70001 program of prevocational training emphasizes basic skills and positive attitudes and tries to develop youths' self-confidence as well as their competence. The objective is not merely to get them placed but to equip them to progress after they are placed. Follow-up counseling is an important part of this effort, in contrast to the "body count" approach of more typical CETA training programs, which merely try to place as many people as possible but do not worry as much about what eventually happens to them.

Although 70001 deals with some "difficult" as well as "easy" dropouts (it gets some who have dropped out of other programs), it is not designed to treat youths who need serious remedial work on basic academic skills or long periods of developing job skills. The "hardest core" youths are those treated by the Job Corps. Most of its training is done in residential settings and lasts an average of six months. The early dropout rate is high, but the results for those who stick it out appear to be lasting. It is an expensive but seemingly effective way of helping some of the youths on the farthest end of the spectrum from where we began.

The size of the various groups along the spectrum is difficult to determine. The majority of youths need no special help, although many would benefit from improved teaching of basic academic skills.

Another large group needs some remedial instruction in English and math or more knowledge of the job market and the responsibilities of a job. These youths are helped by programs such as Jobs for America's Graduates, Youthwork's work-education program, and OIC's Career Intern Program if they are still in school. If they are not, a program like 70001 can help them. A third group—not as large as the others—needs more intensive help of the kind given by the Job Corps if those who are in it are ever to become employable.

There must be some continued public funding of training programs for the second and third groups, especially the third. Industry cannot be expected to take on the responsibilty of instilling in youths the basic aptitudes and attitudes needed for work, although a 1977 Conference Board study estimated that 35 percent of U.S. companies provide remedial education to some of their employees. But there is a large role for the private sector to play in seeing that youths receive the right kinds of training and that work experiences help prepare them for permanent jobs as well as provide some income. The PICs— marked to play a major role under any new CETA legislation—can help to promote effective programs like some of those discussed here, programs designed to serve well-defined groups.

Federal policy has another role to play besides encouraging the right kinds of training and employment programs. It should also remove unnecessary obstacles to youth employment and provide incentives for job creation. The minimum wage reduces the number of unskilled jobs available. European countries that have a legal minimum provide for graduated youth differentials, a policy that encourages employers to hire unskilled youths and bring them up to the minimum as their productivity increases. The United States would be well advised to implement such a policy.

Employers can also be given direct wage subsidies that lower the cost of employing unskilled workers. Although the targeted jobs tax credit has not led employers to hire many youths whom they would not otherwise have hired, direct wage subsidies can be effective if they are limited to private employers and phased out automatically after the worker hired has gained sufficient skills to be worth an unsubsidized wage. The ADVOCAP program developed by Public/ Private Ventures used such subsidies as incentives to get small businesses to hire youths and train them on the job. Even stipends of the kind paid to most CETA enrollees in the past can be justified if they are limited to youths who are performing useful work while being trained, as in Public/Private Ventures' VICI program for training youths in construction skills while they rehabilitate urban buildings.

Private employers can work through such organizations as PICs and industry-education councils to help design training programs as well as provide work experience. Beyond this, they can act more directly by emulating Continental-Illinois Bank, Security Pacific Bank, and Ralston Purina, who run their own work-study or skill training programs and hire some of the graduates. There is not enough CETA or foundation money to reach all the youths who need preparation for the job market, and those who are trained well must still find jobs. Private employers, with incentives in the form of minimum wage youth differentials or wage subsidies of some kind, must act individually and collectively to create employment opportunities. David Mahoney, chairman of Norton Simon Corporation, has urged his corporate colleagues to commit themselves financially to creating jobs for the disadvantaged. Otherwise the problem will fall back into the lap of the federal government, which will be tempted to "solve" it with another public jobs program. The insurance industry has recently pledged to devote more resources specifically to alleviate unemployment, especially among minority youths.

The tax system currently favors youths who go on to college by subsidizing their education while they prepare themselves for better jobs with higher earnings. At least one imaginative analyst of the youth problem has suggested that we consider giving all youths an even break by providing those who enter the labor force directly from high school with the same kind of subsidy; it could be used for vocational training or simply to reduce the cost of hiring an unskilled worker. European countries are already moving toward the objective of providing all youths with education, employment, or training opportunities. Limited subsidies to private employers and greater involvement of employers in the educational system could constitute the basis for an effective human resource development policy—rather than just a short-term effort to reduce "youth unemployment."

Urban Transportation

C. Kenneth Orski

For urban transportation these are, in the words of Charles Dickens, the worst of times and the best of times. They are difficult times because urban transit systems are struggling with record operating deficits as federal transit subsidies are being phased out and cities are confronting a severe fiscal squeeze. They are the best of times because these very pressures are creating unprecedented opportunities for institutional and service innovations that promise to lift transit out of its current predicament and restore its fiscal soundness.

Paradoxically, massive federal operating subsidies have been a mixed blessing. While they have relieved the cities of some of the fiscal burden, they may have done the cities a disservice in the longer run by masking the effect of underlying demographic trends on transit economics, thereby postponing badly needed revision of inefficient transit practices. Conversely, the elimination of the subsidies, far from dealing transit a death blow, may prove to be a hidden blessing by forcing local officials to re-examine the logic of current transportation practices and to seek some fundamental—and long overdue—reforms in America's urban transportation systems.

A combination of forces is radically changing the operating environment of urban transportation:

• Inflation and liberal wage settlements caused nationwide transit operating costs to spiral from $2.5 billion in 1973 to $6 billion in 1980—and they show no evidence of leveling off. This escalation is largely a result of rapidly rising labor costs, which usually compose 80 percent of transit operating expenses. Between 1967 and 1980, transit wages increased 160 percent while the consumer price index rose 146 percent. Today, transit workers are among the highest-paid public employees. Contributing to the wage escalation have been automatic cost-of-living adjustments, restrictive contracts barring part-time drivers, and compulsory binding arbitration agreements. The problem has been compounded by legal provisions in the Urban Mass

Transportation Act, and their administration by the U.S. Department of Labor, that give transit unions an effective veto power over federal grants to local transit agencies, thus enabling unions to obtain concessions that they would not obtain from ordinary collective bargaining.

• At the same time, to lure people back to mass transit, city officials have deliberately maintained low fares. From 1972 to 1978, average fares nationwide, adjusted for inflation, had actually decreased by nearly 17 percent. As a result, farebox revenues, which kept some transit systems profitable as late as 1960, now usually cover only 45 percent of transit operating costs.

• The combination of escalating operating costs and artificially low fares has pushed transit operating deficits to record heights. Deficits of $2 billion in 1978 climbed to $2.7 billion in 1979 and reached $3.2 billion in 1980. According to one estimate, transit systems nationwide may need more than $6 billion in public subsidies to keep running.

• The announced phase-out of federal operating assistance can only worsen mass transit's plight. Although, on the average, federal aid accounts for only 15 percent of transit operating expenses, its discontinuance will remove more than $1 billion annually from transit system coffers and will place greater pressures on the already strained state and local budgets.

• Highway trust fund revenues are also declining, because people are driving less and have shifted to more fuel-efficient cars; at the same time the cost of highway repair and reconstruction has been rising steeply—43 percent in the last four years.

• Concurrently, cities and states face leaner budgets and a reduced capacity to raise additional revenues because of formal spending limitations, growing taxpayer resistance to higher taxes, and the high cost of borrowing funds in the financial markets.

• Above all, there has been a sense of disappointed expectations—a feeling that, despite seven years of sustained national efforts, transit has failed to secure a viable place in urban America. While transit ridership did gain somewhat in absolute numbers since its nadir in the late 1960s, its share nationwide of the urban transportation market has increased only marginally, and in many localities remains virtually unchanged.

Looming in the background are changing perceptions of and attitudes toward government. There is mounting public concern over the ineffectiveness of government programs. Large-scale public bureaucracies are seen as remote, uncaring, and unresponsive. People are groping for less costly forms of service delivery, for new collaborative relationships and approaches to addressing community problems, and for novel ways to use the full range of local resources, both public and private. There is, in sum, a new desire to see closer public/private collaboration in community problem solving.

Together, these forces have set in motion a major reappraisal of urban transportation. The traditional view—that delivery of local transportation services should be the exclusive domain of tax-supported public agencies, sheltered from competition by an array of protective laws and regulations—no longer commands unqualified acceptance. Emerging in its place is a new view of public transportation based on a belief that government itself need not necessarily deliver all the services that citizens have empowered it to provide. This new view is built around the principles of choice, competition, and diversity—diversity of services, of service providers, of organizational and management structures, and of sponsors. It is also a view based on a proposition that efficient transportation service is of enormous importance to the business community, and its provision, therefore, should be a cooperative task and a shared responsibility of the public and private sectors.

The new models of transportation service delivery that have evolved in response to these pressures generally fall into seven categories.

Contractual Arrangements with Private Carriers

Growing numbers of municipalities and transit authorities contract out portions or all of their public transportation operations to private firms to reduce costs and improve productivity. For example:

• The Tidewater Transportation District in southeastern Virginia contracts with a private taxicab company to provide service on demand in a residential suburb previously served by a regular bus route. The taxi service costs the district $16 per hour, compared with $30 per hour to operate its own buses.

• Phoenix contracts out Sunday transit service to a local taxicab company at an annual cost of $140,000; city officials estimate the cost of comparable publicly provided service at $700,000.

• Lexington, Massachusetts, contracts with a private firm to operate its community bus system, paying $16 per hour for bus operation. The private firm owns and maintains the buses so that the town has no capital expenses.

• Under contract with Gainesville, Florida, a private firm, ARA Services, Inc., has assumed complete responsibility for running the city's two garages and a fleet of motor vehicles. The city's transportation budget of $1.2 million for fiscal year 1981 was 11 percent below the amount budgeted for fiscal year 1979 for Gainesville's in-house program. The city has estimated that savings during the first year of contract operations were $296,000.

Interest in contracting is growing. The Advisory Commission on Intergovernmental Relations (ACIR) and the International City Management Association (ICMA) have each conducted surveys to measure cities' reliance on and attitudes toward the use of private firms to provide selected public services. Of 2,650 cities surveyed by ACIR, over 36 percent indicated a preference for contracting with private firms. The ICMA survey found that 60 percent of its respondents were already using private enterprise for public services such as refuse collection, fire protection, street cleaning, snow removal, and road maintenance. The practice of contracting received additional impetus in November 1981 from a National League of Cities resolution recommending private contracting "whenever it is a less costly and more efficient way of providing needed public services."

Despite potential obstacles—lack of suitable contractors and inability to provide adequate public oversight and performance monitoring—the practice of contracting for transportation services is likely to increase. Growing numbers of transit officials have abandoned their traditional reluctance to relinquish control over all aspects of public transportation and have come to view their principal role as one of policy setting: deciding what services are needed and ensuring that these services are delivered in the most efficient and economical manner. They no longer see their agencies necessarily as service producers. Even when regional transit agencies do continue as operating bodies, local elected officials increasingly view them as one among several potential service suppliers and regard themselves as prudent buyers in a competitive market.

Suburban jurisdictions in the Washington, D.C., metropolitan area provide an example of the changing attitudes toward public transportation. Most of the suburban counties contemplate switching to locally managed, possibly privately operated, community transit systems, while continuing to purchase long-haul bus services from the regional transit authority. Other metropolitan areas are adopting an opposite approach: central city transportation services continue to be operated by public transit agencies, but long-distance commuter services are being franchised to private bus operators. Both cases, however, are characterized by the same philosophy: let each level of government manage the transportation services that it can most efficiently deliver.

Entrepreneurial Transit

Private transit services, provided in competition with existing publicly provided services, have sprung up in several metropolitan areas in response to inadequate public transit service or substantial fare increases. The classic example is Chicago, where the number of private subscription buses has greatly increased because of 1981 fare hikes and cutbacks in commuter rail service. Ten private bus companies using 120 buses carry nearly 5,000 daily commuters from the suburbs to Chicago's central business district. The private operators charge $75 a month, which is 10–20 percent less than the cost of equivalent monthly train passes. For $100 a month, Chicago commuters receive deluxe service—air conditioned buses with reclining seats, morning newspapers, and a washroom. Similar services have been operating in New York City, where 550 private buses transport commuters to Manhattan every morning; in northern New Jersey; in Boston; and in Southern California, where the private COMBUS company operates dozens of unsubsidized subscription services at costs far below those of the public Southern California Rapid Transit District. After studying twenty-two express lines in Los Angeles and Orange counties, the Southern California Association of Governments concluded that using private rather than public carriers could reduce operating costs by 50 percent. Converting just those twenty-two lines could result in savings of $5 million a year. Private commuter bus services, often a response to large increases in transit fares and dissatisfaction with the quality of service, are starting up in Atlanta, Houston, and Philadelphia.

Nonprofit Transportation-User Organizations

Nonprofit transportation-user organizations have been formed to cater to specific transportation markets. These organizations can be divided into four types: .

Commuter Bus Clubs and Bus Cooperatives. Commuters in suburban communities often band together to charter buses that will take them to work. In Columbia, Maryland, for example, the Columbia Commuter Bus Corporation, a nonprofit association run by volunteers, operates seventeen buses daily between the community and downtown Washington. The organization has existed for ten years and has an operating budget of nearly $1 million.

Regional Ride-Sharing Agencies. In a number of metropolitan areas nonprofit organizations have been created to provide regional ride-sharing services to the public. They often work closely with major employers and with groups of smaller employers (in office parks, for example) to relieve them of the burden of starting their own ride-sharing programs. The large ride-sharing agencies, such as Caravan in Boston, Rides in San Francisco, Commuter-Pool in Seattle, and Commuter Computer in Los Angeles, each operate from 100 to 200 van pools.

Rural Transportation Agencies. Nonprofit transportation agencies have also been formed to meet the special needs of rural residents. Although often linked with efforts to provide social service transportation to elderly and handicapped persons, in some areas they have assumed a much broader role. In Pennsylvania, for example, the Montgomery County Paratransit Association (MCPA) coordinates twenty private taxicab companies operating in a 624 square mile area sprinkled with numerous small towns and suburban communities outside Philadelphia. Through its members, MCPA offers such collective transportation services as shared-ride taxis, flexible van services, and subscription bus pools. Also, it operates various types of vehicles: taxis, small vans, large vans, buses, and specially equipped vehicles for handicapped persons. MCPA analyzes the transportation needs of its clients and then offers the most appropriate service and vehicle. The agency undertakes all the necessary contracting with its member carriers and presents a single bill to the client, but leaves all operating decisions to its constituent members.

Neighborhood-based Transportation Cooperatives. Public transportation can also be organized within neighborhoods. Neighborhood associations have made several proposals to run jitneys for elderly residents. Neighborhood automobile cooperatives have been proposed (and one demonstration project is under way) that would place at the residents' disposal a fleet of special purpose vehicles such as vans, station wagons, recreational vehicles, and large sedans, which people need only occasionally and could own and use on a shared basis.

Corporate Employee Transportation Programs

By the end of 1981, some 800 private companies were subsidizing company-based employee transportation programs that use car pools, van pools, and, on occasion, buses. Several companies, notably Reader's Digest in Pleasantville, New York, have been running employee work buses for many years.

263

Company-subsidized transportation to work is growing in popularity as an employee fringe benefit. Here is how one company justifies its involvement in an employee ride-sharing program:

- the program eliminates the need to expand parking areas and reduces traffic congestion at the company site by reducing the number of employee cars
- it broadens the labor market by making the company accessible to potential employees from a wider geographical area
- it develops a more productive work force—employees are in a better frame of mind at work when they commute in the comfortable, relaxed atmosphere of a van
- it reduces absenteeism and tardiness—because poolers pay for their rides in advance, they are less likely to miss work; because they are dependent on one another to arrive at work on time, they are more likely to observe established work hours
- it enhances the company's community image—a strong commitment to ride sharing identifies the firm as a concerned and enlightened corporate citizen

Developer Involvement

Involvement of private developers in transportation is also growing. Developers have abandoned their traditional reluctance to cooperate with the public sector and are increasingly sharing in the expense of providing transportation improvements.

Private developers have a history of contributing to finance improvements of roads near their developments. They also have long been responsible for constructing streets within their subdivisions and widening and improving access roads to their developments. What is new is the rapidly expanding scale and nature of their involvement. In Leisure World, California, Las Colinas, Texas, Meadow Lake, New Jersey, and other private residential communities and retirement villages, developers provide collective transportation services for residents to nearby shopping malls and suburban centers. Similarly, developers of corporate office parks and large suburban employment centers and hospital complexes provide shuttle bus services to nearby commuter rail and rapid transit stations (for example, in Harmon Cove Corporate Park, New Jersey, Forrestal Center, New Jersey, Pill Hill hospital complex in Oakland, and Children's Hospital in San Francisco).

Negotiated Transportation Strategies. Large developers and local governments increasingly use negotiated transportation strategies to find a more equitable basis for sharing the expense of highway improvements and transportation services necessitated by the new developments. In some cases developers are granted construction permits or zoning approvals on the condition that they develop and implement programs to minimize the effect of the increased traffic on surrounding roads, through ride-sharing programs, for example. In other cases, notably in Los Angeles, developers and builders who adopt such traffic reduction programs are allowed, in exchange, to provide fewer parking spaces and thus reap the financial benefits of reduced parking construction costs. For example:

• Hartz Mountain Industries, major developers of Meadowlands, New Jersey, contributed $11 million toward highway improvements and the construction of a rail station and an adjoining parking lot that will serve the Harmon Cove Corporate Park and Harmon Meadow development.

• In Nashville, Tennessee, Cousins Properties financed the construction of a $3.5 million highway interchange to provide access to the new Hickory Hollow shopping center.

• In Middlesex County, New Jersey, Lincoln Properties is sharing in the cost of a $7 million highway bypass to accommodate the increased traffic from a new private residential development.

• At Tysons Corner in Northern Virginia, Tycon Developers, Ltd., has offered to build a $3 million four-lane bridge spanning an existing highway to provide direct access to its new $100 million office complex.

• The San Francisco Board of Supervisors recently enacted enabling legislation for a "transit development fee" to fund public transit. The fee will be imposed upon developers as a condition for obtaining a certificate of occupancy for new developments. Similar requirements for local road improvements exist in other communities.

• Fairfax County, Virginia, and the developers of a large integrated office/hotel/retail business park entered into an agreement that commits the developer to: (1) fund $18 million of highway improvements that will provide grade-separated access to the development; (2) establish a ride-sharing program for the tenants and employees of the office park; (3) encourage the use of mass transit through the construction of bus shelters and walkways to transit stops; (4) operate a rush hour shuttle bus to the nearest rail transit station; (5) establish a nonprofit tenants' association to ensure compliance with the terms of the agreement; and (6) implement any additional transportation strategies to ensure that peak hour traffic generated by the development does not exceed a stipulated level.

• A syndicate of prominent real estate developers in Dallas, Texas, recently proposed a $357 million surface "light rail" transit system that would be financed partly by tax dollars and partly by private capital. The proposed twenty-three-mile rail line would link major residential and commercial projects owned by the private developers to other parts of the city and county. Most of the line's right of way would be provided by the developers. This plan marks the first major return of private capital to the rail transit industry, and may signal a reversion to an earlier model of land use and transportation development, when the two processes were intimately related through joint management. Most land development before the 1920s occurred only because of heavy private investment in rail facilities—first in railroads that opened the West to agrarian development, then in "inter-urbans" and electric street railways that stimulated development at the urban fringe, giving rise to the so-called streetcar suburbs. Today, as the federal government divests itself of numerous public responsibilities, including support of mass transit and commuter railways, financially strapped local governments are looking with growing favor on the private sector as a potential partner in financing the transportation infrastructure. Railroad development will have truly come full circle within our own lifetimes.

Business Improvement Districts

Special business improvement districts with the power to raise property taxes to finance local improvements and local services have been steadily increasing in numbers, and many have expanded their responsibilities beyond their traditional focus of promotion and economic development. In New York City business improvement districts have formed nonprofit corporations to manage projects and programs funded through additional tax assessments, which are collected by the city and then returned to the neighborhoods. The additional revenues can be used to maintain existing facilities, fund new capital improvements, manage public spaces, or provide additional services such as security, sanitation, or local transportation. In Denver, a special downtown assessment district is being formed to finance the management of Denver's fifty-square-block core area, developed around its new Sixteenth Street Mall. In Annapolis, Maryland, downtown merchants, hotels, and restaurants have banded together to initiate a weekend shuttle bus service from outlying parking lots to the center of town for the benefit of their customers. A similar service was in operation for two years in Laclede's Landing, a revitalized entertainment district adjacent to the Gateway Arch in St. Louis,

Missouri, where a shuttle bus was operated cooperatively by several hotels and restaurants for their patrons.

Transportation Management Associations

Transportation management associations (TMAs) represent the most advanced and ambitious form of private sector involvement in community transportation. They are nonprofit organizations, formed by local businesses, corporate employers, owner/developers of suburban and downtown properties, and civic leaders to address community transportation problems that can be dealt with more efficiently on a collective basis. Transportation management associations create their own tax bases through assessment fees. Some operate their own services; others contract with independent service providers, either public or private. Some are single purpose organizations formed specifically to address transportation concerns; others are elements of broader multipurpose civic organizations. Some concentrate on downtown or central city transportation problems; others deal with regional transportation needs; still others are suburban in orientation. What follows are the profiles of four transportation management associations, each offering a uniquely tailored solution to urban transportation problems.

The Greater Hartford Rideshare Corporation. Company involvement in employee transportation is a tradition in Hartford, Connecticut. As early as 1957, for example, Connecticut General Life Insurance Company was running employee buses to its suburban headquarters from downtown Hartford. By 1971 the Southern New England Telephone Company had formed 380 car pools among its employees. The oil embargo of 1973 provided an additional impetus. By the late 1970s Hartford's major employers—Connecticut General, Aetna Life, New England Telephone, and Travelers Insurance—all had large-scale employee van-pool programs.

Much of downtown Hartford's business activity, however, involves small firms. Because small companies find it difficult to establish viable company-based ride-sharing programs and are unwilling to assume the cost of setting up individual programs, a large portion of Hartford's labor force was deprived of access to this form of commuter transportation. To overcome these barriers, the state, with the active support and encouragement of the business community— notably Connecticut General—set up the Greater Hartford Rideshare Corporation. The purpose of this independent, nonprofit organization, whose board of directors includes representatives of forty companies in the Hartford area, was to coordinate all public and private efforts to plan, promote, and implement ride-sharing activities within the Hartford area. While the corporation's initial efforts have focused on assisting member companies to form employee van pools, its ultimate objectives are much broader. The corporation is a comprehensive public/private transportation management association, performing a variety of services to ensure personal mobility in the Hartford area. Its activities may include assisting corporate clients in setting up comprehensive employee transportation programs, working with developers on traffic engineering improvements and ride-sharing programs, implementing parking management schemes in cooperation with the city, and performing a host of other transportation-related functions for the public and private sectors.

The Greater Hartford Rideshare Corporation is a dramatic example of an emerging form of cooperation between public officials and business leaders to address local community needs. As Governor Grasso stated during the corporation's inaugural ceremonies:

> We can no longer define our economic and social needs as being either solely public or private responsibilities. We need to recognize that a greater degree of cooperation will be essential if we are to take advantage of the resources of both these sectors to increase our efficiency and effectiveness. The planning, promoting and providing of energy-efficient mobility is both the responsibility of private individuals and private corporations, as well as a concern of the public sector. The Greater Hartford Rideshare Corporation offers a mechanism to effect this cooperative venture.

Private sector involvement in transportation is further strengthened through the imaginative leadership of the Greater Hartford Chamber of Commerce. The chamber and its Transportation Committee serve as an integrating mechanism for the public transportation program, the Rideshare Corporation, and the Downtown Council consisting of civic leaders concerned with downtown development. In Hartford public transportation service has transcended the traditional distinctions between the public and private sectors. What has emerged instead is a melding of the two sectors in a true community partnership.

The Stamford Metropool. In Stamford, Connecticut, as in Hartford, the private sector has played a major role in employee transportation. During the early 1970s Stamford and its immediate surroundings became a prime location for corporate headquarters. The large influx of new companies created a drain on nearby housing and forced many employees to commute long distances to work. This, in turn, led to recruitment problems. By 1979, some corporations were experiencing a 60 percent rejection rate in their recruiting efforts.

As a solution, the corporate community adopted a regional ride-sharing program, covering Fairfield County, where Stamford is located, and adjoining Westchester County, New York. A nonprofit corporation, Metropool, was established, with an initial membership of eight companies (later expanded to twenty) and capital of $100,000, raised through membership contributions. As with the Hartford corporation, members of Metropool consider its mission to be more than just the provision of van-pool services to corporate employers. They view it as an integrated public/private transportation management organization that will eventually offer an array of transportation services to clients throughout the suburban New York region. Here again is a fusion of public and private responsibilities and interests.

Tysons Transportation Association. Twenty-five years ago Tysons Corner in suburban Northern Virginia consisted of a small general store and a gas station. Today, with over 9 million square feet of office and commercial space, Tysons is a bustling suburban mini-city. In addition to a large regional shopping mall, it contains two office parks and a host of hotels, restaurants, banks, and insurance offices. Significantly, it also has some high-rise residential apartment buildings. Tysons's daytime population is 25,000 people, who come to work in 20,000 automobiles, creating gigantic traffic jams twice a day. Despite its traffic congestion, Tysons continues to grow. It is adding 1 million square feet of office space a year, which means 4,000 new employees and 3,000 autos. At this rate, the number of cars coming into Tysons will approach 35,000 by 1986—without any possibility of major road improvements.

This prospect of bigger traffic problems has catalyzed the local business community into action. Fifty of the largest companies at Tysons and the major developers have banded together with the support of the county to form a nonprofit association to take whatever steps may be necessary to improve the transportation conditions within the zone.

The members assess themselves annual membership fees and with the help of that money have launched an area-wide van-pool program for the commuting employees and a free shuttle bus service for the daytime convenience of employees, residents, and visitors. The association's goal is to remove 4,000–5,000 cars from the roads by 1986, while expanding mobility within the center to give it more cohesion and create a greater sense of community.

269

El Segundo Employers Association. The El Segundo/International Airport complex in Los Angeles's South Bay area is emerging as a major high-density urban center. It is estimated that by 1984 the area will have 8 million square feet of office space, over 9,000 hotel rooms, and a daytime population of 168,000. More than $860 million will be spent on 6 million square feet of industrial and office space in the next three years. This development, within a two-mile radius of the airport, will add 194,000 vehicle trips daily to the already over-burdened roads.

Concerned about the worsening traffic conditions, a number of major corporations in the immediate area formed the El Segundo Employers Association (ESEA) to find solutions to the area's growing transportation problems. The founding members represent nearly 70,000 of the 100,000 employees working in the El Segundo area and include such major firms as Hughes, Xerox, TRW, Northrop, and Rockwell.

One of the first tasks of the new association has been the development of a transportation management plan for the area. The aim of the ESEA plan is to offer a variety of traffic improvements and commuting alternatives: the use of reversible lanes to speed up traffic in rush hours, an area-wide car-pool and van-pool program, an employment-oriented bus service with flexible routes and schedules, a co-operative system for scheduling work hours, a bike path system for employees living nearby, and, possibly, a trolley line linking El Segundo with several communities to the south where many of the employees live. Funds for the association's operations come from a voluntary assessment on the participating corporations.

Similar efforts have been made in the suburbs of several other major cities: City Post Oak, near Houston; California's Santa Clara County; and Sacramento, California. Examples of cooperative efforts to solve the transportation problems of downtown areas include the Central City Association of Los Angeles, the Denver Partnership, Inc., and the Newark Renaissance.

Conclusions

As these examples show, a new approach to transportation service delivery is emerging. It is an approach based on community partnership between the private and public sectors. Community partnerships can take many forms, but they all share a common vision: to create an environment that will catalyze and foster expanded involvement of the private sector and closer public/private cooperation in community affairs. Community partnerships are not alternatives to the local political process, nor are they blue ribbon study commissions or discussion groups. They are action-oriented alliances of local governments, businesses, civic organizations, and philanthropic institutions, with well-defined agendas and a commitment to pool public and private resources to solve community problems.

These public/private partnerships may be the vanguard of a new form of governance—a new grass-roots approach to local problems that is neither fully public nor fully private, but is instead a merging of public and private interests in new institutional settings. Transportation management associations may be the clearest manifestation yet of this new form of collaborative grass-roots governance.

Private Meets Public:
An Examination of
Contemporary Education

Marsha Levine and Denis P. Doyle

Adaptation to decline is going to be a very important skill in the years ahead. If we are only adapted to growth, then we are likely to make a tragic mess of decline. There is a strong case to be made for the argument that decline requires greater skill, better judgment, a stronger sense of community, and a higher order of leadership than growth does. It is easy to adjust to growth. If you make mistakes, time will generally correct them. If you put too much into one segment of the system, all you have to do is wait a little while and hold back the growth of the overextended section and the other sections will catch up with it. In decline, however, time aggravates mistakes. It makes it much harder to achieve the proper proportions of the system, as it is the achieving of these proper proportions which is one of the major functions of leadership.

KENNETH BOULDING

Introduction

Government influences our modern mixed economy in many ways, direct and indirect. Frequently the public sector directly operates or finances such services as health care, nutrition, housing, and education; it also influences the way in which the private sector provides services. Governmental regulation of the private sector weaves a complex web of public involvement in private decision making, blurring the distinction between purely public and private and making it difficult to delineate the two sectors precisely.

Nowhere is this more true than in the field of education and training. Government transfer payments to individuals and institutions, government rules and regulations, government-owned and -operated schools—in direct competition with private institutions—are only the most obvious examples of public sector involvement in education. In fact, at one level of analysis, "purely private" education institutions exist at the pleasure of the state: articles of incorporation, the authority to establish and enforce contracts, and the terms and conditions of operation and organization are controlled by government. And in the twentieth century, government's power to tax—or not to tax—extends further control over private education. Eligibility for tax-exempt status and the regulation of private financial transactions —gifts, bequests, and donations—have a powerful impact on the health, even the life, of private institutions. (See figure 1 for an illustration of the mixture of public and private sources in institutions of higher education.)

Moreover, private education is subject to explicit government regulation that varies with the jurisdiction in which the school is located. Health and safety regulations apply to private schools everywhere, and in some states other, more comprehensive regulatory requirements are imposed: licensing of teachers, curricular standards, and the length of the school day and school year are often subject to some measure of government control.

That this should be so is perfectly understandable, if not entirely desirable. Education, at least in the primary and early secondary schools, is central to our political and economic well-being. Education for citizenship is as old as the republic; indeed, it is impossible to imagine a healthy and vigorous republic without an educated citizenry. Historically, however, education has never been a major responsibility of the federal government; states, localities, and private citizens have managed and operated schools since the founding. Today, for example, some 16,000 locally selected school boards and committees set policy for the nation's public elementary and secondary schools. (Approximately 90 percent of children attend public schools, 10 percent private schools; see table 1.) Historical circumstances have led to a situation in which state and local governments provide education by owning and operating schools.

It is possible, of course, to imagine a wholly different set of arrangements from those now in place to accomplish the ends of government support for education—vouchers or tax credits, for example—but national practice is striking in its uniformity. Schools throughout the nation are more alike than dissimilar, even though they are not subject to centralized government control.

FIGURE 1

Revenues and Expenditures of Institutions of Higher Education, by Source and Function

Public Institutions **Private Institutions**

Revenues: Where the Money Comes From

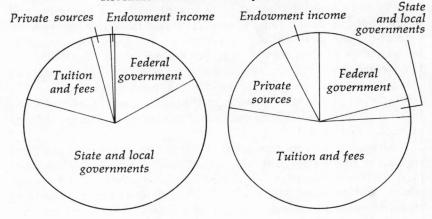

Expenditures: Where the Money Goes

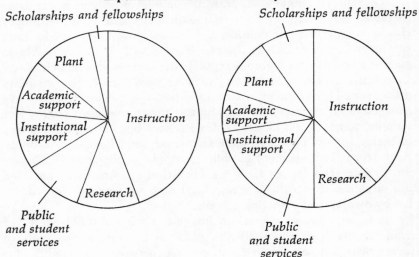

Source: U.S. Department of Education, National Center for Education Statistics, *The Condition of Education, 1981*, p. 171.

TABLE 1

ENROLLMENT, EXPENDITURES, AND NUMBERS OF ELEMENTARY AND
SECONDARY PUBLIC AND PRIVATE SCHOOLS, 1968–1989

			Projected 1988-89	
	1968-69	*1978-79*	Amount	Percent change from 1978-79
Enrollment (millions)				
Public	45.0	42.6	39.3	−8
Private	5.8	5.0	5.6	12
Expenditures ($ billion)				
Public	35.2	89.4	100.6	13
Private	4.0	10.6	14.0	32
Number of schools				
Public	102,026	96,501	n.a.	—
Private	19,946	18,500	n.a.	—

n.a. — not available.

SOURCES: National Center for Education Statistics, *Digest of Education Statistics*, 1981, p. 14; and *Digest of Education Statistics*, 1970, p. 6 (public figures for number of schools are for 1967-1968, private for 1965-1966).

Because of this uniformity, it is useful to examine contemporary practice. Generally, children are received in the early years and move through a linear education progression that eventually leads to the workplace. This is true of the private as well as the public school world. And it is true of those prepared for the learned professions as well as for vocations. Even though time in school and quality of schooling differ markedly for different students, the trajectory from infancy to adulthood and the world of work typically describes the same curve. The principal differences are in the length of the curve, the manual laborer who may drop out of school at fourteen riding a short curve and the neurosurgeon who remains a "student" until the mid-thirties riding as long a curve as one is likely to find.

This obvious point is raised to illuminate two dimensions of American education: its uniformity reflects shared national purposes rather than central government orchestration. One major purpose is education for citizenship, socialization, and acculturation. The other is education as human capital formation, the preparation of men and women to take their place in the nation's work force. The literature of education and political science has treated the question of education for citizenship extensively, and additional comment on this important idea is not warranted here. We are concerned with education as it forms human capital.

We raise the issue of human capital not in the technical sense in which economists might deal with it—that is beyond our scope and purpose—but as policy makers perforce *must* deal with it. Education for what? No school board, no state legislative education committee, no corporate official, indeed no prospective student, can avoid it. We are at this point not interested in the difficult normative question of who should pay for human capital formation. Rather, we are concerned with describing current practice. The questions of who benefits, who gains, and who should pay have been discussed more thoroughly and skillfully by a number of writers, such as Theodore W. Schultz and Milton Friedman;[1] we mention them because they are central to an analysis of private-public interaction in education. If education is viewed in economic terms—as it must be if the private sector is involved—we must sort out in a preliminary way some of its implications for human capital. Friedman makes the point with a modest but powerful example: "It is only in modern times and in a few countries that literacy has ceased to have a marketable value."[2]

Although an important distinction between education for citizenship and human capital formation can be made, we do not make it here. In our recent history, a social decision has been made to educate more and more people for longer and longer periods of time, largely at public expense. But three trends are emerging that have important implications for the future.

The most dramatic is the most recent: major cuts in government aid for education. This can either accelerate the process of greater private investment in human capital or reduce total investment. We do not yet know what the effects will be, but they highlight the second trend.

A less dramatic but even more important trend has been a spontaneous and substantial increase in private sector investment in education and training well before government spending reductions were proposed. These areas of private sector investment in education have just begun to be the focus of systematic research and study. Only recently, for example, have useful data become available for private elementary and secondary institutions; and we can still only estimate the extent of industry-based education and training. Unfortunately, there are no hard numbers available to document growth in industry-based education and training and no aggregate enrollment figures. In fact, one important outcome of this investigation is to

FIGURE 2

EXPENDITURES IN PUBLIC AND PRIVATE INSTITUTIONS OF HIGHER
EDUCATION AND FOR INDUSTRY-BASED EDUCATION AND TRAINING
(billions of dollars)

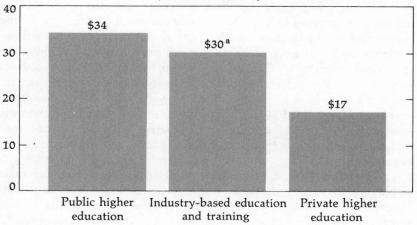

[a] Industry-based figure estimated by American Society for Training and Development.

SOURCE: National Center for Education Statistics, fiscal year 1979, as shown in "College and University Finances," *Chronicle of Higher Education*, August 25, 1980.

show the need for systematic collection of data on education in collaborative and nontraditional settings.

The estimates we do have indicate that the amount of money being invested in education and training by business and industry is approximately equal to the amount being spent in public postsecondary institutions (see figure 2). The $30 billion estimate made by the American Society for Training and Development (ASTD) includes

> expenditures for in-house (employer provided) education and training—instructors' salaries; hardware and software; training facilities; research, design, planning, administration, and evaluation of the training/development function; tuition assistance for employees; seminars and workshops; consultant services, related travel and living expenses; correspondence courses and other forms of self-study media, plus indirect cost of overhead allocation. It does not include the costs of wages and salaries to those being trained.[3]

277

It also does not include the costs of collaborative programs and training. Adding personnel costs would raise the estimate substantially. This illustrates a difficulty in making estimates: not everyone counts the same things.

Although aggregate enrollment figures are not available for industry, a sense of scope can be inferred from figures for public postsecondary institutions, which enroll approximately 9 million students with approximately the same expenditures as industry-sponsored education. The percentage of adult education courses provided by the private sector offers another estimate of extent. Although schools at all levels, including vocational, trade, and business schools, provided 57 percent of all such courses in 1978, the next largest provider was business and industry, with 11 percent (see table 2); and there are indications that the industry sector has grown since then.

When the data on instruction provided by employers for their employees are broken down by category of employer, industry is by far the largest provider. Schools and government agencies are second and third. Another indicator of growth is the increasing membership of the ASTD, which has doubled in the past ten years and is now reported at 40,000.[4]

We discuss this phenomenon at greater length in "Myths and Shadows," but our conclusion bears repeating.[5] The increase in private sector investment in education is related to qualitative deficiencies in public sector education. Too many workers are poorly prepared, and too many public schools are not offering the kind and quality of education employees need. The private sector turned to its own education and training in the 1960s and 1970s not because too few people were being educated but because those who were, were not being educated well enough. The manpower skills employers needed were not for sale in the marketplace.

The third trend is the downward slope of American productivity. Highlighted by efficient foreign competition, decreases in American productivity emerge as a major problem. Because of the importance of human capital to productivity, acquired skills and abilities are central to American economic health.

The changes we have noted, then, were not the product of ideological or political shifts, but were pragmatic responses to real problems. And America is nothing if not pragmatic. It is not too much to assert that our public policies derive from our private practice: when practice changes, so does public policy. That is why we think private sector involvement in education is of the utmost importance.

TABLE 2
COURSES IN ADULT EDUCATION, BY TYPE OF PROVIDER OF INSTRUCTION, YEAR ENDING MAY 1978

	Number of Courses (thousands)	Percentage Distribution
Provider of instruction		
School	16,554	57.3
Elementary, junior, or high school	2,725	9.4
Two-year college or vocational-technical institute	5,321	18.4
Four-year college or university	5,666	19.6
Vocational, trade, or business school	1,933	6.7
Other school	909	3.1
Business or industry	3,165	11.0
Labor organization or professional association	1,086	3.8
Government agency	2,445	8.5
Private community organization	2,394	8.3
Tutor or private instructor	1,338	4.6
Other	1,268	4.4
Did not know	100	0.3
Not reported	544	1.9
Total	28,894	100.0
Employer-provided instruction for employees		
School	1,146	24.2
Business or industry	1,998	42.1
Labor organization or professional association	213	4.5
Government agency	985	20.8
Private community organization	116	2.4
Other	283	6.0
Total	4,741	100.0

NOTE: Details may not add to totals because of rounding.
SOURCE: U.S. Department of Education, National Center for Education Statistics, *The Condition of Education, 1981*, p. 24.

It is, of course, tempting to speculate about the way in which theory informs practice: might an alternative conceptual framework lead to different education arrangements? But that is beyond the purposes of this chapter. Here we are concerned with practice: what is going on, what changes appear to be taking place, and what present trends suggest for the future. This exercise is less prosaic than it might appear at first glance. "What is going on" is not so widely known as one might think; the scope of private sector involvement in education is larger and more varied than is commonly known.

In the first part of this chapter, we report and comment on our preliminary examination of the recent and sustained growth of education in the private sector. We describe some of the myths that characterize and obscure this little-examined field and sketch its size and complexity. We observe that a "shadow" private sector education system is already in place and that it has major public policy significance. We discuss three major elements of education in the private sector. First is the steady and sustained growth of private elementary and secondary schooling just as American public education is entering a period of unprecedented enrollment decline. Second is the growth of business and corporate education and training programs. Third is the emergence of private sector relationships with traditional education institutions, public and private, higher and lower. This section examines a wide range of activities, from private and corporate philanthropy to partnerships between business and schools.

We suggest that these phenomena are linked, that they reflect significant demand for high-quality education, and that they imply the development of long-term trends that may permanently alter American education. We are convinced that the clients of education view it as an investment and act accordingly. Parents who choose to send their children to a tuition-charging school rather than a "free" public school are making an investment in an outcome for their children's future that they prefer to what they believe might result from accepting a free public education. They may be interested in a particular value orientation or in a religious education, but whatever their motives, they are convinced that a difference in quality exists.

The involvement of business and corporations with public school systems reflects a similar orientation. Our research reveals a broad range of motives for partnerships between business and education—from pure public relations to true altruism. It is clear that business and industry are questioning the ability of public schools to produce a competent work force that is adequately and appropriately educated. They are also beginning to assume some responsibility with public schools for meeting those needs. Similarly, research partnerships between industry and universities reflect an investment orientation toward education. Finally, this investment behavior is seen nowhere more clearly than in the enormous undertaking of business and labor as providers of education and training.

In this chapter we examine what education as an investment looks like in actual practice and what it may mean for public policy.

We look closely at several examples of private sector involvement in education to identify motives, processes, and problems. Of necessity, we limited our inquiry to the role of the private sector in certain high-priority areas.

In postindustrial democracy, reliant on high technology, embedded in a complex web of international trade and defense alliances, the areas of highest priority are obvious. Science, mathematics, and communication are basic to the economy, defense, and political life. Related areas—computer science, engineering, basic and applied research—fan out from these.

While that is clearly not the whole story (we still have pressing needs in the humanities and the arts), science and mathematics education offers a manageable analytic task and has two important additional advantages as a subject of study. One, there is national agreement about the importance of these areas. Two, the second-order issues these subjects raise ripple into the education enterprise as a whole. The problems associated with strengthening mathematics instruction in the high school, for example, raise every issue known to analysts of education: teacher licensing, tenure, and salary structure; school organization; management and personnel policies; pedagogy, curriculum, and materials; the economics and public finance of education; and practical questions about taxes and revenues.

The case studies we have selected illustrate three themes: one, a perception, shared by educators and the private sector, of education as an investment; two, the development and utilization of links between education and business to share responsibility; and three, the pooling of resources to invest in the development of human capital.

Our findings lead us to some conclusions about the significance of the role of the private sector in education. We believe that for the 1980s and beyond, relationships between education and business must increasingly be built on mutual understanding of the connection between education and productivity. The development of human capital is the key. Only through shared understanding of education as an investment can the resources of both sectors be tapped. Quality education is necessary both for individual growth and for economic development.

Private Elementary and Secondary Schools: Family Investments in the Future

The first aspect of private sector involvement in education we address is the recent growth of private elementary and secondary education. Unfortunately, public attitudes toward private schools are shaped by myth, but several recent developments permit us to examine private education more systematically and to draw some tentative conclusions about its role in contemporary society. Data are more readily available and of better quality than they have been. The National Center for Education Statistics (NCES) now counts the same things in the private school world as in the public, and it presents the information by type of private school. This simple development is immensely important, for it permits us to separate data on Catholic schools, which constitute about two-thirds of the private school universe, from those on other private schools. Our historical inability to do so produced curious findings, of the kind one would experience in trying to deal with questions about rural New York state if the data base did not permit holding New York City data to one side.

The principal misconception caused by aggregate private school data was that private school enrollments as a whole were declining. They were not. Catholic school enrollments were declining—more than a million students lost in one decade—but they dropped for some of the same reasons the public schools declined: a drop in live births among Catholics, coupled with decisions by the church hierarchy to reduce capital outlays and increase tuition charges in parish schools, made declines in enrollment inevitable. But collecting total data for private schools hid the fact that other, non-Catholic enrollments were increasing in the 1970s (see table 3). And there is very strong evidence that the Catholic decline has leveled off; there is even reason to believe that Catholic school enrollment may increase in the mid-1980s,[6] despite the fact that there are no government programs (except Minnesota's modest tax deduction) that help families meet the cost of tuition in private schools.

For some reason, or set of reasons, more and more Americans are deciding to buy something that is otherwise free. The absolute shift toward private schooling is still not large, but the percentages are impressive. Although public school enrollments are projected to decline by several percentage points a year, the National Center for Education Statistics predicts a private school enrollment increase of 12 percent by 1985.

The percentages sound impressive until one remembers that the base is about 5 million students in private schools, 42 million in public. Nevertheless, the trends are potentially significant because of who the children enrolled in private schools are. If those who enroll are children of the nation's quality-conscious parents, public schools may find themselves losing an important constituency.

TABLE 3
Nonpublic School Enrollment Trends, 1965–1976

	Enrollment		Percent Change
	1965-66	1975-76	
Roman Catholic	5,573,810	3,415,000	−38.7
Lutheran			
Missouri Synod	171,966	165,604	−3.7
Wisconsin Synod	27,448	31,183	13.6
American	8,795	16,121	83.3
Evangelical			
National Association of Christian	32,003	23,185	−27.6
West Association of Christian	11,388	63,131	454.4
Assembly of God	3,110	21,921	604.9
Jewish			
Orthodox	68,800	82,200	19.5
Conservative	3,489	7,965	128.3
National Association of Independent Schools	199,329	277,406	39.2
Episcopal (nonparish)	55,060	71,020	29.0
Quaker	10,878	13,801	26.9

SOURCE: Susan Abramowitz and Stuart Rosenfield, eds., *Declining Enrollments: The Challenge of the Coming Decade* (Washington, D.C.: National Institute of Education, March 1978).

(One important qualification about private school data should be noted. Existing private school data bases do not include so-called Christian academies, the segment of private education that some analysts describe as growing the most rapidly. As a rule, these schools do not appear in the statistical compilations of the National Center for Education Statistics, nor are they members of old-line private education interest groups. Whatever their size, they are clearly an important phenomenon, but we know too little about them to include them in our discussion.)

In a preliminary and tentative way, we are able to address the subtle and important question of school quality. The work of James Coleman and Andrew Greeley in this country and Rutter and his colleagues in England makes a powerful case for school effects, in which it is clear that certain schools have a far stronger impact than others on low-income, low-achieving youngsters.[7] The American findings are surrounded by controversy, not because the authors found that schools have effects but because they found stronger and more positive effects in private schools. The English researchers had the wit or good luck to confine their comparisons to government schools. And their findings were no surprise to parents, teachers, and students. Some schools are better than others. Such schools can be identified. Other things being equal, it is better to attend a good school than a bad one. Most important, poor children—those most likely to fail in school—do significantly better in good schools. Cast in these terms, the issue is hardly controversial, though what public policies are to be adopted as a consequence of this knowledge is not as clear.

In this country, however, the research of Coleman and Greeley, because it compared public and private schools, has not been warmly received by the education establishment. The negative reaction reveals the ideological character of much social science research and demonstrates, in an important way, how threatening private schools are to public school educators.[8]

At one level, the argument about quality in education is moot, because by definition parents who prefer the fee-charging private market to the free public alternative have unequivocally expressed a strong and frequently expensive preference. They believe there is a difference in quality that is worth the price. It is for this reason that public educators find private education unsettling; it is disconcerting to have fewer takers for a free service that in form at least is much like one the client of private education buys in the market.

The growth of private schooling in the face of public school decline is a challenge of such consequence that policy analysts, policy makers, and public school educators cannot afford to ignore it. Even if tuition tax credits for education were not on the nation's agenda, it would be essential to understand the phenomenon of private school growth. Government schools must know what it is their private competition does to attract and hold students.

In examining the growth of private schools, there are three principal elements of interest: opportunity, motivation, and behavior. Because we believe that families' choice of private schools is a form of investment, it is no coincidence that these elements describe investment generally.

First, the opportunity to attend private schools is today greater than ever. Reduced family size, the delay of first childbearing, and the increase in two-income families now make it possible for many more families to consider private schooling as a realistic option. The importance of more women entering the labor force cannot be overemphasized, for it profoundly affects opportunities (both realized and forgone), motivation, and behavior. On average, for example, two-income families earn 20 percent more than single-income families.

Second, analysis of the motives for attending private schools is necessarily speculative but no less useful for that. Among the motives are such obvious reasons as the desire for physical safety and a disciplined environment. Of great importance to many parents is a school that imparts religious and moral values. For some, social status figures prominently in private school decisions.

Whatever the specifics, there is a quality difference that leads to private school enrollment. And that quality difference involves those things schools are especially suited to do well: academic and vocational instruction, building and reinforcing acquired skills, transmitting culture and values, and building character—a slightly old-fashioned, but nevertheless important, goal. In short, parents look to schools to do those things they are organized to do, and they look to better schools to do the job better. The rhetorical fog of research and policy analysis surrounding education must not obscure this simple truth.

There is a final word on motivation: is it linked to antisocial desires for socioeconomic and racial isolation? Here the evidence is mixed: there are, of course, ignoble motives at work in any social institution, but no evidence supports the idea that established private schools are havens for whites escaping their social responsibilities. The evidence suggests that many private schools have met their social obligations more successfully than their public counterparts. And it is from behavior that we must infer motives.

Who actually attends private schools, and how do private schools deal with the larger community? First, private schools charge fees; and the lower a family's income, the more onerous even the lowest fee. It should come as no surprise, then, to discover that private school enrollments are moderately well correlated with income; there are few very poor families in private schools. But there are some, for two reasons. Some families are willing to make heroic financial sacrifices to send their children to private schools, and most poor children in private schools receive private financial aid. This point is hardly noteworthy except when we consider a curious aspect of public elementary and secondary education: no scholarships are available in the public sector. This practice is so deeply ingrained and so commonplace it is taken for granted. Indeed, why do public school districts not offer scholarships? They do charge tuition to nonresidents. They do not provide scholarships because of force of habit rooted in neighborhood assignment to school; could a more rigorous form of exclusivity be imagined?

TABLE 4

ENROLLMENT CHANGES BY ETHNIC BACKGROUND, CATHOLIC
ELEMENTARY AND SECONDARY SCHOOLS, 1970–1981

	1970-71	1980-81	Change	
			Number	Percent
Total	4,363,600	3,106,300	−1,257,300	−28.8
Black	209,500	252,900	43,400	20.7
Hispanic	216,500	256,000	39,500	18.2
Asian	23,500	52,100	28,600	121.7
All minority[a]	449,500	561,000	111,500	24.8

[a] American Indians, who make up less than one-half of 1 percent of Catholic schools enrollments, are not included.

SOURCE: Bruno Manno, "A Statistical Report on U.S. Catholic Schools 1978-81," National Catholic Education Assocation, February 1981.

The second question central to private school interaction with the larger community is that of participation rates by race and ethnicity. When income is controlled for, being black is not negatively correlated with private school enrollment. There is even preliminary evidence that middle-class blacks are overrepresented in private schools.

But the most interesting private school phenomenon of the past two decades is the role of Catholic schools in the inner city. For many black families, the majority of whom are not Catholic, inner-city Catholic schools are an affordable alternative to a public school system in disarray. Gallup poll data consistently show the highest rate of dissatisfaction with urban public schools among inner-city blacks. Many urban blacks therefore want their children to attend Catholic schools, and it is noteworthy that many Catholic schools have responded with enthusiasm (see tables 4 and 5).

Of equal importance is the behavior of private school associations. The principal membership group of private schools, the Council for American Private Education, has strongly endorsed nondiscriminatory admission practices and has filed amicus briefs in court cases that challenge racially discriminatory practices. Today few if any established private schools remain unintegrated, an assertion that cannot be made of comparable suburban public schools. Again, we find private school behavior that runs counter to the conventional wisdom.

TABLE 5
Enrollment by Ethnic Background, Catholic Elementary and Secondary Schools, 1970–1981
(percent)

	1970-71	1980-81
Black	4.8	8.1
Hispanic	5.0	8.3
Asian	0.5	1.7
American Indian	0.5	0.3
All others	89.2	81.6

Source: Manno, "Statistical Report on U.S. Catholic Schools."

What are the implications for policy? Is the growth in private schooling simply an independent phenomenon that has no bearing on the world of public policy, or does it suggest a larger meaning? It seems clear to us that there is some larger meaning. A movement of this kind has at least three kinds of implications.

First is the question of public regulation of private schools. Since they maintain a small but important market share, should they be regulated in some more comprehensive way? The issue will surface even without proposals for public funding, because the vigor of private schools brings them to the attention of policy makers. But the independence and flexibility of private schools are precisely what make them interesting, both as a subject of research and as an opportunity for investment in human capital. Further regulation could do inestimable harm.

Second is the central question of public aid to private schooling, through the tax system or more direct means. America is the world's only advanced democracy that does not provide aid to nongovernment schools. Particularly because private schools are vigorous and growing, pressure will build to provide at least limited public support for them. The debate on this important question must be informed by high-quality data and thoughtful analysis; although data and analysis cannot resolve the discussion, they can give it a civil tone and permit honest differences of opinion to appear. We do not have time or space for thorough exploration of proposals for public aid for private schooling, but the issue may be the most important item on the nation's education agenda in the 1980s because it represents an opportunity to increase the ability of individuals or families to invest in themselves and their children's future.

Third, and most important, is the effect of both private school growth and research and analysis of such growth on the public sector. As private school enrollments continue to increase, will the public sector sit idly by, anxiously wringing its hands, or will it do something more imaginative than complain that private schools have all the breaks? That private schools can hire whom they like, fire whom they dislike, accept or reject students on whimsical or substantive grounds, organize their curricula as they see fit, is viewed with envy and alarm by many public school officials. A more creative response to these issues would be to deregulate public schools—restore some measure of teacher professionalism, student standards, and family choice. In short, public schools should themselves provide a basis for individual investment in schooling. Nonfinancial investments in public schools in terms of parental involvement, commitment, or loyalty are possible—and can be a source of enormous institutional strength.[9]

The notion that public schools have to tolerate deviant and antisocial behavior—that those students who want to learn are prevented from doing so by others who do not care to learn—is public policy run amok. Moreover, the "new knowledge" that at least some schools work, that they have effects on student behavior and outcomes, should act as an incentive and stand as an opportunity for the public schools to improve themselves.

As we have tried to suggest, the myths about private schooling are both substantial and unsubstantiated. The evidence suggests that they are not havens for white flight, the province of elites and hard hats who are avoiding their social responsibility. On the contrary, today's private schools satisfy many of the conditions that make them servants of a larger public. They are racially and socioeconomically integrated; they provide safe physical and academic environments; they demand much of their students; and much is demanded of them.

Although they are far from perfect institutions, they are communities of shared interest—common schools, if you will—that meet an important social need. Dispelling the myths about private schools will do much to improve the quality of discussion about them; it may even permit more evenhanded and sensible public policies toward both public and private schools to emerge. We might begin to think seriously about an accommodation with private education, in which some measure of public support is made available. Of more importance, however, is what the growth in private schools tells us about how Americans view education generally. Given the opportunity, an increasing number of parents are looking at education as an investment, with more desirable returns available in the private sector.

Industry-Based Education and Training

Another dimension of private sector involvement in education is the role of business as a provider of education. Others have studied this area extensively.[10] Our purpose is to describe the kinds of involvement that exist, interpret them in the context of the private sector view of education, and discuss some of their implications for policy.

Our best estimates are that industry spends $30 billion annually on education and training, an amount approximately half of what is spent on postsecondary education. The goal of this investment is to increase productivity and profitability. The amount invested and the form and focus of corporate education and training depend on the answers to two important questions. First, is it cheaper to buy or to make a trained work force? Second, what kind of education and training is needed? The answer to the first question depends on who is available for employment, how much business training costs, and the extent to which costs can be passed on as a cost of production. The answer to the second question is even more problematic. While evidence about declining productivity mounts, the factors that contribute to it are not clear: outdated job skills, declining job satisfaction, and poor employee morale all play a part. As Lynton indicates, the outcome of the debate on productivity will certainly affect the focus and content of corporate education and training.[11]

In the meantime, the steady growth in corporate education and training indicates that industry has reached some tentative conclusions. Some corporate programs are not offered by traditional education institutions. They are job-specific training rather than education. Others overlap the offerings of schools and universities. Industry provides its own because it believes university courses are inadequate or inappropriate. Businesses often need flexible, nontraditional education delivery systems, such as short courses designed to fit into work schedules or career development patterns or courses taught on site at unconventional times.

Course content is also related to the specific technical or management skills needed for the job. With the accelerated pace of change in business practices and procedures, requirements for training increase. This is particularly significant for new high-technology industries, but older industries such as transportation, manufacturing, and insurance are changing too. Employee turnover, expansion of the work force, the need to modify skills to improve effectiveness, and requirements for advancement within a company create a continuing demand for training. In some companies, such as IBM, an extensive retraining program has allowed the corporation to avoid employee layoffs as a matter of policy.[12]

The organization of education and training programs in business and industry is diverse. It is related to the size of the company and the nature of the business. Some programs are designed and implemented in house, some are offered through contractual arrangements with public and private education institutions, and some are cosponsored with unions.

The setting can also vary. Some corporations (for example, IBM, Xerox, Uniroyal) operate full-service residential corporate education centers. The Xerox International Center for Training and Management Development in Leesburg, Virginia, is a model of such a center, providing education and training in sales, service, and management development for Xerox employees. It has a permanent full-time staff of about 500 and a capacity of 980 students, who live on campus. Located on a 2,265-acre site, the center also has recreational and athletic facilities. All new Xerox sales personnel go to Leesburg for a basic sales course and return periodically for additional training. For service technicians, Leesburg offers fifty courses designed by education specialists to emphasize hands-on experience. The program for middle and upper management is taught by successful Xerox managers, themselves specialists in management training, with additional outside experts in specific fields. Since the opening of the center in 1974, 125,000 individual programs have been completed by Xerox employees.

Although most students at the center are Xerox employees, one program, designed to develop preliminary skills and knowledge, is aimed at members of minorities and women who are not Xerox employees. Candidates are recommended by branch offices after initial aptitude screening; there are no academic requirements. All expenses, including transportation and a small stipend, are paid by Xerox. The program, in which students pace themselves, usually lasts four weeks. After completing the program successfully, the students are eligible for employment by Xerox and continued training.

The Xerox center provides in-house training specific to the job and the company. Two other types of industry-based in-house programs more nearly resemble traditional education. At one end of the spectrum is education in remedial skills. A Conference Board study in 1977 found that 35 percent of the companies surveyed provided remedial education for employees. Unlike other education and training programs, these are viewed by industry as necessary but undesirable—forced investments, if you will. Some corporate representatives assert that their basic skills programs should and could be eliminated by more effective public school programs; others see them as an outgrowth of federal affirmative action programs. A few examples show the scale and nature of these activities:

- AT & T has 14,000 employees at any given time taking courses in basic mathematics and writing on company time at an annual cost of $6 million.
- Illinois Bank and Trust Company offers a twenty-week course in spelling, punctuation, and grammar to all new employees.
- Polaroid established its own remedial and bilingual programs for employees ten years ago, after deciding that local schools and colleges could not provide the services the company required.

Even more disturbing as a commentary on education, basic skills programs like these provide instruction for employees with college and advanced degrees as well as for high-school graduates.

At the other end of the education spectrum are corporation-sponsored formal education and degree-granting postsecondary programs. Some were developed to fill a specific void in traditional higher education offerings. Wang Laboratories created the Wang Institute, with a master's program in software engineering, when it could identify only two such programs in the nation. Other companies have developed programs for their specific needs or their employees'. The institutionalization of these programs has already begun. The Wang Institute and the in-house program of the Arthur D. Little Corporation now issue degrees approved by the Massachusetts Board of Education. Although most courses offered by industry still carry no formal academic credit, colleges and universities are under some pressure to accept such courses as credit toward degrees. The Program on Non-Collegiate Sponsored Instruction of the American Council on Education has identified 2,000 courses at 138 corporations that it recommends as suitable for credit. The New York State Board of Regents supports this effort. The regents' external degree program awards credit for such approved courses.

While programs like these compete directly with traditional post-secondary institutions, there are also collaborative efforts of industry and universities to develop degree programs. These are described in the next section. They are growing in number, and they promise more efficient use of resources. They may offer creative solutions to the problem of providing appropriate education and training of high quality.

Various reasons have been advanced for industry's increasing investment in education and training. Some analysts see it as a vote of no confidence in the ability of traditional education institutions to respond to preemployment and employee development needs. Another interpretation focuses on the size of the market: it is so large that it requires the response of both traditional institutions and business. Healthy competition for traditional postsecondary institutions may force higher education to reshape itself—perhaps into a bifurcated system of traditional universities and new "relevant" institutions, with unresponsive institutions going out of business.

There is truth in each interpretation. And it is equally true that continued growth will occur as long as corporations believe that development of human resources pays. Some larger corporations are convinced of that and include human resource development in their long-range strategic planning. The aging of the work force and changes in technology that require training and retraining accelerate movement in this direction. Further incentives could be provided to increased training and education by corporations. Tax incentives for human capital investment (comparable to those available for traditional capital equipment) or direct federal subsidies for corporate on-the-job training of the unemployed are possibilities. We return to these questions in our concluding section.

Partnerships between Industry and Education

The third aspect of private sector involvement in education is partnership between business and traditional education institutions. These relationships exist at all levels of education, involve small businesses and multinational corporations, and include public as well as private institutions.

Industry's involvement extends from philanthropic donations to private colleges to the joint development of a public high school for science and technology. The motives for involvement range from public relations to a recognition that investment in education produces returns in the form of a strengthened community or a more adequately prepared work force.

In this section we discuss the kinds of relationships that exist between sectors at the postsecondary and precollegiate levels and give examples. We conclude the section with a discussion of what these partnerships reveal about the potential of industry-education relationships and what role public policy may play to encourage them.

Partnerships between Institutions of Postsecondary Education and Industry

Private sector philanthropy, in the form of both direct grants to institutions and scholarship programs, has a long history. Corporate support of higher education continues to grow: the Council for Financial Aid to Education estimated it at $870 million in 1979,[13] more than double such support in 1975. Corporate giving, however, constitutes less than 2 percent of total spending on higher education. Industry's expanded interest in this area takes forms other than dollar investment.

University-Corporate Alliances. Corporate partnerships with universities in specific areas of basic and applied scientific research are growing. The gradual decline over the past ten years in federal support for research, coupled with soaring research and development costs and the potential for commercial profits, has led universities and corporations to join forces to perform research and development with commercial applications.

The issues before the university community are much the same as those raised by government support, which grew dramatically after World War II, with one important exception: corporate support gives universities an opportunity to reap substantial economic benefits.

Universities find corporate funding attractive not only because federal funds are diminishing but because the long-term effects of government funding are problematic. Government administration and regulation present serious problems. Moreover, corporations find private sector collaboration attractive because of potential applications in such fields as genetic engineering and microelectronics. Corporations see jointly sponsored basic research as an attractive way to "gain a window" on new technologies. For a relatively small grant or a share in potential profits, they gain access to leading researchers and an opportunity to be in on the ground floor. Furthermore, universities may provide a pool of qualified technical talent if the venture has commercial potential.

Companies and universities that have embarked on such partnerships include the Massachusetts Institute of Technology and Exxon in combustion research; Monsanto and Harvard Medical School in cancer research; IBM, Xerox, and Burroughs with the California Institute of Technology in integrated circuit technology; du Pont and Harvard Medical School in genetic engineering; and Control Data, Burroughs, and 3M with the University of Minnesota in integrated circuits.

Each arrangement is unique and involves a learning process for both sides. Typically, however, each partnership finds it is dealing with a similar set of problems: how to distribute the rewards from new discoveries, what methods to use for licensing potential inventions, and how to achieve an appropriate balance between scholarly

293

inquiry and industrial needs for proprietary advantage. Moreover, questions of shared financial support, outside reimbursement of faculty members, and the prospect of corporate influence on academic life raise profound ethical and moral problems. Consideration of institutional autonomy and integrity are important: will research priorities be guided by profit rather than traditional standards of disinterested inquiry? Similarly, how will the professional lives and roles of research professors and students be affected? Will status and rewards accrue to faculty members who develop commercial applications or to those who pursue more traditional paths?

These issues, of course, are not unique to corporate-sponsored research. They are present in the context of government-sponsored research as well; for example, is it consistent with the vision and purpose of a university to engage in weapons research?

It may be that we are witnessing the final stage in the maturation of the modern university symbolized by Enrico Fermi's creation of the first self-sustaining chain reaction in the early 1940s at the University of Chicago's Stagg Field. That day a dramatic product of government funding and university research emerged, introducing a new era. The advent of the corporation-university partnership is one more chapter in that book.

The relations that are being forged today will continue to be subjected to serious scrutiny and much soul searching; they will be filled with controversy as well as promise; and they warrant close examination in the future.

Shortages. A growing shortage of scientists and engineers and the poor quality of technical faculties leads to the second area of expanded corporate involvement with higher education. The boom in enrollments in undergraduate engineering programs and the shortage of graduate students and engineering teaching faculty result from the growth in high-technology industry and its ability and willingness to pay high salaries. They also reflect the limited ability of universities to respond to changes in demand and their limited financial resources. They are a dramatic illustration of the interlocking relation between education and manpower. Since 1970 the number of undergraduate engineering students has doubled (to over 360,000 in 1980), but the number of Ph.D.'s has declined from about 3,000 to 1,800.[14] The statistics on teaching faculty are similarly alarming. Roughly 10 percent of the 16,000 faculty engineering positions are vacant, and vacancy rates are even higher in specific areas such as computer science. In addition, many of America's engineering schools are equipped with obsolete laboratories and equipment.

Cuts in government funding and a concern over the nation's productivity and the role that technology plays in economic development have made this situation the focus of attention. A 1977 study by the National Science Foundation reported that high-technology industries had "twice the productivity, triple the real growth, six times fewer price increases, and nine times more employment" when compared with low-technology industries.[15] High technology, however, is highly dependent on highly skilled manpower. Because the stakes are so high, creative responses from government, industry, and academia are emerging.

The legislatures of a number of states are looking at the ability of their state universities' engineering education and research facilities to serve the high-technology industry they want to attract and retain. These states include Wyoming ($18 million budgeted to expand the engineering program), North Carolina ($24 million for the development of a microelectron center), New Mexico (developing a new engineering program in the state university), and Arizona (developing a $32 million Center for Excellence in Engineering). The last is a partnership of government, industry, and academia with contributions from such local industries as Motorola, Garrett Turbine, Honeywell, and Sperry Flight Systems. The money will increase the salaries of engineering faculty, add faculty, increase student enrollments, and build a center for research.[16]

Similar partnerships are being developed elsewhere. Stanford University and Texas Instruments, Hewlett-Packard, Xerox, and Fairchild Camera are developing a $72 million Center for Integrated Systems. At Carnegie-Mellon, Westinghouse, Digital, and the Office of Naval Research are sponsoring a Robotics Institute.

In addition to these partnerships, industry is encouraging initiatives that will provide both short-term remedies and a long-term resolution to the problem. To these ends, the American Electronics Association (AEA) has established the National Engineering Education Foundation. To ease the current crisis, it urges its members to contribute to the expansion of educational resources by increasing faculty through adjunct and visiting professors, establishing AEA teaching chairs, and providing industry consultancies for new faculty members to supplement their teaching income. It encourages the upgrading of university equipment through grants and equipment transfers. To promote systemic change and increase resource development, the fund encourages graduate student fellowships and loans to increase the number of engineers with doctorates; loan forgiveness clauses are included for recipients who become teachers. It is urging legislative action to increase budgets for equipment and facilities and salaries of engineering and computer science faculty in public universities.[17] A bill was recently introduced in California to create a salary differential for members of engineering faculties, putting them in a special category with medical school and law faculties. Although the bill was not enacted by the legislature, the Board of Trustees of the California State Universities has adopted special salary schedules for assistant professors in engineering, computer sciences, and business administration, designed to recruit and maintain junior faculty by making salaries more competitive with the private sector.

Individual corporations have established special funds to increase the numbers of engineering faculty and their salaries. The Exxon Education Foundation has established a $15 million program that will award grants to over sixty colleges and universities to support doctoral students in engineering and supplement salaries of untenured faculty members. Some corporate initiatives motivated by a concern for increasing the pool of qualified engineers focus on increasing the number of women and minority students in engineering. Du Pont and Dow Chemical have developed such programs.

Even from this brief survey of private sector initiatives in postsecondary engineering education it is clear that business is playing an important role in addressing a national problem. There are also indications that the private sector does not assume that the problem will be solved by money alone. Partnerships among government, industry, and universities (including the sharing of human, material, and financial resources) will require coordinated policy action by all three.

Cooperative Programs. The third area of corporate involvement with postsecondary education concerns cooperative programs for the education and training of employees. Some companies have turned to local two- and four-year colleges to provide specialized courses for their employees. These arrangements can make better use of resources and facilities, but, if they are to work, important issues must be settled. Often industry requires multidisciplinary courses, which are sometimes difficult for colleges to arrange. It requires curricula that encourage the transition from theory to practice, and often the traditional institutions are too theoretical in their approaches. In addition, industry requires flexibility in delivery systems—courses taught at odd hours or on site.[18]

Finally, major questions about academic autonomy, industry-developed curricula, and the appropriateness of noncredit offerings arise.[19] When industry and education deal creatively with these

LEVINE AND DOYLE

issues, new roles and the potential for substantial program diversity can result. The following are examples of such cooperative programs:

- AT & T and Pace University in New York have jointly developed an M.B.A. program for AT & T employees.
- The INA Corporation and the University of Pennsylvania have created a program in which INA employees can earn liberal arts degrees by attending University of Pennsylvania classes taught at INA corporate headquarters.
- John Wood Community College and the Harris Corporation in Illinois have an arrangement through which Harris provides technical instruction, facilities, and equipment and the college provides administrative services, counseling, and remedial education. A four-year college is under contract to provide liberal arts and general education to meet the needs of employers and the community.

Partnerships between Institutions of Precollegiate Education and Industry

While industry-based education and training are well established, the involvement of business in support of public schools is only beginning. Corporations are involved nationally in providing financial support, links to community resources, facilities, teacher development, curriculum development, advisory and planning assistance, and budget and management expertise in addition to volunteer activities that provide direct support to schools.

These activities have various purposes: to facilitate school-to-work transitions; to develop career awareness; to encourage business, economics, or free enterprise education; or to strengthen general or basic education. All these activities are in addition to the traditional involvement of industry in vocational education through cooperative education and work-study programs.

Involvement takes many forms: adopt-a-school projects, corporate volunteer programs, executive loans, Junior Achievement programs, teacher internships, special curriculum projects, and joint development of magnet schools. Some are short-term commitments; others reflect a commitment to long-term development of human resources.

Corporate involvement may serve interests from public relations to corporate social responsibility. It is fair to generalize only to the extent that some form of self-interest, whether immediate or indirect and long-term, is a primary motive. It is in the self-interest of the private sector to support a school system that can produce a pool of employable graduates, help retain valued employees in the community, and attract new employees. It is clear that many corporations recognize the relationship between a strong school system and meeting their short-term employment needs. It is less clear that they link support of the school system to their concern for long-term manpower needs.

A few examples of private sector–public schools partnerships and programs illustrate the activities and roles the private sector has assumed:

• ARCO/Joint Educational Project is sponsored by the Atlantic Richfield Company, the University of Southern California, and the Los Angeles Unified School District. It is aimed at improving high-school students' basic skills and assisting their parents. Employees are trained as volunteers by university faculty, and all volunteer activity is on company time.

• Private Initiatives in Public Education (PIPE) is sponsored by the Seattle Chamber of Commerce, the Seattle Teachers' Association, and several community organizations. Its main objective is to provide a mechanism by which the community resources of Seattle can be allocated to the public schools. Each school is paired with a major local business, and jointly they assess the school's needs and the resources available in the community to help meet them.

• Kaiser Aluminum and Chemical Company in Oakland, California, has contributed the time of 100 volunteers and over $400,000 in the last three years to establishing reading, career, and mathematics centers.

• Eastman Kodak Company in Rochester, New York, has more than 150 employees involved in programs designed to interest students in mathematics and science careers.

• Through the Allegheny Conference, a civic association of Pittsburgh business leaders, the private sector has contributed over $750,000 to an education fund to support Pittsburgh schools. Projects include school-business links, provision of computer services, in-service education for teachers in company-sponsored courses, student visits to corporate facilities, and direct financial support for innovative programs.

• Westinghouse Corporation, C & P Telephone, and ten southeast Washington, D.C., public schools are involved in a project aimed at improving schools through increased involvement of parents. The corporations match funds donated or raised by the parents for school improvement projects.

• Impact II, a project of the Exxon Education Foundation, focuses on the identification and dissemination of innovative teaching practices in New York City schools. Begun in 1980 through an arrangement with the Economic Development Council in New York City, the project distributes small grants to individual teachers to help develop and disseminate teacher-developed curricula and instructional innovations.

• Many school districts have adopt-a-school programs, which focus on channeling resources of the private sector to meet self-identified needs of individual schools and teachers. Sometimes called education-business partnerships to emphasize the mutuality of the relationship and shared responsibility, these programs can be found across the country. They may be initiated by school districts, chambers of commerce, or other local business groups. They typically have the support and involvement of the top leaders in both sectors. Adopt-a-school projects bring corporate personnel into schools as aides, tutors, technical assistants, curriculum advisers, and speakers.

We have described three arenas of private sector involvement in education: private elementary and secondary schools, industry-based education and training, and industry-education collaborations at the postsecondary and precollegiate levels. We have tried to indicate the breadth of activity and interpreted it as a response to increased demands for quality and diversity. We have also concluded that much of the growth in this area is viewed by families and industry as an investment in the development of human resources.

Unless public policies are adopted that will stimulate private school enrollments and industry-based training and education, further growth will be checked by self-limiting factors. Industry-education partnerships, however, may be more open ended, and their potential impact on public and private institutions may be very great.

To determine what potential these cooperative activities have for the future, we must understand the issues and the processes involved. To this end, we will explore some examples in greater detail. We are particularly interested in the critical problem of deficiencies in science, mathematics, and computer education and how they involve industry and the public schools. We have selected these examples for two reasons. First, we need to understand the potential for private sector initiative to improve public schools because they are the nation's most important agent for the development of human capital in the early years. Second, these partnerships should improve the quality of general education, in addition to addressing the narrower issue of training. We have selected examples from a broad field on the following bases:

- They are examples of different kinds of linkages.
- They address a variety of issues: in-service training for teachers, curriculum development, provision of facilities or equipment, volunteer programs, financial support.
- They are informative about the motives, processes, and problems as well as the outcomes of such partnerships.

Computers and Education. The introduction of computers and other communications technologies into schools is occurring in two ways: one, as an instructional system with rich potential for reinforcing and expanding the learning process and, two, as a curriculum area for professional and vocational development. The gap between the growing use of computers in industry and for personal use and the availability of computer education is widening[20] (see figures 3 and 4). The following private sector initiatives address this problem.

Industry-Education Council, Santa Clara County, California. Industry-education councils have sprung up in many states across the country as a result of business interest in better coordination with education and labor. Approximately 150 such councils exist.[21]

In Santa Clara County (which includes part of Silicon Valley), the Industry-Education Council (IEC), part of a statewide council supported by private industry, surveyed local businesses and found that 80 to 90 percent of their new employees need to understand how to use a computer system. Few schools, however, have the financial resources to provide the equipment and programs to build these skills. Since 1981 the IEC has sponsored a mobile computer facility to provide hands-on experience for district students. Actual computer time helps develop computer awareness and comfort, serves as a model for school programs, and provides market exposure to the equipment used. The project brings together the resources of the IEC; Atari equipment; members of Computer-Using Educators (CUE), a grass-roots organization of teachers who write the curriculum; and Mission College and San Jose State University, which staff the project. The van visits schools and college campuses at a minimal charge and serves both students and teachers.

FIGURE 3

Employment in Computer Occupations, 1970, 1980, and 1990

Thousands of persons

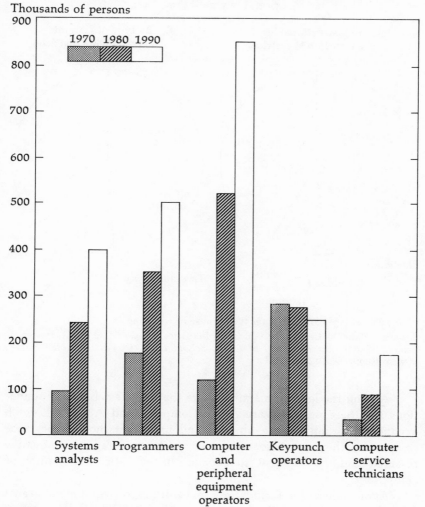

Source: Bureau of Labor Statistics.

Education foundations and corporate giving programs. Because equipment costs are a significant barrier to extensive use of computers in education, donations of computer equipment by manufacturers are important. In earlier days this was an informal practice, but new computer foundations formally donate equipment and encourage the development of software and innovative computer uses.

FIGURE 4

Districts Providing Students with Access to Computers for Instruction, United States, Fall 1980

A. By instructional level
(N = 15,834 districts)

B. By type of computer
(N = 15,834 districts)

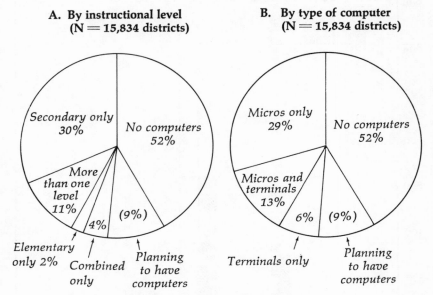

NOTE: Percentages may not total 100 because of rounding.

SOURCE: National Center for Education Statistics, *Student Use of Computers in Schools, Fall 1980: A Survey of Public School Districts*, Fast Response Survey System Report No. 12., p. 11.

Among the leading manufacturers that have established foundations for these purposes are Apple Computer and Atari. Although expanded markets are an obvious and important motive for these companies, they are also concerned with encouraging innovative research and development to expand the educational potential of computers.

Apple Education Foundation concentrates on equipment grants for software development. In its brief history, the Apple foundation has awarded equipment worth $900,000 for 146 proposals—10 percent of the applications—representing subjects from reading projects to art education. Awards are made to skilled professionals in nonprofit institutions to encourage broader application of computers for educational purposes.

The Atari Institute for Educational Action Research also makes awards to nonprofit institutions and individuals for the development of innovative uses of computers in education. With the participation of a twelve-member advisory board, the Atari Institute awarded half a million dollars in 1981 in equipment and cash stipends for the development of computer use in nonschool educational settings. The Lawrence Hall of Science Computer Education Project of the University of California at Berkeley and the Future Center at the Capital Children's Museum, Washington, D.C., are the recipients of two major cash and equipment grants. The institute plans to establish themes for each year's awards. Education in nonschool settings was the first theme; teacher training and early childhood applications might be themes for future years.

Broad areas are identified by the foundations' award makers, but the recipients are not limited by particular research questions; they define their own interests and needs. The manufacturers' marketing motive contributes to the development of innovative uses of computer technology in educational settings. The foundations can serve as a link between educators and industry. They can function as a clearinghouse for information, and they can facilitate cooperative projects among institutions, individuals, and industry.

Science, Mathematics, and Technology. The story of the declining quality of science and mathematics teaching and learning has been told from many perspectives. Schools report inadequacies in the preparation of teachers, minimal course requirements for graduation and for college admissions, archaic equipment and facilities in teaching and research laboratories, and declining performance by students on standardized tests. Industry reports deficiencies in skills and knowledge of entry-level employees, critical shortages of skilled workers, and projected needs for technically trained employees that at current rates of increase will continue to be unmet. A third perspective is the growing need to develop a science, mathematics, and computer literate population. As these areas become more a part of everyday life, a solid knowledge base is needed for informed decision making.

A National Research Council study, "The State of School Science," defines the problems in precollegiate science education. The statistics are in some cases startling. Two-thirds of our high schools offer only one year of science or of mathematics. Half of all high-school graduates have taken only one year of biology (their total science education) and have completed mathematics study with simple algebra. Calculus is studied by only 105,000 high-school students in the United States, and laboratory experience for those studying science has been effectively cut in half in the last decade by shortages of facilities and equipment.[22] National Assessment of Educational Progress studies show a decline in mathematics achievement of students of 1 to 4 percent between 1973 and 1978.

There are 10,000 physics teachers for 17,000 school districts in this country. Every state reports a shortage of mathematics teachers, and the National Education Association reports that the average beginning salary for a new mathematics teacher is 73 percent of what is being offered by industry.[23]

The following case studies address some of these critical problems.

Project to Increase Mastery of Mathematics. The Project to Increase Mastery of Mathematics (PIMM) in Connecticut is a model of interinstitutional collaboration, which addresses a specific, pervasive, yet elusive problem. Incorporating the architectural principle that form follows function, PIMM's organizational structure, its membership, and the processes and principles that guide its operations are consistent with the issue it addresses. The problem is the low level of mathematical understanding and competence among students and adults. Evidence of the problem can be found in students' performance on standardized tests, the number of job applicants turned away for lack of knowledge of arithmetic, algebra, and geometry, and the declining competence in mathematics among students entering colleges and universities.

Although the problem of declining mathematics competence can be simply stated, the factors that contribute to it are complicated, diverse, and difficult to address. It is affected by the behavior of individuals and organizations across society—parents, school administrators, teachers, colleges and universities, educators of teachers, legislators and public sector institutions, business and industry. Many people, for example, believe that mathematics is difficult, and an inability to perform mathematically is socially acceptable. In addition, there is a widely held view that boys are better than girls at mathematics. Parents reinforce these myths by not emphasizing the study of mathematics for their own children and by having relatively low expectations for their achievement. Teachers themselves are often victims of these myths and project negative attitudes and low expectations for their students' performance. The attitudes of parents and teachers, then, shape students' experiences and are reinforced by the society at large. Lack of awareness of the relevance of mathematics to life and job skills is another contributing factor. Motivation for learning is seriously weakened when the student is not aware of the relevance of the curriculum to his or her future needs. That this relevance is increasing rapidly is creating a critical problem.

Economic factors contribute as well. Computer facilities and equipment are costly. Critical shortages of skilled people in industry and the resulting high salaries cause a drain of good teachers from classrooms into industry. Finally, curricular and instructional factors contribute significantly to the lack of student mastery: too little time on problem solving, the too rapid introduction of abstract concepts, too little attention to the relations between applied and theoretical mathematics.

The question is how to tackle the problem. The PIMM response builds on the problem's breadth; even more to the point, it builds on individuals and organizations that both contribute to and are concerned about the problem. PIMM is a coalition—a joint effort of business and industry, teachers and school administrators, and university mathematicians concerned about the inadequate understanding and competence in mathematics of Connecticut school graduates. The basis for their concern varies: business and industry depend on a well-educated, skilled pool from which to draw employees; high-ranking academic institutions need to be able to maintain their high standards for admission and support their rigorous curricula; research depends on well-trained people; and school teachers and administrators need to provide instruction that can serve as a basis for the students' vocational goals and for their ability to function as responsible citizens.

These concerns arise from different needs, but they have the same objective. PIMM's strength is its ability to recognize that diversity of interest is an asset—it stimulates activity at different levels and in several directions by picking up many strands. Beyond that, the broad base of the coalition provides greater financial aid and human resources, extends its impact in many directions, and enables the various participants to understand each other better.

In the selection of projects, PIMM has capitalized on the interests of individuals and the concerns of the organizations or institutions they represent. In this way individuals feel they can work on their particular issue and bring their expertise and resources to bear on what is part of a multifaceted problem. Using this process, PIMM has established task forces on communications between education and business-industry-labor, teacher education, economic factors, attitudes toward mathematics, and the structure of instruction. Among their accomplishments PIMM cites the following projects:

- the preparation and distribution of a job analysis
- the development of a speakers' bureau
- the preparation and distribution of a guidance counselors' packet
- the offering (with financial help from the Joint Teacher Education Commission, the city of Middletown, and Wesleyan University) of an in-service mathematics course for elementary-school teachers in Middletown
- the sponsorship of a series of conferences throughout the state to discuss the role of computers in the schools: hardware and software, financing, levels of instruction
- the preparation of "real life" problem lists: problems, carefully arranged for different grade levels, illustrating topics of mathematics that relate to the workplace
- the offering of two in-service workshops in West Hartford—one for high-school teachers and the other for elementary-school teachers—to decrease math anxiety and increase math confidence

PIMM plans additional activities to increase the base of support from local businesses and industry. Currently financial support is received from Pratt and Whitney Aircraft, a division of United Technologies Corporation; Connecticut General Insurance; General Electric; and Wesleyan. The budget is modest—the major investment has been the commitment of the individual members.

The viability of a collaboration such as PIMM rests ultimately on individual commitment and the support individuals get from their institutions. The significance of institutional support varies: university participants are involved largely on their own initiative. They require little financial support from the university and can usually obtain whatever support they need. Individuals representing businesses, however, need concrete support. Two very large corporations are represented among the core leadership of PIMM. In each case the individual has a strong belief in the critical need to solve the problem PIMM is tackling.

The reasons for corporate support are varied. Pratt and Whitney Aircraft has a policy of support to education through service and involvement in addition to philanthropy. The company needs employees with mathematical competence at many levels and has an extensive program of in-house technical training and management development. Convinced that the mathematics competence of its new employees has declined over the last few years, Pratt and

Whitney has been forced to offer them basic mathematics courses. It supports PIMM through the commitment of financial and human resources as an investment that, if successful, will improve the quality of the available employee pool in Connecticut.

IBM also supports the involvement of one of its professional employees. Its support reflects a corporate philosophy of encouraging the volunteer community involvement of its employees. That there might be direct returns to IBM in the form of mathematically better trained employees is incidental. IBM's focus is on the return it gets from contributing to community involvement; it can attract good people by offering a good place to live. PIMM thus illustrates the varied reasons for corporate involvement, even within one collaborative effort.

The collaboration performs some very specific functions and provides some special opportunities that neither individuals nor institutions working alone could achieve. First, it can capitalize on the networks of each participating institution for financial and human resources and through those networks can heighten statewide awareness. Second, it provides an environment for communication, a context for creative problem solving; it brings together theoretical and applied mathematics and its uses; and its flexibility and acceptance of different approaches are a strength.

Last, PIMM's functions are part of a process of *change:* mathematics competence is not exclusively the educator's problem. It is a larger problem. Because the public and the private sectors share a concern about lack of competence in mathematics, because it has many contributing causes, and because solutions require a comprehensive and long-term investment, public and private resources are needed. A narrow offensive will not solve the problem, and society cannot afford to leave it unsolved.

Honeywell, Inc. Both the Honeywell Fund and the Honeywell Corporate and Community Responsibility Department focus on education. Honeywell's involvement grows out of a corporate philosophy of commitment to employees. Some 45 percent of Honeywell Fund's annual giving goes to education. In 1981 a special five-year, $5 million program began to award grants to institutions of higher education. Employees are encouraged to volunteer in the community and provide technical assistance, tutoring, mentor, and training services in schools, while Honeywell provides financial assistance, equipment, buildings, and space. Educational projects in which Honeywell employees and resources are engaged are located in schools and other settings; they serve a variety of populations, including gifted elementary and secondary students and handicapped, economically disadvantaged, minority, and institutionalized youth; and they concern many areas, including science and technology, the development of work habits and basic job skills, basic and remedial studies, career identification and job-seeking skills, knowledge of business and free enterprise, and role models and mentors.

The company's most recent and extensive education program involves the Minneapolis public schools. Over the years a partnership has developed between Honeywell and the Minneapolis public schools, culminating in a science and technology magnet school, Summa Tech. The origin and development of that project further illuminate the guiding corporate philosophy and may be instructive for others interested in similar endeavors. Strategic planning in both the school system and Honeywell led each to decisions setting the stage for partnership. That the project is a product of strategic planning in both the public and the private sectors is important to Honeywell, because it views involvement in such a venture as an investment.

The Minneapolis school system, with the financial support of several corporations including Honeywell, had developed a long-range plan for the school district that included development of a science and technology magnet school for grades nine to twelve. An analysis of Honeywell's earlier education involvement persuaded corporate management to make a deeper commitment to public schools, and the school system worked with Honeywell to develop a proposal that involved Honeywell in the planning and implementation of the school. Honeywell found the project attractive for several reasons: it met Honeywell's criteria for educational involvement; it was consistent with Honeywell's analysis of the educational changes required by projected demographic and occupational trends; and it was compatible with Honeywell's ideas of how to create more effective links between secondary-school education, the workplace, and postsecondary institutions. The partnership offered the schools the opportunity and challenge of using a broad range of Honeywell's financial, technical, human, and material resources.

Honeywell provided funds for one-half of the project coordinator's salary for two years plus several thousand dollars for start-up costs. Twenty-seven Honeywell employees and one spouse of an employee are engaged as volunteers in the planning and development of Summa Tech. Although it is sponsored by the Corporate Technology Center, expertise from the corporation as a whole is available.

This relationship is carefully nurtured because the partnership is viewed as a developmental process. The school district and the company each provide resources—financial, staff, material, and facilities. The interplay of these resources is designed to develop a school program that satisfies the needs of students, the school system, and the community and the interests of Honeywell. Honeywell is willing to make a commitment when a project meets the school's needs and is in the interests of the community.

An equally important factor in the partnership is Honeywell's commitment to its employees' volunteer experience. This priority, which is the foundation of all Honeywell's community involvement, serves each project well. Concern for individual effectiveness requires careful planning, implementation, and evaluation.

Organizational factors and structural differences between schools and corporations are a major challenge in creating effective partnerships between them. The process of getting such different systems to work creatively together requires sensitivity to differences, constant feedback, and nurturing—in other words, a developmental orientation. Both partners must be aware of their differences in organizational structure and management style. Honeywell's commitment to its employees suggests a particularly effective developmental orientation, reflected in its sensitivity to the ingredients of an effective volunteer program.

Urban public school system. The Houston business/school partnership is best characterized by the superintendent for instruction of the Houston Independent School District. She maintains that a school district cannot be a closed system if it is to solve hard problems. Not to use the knowledge, concern, and interest available in the greater community is shortsighted.

The involvement of the business community in the Houston schools includes a variety of activities and is based on a variety of motives. Business and industry provide regular and occasional volunteers, coordinated through the Volunteers in Public Schools Business/School Partnerships. Volunteers serve as bilingual tutors and teacher partners in elementary and secondary schools. Some teacher partners work on basic skills; others offer expertise in science, computer technology, drafting, and electrical engineering. In addition, several large corporations offer internships, summer teacher workshops, occasional guest speakers, and field trips. The school district is particularly interested in evaluating changes in the attitudes and expectations of the volunteers as well as the program management and its effects.

An interview with the chief executive officer of one corporation supporting a significant volunteer program in the Houston schools indicates that the company's commitment to the community and to its employees is an important reason for its support of such an effort. Initial requests come from individual schools, and principals and teachers match their needs with a company's available resources. The coordinator also ensures that the volunteer program has the support of top management and that communications and management systems are identified to carry it out.

The business community has also been extensively involved in the creation and development of some of Houston's magnet school programs. The High School for Engineering Professions program, for example, began in 1975 after one year of intensive planning, which included business and industry. It addressed two critical problems in the field of engineering identified by chief executive officers of major corporations: a shortage of engineers and underrepresentation of minorities and women. While it is clearly in the self-interest of energy and technology corporations to increase the pool of qualified engineering applicants, that goal is consistent with the twin objectives of the magnet school program—the pursuit of excellence and equity.

The engineering high school is unique in that it deals with a pre-engineering curriculum and minority students. The curriculum, for which guidelines were established by a group of deans of engineering schools, focuses on understanding rather than technician training. Industry plays an advisory role and provides financial support, technical assistance, equipment, and the loan of personnel. During the 1981-1982 school year an IBM engineer was on loan full-time as a regular faculty member, carrying a full teaching load and doing some in-service work with teachers. He believes that his industry perspectives add an important dimension to the high-school program.

Industry supports a stronger mathematics and science curriculum in other ways. Through the Gulf Coast Alliance for Minorities in Engineering, twenty companies are involved in junior high school programs that focus on career awareness and motivation for continued study in mathematics and science. Houston also has five elementary magnet schools that focus on mathematics and science.

The Houston school district staff views business-education partnerships as a way to nurture and stimulate change in school environments. It is eager to emphasize, however, that the school system determines the direction of change and that is the key to successful partnerships. The Houston experience suggests that the business community is motivated by a desire to participate in the solution of problems; it does not want to assume the burdens of the schools. When the school system identified ways in which businesses could make a constructive contribution, they were more inclined to make a commitment.

Another magnet school in Houston, the High School for Health Professions, was initiated by Baylor College of Medicine and developed through the cooperative efforts of the school district and Baylor. The curriculum, developed jointly, offers a four-year health science training program in addition to electives in foreign language, advanced mathematics and science, and business education. The only high school originated and sponsored by a medical school, it has developed functional links between the school system and Baylor's Center for Allied Health Manpower Development. The structure includes a steering committee of representatives of both institutions to review broad policy and new operational policies; the principal of the high school holds a faculty appointment in the Department of Community Medicine at Baylor; the allied health center director develops Baylor policy while the school principal implements general school district policy. The high school is a successful example of inter-institutional collaboration with a limited set of objectives.

Lessons Learned. Although drawing conclusions from a few examples of commitment and success is risky, we believe that certain lessons can be learned from these illustrations.

First, there is not one formula, one model, or one structure that works. Each of the examples shows a unique relationship, a different kind of structure—each successful in what it attempts to do.

Second, the initiative for a partnership may come from the private sector, from schools, or from universities; the success or failure of any particular partnership cannot be predicted from its source.

Third, a broad range of motives can be associated with any one partnership—public relations, community responsibility, and enlightened self-interest may contribute to corporate involvement in an education project.

Fourth, it is important for educators to determine their needs and their objectives and to articulate ways in which the private sector can share in meeting them. Corporations want to participate in solutions; they do not want to take responsibility for a set of problems. Specific objectives that will allow for incremental, identifiable successes are necessary.

Fifth, individuals make a partnership succeed or fail. Personal commitment by the top leadership is necessary. There also is a good deal of diversity in how the leaders of different companies view the role their organization can play. One corporation may support education solely through philanthropic giving while another gives material and human resources as well as financial support. Although philanthropic giving constitutes a generous and important source of support, it is limited and is typically directed toward higher education. The creation of partnerships, however, extends to all levels of education and is far more open-ended.

Sixth, these partnerships reflect one common thread: investment in human capital. They are built on a recognition of the interdependence of education and manpower and the recognition that corporate well-being is tied to the health of the community.

Seventh, these examples illustrate a hypothesis about management style in corporations. We encountered a developmental focus in the corporations we examined. The importance of this is hard to assess, but it appears to be linked to recent criticism of certain corporate behavior over the past several decades. Short-term goals, early profit taking, limited investment in research and development, and short-term personal commitments have placed some American corporations at a disadvantage in international competition. Japanese corporate behavior, in particular, appears to avoid these pitfalls. Long-term corporate growth and investment in education require long-term planning and commitment. Corporate leaders with a developmental focus, of the kind described by Michael Maccoby in *The Leader*, may be necessary for such investment.[24] This suggests that substantial changes in corporate attitudes are needed to increase the involvement of industry in partnerships with education.

Finally, we are concerned with the role of educators in partnerships. Only when educators view education as an open process, not a closed system, and when they acknowledge that they do not have a monopoly on teaching and learning, will communication and collaboration proceed.

Policy Prospects

We have identified and discussed three broad areas of private sector involvement in education and training: traditional elementary and secondary schools; industry-based education and training; and private sector–public sector collaborative efforts. A set of common themes ties these three elements together. First, they represent investment in human capital. Second, they are a product of spontaneous growth; that is, they are not the product of government planning or funding, but are a response to objective conditions. Third, they occurred in a period of relative government abundance. In collateral areas, the government was designing programs and spending money at a very high rate. The 1970s were a decade in which all levels of government spent more and more heavily on education and training but *not* in the segments we have identified.

Thus private school enrollments and industry training in basic skills were climbing precisely as government was spending ever more for public education. The three areas we have identified, then, were not related to government cuts; but now that government cuts have occurred, they are all the more important.

Private Elementary and Secondary Schools. This traditional segment of American education has rarely, if ever, been more vigorous. Barring an unforeseen sharp economic downturn, all signs point to continued vigor. Enrollments continue to increase, and most analysts are convinced that private schools will continue to command a small but important part of the market. Not long ago there was concern that private schools were in jeopardy—because of a pattern of enrollment declines that did not bottom out until the late 1970s. Ironically, certain private school analysts today are concerned that if private schools are at risk, it is because of their strength; as private schools assume a more important role in educating the nation's students, they are more likely to be targets of proposed legislation and regulation. Whether or not this is a legitimate concern remains to be seen, but it is clear that private elementary and secondary schools will continue to be viewed by their clients as important ways to invest in children.

What policy significance attaches to private elementary and secondary education? First, as we have pointed out, established private schools are meeting their social responsibilities. They are not bastions of elitism or racism. The available evidence suggests that they have made and will continue to make major contributions to racial and socioeconomic integration. And the recent work by Coleman and Greeley indicates that academic performance is higher for certain students in private than in public schools. Taken together, this information suggests that government should leave private schools to their own devices. More regulation would be undesirable and counterproductive.

What, however, of proposals for public support? Should private school students and their families receive tax relief or other forms of government support? That is a discussion too value laden and politically charged to be reopened here except to make two points: one, there is no compelling reason to believe that the only way for government to support education is to own and operate schools; two, if a public policy decision is reached to give government aid to private education, the ideas to implement such a decision are close at hand. Tax credits and tuition vouchers are the most obvious.

Industry-Based Training and Education. Industry-based education and training are also forms of investment in human capital. But much of that investment is reluctant: industry would prefer to hire employees already trained and educated. This is particularly true of basic skills, an area in which many industries now find themselves involved. More advanced or job- or company-specific training is clearly a cost of production, and its availability is a function of corporate and union resources and desires. But basic skills training raises a special question: Are the public schools doing their job if their graduates are unemployable without further business-sponsored training?

It may be that, for reasons of employee motivation, businesses are better suited to provide certain kinds of education and training. If this were so, it would be useful to investigate which institutions are best equipped to handle certain kinds of education—public schools or employers. So far, business-sponsored education in basic skills is small enough to be suggestive rather than definitive, but it is clearly a trend that should be followed closely in the 1980s. This is an area that is likely to find a natural equilibrium without government intervention. Because it is investment-based, it bears fruit or it does not, and the private sector will continue its activities as long as there is a need to do so. If public schools are able to increase the competence of their graduates, employers will no longer find it necessary to offer remedial training. But education and training for job- or company-related objectives will continue and almost certainly increase.

Our primary policy interest is whether or not there are barriers or incentives that should be modified in the interests of greater activity by employers in this area. Insofar as employer-sponsored education and training are simply costs of production, there are no major structural barriers to them.

One area bears further examination and analysis: business-sponsored training and education have been designed to serve the specific needs of employers. But the skills and capacities of the trainers may have applications beyond the needs of the host business. Some commercial market exists for certain kinds of business-developed training that goes beyond the narrower interests of the business's own employees. The development of the Wang Institute is a prime example. Other applications might be appropriate, such as school-business contracts for the teaching of basic skills, mathematics, or science by private providers within public schools. Such a development hinges on the willingness of public schools to explore and implement such programs.

School-Business Collaboration. Our site work and review of the literature reveal a wide variety of school-business collaborative activities, ranging from the provision of material or employee volunteers to complex contractual relationships between chemical companies and major research universities.

Examples from either end of the spectrum lend themselves to clear interpretation. At one end, modest activities with high visibility serve public relations purposes, while at the other end corporate-university contracts are based on determinations of long-term profitability. It is the examples in the middle that are both more interesting and more difficult to assess. Will the Connecticut mathematics project continue and bear fruit? Will the Houston public school–private sector partnerships continue? And might others like them appear in other communities?

It should be clear that we are convinced that the long-term implications for public policy are numerous; unfortunately, the short-term implications are unclear. We are able to see overarching themes, but specific public policies are difficult to identify. It may be that this sense of uncertainty is appropriate to the subject. We are witnessing the emergence of long-term structural changes, driven by changing attitudes and social forces that have not yet worked themselves out. In such a situation, caution is a virtue. Nevertheless, several general points are appropriate.

One theme that emerges is that the public sector has a good deal to learn from the private. The virtues of private elementary and secondary education flow from a few simple variables. First, private schools are voluntary associations of teachers and taught; typically they are heterogeneous in student body but homogeneous in values. Second, they are virtually unregulated and nonbureaucratic: the exercise of informed judgment by all members of the private school community is expected as a matter of course. Third, they are almost uniformly smaller than public schools.

Similarly, the lessons of business education and training are clear. The link between motivation and accomplishment is strong.

Artificial institutional barriers to teaching and learning are few. Productivity, efficiency, and success are stressed. The keys are decentralization, flexibility, and measured output.

Taken together, these attributes suggest two things for public schools. One, public schools would be well advised to look to the private sector for examples of administrative and organizational flexibility as well as pedagogical insights. This is true whether or not public schools hope to forge partnerships with the private sector. The second point is equally important: if public schools wish to collaborate with the private sector, they must be prepared to support major changes in the ways they are organized and operated. Private sector involvement will not work in a business-as-usual environment.

If business-school collaboration is to have staying power, it must satisfy the interests of both parties; more important, it must pay off in ways that make sense to both the private and the public sectors. Our overarching theme has been investment in human capital: this is the telling element of school-business collaboration. If business is convinced that such an investment is worthwhile, it will continue; if not, it will wither and disappear. Simple altruism or a desire to demonstrate "good corporate citizenship" will not be sufficient to sustain collaboration over the long haul. These impulses can be satisfied in a wide variety of ways, and the nation's public schools are by no means the sole or even the preferred candidate for such corporate attention. Museums, performing arts centers, and charitable and welfare programs also exert strong claims on corporate resources and consciences.

Two elements are necessary to cement school-business collaboration. First, business must be convinced that support pays off in the form of improved schools and a better product. Second, public schools must demonstrate their willingness and ability to work with business in ways that run counter to much that schools have traditionally done.

This confluence of events represents a historic opportunity. The issue is not that schools should become the staging ground for corporate America, producing a docile and skillful work force to keep the wheels of industry turning. Nor is it the more subtle, but no less undesirable, idea that public schools should sacrifice education for training, substituting narrow skill building for the development of the mind as a whole. The issues are at once more prosaic and more important. And because we are dealing with education issues, as well as political and economic ones, we must turn to a short discussion of school organization, staffing, and teaching.

School organization. Public schools are not well designed to take advantage of collaborations with business. A practice as conventional and accepted as exclusive reliance on summer vacations severely limits the ability of schools to develop cooperative work-study placements in business and industry for teachers, students, and private sector employers. More important, the large, centralized bureaucratic structures of contemporary urban school districts severely limit the flexibility needed to capitalize fully on the possibilities for school-business collaboration.

Large school districts, in particular, tend to be rigid, centralized hierarchies, reflecting an older industrial and bureaucratic model inappropriate to the modern world. The decision-making chain is often so long and complex as to be inaccessible to all but initiates. As a consequence, no one and everyone is in charge. William Mc-Cready of the National Opinion Research Center of the University of Chicago observes that Chicago's public schools, with 500,000 students, employ 3,500 administrators while Chicago's Catholic schools, with 250,000 students, employ 35 administrators. Private schools employ fewer administrators not because they are more virtuous (though the consequence is virtue) but because they cannot afford more.

In this case, financial austerity is a blessing in disguise, because it forces Catholic schools to be nonbureaucratic. This reinforces that sense of community essential to effective schooling, makes for institutional flexibility, ensures greater professionalism among teachers who are leaders of their classrooms, and inhibits or even eliminates buck passing. Short of the cardinal, there is almost no one to whom the buck can be passed. It is no surprise that the flat organization chart of Catholic schools looks much like that of successful modern commercial and industrial concerns. In theological terminology, the principle is "subsidiarity": the lowest unit of organization that can do the job does it. In politics, the term is local control; in business, it is decentralized decision making.

The flexibility private schools enjoy may be fortuitous, but the insight it affords is not. It is more than accident that public schools must learn from private schools if they are to deal effectively with the private sector. This is not to suggest that they lose their purpose or change their mission; rather, we are convinced that they must change their behavior if they hope to retain their character and sense of purpose.

Staffing. The problems and opportunities raised by staffing are highlighted by the issue of mathematics and science instruction. In most jurisdictions, only one category of mathematician or scientist may teach in public schools: those licensed by the state. And a license, we must remember, is "permission to do something otherwise prohibited." All other scientists and mathematicians—including university and college professors as well as researchers and practitioners in the public and the private sectors—are ineligible to teach in public elementary and secondary schools. This structural barrier is formidable, and the problem it poses cannot be overemphasized. Although licensing systems are designed to screen out the incompetent, the effect of most teacher licensing systems is to screen out the above average as well. Unfortunately, licensing barriers and existing salary schedules create a sort of negative synergy, making it progressively more difficult for public schools to find and employ "qualified" mathematicians and scientists. The salary attractions of the private sector—along with its ambiance and other amenities—make it extremely difficult for the public sector to compete.

Serious problems flow from these barriers to public sector employment. The Discovery Math program, for example, a private sector project in which trained mathematicians from universities and private industry teach college-level algebra to disadvantaged elementary-school students, is severely hampered by licensing restrictions. Senior mathematicians at the University of California, Stanford University, and private corporations in Silicon Valley are not licensed to teach in California public schools. They may conduct public school classes, but only in the presence of licensed teachers. A university professor may be a teacher of teachers, but not a teacher of elementary or secondary students. The situation is virtually incomprehensible from the standpoint of the private sector, where performance is more important than credentials. If the situation is to be remedied, public schools and public officials must take the initiative.

At the same time, public school salaries have become insulated from the market. The uniform salary schedule, once thought of as a reform of great virtue, treats all teachers equally, as interchangeable parts moving slowly upward on a seniority ladder. The situation gives rise to the old truism that teachers are simultaneously the best and worst paid of the professions: when the weakest teacher is paid what the best is paid, the poor teacher is as grossly overpaid as the best is woefully underpaid.

For years, halting attempts have been made to introduce merit pay for teachers, an idea so unpopular in the education establishment that it is probably politically impossible to initiate such a program. But other forms of salary distinction might be possible, such as split schedules based on the subject taught. Public schools could do what many universities do, pay faculty members in short supply more than those in fields that are easily staffed. If medical and law school faculties earn more than English teachers, is there any reason not to pay science and mathematics teachers more than teachers in disciplines that are overrepresented? Indeed, relating salaries to market conditions could do much to balance supply and demand and avoid serious shortages in critical areas. The message is simple but strong: the public sector should introduce some market mechanisms into its own world if it hopes to deal with the private sector, indeed, if it hopes to succeed at all.

The idea is no less interesting in light of one strong possibility: over the long haul, a split salary schedule would probably drive salaries up across the board. Except during major depressions, professional salaries tend to be "sticky" and do not float downward. But in a period of financial austerity, across-the-board increases are highly unlikely, especially in large school systems in which expenditures for salaries are very large. Over time, the high end of a split salary schedule might pull lower salaries with it, an effect to be welcomed by teachers even as school boards and taxpayers lament.

Teaching and learning. In first discussing the organizational and staffing implications of private sector–public sector collaboration, we have left till last the most important element of school: teaching. It is a mysterious process, the interaction of teacher and taught, and brooks no facile analysis. Indeed, in the presence of such an issue, one does well to ponder Mencken's comment: "For every complex problem, there is a solution which is simple, direct, and wrong."

With that warning in mind, it is still important to observe that if teaching is a profession, certain prerogatives and obligations follow. Teachers should be expected to reassert their role as classroom leaders. Indeed, it is useful to turn to the more traditional nomenclature of Great Britain, where principals are "head masters" and teachers "masters," for it nicely illuminates the role of teachers. Buried in a modern bureaucracy, burdened with forms and procedures, responding to numerous administrators and more numerous demands, today's teacher looks more like a production-line employee than a professional. Increasing teachers' flexibility, restoring the place of informed judgment, rationalizing salary schedules, and loosening licensing requirements are devices that both improve teaching and make public schools more like private ones.

Conclusion

In addition to the policy prospects we have noted, our examination of the private sector's role in education and training points up three major trends:

- Private elementary and secondary schools are vigorous and growing. They should continue to grow until the end of the decade.
- Business and industry have made a heavy commitment to employee education and training.
- Business-school collaboration is emerging as a significant activity.

The first two trends are well documented and fit conceptual models of human capital formation: in the first, clients (private school parents) make deliberate decisions to invest in the "quality," or human capital, of their children; in the second, education and training constitute a direct investment strategy designed to improve human capital so as to increase productivity.

In each case, if the public sector offered higher-quality schools, both as places to send children and as producers of trained and educated workers, some shift from the private to the public sector would occur. Instead, just the reverse has occurred: the shift to private education reflects the belief that there are serious shortfalls in the public sector.

This shift is not wholly undesirable. It reflects some real measure of market responsiveness; it reveals a fundamental belief in the value and importance of education; it puts the public sector on notice that there are quality-conscious clients who will not tolerate indifferent education; and it reveals trends that will, in some measure, shape the future. It also helps to explain the third trend: the nascent movement toward business-school collaboration. This trend is in some ways the most important because it symbolizes—as well as actualizes—the need for major shifts in institutional roles and responsibilities for education in the twenty-first century.

The first two developments—the growth of private schools and the concurrent expansion of industry-based training and education—occurred in a period of government growth. They were not funded by government, but neither did they occur as a response to government cuts. They represent qualitative rather than quantitative responses by the private sector to publicly provided education.

Even though they were not a product of government largess, their potential for further expansion is related to government policies. A generous program of human capital tax write-offs, similar to those available for physical capital, could profoundly affect additional developments in private sector education and training. Without such a program, private sector education will reach some "natural" lower equilibrium point. The policy issues and the instrumentalities that could be employed to encourage further private sector growth are relatively straightforward and well known. Tax credits, tax deductions, tuition or training vouchers, and similar ideas have been widely discussed and analyzed. Enough is known about them to move in that direction if public policies shift toward programs of support of private sector education and training. This essay is not the place to pursue these ideas. Rather, we are concerned about public policy—and private practice—in the context of business-school collaboration.

This is so for several reasons. First, although private sector involvement in education and training is vigorous, the public sector remains by far the largest provider of education and training. Even assuming linear extrapolation of private sector trends until the twenty-first century—2 percent per year growth in private schools, for example—the public sector will remain the dominant provider of education.

Second, large infusions of additional public money into public sector education are highly unlikely. The public mood does not appear to support large new programs, and it is clear that the administration, the Congress, and state legislatures and governors do not. The reasons are too numerous to detail here: suffice it to say that in an era of scarcity, with an aging population, there are more demands for social programs than there is public funding available. In this environment, education will not be as high on the nation's agenda as it was during the period of the baby boom.

The Question of Who Should Pay. In the preceding narrative, we have deliberately not discussed the question of who should pay for human capital formation. Instead we have described who is paying and identified policies that might be an incentive to further investment by the private sector in education.

We are now faced with the prospect of reduction or leveling off of government funding, and we may be approaching the natural limits of private investment. The question of who should pay for human capital investment, then, must be addressed—if only tentatively. A strong case can be made that the beneficiaries of human capital investment should pay much, if not all, of the cost.

The issue is important for a number of reasons. First, traditions of public support of education and training have been justified on implicit theories of social justice, which stress access and equity for the less fortunate. But there are many ways to ensure social justice, and direct government subsidies are not necessarily the most efficient or desirable. Government could play a brokerage or stimulative role, acting as a human capital banker or providing indirect subsidies through the tax system. The important point is that a dollar cut from federal programs is not necessarily a dollar lost to human capital investment. This is not a defense of budget cuts, but government budgets and programs do not tell the whole story. Indeed, poorly conceived government programs can induce overinvestment in human capital when distortions in investment patterns are taken into account. A heavily subsidized program for support of a particular field of study can attract inappropriately high investment in that field, just as undercapitalization produces underinvestment. Since the postwar period, we have observed this situation on several occasions. In response to Sputnik, engineering and related disciplines received heavy government funding, which led to a transient oversupply. Similarly, we now face a significant oversupply of Ph.D.'s in arts and letters.

Supply and demand in the skilled crafts and trades—and in the several advanced disciplines and learned professions—are never likely to reach perfect equilibrium, but there is no a priori reason to assume that it will be more beneficial to rely on government planning than on market forces. A more promising course of action would be some form of government brokerage that relies on market mechanisms—a more deliberate and thoughtful version of the programs that now exist. A federally sponsored human capital bank or federal human capital tax credits, both for individuals and for employers, are worth serious consideration.

While there is no consensus about who should bear the costs of human capital formation, there is emerging agreement about the importance of the issue. Properly defined, the problem of who should pay may become the subject of public debate and decision making.

Summary. To summarize, then, this chapter has attempted to make a few simple points. Human capital investment is becoming a self-conscious enterprise in American society. Clients of education—families of private school students—and business and industry are investing more and more heavily in education and training. This market has natural limits, however, and the public schools will continue to play a major and needed role in human capital formation.

The exigencies of the present make it progressively more difficult for the public schools to secure more public funding. For better or worse, this forces them to turn to new and innovative solutions to their problems. One promising solution is to develop lasting partnerships with the private sector.

We do not believe that such relationships can be built on private sector altruism and public sector business-as-usual attitudes. The private sector must be convinced that what it is doing is worthwhile. Institutions as well as people get what they pay for, and lasting public-private relationships must be built on mutual expectations of mutual benefit.

At the same time, public schools, if they are to succeed at establishing relationships with the private sector, must be prepared to change. They must look to private schools as models of behavior, organization, and pedagogy, and they must look to the business and corporate world for models of staffing, salaries, and habits of entrepreneurship.

The stakes are high. A worst-case scenario combines inflexible public schools and a hesitant private sector. In that case, we can expect a continuing shift to private elementary and secondary schools among quality-conscious families; increasing reliance by business and industry on in-house training and education for their employees; and a public school system further adrift, remote from its natural constituency, and unwilling and unable to change. A more hopeful scenario is the emergence of long-term relationships between the private sector and the public schools, characterized by flexibility, imagination, and inventiveness, in which both parties are convinced that the arrangement is mutually beneficial.

The task ahead, then, is to nurture those collaborative relationships already in place, observe them, learn from them, and hope that today's lessons are tomorrow's promise.

Appendix: Research Notes and Bibliography

Some of the supporting material for this chapter was drawn from informal conversations with persons already studying some aspect of private sector involvement in education. Discussions about work in progress with Michael Timpane, former director of the National Institute of Education and now dean of Teachers College, Columbia University, and Beth Brown, consultant, Office of Technology Assessment, U.S. Congress, contributed significantly to the development of sections of the chapter. Mr. Timpane's study for the Carnegie Corporation focuses on private sector involvement in public schools; Ms. Brown's studies for OTA examine industry- and labor-based education and training. The work of Ernest A. Lynton for the Ford

Foundation on the role of colleges and universities in corporate education also provided a basis for some of the observations.

The following groups or organizations either have been or are involved in work related to the areas touched on in this chapter. The list is by no means complete—indeed, the number of organizations and individuals concerned with these issues is growing steadily. We apologize for any omissions we may have made.

The Conference Board, Inc. An independent, not-for-profit research institution, the Conference Board serves business, government, labor, and other institutions through studies and research reports on management and economics issues. Some 4,000 worldwide associates include corporations, national and regional governments, labor unions, universities, associations, public libraries, and individuals. Among its many publications, three are particularly relevant to this study:

The Conference Board and Council for Financial Aid to Education. *Annual Survey of Corporate Contributions, 1981 Edition.* New York, 1981. 27 pp.

Lusterman, Seymour. *Education in Industry.* New York: Conference Board, 1977. 97 pp.

Lusterman, Seymour, and Gorlin, Harriet. *Educating Students for Work: Some Business Roles.* New York: Conference Board, 1980. 62 pp.

National Institute for Work and Learning (NIWL) (formerly the National Manpower Institute). The National Institute for Work and Learning is a private, not-for-profit policy research and demonstration organization, established in 1971. The focus of its work is on integrating education, employment, training, and economic policy in the private and public sectors to maximize the individual's work and learning experience. Among its many publications are policy research monographs, case studies on effective tuition-aid programs, and research analyses. The following are of particular relevance to this chapter.

Fraser, Bryna Shore; Gold, Gerard G.; Rankin, John; Rudick, Lois; and Ward, Ronnie C. *Industry-Education-Labor Collaboration: The Literature of Collaborative Councils.* Washington, D.C.: NIWL, 1981. 143 pp.

Gold, Gerard G.; Fraser, Bryna Shore; Elsaman, Max; and Rankin, John. *Industry-Education-Labor Collaboration: A Directory of Collaborative Councils.* Washington, D.C.: NIWL, 1981. 336 pp.

Goldstein, Harold. *Training and Education by Industry.* Washington, D.C.: NIWL, 1980. 80 pp.

Wirtz, Willard. *Tuition-Aid Revisited: Tapping the Untapped Resource.* Washington, D.C.: NIWL, 1979. 31 pp.

National Association for Industry-Education Cooperation (NAIEC).
The NAIEC is a national organization whose membership includes representatives of business, industry, education, government, and labor. Its purpose is to promote increased communication and cooperation across sectors. Among its publications are handbooks and manuals to facilitate industry-education cooperation and the *Journal of Industry-Education Cooperation.*

National Institute of Education, U.S. Department of Education (NIE).
Over several years the NIE's Education and Work Group has defined specific and relevant study areas, which have led to a systematic exploration of issues related to private sector education. The most current area of study being funded is the impact of public policy on private sector education and training programs.

Council for Financial Aid to Education (CFAE). The Council for Financial Aid to Education is a nonprofit service organization, established in 1952 and financed by over 350 corporations. Its purpose is to encourage financial support of higher education, especially by the private sector. In addition to studying educational philanthropy, it provides a consulting service to corporations and academic institutions, conducts a national public service advertising campaign, and produces publications relevant to corporate support of colleges and universities. It is the cosponsor, with the Conference Board, of the *Annual Survey of Corporate Contributions.* Among its many publications are:

Council for Financial Aid to Education. *How to Develop and Administer a Corporate Scholarship Program.* New York, 1981. 51 pp.
―――. *How to Develop an Effective Program of Corporate Support for Higher Education.* New York, 1979. 23 pp.
―――. *Interface—Growing Initiatives between the Corporation and the Campus toward Greater Mutual Understanding.* New York, 1977. 67 pp.
―――. *Voluntary Support of Education, 1979–80.* New York, 1981. 68 pp.

Chamber of Commerce of the United States. A national organization with over 2,800 local and state chapters, the Chamber of Commerce has a long history of involvement in education. The national organization and many local chapters have education, training, and manpower committees. The Chamber of Commerce network provides information to member organizations on business-education partnerships and ways in which the business community can provide support to local school systems. Among its many publications are:

Chamber of Commerce of the United States. *Career Education: What*

It Is and Why We Need It, from Leaders of Industry, Education, Labor, and the Professions. Washington, D.C., 1975. 18 pp.

———. *Contact: A Directory of Business and Economic Education Programs.* Washington, D.C., 1980. 129 pp.

———. *A Source of Funds for Training Workers: The New Private Sector Initiative Program.* Washington, D.C., 1979. 36 pp.

National School Volunteer Program (NSVP). The National School Volunteer Program promotes voluntarism in schools. It provides training for local volunteer organizers, functions as a clearinghouse for local programs, and facilitates volunteer–school district coordination. It has a particular interest in developing ties between schools and local businesses. Among its many publications is:

Purcell, E. A.; Alden, J. W.; and Nagle, T. L. *Partners for the 80's: Business and Education.* Alexandria, Va.: NSVP, 1981. 59 pp. (Profiles of business-school partnerships nationwide.)

American Society for Training and Development (ASTD). The American Society for Training and Development is a professional association of specialists in training, adult education, and human resource development. The society has headquarters in Washington, D.C., and over 100 local chapters. It serves its membership with conferences, institutes, and seminars and publishes a monthly journal and the *National Report for Training and Development.* Among its many publications it includes a research series and practical guides and handbooks for practitioners. A recent publication is:

ASTD Directory of Academic Programs in Training and Development/Human Resource Development. Washington, D.C.: ASTD, 1981.

Other Organizations. Other groups concerned with issues related to private sector involvement in education include the Council for the Advancement of Experiential Learning; the National Alliance of Business; Junior Achievement; the National Association of Manufacturers; the American Council on Education; the American Association for Higher Education and other professional education associations; and local, state, and federal education, labor, employment, and training agencies, groups, and associations.

Other Sources. In addition to the publications cited above or in the text, the following sources are relevant. It should also be noted that anecdotal reports and articles on business-education partnerships appear regularly in the media.

Benson, Charles, ed. *Education Finance and Organization: Research Perspectives for the Future.* Washington, D.C.: National Institute of Education, January 1980.

Berger, Peter L., and Neuhaus, Richard John. *To Empower People.* Washington, D.C.: American Enterprise Institute, 1977.

Burt, Samuel M., and Lessinger, Leon M. *Volunteer Industry Involvement in Public Education.* Lexington, Mass.: Heath-Lexington Books, 1970.

Callahan, Raymond C. *Education and the Cult of Efficiency.* Chicago: University of Chicago Press, 1962.

Cohen, David K., and Farrar, Eleanor. "Power to the Parents? The Story of Educational Vouchers." *Public Interest,* no. 48 (Summer 1977): 72–97.

The Condition of Education, 1979. Washington, D.C.: National Center for Education Statistics, 1979.

The Condition of Education, 1979: Part 2. Washington, D.C.: National Center for Education Statistics, 1979.

The Condition of Education, 1980. Washington, D.C.: National Center for Education Statistics, 1980.

The Condition of Education, 1980: Part 2. Washington, D.C.: National Center for Education Statistics, 1980.

The Condition of Education, 1981. Washington, D.C.: National Center for Education Statistics, 1981.

Denison, Edward F. *Accounting for Slower Economic Growth: The U.S. in the 1970s.* Washington, D.C.: Brookings Institution, 1979.

Doyle, Denis P. "Can Confidence in Public Schools Be Restored?" *Seattle Times,* May 11, 1980.

————. "Education and Values: A Consideration." *College Board Review,* no. 118 (Winter 1980–1981).

————. "The Flight from Public Schools: It's Not Racial, It's Middle Class." *Los Angeles Herald Examiner,* June 20, 1980.

————. "Going Private." *London Times Educational Supplement,* April 4, 1980.

————. "A New Decade for U.S. Education: Who Pays, Who Gains, Who Loses?" *Los Angeles Times,* December 30, 1979, opinion section.

————. "The Politics of Choice: A View from the Bridge." In *Parents, Teachers, and Children: Prospects for Choice in American Education,* edited by Lawrence Chickering. San Francisco: Institute for Contemporary Studies, 1977.

————. "Public Policy and Private Education." *Phi Delta Kappan* 62, no. 1 (September 1980).

Doyle, Denis P., and Levine, Marsha. "Myths and Shadows: Some Preliminary Observations on Education and the Private Sector in an Era of Limits." Paper prepared for Public Policy Week, December 1981, American Enterprise Institute, Washington, D.C.

Drucker, Peter F. "The Coming Changes in Our School Systems." *Wall Street Journal,* March 3, 1981, p. 13.

Education Finance Center. *School Finance Reform in the States: 1981.* Denver: Education Commission of the States, January 1981.

Elam, S. M. *A Decade of Gallup Polls of Attitudes toward Education, 1969–1978.* Bloomington, Ind.: Phi Delta Kappan Education Foundation, 1978.

Erickson, Donald A. "Should All the Nation's Schools Compete for Clients and Support?" *Phi Delta Kappan* 61, no. 1 (September 1979).

Finn, Chester E. "A Call for Quality Education." *Life* (March 1981).

"How State Governments Are Promoting Literacy." *Electronic Learning* 1, no. 2 (December 1981).

Kraushar, Otto F. *Private Schools: From the Puritans to the Present.* Bloomington, Ind.: Phi Delta Kappan Education Foundation, 1976.

Moynihan, Daniel P. "Government and the Ruin of Private Education." *Harper's* (April 1978): 28.

———. "What Do You Do When the Supreme Court Is Wrong?" *Public Interest,* no. 57 (Fall 1979): 3.

National Center for Education Statistics. *Student Use of Computers in Schools, Fall 1980: A Survey of Public School Districts.*

National Science Foundation and U.S. Department of Education. *Science and Engineering Education for the 1980s and Beyond.* Washington, D.C., 1980.

Newitt, Jane. *Future Trends in Education.* Lexington, Mass.: Lexington Books, 1979.

Ravitch, Diane. "The Schools We Deserve." *New Republic,* April 18, 1981.

Schultze, Charles L. *The Public Use of Private Interest.* Washington, D.C.: Brookings Institution, 1977.

Stauffer, Thomas M., ed. *Agenda for Business and Higher Education: Business-Higher Education Forum.* Washington, D.C.: American Council on Education, 1980.

"Survey of Continuing Education." *New York Times,* August 30, 1981.

Tomlinson, Tommy. "The Troubled Years: An Interpretive Analysis of Public Schooling since 1950." *Phi Delta Kappan* 62 (1981): 373–76.

Useem, Elizabeth. "Education and High Technology Industry: The Case of Silicon Valley." Paper prepared for the Institute for the Interdisciplinary Study of Education, Northeastern University, August 1981.

Notes

1 See Theodore W. Schultz, *Investing in People: The Economics of Population Scarcity* (Berkeley: University of California Press, 1981); and Milton Friedman, "The Role of Government in Education," in Robert E. Solo, ed., *Economics and the Public Interest* (New Brunswick, N.J.: Rutgers University Press, 1955).

2 Friedman, "Role of Government," p. 126.

3 Robert L. Craig and Christine J. Evers, "Employers as Educators: The Shadow Education System," in Gerard Gold, ed., *New Directions for Experiential Learn-*

ing: Business and Higher Education—toward New Alliances, no. 13 (San Francisco: Jossey-Bass, 1981), p. 31.

4 Ibid., p. 32.

5 Denis P. Doyle and Marsha Levine, "Myths and Shadows: Some Preliminary Observations on Education and the Private Sector in an Era of Limits" (Paper prepared for Public Policy Week, 1981, American Enterprise Institute, Washington, D.C.).

6 For a more detailed discussion of private school enrollments, see Denis P. Doyle, "A Din of Inequity," *Teachers College Record,* vol. 82, no. 4 (Summer 1981).

7 James Coleman, Thomas Hoffer, and Sally Kilgore, "Public and Private Schools," unpublished paper, University of Chicago, 1981; Andrew Greeley, "Minority Students in Catholic Secondary Schools," unpublished paper, University of Arizona, 1981; and Michael Rutter et al., *Fifteen Thousand Hours* (Cambridge, Mass.: Harvard University Press, 1979).

8 See Chester E. Finn, Jr., "Trashing the Coleman Report," *Education Week,* vol. 1, no. 1 (September 7, 1981).

9 See David S. Seeley, *Education through Partnership: Mediating Structures and Education* (Cambridge, Mass.: Ballinger, 1981).

10 See, for example, Seymour Lusterman, *Education in Industry* (New York: Conference Board, 1977); American Association for Higher Education, *Current Issues in Higher Education: Partnerships with Businesses and the Professions.* 1981; and Gerard Gold, ed., "New Alliances: Business and Higher Education," *Phi Delta Kappan,* vol. 61, no. 5 (January 1980).

11 Ernest A. Lynton, "A Role for Colleges in Corporate Training and Development," in American Association for Higher Education, *Current Issues in Higher Education,* p. 9.

12 Beth Brown, consultant, Office of Technology Assessment, U.S. Congress, informal communication.

13 Council for Financial Aid to Education, *Voluntary Support of Education, 1979-80* (New York, 1981).

14 "Why Engineering Deans Worry a Lot," *Fortune,* January 11, 1982, p. 84.

15 Cited in American Electronics Association, *Plan for Action to Reduce Engineering Shortage—with Supporting Data,* 1981, p. 22.

16 Thomas W. Lippman, "Government, Industry, Academia: Engineering Shortage Sparks a Once-Unlikely Merger," *Washington Post,* December 27, 1981.

17 American Electronics Association, *Plan for Action.*

18 Lynton, "A Role for Colleges," pp. 8-15.

19 See K. Patricia Cross, "New Frontiers for Higher Education: Business and the Professions," in American Association for Higher Education, *Current Issues in Higher Education,* pp. 1-7.

20 See U.S. Department of Labor, Bureau of Labor Statistics, *Employment Trends in Computer Occupations,* October 1981.

21 See Gerard Gold et al., *Industry-Education-Labor Collaboration: A Directory of Collaborative Councils* (Washington, D.C.: National Institute of Work and Learning, 1981); and Bryna Shore Fraser et al., *Industry-Education-Labor Collaboration: The Literature of Collaborative Councils* (Washington, D.C.: National Institute of Work and Learning, 1981).

22 D. Allan Bromley, "The Other Frontiers of Science," *Science,* February 26, 1982, p. 1037.

23 "Science at School," *Economist,* October 10, 1981.

24 Michael Maccoby, *The Leader: Managing the Work Place* (New York: Simon and Schuster, 1981).

329

Housing Lower-Income Families and Individuals

John C. Weicher

For almost fifty years the federal government has been involved in attempts to improve the housing of lower-income Americans, typically by building new housing specifically for them. Increasingly the costs of these attempts have risen, and the sense of accomplishment has diminished: the government's efforts have been roundly criticized from a wide variety of perspectives. At present, it seems fair to say that there is a general public perception that the programs have not worked satisfactorily, and that some other policy should be tried.

Against this background, a number of private organizations have begun to develop their own approaches to housing for the poor, working outside the framework of the federal government's programs. These include both profit-making firms and nonprofit corporations and agencies, such as churches and neighborhood groups. Their efforts may point the way to future directions for public policy in housing, with new roles for both the private and the public sectors.

This chapter discusses these initiatives and possibilities. It first summarizes the present housing situation of lower-income Americans to identify the progress made toward decent housing for everyone and the problems that remain. It then analyzes two recent federal programs that have relied on the private sector to provide adequate housing for the poor—and on the poor to find that housing for themselves. Finally it describes several private sector initiatives that exemplify, but by no means exhaust, the range of activities undertaken by concerned citizens, acting as individuals and through local organizations of all sorts.

The author would like to thank Larry Ozanne and Rudolph G. Penner for helpful suggestions, and Richard B. Clemmer for providing unpublished tabulations of housing data from the Annual Housing Survey.

Housing Conditions among the Poor

The present housing situation of lower-income Americans can be summarized in a few sentences.[1] The overwhelming majority are housed *privately*, rather than by government or with government assistance. They are housed *adequately*, in terms of quality. But they are housed *expensively*, in the sense that the cost of adequate housing puts a severe strain on their budgets. These facts suggest a number of ways in which the private sector can be utilized to help low-income families improve their housing.

Basic Concepts in Housing Policy. Before amplifying these short statements about the housing problems of the poor, it is useful to define briefly three key terms: "poor," "adequate," and "expensive." All of them have specialized meanings in housing legislation and policy analyses.

Income. The definition of "poor" is based on the income criteria used to determine eligibility for housing subsidies. Since 1974, the upper limit for assistance under the major programs has been 80 percent of median income in the market area (generally defined as a standard metropolitan statistical area or a nonmetropolitan county). This variable local limit has been adopted, instead of a single fixed dollar amount, because the United States comprises many local housing markets, not one national market. Moreover, housing costs vary widely across the country, but are generally high where incomes are high.

Within the category of eligible households, a further distinction is commonly made between "very low income" (50 percent or less of the local median) and "moderately low income" (between 50 and 80 percent of the median). As of 1980, "very low income" meant, on the average for the country as a whole, approximately $10,500 or less. This is about 25 percent greater than the poverty level of $8,400. "Moderately low income" households received between $10,500 and $16,800. All these figures apply to a family of four; both the poverty level and the income limits are adjusted for household size, in similar ways.

The income limits have been gradually rising over time. In 1966, for example, the typical income limit for a four-person family was about $3,900, which was about 52 percent of median family income.[2] In 1968 Congress enacted two subsidy programs explicitly designed for "moderate income" families (Sections 235 and 236); these had income limits of about 70 percent of the median.

331

Housing cost. Housing has typically been considered "too expensive" if the cost of occupying it takes more than some specified fraction of the household's income. Traditionally, an expense/income ratio of 0.25 has been considered the dividing line, with higher ratios taken as evidence of financial hardship. This ratio was generally used by mortgage lenders in evaluating loan applications: if the mortgage payment and property taxes exceeded 25 percent of the household's monthly income, the mortgage application was likely to be rejected. A similar ratio for renters has been used by family financial advisers. Tenants in subsidized housing have usually been required to contribute up to a quarter of their income toward their rent, the remainder being met through subsidy.

Within the last few years, the very high nominal interest rates facing potential home buyers have resulted in the relaxation and gradual abandonment of the traditional ratio. Mortgage expense/income ratios of 30 to 40 percent are not uncommon. At the same time, alternative rent/income ratios have been utilized in various analyses of the housing problems of the poor.[3] In 1981 Congress raised the required payment from 25 to 30 percent of income for those tenants in the moderately low income category. In this chapter, an expense/income ratio greater than 30 percent is used to indicate "too expensive" housing.

Housing quality. Defining the physical "adequacy" of housing is more complicated. At present, there is no generally accepted standard for housing quality in the United States, but fortunately the various criteria developed in recent years are quite similar.

From World War II to 1970, the consensual definition of housing quality could be simply stated: a housing unit was considered substandard if it was in poor structural condition ("dilapidated" or "needing major repairs") or if it lacked complete plumbing facilities. However, because it was difficult to identify precisely which housing units were "dilapidated," the Census Bureau stopped asking questions about overall structural quality after 1970. This left only the presence of complete plumbing, which was widely regarded as an insufficient indicator of standard quality housing.

Since 1973, new measures of housing quality have become available in the Annual Housing Survey (AHS) and have been used to construct new measures of adequacy.[4] The AHS collects data on some thirty different kinds of housing deficiencies—far more than have previously been available in any data source—for approximately a 1-in-1,000 sample of the housing stock. Questions are asked not only about the presence of facilities but also about their functioning—for example, not only "Do you have plumbing?" but also "Has it broken down in the last year? If so, how often? For how long?" Similar questions are asked about the heating, electrical, and other major systems of the unit. Instead of asking a single question on overall physical condition, the survey covers a number of specific structural problems, such as leaky roofs, holes in the floors or walls, and missing stairs in apartment buildings.

A number of government agencies—including the Department of Housing and Urban Development (HUD), the Office of Management and Budget (OMB), and the Congressional Budget Office (CBO)—have used the AHS in an attempt to find a new standard for housing quality. This chapter uses the most recent CBO definition to measure the number of inadequate housing units. This definition, more complicated than the traditional criterion, is presented in table 1. It is typical of those developed by the other agencies; all show about the same number of inadequate units and the same patterns within the housing stock.

As the table shows, the CBO definition divides housing defects into two categories. The first seven are either structural deficiencies that would probably be corrected only in the course of major rehabilitation, or continuing serious breakdowns in the plumbing or heating system. Any of these defects is fundamental. The last eight items in the table are probably less serious. These problems may arise periodically in any housing unit; when they do, they are usually repaired in the normal course of maintenance. Generally, the same units do not suffer from these defects each year; for example, 89 percent of the houses with leaky roofs in 1974 no longer had that problem by 1976.[5] Thus a single deficiency in this category does not seem sufficient to characterize a unit as "inadequate." The criterion that two such defects must be present at the same time is an attempt to distinguish units needing normal maintenance—and likely to get it—from those actually in need of major rehabilitation or replacement.

Current Housing Problems. For both housing quality and cost, two facts stand out: problems are far more common among renters than among owners, and they are concentrated at the bottom of the income distribution.[6] Problems are also disproportionately found among certain types of households, such as those consisting of blacks or the elderly or headed by women. To a very large extent, however, the housing problems of these groups are the consequence of their generally having lower incomes than the rest of the population. When adequacy and cost burden are compared for different household types holding income constant, the elderly usually live in better housing

TABLE 1

CONGRESSIONAL BUDGET OFFICE DEFINITION OF HOUSING INADEQUACY ("NEEDING REHABILITATION")

A unit is classified as needing rehabilitation if it has at least one of the following conditions:

1. the absence of complete plumbing facilities
2. the absence of complete kitchen facilities
3. the absence of a public sewer connection, septic tank, or cesspool
4. three or more breakdowns of six or more hours each time in the sewer, septic tank, or cesspool during the prior ninety days
5. three or more breakdowns of six or more hours each time in the heating system during the last winter
6. three or more times completely without a flush toilet for six or more hours each time during the prior ninety days
7. three or more times completely without water for six or more hours each time during the prior ninety days

or if the unit has two or more of the following conditions:

1. leaking roof
2. holes in interior floors
3. open cracks or holes in interior walls or ceilings
4. broken plaster over greater than one square foot of interior walls or ceilings
5. unconcealed wiring
6. the absence of any working light in public hallways in multi-unit structures
7. loose or no handrails in public hallways in multi-unit structures
8. loose, broken, or missing steps in public hallways in multi-unit structures

SOURCE: Congressional Budget Office, *Federal Housing Policy: Current Programs and Recurring Issues*, 1978, p. 6.

than younger households with the same income, and female-headed households are about as well housed as male-headed ones. More blacks live in inadequate housing than whites with similar incomes, suggesting that discrimination may linger in the housing market, but fewer very low income blacks have a high cost burden.

These differences between demographic groups are minor, compared with the differences by income class for members of any particular group; higher income blacks, for example, have cost and adequacy patterns much closer to those of higher income whites than to moderately low or very low income blacks. Accordingly, this analysis focuses on housing problems on the basis of household income and tenure. In looking at the poor, the classification into very low income and moderately low income proves to be useful: the two groups have rather different housing circumstances.

Very low income. About 9.3 million very low income families and individuals rented private housing in the United States in 1977. About 60 percent of them—5.5 million—lived in private housing that was adequate in quality, but they had to pay more than 30 percent of their income as rent in order to do so. Some 2 million lived in physically inadequate housing; well over half of them, 1.3 million, also suffered a high rent burden. About 1.8 million households suffered neither problem. Clearly it is very hard for the poorest renter households to avoid housing problems without government assistance, but most of them have been able to find and occupy decent housing.[7]

The situation among very low income owners is quite different. It is perhaps surprising to note that there are some 9.7 million very low income households that own their own homes. This is 46 percent of all very low income households. However, the majority of the owners, 5.0 million, are elderly; presumably most bought their homes when they were younger and their incomes were higher.

Very low income owners have fewer housing problems than renters do. This is to be expected, since homeowners have much more control over the quality of their housing; when a problem occurs, it is easier for the owner to hire someone to fix it, or even do it personally, than for the renter to make arrangements with the landlord for the repairs. In the very low income category, more than twice as many renters as owners live in inadequate housing (19.2 percent and 9.4 percent, respectively, including those in subsidized housing). Cost is a much more prevalent problem for owners, though still less serious than for very low income renters. Just over half of the owners have to pay a high share of their income to meet their mortgage and other housing expenses. The remaining 42 percent of very low income owners live in adequate housing without having to pay a large share of their income for it. Most of these are elderly.

"Permanent" and "temporary" poverty. These conclusions are not substantively changed if the population under study is restricted to "permanently" poor, eliminating those who have low incomes for some temporary reason, such as ill health, cyclical unemployment, or bad weather (for farmers). A recent attempt to separate the permanently poor from the temporarily poor households established that, among permanently poor renters, high rent/income ratios were twice

as common as physically inadequate housing. More than 83 percent had the former problem, compared with the 40 percent who had the latter. Surprisingly, a majority of the permanently poor (53 percent) lived in adequate housing, but paid more than 30 percent of their income for rent.[8] The percentage in this category is not much less than for all very low income renters. A much greater difference occurred in the instance of inadequate housing: about 40 percent of the permanently poor renters had this problem, compared with 19 percent of those with very low incomes. Fewer than 10 percent suffered neither problem. Permanently poor owners were much better off: 45 percent had neither problem, 35 percent lived in inadequate housing, and 20 percent lived in adequate housing with a high expense burden.

The income cutoff used in this study was the poverty level, rather than the very low income measure common to housing policy; since the poverty level is lower, a greater incidence of housing problems would be expected. Less to be expected is the predominance of housing cost as the most common problem; apparently permanently poor households have made permanent adjustments to their expenditure patterns in order to live in decent housing, at the expense of food, clothing, and other goods and services.

Moderately low income. Housing conditions improve markedly with income. Both inadequacy and high expense burdens are much less common among moderately low income households than among the poorest. About 11 percent of renters in this income category live in inadequate housing; 7 percent have a high rent/income ratio. Only 2 percent have both problems. Nearly all of these families and individuals have found their housing on the private market; less than 7 percent receive housing subsidies.

More than half (55 percent) of all moderate-income families own homes. Less than 5 percent of the 8.5 million owners have an adequacy problem. About a quarter have a high expense burden, while over 70 percent have neither problem. Owners in this category are much more nearly a cross section of the population, in age and household composition, than are very low income owners.

Other households. Among middle- and upper income Americans, physical housing problems are uncommon if not rare. Less than 9 percent of renters, and less than 3 percent of owners, live in inadequate housing. Less than 5 percent of renters, and 13 percent of owners, suffer a high expense burden.

As these percentages might suggest, high housing expense/income ratios are not confined to very low income renters. Of the

20.6 million households spending more than 30 percent of their income for housing, only about 7.5 million are very low income renters. Another 1.5 million are moderately low income renters, and 500,000 are renters with higher incomes.

More homeowners than renters—11.1 million, as compared with 9.5 million—have high housing expenses in proportion to their incomes. About 4.6 million are very low income owners. Most of the rest are young or recent home buyers, who can reasonably expect their incomes to rise and bring down their expense/income ratio. But more important is the fact that these households differ from the poor in that they do not *have* to pay a high share of their income to occupy physically adequate housing; instead, they choose to incur this burden in order to own their own homes. In most cases, their homes are much better than minimally adequate. The problems middle- and upper-income families face in becoming homeowners are important, but lie outside the scope of this study of private sector initiatives.

Trends in Housing. The direction and rate of change in housing conditions are almost as important as the current number of households with problems, for purposes of assessing housing policy and describing the role of the private sector.

Quality. Over the entire postwar period, there has been a steady improvement in quality. By every available measure, fewer and fewer households have suffered from physical inadequacy. Almost half the housing stock in the country was classified as substandard according to the traditional definition in 1940; by 1970 this had declined to less than 10 percent.

Among minorities, the trend is the same. Some 80 percent of nonwhite households lacked complete plumbing in 1940, for example, compared with 7 percent of black households in 1977. National data on the Hispanic population became available only with the 1970 census, but the figures since then show the incidence of incomplete plumbing cut in half by 1977. This is about the same as the rate of improvement among blacks and the poor. The limitations of the data for these and other groups are frustrating, but do not appear to invalidate the general impression: in each case, housing remains somewhat worse for the group than for the population as a whole, but the incidence of inadequacy has declined steadily.

The data from the Annual Housing Survey are of too short a duration to establish any real pattern, but the figures show continuing improvement since the first year. In 1973, some 8.1 percent of all housing units were inadequate, by the definition used here; by 1977, this had fallen to 7.5 percent.

Cost. Housing costs for renters show the same steady improvement over the postwar period. This improvement is not often recognized because the most common measure, the rent/income ratio, does not take into account either the shift to homeownership or the changing quality of the housing stock. Rent/income ratios have risen: in 1950, some 32 percent of all renters paid more than a quarter of their income for rent, while by 1979 the fraction rose to 51 percent. Much of this increase can, however, be attributed to the shift of better-off renters to ownership. In 1950, 45 percent of the population rented; by 1979, only 35 percent did. The decline was especially pronounced among higher-income households, who generally had much lower rent/income ratios.

Part of the increase in the ratio is also due to the higher quality of rental housing. The reported rent increases that have occurred over time reflect improved quality and greater space, as well as higher costs for adequate housing. One appropriate way of evaluating rental costs is to compare the change in income with the change in rent for the same quality of housing over time. The best-known measure of the latter is the residential rent component of the consumer price index (CPI), which is derived from rents on the same dwellings resurveyed from year to year. Between 1950 and 1979, this index increased by 200 percent; that is, rents for housing of the same quality tripled. (Actual rents rose by 400 percent, which means that quality improvements accounted for about as much of the higher rents as did cost increases.) By comparison, income for the typical family rose by 491 percent in the same three decades, and income for the poorest families by 493 percent.[9] Thus the typical household, and the typical poor household, were able to afford better rental housing.

A similar procedure can be used for homeowners, although data are available only for a much shorter period. Here the pattern is somewhat different. From 1963 to 1979 the cost of a newly built home of constant quality rose by 7.4 percent annually according to the Census Bureau's *Price Index of New One-Family Homes Sold.* This is almost the same as the increase in median family income over the period. For owner-occupied housing, however, the mortgage interest rate is an important component of cost, in addition to the sales price. Mortgage rates have historically had a very pronounced cyclical pattern; in recent years, as inflation has worsened, they have gone up dramatically. Thus the monthly mortgage payment for a house of constant quality, as a fraction of the typical family's income, fluctuated between 20 and 25 percent until the mid-1970s, then rose sharply to more than 35 percent by 1980.

Since the vast majority of homeowners have fixed-rate mortgages, the rise in interest rates affects them directly only if they wish to buy or sell. Even the high interest rates may not be much of a problem for many elderly owners, who may "trade down" to a smaller house, and can afford to do so without a mortgage. Thus low income families may be largely unaffected by the current high rates if they already own their own homes; but they probably cannot afford any kind of home if they do not.

Tenure. The different trends in costs for owners and renters might lead one to infer that homeownership has been decreasing over time. In fact, the opposite has happened. In the postwar period, ownership has steadily and dramatically increased, from less than 55 percent of all households in 1950 to over 65 percent in 1979. Nearly 80 percent of all married couples are owners. It is more accurate to say that strong demand for homeownership has pushed up the costs of owning than that rising costs have inhibited ownership.

This trend to ownership embraces virtually all segments of American society, with one important exception. Among very low income households (those with incomes less than 50 percent of the national median), ownership has declined slightly. Just over half, 51 percent, were owners in 1950; less than half, 48 percent, owned in 1979.[10]

The trend in ownership is one important difference between very low income and moderately low income households. For the latter, ownership rose from 50 percent in 1950 to 60 percent in 1979, paralleling the increase in the population as a whole.

The decline among the poorest is a matter of some concern. Homeownership has traditionally been an important source of asset accumulation for lower as well as middle income Americans. During the inflation of the past fifteen years, the importance of homeownership has been enhanced as it has proved to be the best hedge against inflation for most families. The poorest households, however, have been less able to take advantage of homeownership, even as its importance has increased.

Expanding the Role of the Private Sector

This review of the current housing situation of lower-income households indicates that the poor place a high priority on living in decent housing and that the private sector can in fact provide it for them. Indeed, the private sector is now doing so, to an unprecedented extent. But the housing is expensive from the standpoint of the poor; to pay for it, they must use such a large share of their income that they have little left to pay for other goods and services. Stated simply, the housing problem of the poor results basically from their poverty, not from special circumstances in the housing market.

Historically, federal housing policy has been based on quite a different perception of the problems confronting the poor: the premise that the private sector was not providing and probably could not provide adequate housing, and that it was therefore up to the federal government to make decent housing available. The federal government began in the mid-1930s to act on this perception by providing money for the construction of housing designed specifically for occupancy by low-income families. Little of this has been built directly by the federal government. Instead, the federal government has made payments to local government agencies, under the public housing program, or to individual builders, through various mortgage subsidy mechanisms; these entities have then built and operated the housing. But the federal government has exercised the right to approve each project before funding it and has thereby played a major role in determining the characteristics of the housing built for the poor. The tenant's choice of housing has been restricted to the specific units produced under the subsidy programs—sometimes to only one such unit—if he or she is to receive any housing assistance from the government.

Such a program may have been desirable at a time when perhaps half the housing in the country was substandard, although there were advocates of greater reliance on the private sector even in the 1930s. But it makes little sense now, when a small and declining share of the stock is inadequate and the chief housing problem facing the poor is financial. Nonetheless, the general approach devised in the 1930s has remained the basic concept underlying federal housing policy ever since.

In the past decade, however, two federal housing initiatives have used the private sector to provide decent housing for the poor. These are the Experimental Housing Allowance Program (EHAP) and the Section 8 existing housing program. The former was an extensive experiment, begun in 1973; the latter, an actual operating program, enacted in 1974. In both, poor individuals and families have selected the private housing that they want to live in, and the federal government has provided funds to enable them to do so. These initiatives have produced much information about how well the private sector of the economy can in fact provide decent housing for the poor and what the appropriate role is for the federal government.

These are not private sector initiatives in the literal sense; private organizations have not undertaken to solve the housing cost problems of the poor. Nor is it likely that they would; after all, the basic problem is that the poor have inadequate incomes to afford decent housing, and income redistribution is essentially a governmental role and responsibility. But Section 8 existing housing and the housing allowance experiments have operated by expanding the role of the private sector, relying on private landlords to provide adequate housing for the poor more efficiently than the government has been able to do. Thus they exemplify a kind of public-private partnership that fits within the broad scope of activities that can appropriately be termed "private sector initiatives." In many ways they are analogous to "voucher" programs designed to expand the choices of low-income and other households in education and health.

Both the experiments and the program activities have been studied intensively since their inception. This section summarizes the results of that research.[11] The most important finding appears to be that poor households are able to use their payments to meet their biggest housing problem: they can bring down the cost of housing to a manageable share of their budgets. Rents have not been driven up when the poor have more buying power as long as they have a financial incentive to bargain with the landlord. With respect to housing quality, there has been a large volume of minor repair and improvement to meet the standards; however, those living in the worst housing tend to stay out of the program, even when it would be in their financial interest to participate. When low-income owners are eligible, the same improvements in cost burdens and quality occur. The allowance does little, however, to encourage homeownership among the poor. National concern about discrimination raises the issue of whether the private housing market works satisfactorily for low-income minority households. Apparently it does; blacks and other minorities have participated successfully in proportion to their numbers in the eligible population. Finally, reliance on the private sector has proved much less expensive than the traditional government programs.

Each of these findings is discussed in more detail after a brief description of the two initiatives.

Housing Allowance Programs. Under a "housing allowance" or "demand-side subsidy" program, the poor are given money (the housing allowance) and permitted to choose their own housing, rather than having the housing built for them as under the traditional approach. Serious policy discussion of the housing allowance dates from 1968, when the President's Committee on Urban Housing recommended that it be tested; Congress subsequently called for an experimental demonstration in the Housing and Urban Development Act of 1970, and HUD therefore began the housing allowance experiments. Drawing on the initial experience in EHAP, Congress created an existing housing component in the Section 8 program, established in the Housing and Community Development Act of 1974. This program has grown rapidly and now serves about 630,000 households.

Section 8 existing housing. Because Section 8 is more precisely structured, it is easier to describe than the housing allowance experiments. Under Section 8, a lower-income household first applies for a subsidy from the local agency administering the program. If the household is selected to participate, it is given a certificate promising that it will receive a rent subsidy to enable it to live in a decent housing unit—one that meets the local authority's quality standards and rents for no more than the "fair market rent" established by HUD for the area.

Typically, the household has sixty days in which to find an acceptable unit, after which the certificate lapses and is offered to another household. The local agency must approve any unit that the household chooses, on the basis of standards for heating and plumbing services, structural condition, space, and other attributes. If the agency approves the unit, it then signs a contract with the landlord, promising to pay a portion of the rent each month. This portion is determined by the difference between the rent and 25 percent of the household's income; the tenant pays the rest. Even though the subsidy goes directly to the landlord, it is portable in the sense that the tenant can subsequently choose another dwelling that meets the quality standards anywhere within the jurisdiction of the administering agency, and the subsidy goes with him or her to the new unit.

Eligibility is determined by income and family size. Income limits range from 50 percent of the area median income for a single person to the median itself for a family of eight or more. The limit for a family of four is 80 percent of the median, commonly referred to as "the" income limit and used in that sense in this chapter. Until 1978 nonelderly single persons were excluded from the program.

An unusual feature of the Section 8 existing housing program is that the household can receive a subsidy without having to move if its home meets the quality standards or is upgraded to meet them. In every previous housing subsidy program, families have had to move to a particular unit or project if they were to receive any assistance. About half the households in Section 8 have remained in place. This high proportion is further evidence that the physical condition of housing of lower-income families is generally adequate; it is consistent with the data from the Annual Housing Survey cited in the preceding section.

The housing allowance experiment. There was a more complicated structure in EHAP. The experiment had three components: the "supply experiment," in the Green Bay and South Bend metropolitan areas, in which assistance was offered to all low-income households in order to see what effect the allowance would have on the entire housing market, particularly the lower-income part of the spectrum; the "demand experiment," in Pittsburgh and Phoenix, in which different funding formulas were tested in the same market to see how the responses of recipients might differ; and the "administrative agency experiment," in which a different type of agency was given responsibility in each of eight markets for administering a small allowance program.

The housing allowance experiments differed from the Section 8 existing housing program in several important ways. The subsidy was paid directly to the tenant, who negotiated the lease with the landlord independently. The allowance is therefore sometimes termed "direct cash assistance" or, less accurately, a "housing voucher." The payment to the tenant was based on the estimated rent of a decent housing unit, equivalent conceptually to the "fair market rent," not the actual rent of the unit. If the tenant found a unit meeting the program's quality standards at a lower rent, he or she could keep the difference. Rents could also exceed the cost of decent housing if the tenant wished to spend a larger share of income to obtain housing of still better quality.

Housing Cost. The Section 8 existing housing program has particularly helped families and individuals with especially severe problems of housing cost. Some 89 percent of program participants were in the very low income category; such households are very likely to be paying high fractions of their income for rent. Four-fifths of the assisted households were paying more than 35 percent of their income before they participated in the program. The housing allowance experiments also reached households with high costs to a substantial extent; more than half had a rent/income ratio greater than 35 percent.

Participants used their subsidies to bring down housing costs and reduce the strain on their budgets; in Section 8, the typical rent/income ratio was reduced from over 50 percent to about 25 percent, which was the target ratio established in the payment formula. The fact that subsidy recipients can avoid the cost and bother of moving, if their housing is physically adequate, is a major reason why both Section 8 and EHAP have been successful in solving the housing cost problem of the poor. The elderly in particular have taken advantage of this opportunity.

Before the experiments began, there were fears that housing allowances would drive rents up by increasing the effective demand for a fixed supply of adequate housing. This would undermine the value of the allowance for participants and leave low-income nonparticipants worse off by confronting them with higher rents. Rent inflation has not occurred, however, either in the experiments or under Section 8. The increases incurred by subsidy recipients have been just a few percentage points when adjusted for quality changes. The allowance does not drive rents up partly because only about half the eligible households choose to enroll, partly because many of those who do participate do not spend a large share of their subsidy for better housing, and partly because the quality of the existing stock can be upgraded rather easily. In Section 8, concentrations of as many as 20,000 program participants in the larger cities have been successfully absorbed without rent inflation; and in the supply experiment, where the largest impact has occurred in relation to the overall market, rents have risen by less than the general inflation rate, and less than rents in other areas. There has been little increase even in tight housing markets: inflation was equally negligible in Green Bay, with a 4 percent vacancy rate, and in South Bend, with a 10 percent rate.

The absence of rent inflation illustrates the effectiveness of free competition in the rental market, even in its low-income segment. There are a large number of landlords in any metropolitan area, most of them with a small number of apartments. It would be very difficult if not impossible for these small businesses to collude in order to raise rents without providing any higher quality housing. Even if they tried, the attempt would break down quickly. Costs of moving are low enough so that individual tenants could force landlords to choose between upgrading their apartments and having vacancies; for a small landlord with perhaps one building, a single vacancy for an extended period of time is likely to be a severe financial drain. It is cheaper to provide better housing and have the apartment occupied.

Housing Adequacy. Typically, but not invariably, housing allowances appear to generate significant improvements in quality. The most thorough evaluation of the Section 8 existing housing program found that 19 percent of the subsidy recipients originally lived in inadequate housing, as measured by the CBO criterion. This is the same as the incidence of inadequacy among all lower-income renters; thus Section 8 has been reasonably successful in reaching people with housing quality problems. Even after they began receiving subsidies, however, 6 percent still lived in inadequate housing. For comparison, the incidence of inadequate housing for households in the companion Section 8 new construction program fell from 20 percent to 1 percent—a greater improvement but achieved at a substantially higher cost, as will be shown later in this section.

That any assisted households stayed or moved into deficient housing is both surprising and a violation of program rules—the more so since the CBO criterion is less stringent than the standard of quality required for acceptability in the program itself. But there have been analogous (and markedly worse) administrative problems in the early years of previous HUD programs, such as Sections 235 and 236.[12] Part of the explanation may lie also in the problem of defining and measuring inadequate housing. In evaluating the housing allowance experiments, HUD has reported that sometimes "it takes a trained inspector to detect defects," which otherwise "often go unnoticed by renters, landlords, and homeowners."[13] This raises the question whether the standards are too strict.

An alternative measure of housing improvement is the tenant's subjective assessment of the quality of his or her own housing. Satisfied tenants, those rating their housing "good" or "excellent," increased from 65 percent before participating in Section 8 existing housing to 79 percent afterward. The high initial percentage is consistent with the evidence that most privately housed poor people live in decent housing.

Those who originally live in physically inadequate housing have three options. They can move to standard housing; they can fix up their present home so that it meets program standards; or they can drop out of the program. There is little evidence on the proportion who chose to drop out, but the information on those remaining in the program indicates that 58 percent moved and 42 percent chose to improve their present housing. Generally, movers were originally living in units with more numerous and serious problems. Most "stayers with repairs" reported that they, or their landlords, spent less than $200 to bring their housing up to the program requirements.

The housing allowance supply experiment yielded similar results, with much more detail about the change in the quality of housing for those originally living in inadequate units. ("Inadequacy" in the experiment does not necessarily correspond to the CBO criterion.) About 60 percent chose to make repairs, 20 percent moved, and the remaining 20 percent dropped out of the experiment. Again, the repairs actually undertaken were generally minor and inexpensive. The average cash outlay was about $70 for materials, the work being done either by the tenants or by the landlords. This small effort was enough because few of the units were severely inadequate.

The experiment also had a continuing effect on the quality of low-income housing. Some 40 percent of all substandard units in the Green Bay and South Bend areas were brought up to standard, at modest cost, by program participants during the first five years of the experiment. Further, annual housing inspections led to repairs for units in which defects developed after occupancy. Inspections after the first year found that 20 percent of the assisted units in Green Bay and 40 percent in South Bend had become physically substandard; repairs were made in 90 percent of these units, and they remained in the program. The allowance thus encouraged maintenance and upgrading of the existing housing stock, so that some units that would have become substandard in the absence of the allowance program remained in good condition.

Those who dropped out of the experiment generally had more severe housing quality problems, however, or several problems simultaneously. Families in the worst housing apparently were least likely to participate in the experiment or, presumably, in a full-scale program relying on the private sector to provide decent housing. The low participation rate occurred even though the allowance payments were greater than the cost of repairs, or the cost of renting and moving to a better-quality house or apartment.

In this light, it is worth noting that the choice of a standard has a significant impact on participation by those in inadequate housing. The higher the standard, the more housing units will fail it, and the more households will choose not to participate. In the demand experiment, which had more stringent quality standards, only 17 percent of participants' housing units met the standard initially, as compared with half in the supply experiment. Further, 60 percent of those originally in inadequate housing ultimately dropped out of the demand experiment, compared with only 20 percent in the supply experiment. The choice of quality standard also apparently affected participation by various types of households. In the demand experiment, those most likely to be in inadequate housing—very low income households, large families, and minorities—were least likely to receive an allowance. In the supply experiment, such households participated in proportion to their numbers in the eligible population.

Discrimination. There has been special concern over the ability of members of minority groups to find decent housing under a housing allowance program. To the extent that private landlords attempt to discriminate against minorities, the private housing market will work imperfectly, and these households will be less than fully able to use their subsidy payments to obtain better housing. This kind of problem is generally regarded as much less serious in the traditional programs.

Evidence from both the Section 8 existing housing program and the allowance experiments indicates that minorities have been able to participate effectively. In Section 8 they are represented in proportion to their numbers in the eligible population and appear to experience about the same degree of housing improvement as other households; they are able to find structurally adequate housing at reasonable rents. In the housing allowance supply experiment, minority households participated at a somewhat higher than proportional rate.

A further question is whether minority households are able to move into desirable neighborhoods as well as into decent housing. The best evidence on the locational choices of minority households comes from the housing allowance experiments, in which households that received subsidies were compared with those that did not. The allowances may have resulted in a very slight increase in racial integration and in freedom of locational choice, but the results can also be interpreted as indicating that there was no effect. They certainly did not *reduce* integration, however. Allowance recipients were found to move about as frequently as other low-income households, and to similar neighborhoods. When people in either group moved outside their own neighborhoods, they went to neighborhoods that had similar concentrations of low income households but were slightly more integrated racially.

Housing allowances seem unlikely to alter existing patterns of racial segregation. When blacks or whites in the Pittsburgh demand experiment searched for a new place to live, for example, they limited their search largely to neighborhoods with racial composition similar to that of their present neighborhood.

Because program beneficiaries move about as often and to the same locations as unassisted households, allowances are unlikely to affect neighborhood composition or stability. Only in the supply experiment were enough households enrolled to affect whole neighborhoods, but after five years of operation during which one-fifth of the recipients moved, no measurable change occurred in the racial or economic composition of neighborhoods.

Evaluations of Section 8 have not included any "control group" of unassisted low-income households against which to measure the locational changes of subsidy recipients, but they do provide information on the locational choices of the recipients, so that the actual moves can be studied. Moreover, the Section 8 new construction and existing housing programs can be compared with each other. It appears that both lead to greater integration, but in quite different ways and to different degrees. New construction projects are located predominantly in white neighborhoods and they have a high concentration of white tenants. However, those minority households who want to live in an integrated project and who succeed in getting in, do experience a marked decrease in minority concentration. The pattern is almost the opposite in Section 8 existing housing: a higher proportion of participants are black or Hispanic, and most of those who move go to neighborhoods with smaller minority concentrations, but the racial and economic differences between the original and the new neighborhoods are small.

In sum, a housing allowance program would not greatly expand —but would certainly not reduce—the freedom of locational choice already available to unassisted persons; nor would it particularly alter the racial or economic composition of neighborhoods. But compared with traditional housing subsidy programs, it would provide substantially greater freedom of locational choice for most households.

Homeownership. A housing allowance does little to encourage homeownership among the poor. The supply experiment was open to owners, and renters could use their allowance payments to help them purchase homes if they chose. This did not happen, for several reasons. The ten-year life of the experiment, while long enough for most research purposes, was much shorter than the life of any mortgage, confronting lenders with a substantial risk that the buyer would be unable to continue meeting mortgage payments in later years. In addition, the allowance payment was much less than the required monthly mortgage payment, and the experiment provided no help with the down payment. The first of these problems would disappear in a full-scale allowance program, but the others would not.

Program Cost. A final question concerning housing allowances is their cost to the government, particularly in relation to that of the traditional construction programs. Here the allowances have a substantial advantage that is particularly important in an era of high and rising budget deficits. Roughly twice as many households can be served at any level of budget expenditure under the allowance as under the traditional programs. The latter are more expensive in part because the quality level is higher. Section 8 illustrates the difference: the units in the existing housing program generally are adequate, but the

TABLE 2

COMPARISON OF SUBSIDY COSTS FOR THE SECTION 8
NEW CONSTRUCTION AND EXISTING HOUSING PROGRAMS, 1979
(dollars per month)

Cost Category	New Construction	Existing Housing
Gross rent	362	240
Tenant payment	112[a]	110[a]
HUD subsidy (gross rent minus tenant payment)	250	130

[a] Average tenant payments are slightly different in the two programs because average tenant incomes differ.

SOURCE: President's Commission on Housing, *Interim Report*, 1981, p. 32.

newly constructed units are substantially better than adequate. In addition, the private sector is clearly more efficient than the government in providing housing.

These findings are most conveniently illustrated in the Section 8 program, where new construction and existing housing can be directly compared. Table 2 shows that the differences in rents between the programs result in federal subsidies that are nearly twice as high for new construction as for existing housing for tenants of similar income.

The new construction rents are at the high end of the distribution for the entire rental housing stock. The average program rent of $362 is half again as great as the average for all private rental units of about $242. Only 11 percent of all renters in 1979 paid more than $350 per month. These comparisons even understate the cost difference, because three-quarters of the new subsidized units are either efficiency or one bedroom apartments; only 4 percent of the private units in these categories rented for more than $350.

Part of the high cost stems from government inefficiency. The true rental value of the project units has been estimated, on the basis of their characteristics and location, at $291 per month, rather than $362.[14] This is the rent such apartments could command in the private market. Thus the actual rent of $362 was 24 percent higher than the estimated market rent; the difference of $71 is a measure of the inefficiency in the subsidy program. But even on the basis of their market value rather than their cost, the Section 8 apartments are of high quality compared with what moderate income families could afford; unsubsidized households just at the income limit for Section 8 normally spent about $200 per month for rent. The market value of the average Section 8 existing housing unit, by comparison, is about $231. The new construction program produces housing that is about 25 percent better, as valued in the marketplace, than the houses and apartments subsidized under the existing housing program, even though the latter are typically physically adequate and are about 15 percent better than the housing occupied by unsubsidized moderately low income families.

There are further costs associated with both the new construction and the existing housing programs, for depreciation, administration, and special financing for many of the new units. These add about $48 to the cost of a new apartment and $26 to the cost of an existing one; subtracting the tenant's rent, the total government cost is $298 for a new unit and $156 for an existing one.

The same conclusions hold for other construction programs besides Section 8. Total costs for new public housing have been estimated at $500 per month or more.[15] Moreover, an analysis of West German housing programs found a similar cost pattern for production and allowance programs there.

Rehabilitation

Despite its many merits, the housing allowance does not fully solve all the problems of lower-income families. In particular, it is not likely to bring about complete elimination of the relatively small number of physically inadequate units remaining; on the contrary, some of the worst housing will not be directly affected by the program, because the occupants will not participate. The issue of housing improvement and rehabilitation is particularly important because of the increasing emphasis in public policy, and in society at large, on using the existing stock of housing more effectively. There has been a gradual shift in focus away from demolishing existing housing to make way for new construction and toward maintaining and upgrading it as much as feasible. Thus to the extent that the housing allowance fails to promote improvement, particularly at the worst end of the quality distribution, it fails to satisfy one of the major current concerns of housing policy.

This shortcoming of a housing allowance is not an argument for the traditional government housing subsidy programs. By and large the federal government has a weak record of performance in encouraging housing rehabilitation, despite increasing rhetorical emphasis on rehabilitation in policy statements and even legislation for more than twenty years. One of the principal criticisms of the traditional policy approach has been that it operates through the demolition and replacement of existing housing rather than its maintenance and improvement.[16]

While government programs have done relatively little, the private sector has done a great deal. A very large and increasing volume of maintenance and improvement has been undertaken by individual homeowners, landlords, and tenants, and housing rehabilitation has been the subject of organized efforts by neighborhood groups, churches, business firms, and hybrid organizations set up specifically to deal with housing problems. Indeed, it seems fair to say that rehabilitation has been one of the most important areas of activity for private sector initiatives in housing.

The next section of this chapter describes specific activities undertaken through a variety of private sector initiatives. First, however, it is useful to present a brief discussion of overall rehabilitation activity, as the general background against which to assess these initiatives.

The volume of housing maintenance and repair activity increased rapidly during the 1970s. Total expenditures rose from about $14.8 billion in 1970 to $42.2 billion in 1979, expenditures per housing unit from $219 to $500. Even after taking account of inflation, expenditures per unit increased by 22 percent over the decade, from $219 to $267 in 1970 dollars.[17] The vast bulk of this activity was purely private. Government-supported activity totaled less than $700 million in 1970 and less than $3 billion in 1979. In both years FHA insurance of Title I property improvement loans accounted for most of the government's share; actual loans and grants amounted to only $78 million in 1970, and $910 million in 1979. The increase is almost entirely due to loans and grants made by local governments with funds from their community development block grants rather than to direct federal outlays. As a share of the total, federal activities grew somewhat during the decade, but remained small; they were 4.7 percent in 1970 and 6.9 percent in 1979, or 0.5 and 2.3 percent, respectively, excluding Title I insurance.[18]

Owner-occupied houses receive a disproportionate share of total maintenance expenditures, $638 for each in 1979 as against $370 per unit for all other housing, including cooperatives and condominiums as well as rental houses and apartments. This pattern has prevailed throughout the decade. There is a strong relationship between expenditures and incomes for homeowners; very low income owners spent about $360 each in 1979, moderately low income owners about $690, and homeowners making more than $25,000 about $750. But even the figures for the low-income owners are about the same as for the remainder of the housing stock, which is by and large occupied by families and individuals with somewhat higher incomes.

Much less information is available about the outlays of landlords for rental housing, but the evidence suggests that they spend about two-thirds as much as homeowners. Expenditures appear to be greater for units in smaller buildings and greatest in rental single-family houses; in fact, outlays are about the same for all houses, regardless of tenure.

Research on the investment behavior of individual landlords indicates that they are more willing to make maintenance expenditures when they believe that their neighborhood is improving, and that they are ready to use loans when private lenders make them available.[19]

The concentration on single-family houses exists in government programs as well as in private activity; both community development block grants and direct federal outlays have been spent predominantly on owner-occupied houses, even though they are intended to serve primarily low- and moderate-income families. Over 80 percent of the block grant rehabilitation funds have been devoted to homeowners.[20]

Private Sector Initiatives

Although the range of organizations and activities falling under the rubric of "private sector initiatives" in the field of housing is vast, some generalizations are possible.

The common emphasis on rehabilitation has already been noted. A number of organizations have combined homeownership with their rehabilitation efforts, enabling lower-income families to afford not only to live in decent housing but also to own it. These programs provide a range of ownership opportunities, depending on their location and emphasis. Some offer older single-family detached homes for households that have incomes slightly higher than the eligibility limits for federal rental housing subsidies. Others convert rental apartment projects to cooperative ownership, sometimes for very low income families and individuals.

Perhaps an even stronger characteristic is the neighborhood orientation. To a much greater extent than seems true of private sector initiatives in almost any other field, the organizations concerned with housing address the problems of a single neighborhood. Sometimes the geographic focus is as narrow as a few blocks. Some larger organizations operate in several neighborhoods, but they typically have started on a small scale and then expanded, one neighborhood at a time.

But although the orientation is location-specific, it is frequently not housing-specific. Most organizations concerned with housing are also concerned with other attributes of their neighborhoods. In particular, they seek maintenance and upgrading of the services provided by city governments at the same time that they try to improve local housing conditions. Successful initiatives typically have been able to induce the local government to upgrade services. The focus of this chapter is on housing, and the other concerns of neighborhood groups lie outside its scope; however, some of the most important topics, such as crime and schools, are discussed in other chapters.

Partly because of their broad interests in the neighborhoods, local organizations have often developed unusual working, and even formal, relationships with local government. Moreover, a number of initiatives have involved unusual roles for federal government housing agencies and have used federal housing assistance in imaginative ways. The boundary between the public and the private sectors is difficult to delineate.

The examples in this section illustrate these generalizations. They can best be described as complementary to housing allowances. They tend to serve families close to, or just above, the income limits for federal housing subsidy programs or to engage in activities that the federal government does not. Thus the allowances provide support for the poorest households to afford modest but decent rental housing, while these private sector initiatives focus on the next level of housing progress, providing better housing and ownership opportunities for those who are slightly better off.

It is perhaps worth noting that these examples are not meant to represent all of the housing activities undertaken by private organizations. Many have worked through the various federal government subsidy programs of the past twenty years, building and operating projects for very low and moderately low income families. In this endeavor, they have on average met with neither more nor less success than public agencies and profit-making firms; all have had about the same problems and incurred about the same costs in providing housing.[21] Building new housing specifically for the poor is an expensive way to improve their housing, even when private nonprofit organizations undertake the projects instead of the government.

Neighborhood Housing Services. One of the best-known, and possibly the most extensive, private sector initiatives in the field of housing began in opposition to a federal program.[22] In 1966 residents of the Central North Side neighborhood in Pittsburgh found themselves surrounded by urban renewal projects and decided to try to "do something" to forestall any project from happening to their neighborhood. Two neighborhood citizens' groups and one local business organization began an intensive discussion process that lasted for two years and ultimately involved the city government, the Pittsburgh financial community, and Pittsburgh philanthropic organizations, and this process culminated in the establishment of a new kind of housing initiative, Neighborhood Housing Services (NHS). The initiative had three components: the city provided improved municipal services and housing code enforcement; the lending institutions agreed to use the same criteria as elsewhere in the city in making home improvement and mortgage loans (that is, there would be no redlining); and, for borrowers not deemed creditworthy by the financial institutions, a special high-risk loan fund was established, financed by a grant of $125,000 from the Sarah Scaife Foundation in Pittsburgh. The loan fund was to be administered by a board consisting of both neighborhood residents and representatives of financial institutions, with the former in the majority. This board could make home improvement loans at whatever interest rates and terms they considered reasonable for any particular borrower, postpone or waive repayments in cases of hardship, and bring the full force of informal neighborhood pressure to bear on those who failed to make payments without a good reason.

The program succeeded in stabilizing the neighborhood and upgrading its housing. The revolving loan fund experienced a delinquency rate of about 15 percent, which was low enough to enable it to continue making loans, using repayments of principal and interest. The private lenders found that their loans were good risks, with no special delinquency problems.

In 1972 a federal agency became interested in NHS. The Center for Executive Development of the Federal Home Loan Bank Board conducted a workshop on NHS, as one approach to neighborhood preservation that appeared to be working. The idea attracted attention within the Federal Home Loan Bank System (consisting of the board, the twelve regional home loan banks, and the nation's federally chartered savings and loan associations), and the center began to provide technical assistance to groups in other cities that wanted to start NHS organizations. By mid-1974 NHS programs were operating in four cities besides Pittsburgh and were in the development stage in nine more. At that point HUD began to participate through a joint agreement with the bank board to establish the Urban Reinvestment Task Force; HUD provided a minimal amount of necessary funding, less than $3 million yearly, and the board continued to provide the expertise. The task force replaced the center; William Whiteside, director of the center, became executive director of the task force. In 1978 the task force was replaced by the Neighborhood Reinvestment Corporation, chartered by Congress. By that time four other federal financial regulatory agencies were also involved. At the end of 1981, there were 137 NHS programs in 107 cities, and 45 more were being developed.

Federal involvement consists primarily of providing technical expertise to enable local NHS programs to get under way and in some locations providing part of the funding for the high-risk loan fund. The task force ceases to be involved after a local NHS director is hired and trained. The impetus for specific programs typically comes from the city government, which identifies neighborhoods in which NHS seems likely to work; before the establishment of the task force, the regional federal home loan bank often played this role.

NHS, however, is not a federal program in any conventional sense. Local organizations are formed only if local groups and individuals are able and willing to participate; neighborhoods without community organizations are not selected unless it appears likely that such groups can be established. Local residents become members of the board governing the NHS; usually they constitute the majority.

Indeed, NHS has retained much of the strong antigovernment attitude that led to the original Pittsburgh program. Local residents, financial institutions, and foundations have stressed that they would be unwilling to participate if the federal government were more than peripherally involved.

> The desire to minimize direct federal involvement emanates from a fear of red tape, bureaucracy and poor administration which combine to make a program unresponsive to the needs of those it is trying to serve. The appeal of the NHS program is just the opposite. It was the flexibility, the self-help nature and the local control of the program that made the financial institutions, citizens and funding sources want to become involved.[23]

Following the Pittsburgh example, the typical NHS neighborhood consists primarily of small structures with a significant proportion of resident ownership. Typically three-fourths or more of the housing units are in buildings with one to four units, and from 30 to 60 percent are owner occupied. These include landlords who live in one unit of a small building and rent out the others; more than half the structures, including both houses and apartments, have resident owners. Generally the neighborhoods have below-average incomes for the city, but they are not the poorest areas. NHS can help people afford better housing through its revolving loan fund, but it does not, and does not pretend to, help the very poorest; it is not a vehicle for redistributing income. It serves a clientele somewhat different from that served by the housing allowance and the subsidized housing programs. The average NHS neighborhood is small—about 2,300 residential buildings, 5,000 housing units, and 12,500 residents—with well-defined boundaries. Thus the program is not, and does not claim to be, a panacea for all urban neighborhoods. However, the Neighborhood Reinvestment Corporation is beginning to concern itself with possible programs for renovation and development of rental housing.

Precise statistics on NHS accomplishments have not been compiled, but a recent evaluation concluded that annual housing investment by homeowners amounted to about $1 million in the typical NHS neighborhood.[24] This does not include investment in rental properties or expenditures in nonresidential structures. It appears that owner-occupied homes constitute about two-thirds of the total number of residential properties in which investment occurs, but the dollar value for rental units is not available. The estimate includes investment that would have occurred in the absence of NHS and thus overstates the effect of the program. But the average 1979 investment of about $690 per owner-occupied house in NHS neighborhoods is well above the $500 spent by all lower-income owners; the difference is perhaps the simplest way to measure the net investment generated by NHS, at least for homeowners.

Housing Opportunities, Inc. A few years after Neighborhood Housing Services was created, a somewhat different initiative developed in another part of the Pittsburgh area. Housing Opportunities, Inc., as it eventually came to be called, drew in part on the experience of NHS, but put emphasis on helping lower income families become homeowners as a way to improve neighborhoods.[25]

Housing Opportunities developed out of the McKeesport Neighborhood Ministry, an antipoverty agency founded in the mid-1960s by a coalition of local churches that received much of its funding from the Presbyterian church. McKeesport is a lower-income blue-collar suburb of Pittsburgh, in the Monongahela Valley south of the city.

One of the ministry's supporters was Edward M. Ryan, founder of Ryan Homes, among the largest home builders in the country. James V. McDonough, head of Ryan Homes's mortgage subsidiary, became dissatisfied with the firm's experience with HUD's Section 235 lower-income homeownership program, and conceived a new method for helping lower-income families become owners. Meanwhile James P. Butler, a social worker with the ministry, was increasingly concerned about the importance of housing problems among the ministry's clients. McDonough and Butler approached Ryan separately at the same time, and their ideas fused into the new initiative.

The concept combines rehabilitation and homeownership. McDonough was particularly concerned with homeownership, and his idea became known as the Earned Home Ownership Program (EHOP). It stresses motivation rather than "the give-away, something-for-nothing philosophy of government subsidy programs," as McDonough viewed it.[26] In EHOP, families that want to become homeowners must first receive intensive counseling in money management over a period of six to eighteen months. The family is thus able to establish a record of effective money management and also to identify the amount it can afford to pay for housing. Housing Opportunities then helps the family secure a conventional first mortgage from a participating Pittsburgh financial institution, at a rate of two or three percentage points below the market. There are no cosigners and no mortgage insurance. To the extent that the first mortgage does not cover the full costs of the home, Housing Opportunities offers a second mortgage, tailored to fit the family's situation. The down payment and closing costs are typically financed through the second mortgage, which is likely to carry an interest rate of about 2 percent over a ten-year life. Obviously, such mortgages are well below the market rate. The money for them comes from a revolving loan fund, much like that used in NHS; the fund was initiated with a donation from the Pittsburgh Foundation, a community trust that awards grants to nonprofit organizations in the area. Other contributors include the Pitcairn-Crabbe Foundation and the Campaign for Human Development of the United States Catholic Conference.

Counseling and financing are only part of the process. Housing Opportunities itself first buys and rehabilitates the houses that are then purchased by its client families, and serves as the general contractor for the rehabilitation. In mid-1981, the organization had almost $800,000 invested in the houses it owned. Recently it has expanded its efforts by becoming a builder and has launched a profit-making subsidiary, Quality Craft, Inc., specializing in energy-efficient rehabilitation and operating outside as well as within the Monongahela Valley.

These activities were first conducted through the housing division of the McKeesport Neighborhood Ministry, starting in 1972. Three years later, they were spun off into a separate organization, the Housing and Community Development Corporation, which became

357

Housing Opportunities, Inc., in 1978. From its beginning in McKees-port with a staff of one—Butler—working on one house, the organization gradually expanded into five Monongahela Valley suburbs and five Pittsburgh neighborhoods. In 1980 the Allegheny County Department of Development contracted with Housing Opportunities to provide EHOP in an additional eighteen communities. It is also helping to develop a similar program in Altoona, Pennsylvania. Butler has served as executive director since the start; he now has a staff of sixteen.

During its first four years, the organization received no government funds. Its largest source of private contributions has been lending institutions, followed by builders and then other corporations, such as U.S. Steel and Westinghouse, the largest employers in the target communities. A significant avenue of corporate philanthrophy has been Pennsylvania's Neighborhood Assistance Program, which allows corporations donating money, property, and time or expertise to community betterment groups to claim a state tax credit of 30 percent for each dollar contributed. Since the highest federal corporate income tax rate is 46 percent, this means that the corporation is able to write off up to 76 percent of its contribution. (For community betterment agencies with a comprehensive range of activities, the tax credit is 40 percent, and the total write-off, 86 percent.)

The absence of direct government support also meant the absence of government restrictions, enabling Housing Opportunities to develop its own programs, which it subsequently offered to government agencies on a contract basis. This has provided a significant minor fraction of income in recent years, but general contracting and private contributions are more important sources of funding.

In a normal year, Housing Opportunities is able to bring about seventy families to the point of buying a home. The families are "all working people," says Butler; the most common occupation is steel-worker. Inflation has affected the program in a number of ways. In 1975 the average house cost less than $20,000, the mortgage rate was 8 percent, and the typical family earned less than $8,000; by 1981 the average house cost $32,000, the mortgage rate was 11¼ percent, and the typical income was close to $18,000. This is still significantly below the national median family income, which was $21,000 in 1980. There used to be a significant number of female-headed families in EHOP, but this has dwindled to a few, because of rising housing costs and interest rates. About 35 percent of the families have come from public housing. There has been one foreclosure in the ten years of operation. The program has contributed to the revitalization of the neighborhoods in which it operates; more homes are being upgraded, and fewer are allowed to deteriorate or to be abandoned. Two families in the program have sold their homes, both at a profit.

Housing Opportunities brings together persons with a wide range of backgrounds to make its programs work. Butler, himself a social worker, notes that "when we do something, we start with builders, bankers, attorneys, and social workers in the same room." The last three presidents have been a priest, a builder, and an accountant. The board of directors has a number of "consumer" representatives who have been helped by the program; in recent years they have included a bus driver, a cook, an electrician, and the operator of a beauty salon, along with the businessmen, ministers, and interested volunteers.

Lincoln Life Improved Housing. A different way to promote rehabilitation and homeownership simultaneously in a deteriorating neighborhood has been developed by Lincoln National Corporation, parent of the Lincoln National Life Insurance Company. In 1973 Lincoln National formed a subsidiary, Lincoln Life Improved Housing, Inc., with the goal of rehabilitating housing in Fort Wayne, Indiana, the headquarters of the firm.[27] Lincoln Life Improved Housing chose to concentrate on a small neighborhood near downtown Fort Wayne. The neighborhood, consisting of six square blocks in the east-central part of the city, contained 105 houses. These were generally structurally sound, but many were badly deteriorated, and some were abandoned.

Within the neighborhood, the corporation bought unoccupied houses for about $2,000 to $4,000 and rehabilitated them, gutting the houses and redoing the exteriors, the major systems (heating, plumbing, electrical), and the kitchens and bathrooms. After rehabilitation, Lincoln Life Improved Housing secured a mortgage for 50 percent of the purchase and rehabilitation cost from one of the five major Fort Wayne banks. The mortgages run for fifteen years at a below market interest rate, currently 9½ percent.

The corporation then leases the houses for five years to lower income families interested in becoming homeowners. The rent has averaged $125 per month, covering taxes, insurance, and maintenance as well as the mortgage payment. After five years the tenant can buy the house for one dollar and assume the remaining ten years of the mortgage. The reason for this lease-purchase combination lies in the U.S. tax code. Section 167 (k) provides a five-year accelerated depreciation write-off on rehabilitation expenditures for lower income rental housing. By becoming the landlord for five years, the corporation could reduce its costs by about 40 percent; its total initial investment of $500,000 was cut to $300,000 after tax benefits. In addition to generating the tax savings, the corporation's role as rehabilitater and mortgagor for the first five years has apparently been one important reason why local banks have been willing to make conventional mortgage loans in the neighborhood.

The city government has also been involved in the area. It has spent about $125,000 for capital improvements—particularly for streets and street lighting. It also has established a policy of quickly instituting condemnation proceedings on deteriorating and abandoned property, to minimize the problem of additional blight in the neighborhood.

The new occupants of these houses would generally be considered unlikely candidates for homeownership. Their incomes are usually in the moderately low income category. The typical family has two or three children, and half the families have only one parent. All but one are black; the only white family in the program is also the only one that has been evicted. An important part of the program has been counseling and education stressing home maintenance and family budgeting. The corporation has employed as resident coordinator a professional social worker who provides much of the counseling on a one-to-one basis.

Seventy-eight families have participated in the program. Of these, forty have become homeowners after completing the five-year rental period, twenty-five are renting, and thirteen have dropped out before acquiring title. The program has expanded into an adjacent six block area and is beginning in two more neighborhoods covering approximately twelve more blocks. Revitalization in the neighborhood is evidenced by a substantial reduction in the crime rate and a sense of community among the residents.

Conclusion

Some twenty years ago the urban critic Jane Jacobs noted that public housing projects were built on the mistaken notion that the poor

> *cannot be housed by private enterprise,* and hence must presumably be housed by someone else. Yet in real life, these are people whose housing needs are not in themselves peculiar and thus outside the ordinary province and capability of private enterprise, like the housing needs of prisoners, sailors at sea, or the insane. Perfectly ordinary housing needs can be provided for almost anybody by private enterprise. What is peculiar about these people is merely that *they cannot pay for it.*[28]

That statement, valid then, is still more valid today; its validity is increasingly being recognized. What is not as well recognized is the large role that the private sector is already playing—successfully—in housing the poor. The evidence from the housing allowance experiments and the Section 8 existing housing program indicates that the private sector could play a still larger role, housing more of the poor at less cost than the federal government has been able to do.

In addition, neighborhood organizations have developed a number of initiatives that deal successfully with aspects of housing not fully addressed by the housing allowance, notably the rehabilitation of low-quality units and the creation of enhanced opportunities for homeownership for lower income families that really want to own. New approaches will undoubtedly be devised in the future; the oldest of the efforts described in this chapter goes back only to the mid-1960s. An appropriate federal housing policy would be to provide assistance to enable the poor to afford decent housing and simultaneously to establish an economic and social climate in which private sector initiatives, for the poor and the near-poor, have the opportunity to develop further.

Notes

[1] For a more extensive discussion of housing quality, see John C. Weicher, *Housing: Federal Policies and Programs* (Washington, D.C.: American Enterprise Institute, 1980), chap. 2.

[2] National Commission on Urban Problems, *Building the American City*, 1969, pp. 132-33.

[3] For example, David Birch et al., *America's Housing Needs: 1970 to 1980* (Cambridge, Mass.: Joint Center for Urban Studies, 1973), pp. 4-4 to 4-6. This report uses a rent/income ratio of 0.35 or more for elderly or single-person households, and 0.25 for all other households, to measure "high rent burden."

[4] U.S. Department of Housing and Urban Development and U.S. Bureau of the Census, *Annual Housing Survey: United States and Regions*, Series H-150, Part B.

[5] Kenneth F. Wieand, "Analysis of Multiple-Defect Indicators of Housing Quality with Data from the 1976 Annual Housing Survey" (paper prepared for U.S. Department of Housing and Urban Development, 1978).

[6] Data in this section are taken from the President's Commission on Housing, *Interim Report*, 1981; and Weicher, *Housing*, chap. 2.

[7] The Annual Housing Survey also reports that some 1.9 million very low income renters lived in subsidized housing. Of these, 200,000 lived in substandard housing; 600,000 in standard housing with a rent/income ratio greater than 30 percent; and 1.1 million with neither problem. The rent burden figure is surprising and implausible, because government housing subsidy programs almost invariably limit the tenant's rent contribution to 25 percent or less of income. It seems likely that most of these 600,000 are welfare families living in private housing and receiving a "shelter allowance," rather than tenants of subsidized housing. Any reasonable adjustment of the reported data will result in a higher proportion of privately housed very low income renters living in adequate housing with a high rent burden; this will strengthen the conclusion in the text.

8 Sandra Newman et al., *Poverty, Housing Deprivation, and Housing Assistance*, Project Report 3089-01 (Washington, D.C.: Urban Institute, January 1982).

9 There is some downward bias in the CPI rent index, because it does not adjust for depreciation within the housing stock, but the bias is far too small to affect the basic conclusion.

10 The 1979 figure in the text does not correspond to the 46 percent used earlier in this section, because it refers to a somewhat different group. The lower figure is the incidence of ownership among households with less than 50 percent of their *area* median income; the higher, among those with less than 50 percent of the *national* median. The latter includes a larger proportion of rural households, who generally have lower incomes and also are more frequently homeowners. It is necessary to use the national figure to make comparisons over time.

11 A summary of the research findings is contained in President's Commission, *Interim Report*, chap. 3. For more detail, see James E. Wallace et al., *Participation and Benefits in the Urban Section 8 Program: New Construction and Existing Housing* (Cambridge, Mass.: Abt Associates, Inc., 1981); Raymond J. Struyk and Marc Bendick, Jr., eds., *Housing Vouchers for the Poor: Lessons from a National Experiment* (Washington, D.C.: Urban Institute Press, 1981); Stephen D. Kennedy, *Final Report of the Housing Allowance Demand Experiment* (Cambridge, Mass.: Abt Associates, Inc., 1980); and U.S. Department of Housing and Urban Development, Office of Policy Development and Research, *Experimental Housing Allowance Program: Conclusions, the 1980 Report*, Washington, D.C., 1980.

12 Cited by A. Thomas King, "Comments," in Katharine L. Bradbury and Anthony Downs, eds., *Do Housing Allowances Work?* (Washington, D.C.: Brookings Institution, 1981), pp. 282-83.

13 U.S. Congress, House, Committee on Banking and Currency, *Interim Report on HUD Investigation of Low- and Moderate-Income Housing Programs*, 92d Congress, 1st session, March 31, 1971.

14 The estimated market rents for Section 8 new construction units are calculated from hedonic indices of housing services, in which implicit market values for the various attributes of the housing are derived through a multiple regression analysis of rents against the attributes. The technique is discussed in detail in Wallace et al., *The Urban Section 8 Program*, vol. 2, app. 5.

15 Weicher, *Housing*, pp. 59-60.

16 For a discussion of the development of rehabilitation as a component of housing programs, see John C. Weicher, *Urban Renewal: National Program for Local Problems* (Washington, D.C.: American Enterprise Institute, 1972), chap. 6.

17 U.S. Bureau of the Census, *Residential Alterations and Repairs*, Construction Reports, Series C-50.

18 U.S. Department of Housing and Urban Development, *1979 HUD Statistical Yearbook*, 1980.

19 Neil S. Mayer, "The Roles of Lending, Race, Ownership, and Neighborhood Change in Rental Housing Rehabilitation," Contract Report No. 1131-1, Urban Institute, February 1979.

20 U.S. Department of Housing and Urban Development, Office of Community Planning and Development, *Sixth Annual Community Development Block Grant Report*, Washington, D.C., 1981, p. 59.

21 U.S. General Accounting Office, Comptroller General, *Section 236 Rental Housing: An Evaluation with Lessons for the Future*, 1978.

22 Discussions of Neighborhood Housing Services are contained in Roger S. Ahlbrandt, Jr., and Paul C. Brophy, *Neighborhood Revitalization* (Lexington, Mass.: Lexington Books, 1975), chap. 9; and Roger S. Ahlbrandt, Jr., Paul C.

Brophy, and Jonathan E. Zimmer, *The Neighborhood Housing Services Model: A Progress Assessment of the Related Activities of the Urban Reinvestment Task Force* (Washington, D.C.: U.S. Department of Housing and Urban Development, 1975).

[23] Ahlbrandt, Brophy, and Zimmer, *The NHS Model*, p. 51.

[24] Philip L. Clay, *Neighborhood Partnerships in Action* (Washington, D.C.: Neighborhood Reinvestment Corporation, August 1981), chap. 5.

[25] Information on Housing Opportunities, Inc., is taken from the annual reports for the years 1978 to 1980 and from conversations with James P. Butler, executive director.

[26] Quoted in Housing Opportunities, Inc., *Annual Report 1978*, p. 2.

[27] A more extensive discussion of Lincoln Life Improved Housing is contained in Neil S. Peirce and Oliver W. Cromwell, *Lincoln Life Improved Housing: A Case Study in Corporate Social Responsibility* (Washington, D.C.: Clearinghouse on Corporate Social Responsibility, 1979).

[28] Jane Jacobs, *The Death and Life of Great American Cities* (New York: Random House, 1961), pp. 323-24; emphasis in original.

Containing Health Care Costs

Patricia W. Samors and Sean Sullivan

The sharp increase in health care costs in recent years has led to new public policy initiatives designed to contain these costs. Many new government regulations pertaining to reimbursement of doctors and hospitals, expansion of facilities, and utilization of services have been established, and a variety of comprehensive national health insurance plans have been proposed. Congress is considering several "procompetition" plans, emphasizing incentives for consumers and providers to lower costs. The numerous private sector initiatives developed to reduce the rate of increase in health care costs are often overlooked in the debate over market-oriented versus regulatory approaches to public policy. Frequently these initiatives are taken by employers whose soaring costs of providing employee health benefits correspond to the steep rise in the national health bill. For instance, Ford Motor Company's health costs rose from $68 million in 1965 to $550 million in 1980, doubling roughly every five years. Deere and Company estimated that its bill rose over 300 percent from 1972 to 1977. And health costs for Caterpillar Tractor Company grew from $35 million in 1973 to $100 million in 1978. This growth does not reflect an increase in employees covered or in benefits offered.

This paper examines a selection of private sector initiatives surveyed in a one-year AEI study of health care competition proposals under a grant from the John A. Hartford Foundation. Under this grant, procompetition legislative proposals for reforming the health care system have been analyzed, and their potential for stimulating a more competitive health care industry has been evaluated. The areas of study under the grant include legal issues raised by the proposed changes; obstacles posed by state and federal regulations to the development of competition; administrative issues raised and possible burdens created by the proposals; the effects of proposed changes in federal tax subsidies on federal revenues; and the potential cost savings from a more competitive health care market.[1]

Thus, this survey has evaluated both private efforts to contain rising health care costs and proposals for changing federal and state tax and regulatory reimbursement policies to make the health care market more responsive to economic incentives. Private sector initiatives must be considered with these proposals in mind because changes in government policies can be crucial to the effectiveness of private efforts. Unless accompanied by such changes, private efforts to curb rising costs might be futile.

Private sector activities in the health care field span a wide range; some are sponsored by individual employers, some by unions, and some by insurers and providers. Other efforts involve coalitions of interested parties in a given community.

Some of these initiatives correspond more closely to the thrust of the current procompetition proposals than others. Some, for instance, by trying to change consumer or provider incentives exhibit thinking similar to that in proposed procompetition legislation.[2] Others, however, attempt to improve the existing system without altering the basic incentives.

Flexible Benefits

A prime example of the incentives approach is the "cafeteria plan" offered by several employers around the country. Cafeteria plans or flexible benefits allow employees to shape their benefits to meet their individual needs while giving them incentives to alter their health care consumption patterns. Several companies offer these plans. TRW Corporation originated the concept in 1974 at its California branch, where 18,000 employees now have a choice of three health plan options as well as a Health Maintenance Organization (HMO). Employees who choose the low-option plan are given credits that can be used to "purchase" other specified benefits or—under limited conditions—can be converted to taxable cash payments. Only 5 percent of employees had chosen this option as of December 1981.

American Can Company offers a choice of four plans, with credits determined by subtracting the value of a core set of benefits from the value of the old company plan. The credits can be applied to three other plans that vary deductibles, copayment shares, and stop-loss catastrophic limits, or to other specified benefits. Fewer than 10 percent of American Can employees are in the old plan now; about half are in the next most expensive plan; and fewer than 5 percent are in the low-option plan. The company expects more employees to choose the least expensive plan and to apply their extra credits to other benefits.

Educational Testing Service (ETS) has a plan under which its employees are offered essential coverage in medical care, life insurance, and disability income replacement, as well as vacation, education, and retirement benefits. ETS pays all or the major portion of the cost of these programs. Each year each employee is allotted flexible credits based on calendar years of service with ETS and determined by a percentage of the employee's salary. Employees can use their flexible credits to buy optional benefits to supplement the traditional benefit program or they can receive these credits in cash.

Incentive Plans

A few plans incorporating cost-saving incentives are especially intriguing. Mobil has a bonus plan that may be unique in American industry. Rather than providing their employees with specified health benefits, oil companies contribute a flat monthly amount toward health insurance. Mobil self-insures and compares its total monthly cost per employee with the flat-rate monthly contribution. For each month that the cost is below the contribution, employees are credited with the difference; there is no offset for months in which costs exceed contributions. The plan covers 29,000 active Mobil employees (80 percent of total domestic employment), who are grouped into nine geographical "experience" units. Calculations are made separately for each unit; bonuses vary among units but are uniform within a unit. The plan was introduced in 1977, and bonuses have been paid to nearly all eligibles each year. The average annual bonus in 1980 was $154, and the largest was $255. This plan has two of the principal elements of the procompetition bills—fixed employer contributions and cash rebates.

Another interesting plan is offered to employees of the Mendocino County Schools Office north of San Francisco. Although not strictly a private sector initiative, it merits attention for its originality. For the past two years the schools office has administered a stay-well self-insurance plan instead of purchasing full first-dollar coverage from an outside insurer. It now deposits $500 for each employee in a local account, to be used for the first $500 of medical expenses during the year. At the same time, it purchases a $500 Deductible Group Major Medical Policy from Blue Cross to cover employees after the first $500 of expenses. Any portion of the $500 deposit not used by an employee is carried over to the following year, when another $500 is deposited for him. Any unused portion of this second $500 is also carried over; if his expenses in the second year exceed $500, however, the excess is paid under the group major medical policy and not out of his first-year carryover. When the employee leaves the schools office, he may keep any unspent amounts that have accrued or use them to purchase continuing coverage. This plan encourages employees to stay well and to use discretion in incurring medical expenses. Some choose to pay part of their medical costs themselves rather than spend their allowances, thereby gaining tax benefits. The schools office retains any interest accruing on unspent balances. The record so far shows a quarter of the employees with no medical expenses at all, a quarter with expenses exceeding $500, and half with some expenses but less than $500. Plans similar to the Mendocino plan will be tried on a test basis by the Bank of America and the California state legislature beginning in 1982.

Another interesting although not strictly private sector program operates in Monterey and Santa Barbara Counties, California. Instead of inducing consumers to alter their use of health care, this initiative provides incentives to physicians for cost containment. California's Medi-Cal program, which provides health care for the poor, has historically been plagued by high costs and unsatisfactory medical care. Responding to these problems, the counties have devised a new health insurance system, which is being funded in its developmental stage by the John A. Hartford Foundation of New York. In this system all eligible persons register with a primary-care physician who receives an annual sum calculated to cover the average person's medical needs. Any cost savings are shared by the participating physicians and the county, both of whom are also responsible for any cost overruns.

Sun Company offers its employees several health care options. Sun pays a portion of the premium for a traditional health insurance package, but absorbs the entire cost of the premium for a second fee-for-service option. This latter plan contains specific cost-containment features. For instance, in order to induce the employee to obtain care outside the hospital, only 90 percent of semiprivate hospitalization costs are covered—as opposed to 100 percent for ambulatory surgery. Also, to eliminate unnecessary Friday and Saturday hospital admissions, only 80 percent of such costs are covered except for emergencies.

As mentioned before, there are also those employer- and union-sponsored plans such as wellness programs and direct care, which do not include built-in incentives to reduce costs. They must be included, however, because they are innovative approaches that attempt to control the costs of providing health care coverage.

Health Management

Several companies have initiated large-scale wellness or health management programs. The objective of these programs is to promote the health of a company's employees, thereby reducing absenteeism, increasing productivity, and slowing the rate of growth of health care costs. Kimberly-Clark Corporation established a preventive health maintenance effort in 1977 called the Health Management Program. Through the program, employees are helped to recognize their health risks and to control them. The company encourages lifestyle changes and provides an exercise facility and health education classes. This program, which is offered in two locations, is expected to achieve significant annual savings within ten years.

For two years, Control Data has offered a Staywell Program, which is gradually being offered to nearly all of its 60,000 U.S. employees. Each employee fills out a questionnaire on family health history and personal life-style. Computers process the results to appraise the ten greatest risks to the employee's health, and steps are suggested for reducing them. This program also offers courses in stress reduction, smoking cessation, weight control, nutrition, and fitness.

IBM offers the Plan for Life program of health promotion for its employees and their dependents. In addition to exercise facilities at some of its locations, IBM has a national contract with the YMCA/YWCA that allows employees and their families to use local facilities at no charge. An interesting aspect of IBM's health management program is that tuition is reimbursed for local college adult education courses that fit into the Plan for Life program.

New York Telephone and Johnson and Johnson also conduct wellness programs. New York Telephone's Lifestyle Management Strategies saved the company $2.7 million in 1980. Despite this apparent success, one criticism of these programs is that while they may reduce the demand for health care services, they do not alter consumer incentives and, therefore, will have limited impact on health care costs.

Employer as Provider

Several companies have recently begun to provide direct care for their employees as a way of controlling costs. The Gillette Company, a forerunner in this area, provides health care to more than 90 percent of its work force. The program provides primary care and some specialty care at three clinics staffed by fourteen physicians and ten nurses and technicians. Some of the physicians are on salary, and others are reimbursed on a fee-for-service basis; most maintain outside office practices as well. By providing peer review, monitoring utilization, and stressing preventive and primary care, Gillette provides its employees with quality comprehensive care, while saving an estimated $1 million or more annually.

R. J. Reynolds developed a staff-model HMO (that is, the physicians are employees of the HMO, rather than independent contractors) that serves only its employees and their dependents. The company's Winston-Salem Health Care Plan provides regular HMO services and refers patients to outside specialists and hospitals as needed. Again, utilization—including decisions on surgery—is monitored. With 85 percent of its employees enrolled, Reynolds has saved money on the plan because of the emphasis on preventive care and the lower hospitalization rate commonly found in HMOs.

Unions have historically been involved in the delivery of health care through HMOs and union-sponsored delivery systems. This approach to cost containment has declined, however, as a result of the demand for free choice of physicians and location of care, residential shifts away from the urban areas where the centers were located, and the geographic service limitations of the centers. Many of the centers did exhibit a high degree of efficiency—the United Mine Workers Association's program cost $360 per beneficiary in 1976 compared with a national average of $551.[3]

In addition to providing direct care, labor unions and management have negotiated cost-containment provisions in collective bargaining agreements. United Auto Workers' contracts establish pilot programs for hospital, professional, and drug utilization reviews, for second surgical opinions, and for hospital preadmission testing. Labor-management committees have been established to oversee these programs. In another case, the United Department Store Workers Union mandates that its members receive a second opinion for surgery. In the ten years since this program was initiated, there has been an 18 percent drop in surgery.

Self-Insurance

Mention must be made of the growing trend toward employer self-insurance. Since self-insurance does not attempt to contain costs by altering consumer or provider incentives, it is not clear whether pro-competition legislation would help it or hinder it. Self-insurance does reduce employers' administrative and financial costs, however, and now accounts by one estimate for nearly 20 percent of the health insurance market—an increase from 5 percent in 1975.

Some employers insure against and administer all claims themselves; some self-insure but contract with insurance companies or claims administrators for administrative services only (ASO); and others self-insure against some but not all claims. The Health Insurance Association of America, the trade association of large commercial insurers, estimates that more than 25 percent of all group health benefits are self-insured. A survey by Hay Associates of more than 500 companies shows that nearly 40 percent are either self-insured or combine self-insurance with some degree of commercial coverage. (Hay surveys mostly large firms, which are more likely to self-insure.) Examples of the trend are Caterpillar Tractor, Deere and Company, and Mobil, which are fully self-insured and self-administered. Honeywell is self-insured but contracts with Blue Cross/Blue Shield and commercial insurers for administrative services. Citicorp self-insures against medical claims, while taking advantage of Blue Cross's negotiated discount with hospitals in New York.

The Employee Retirement Income Security Act (ERISA) exempts self-insurance from all state regulation of insurance plans, letting the companies avoid premium taxes and reserve requirements. As a result, employers avoid the "tax costs" of insurance and the loss of earnings on funds held in reserve.

Another benefit that accrues to firms that self-administer the medical claims of their employees is the collecting of data that enables them to determine how and where their money is being spent. An employer can then negotiate with providers, such as hospitals serving the firm's employees, for price discounts, and it can identify providers that are overusing procedures. Control Data, after being self-administered for two years, is just beginning to use data for these purposes.

The private sector initiatives surveyed above all help contain employer health care costs, but they are primarily individual company or union efforts. The following activities bring the major participants together to work jointly toward a reduction in the cost of health care.

Coalitions

The most visible of the joint cost-containment activities has been the formation of health care coalitions. Of the forty to sixty coalitions in existence, only about twenty are actually carrying out their programs. The majority are still forming their agendas.

Membership in the coalitions always includes business and sometimes government, labor, universities, providers, and insurers. Blue

Cross/Blue Shield is involved in twelve coalitions and initiated three of them. Coalitions work on several fronts—promoting and developing HMO alternatives; collecting cost and utilization data for employers using different providers; working with insurers to redesign health benefit plans to encourage less costly utilization practices; participating in local health planning activities through involvement with Health Systems Agencies (HSAs); educating companies, employees, and local hospital board members on health care cost-containment programs; and negotiating with providers and suppliers to contain costs. In addition to their involvement in coalition activities, business and labor often work independently on similar fronts to contain costs.

HMO Development. The Twin City Health Care Development Project was initiated by major Minneapolis–St. Paul employers such as General Mills, Honeywell, Control Data, and Cargill even before the federal HMO act was passed in 1973. This project put up seed money and helped to get HMOs operating. The Group Health Plan already existed, with 36,000 enrollees, but as a result of the project there are now seven HMOs with a total enrollment of more than 300,000, or 15 percent of the metropolitan population. Honeywell has about two-thirds of its 18,000 local employees enrolled in six HMOs, and General Mills has four-fifths of its 3,000 employees in three plans. After five HMOs were formed, many of the remaining physicians signed up with Physicians Health Plan, an IPA (Independent Practice Association) HMO established by the Hennepin County Medical Association as a response to the growth of the prepaid group practices.

Individual companies have occasionally supported the establishment of HMOs in their localities. Ford Motor Company was active in launching a new HMO in Detroit (Health Alliance Plan of Michigan) and tries to offer new plans each year at various locations. Sun Company helped finance the Greater Delaware Valley HMO in Philadelphia. Deere and Company provided money to start an HMO in its home office Quad City area in Illinois and worked to gain support from a major segment of the community's two medical societies. As of December 1981, the plan had operated for only a year and a half, yet had enrolled 30 percent of Deere's work force (12,000 employees) and 40 percent of the community's physicians. Deere is working with the business and medical communities to set up similar prepaid plans at its two major locations in Iowa. Caterpillar Tractor financed a feasibility study for an HMO in York, Pennsylvania, but decided against it because of provider opposition. After a similar study, it is going ahead with an IPA-type HMO at its headquarters in Peoria. And, as mentioned above, in 1976 R. J. Reynolds developed a staff-model HMO for its employees and their dependents. As of the end of 1981, 85 percent of its employees were enrolled in the plan. IBM has also worked diligently to offer employees a choice of several options; it has a total of 135 HMOs at its various branches.

Digital Corporation has taken an innovative approach to providing its employees with information on health plans by commissioning an independent firm to identify the HMO options available at each company location and then making that information available to its employees. Since the study there has been a two percentage point increase in HMO enrollment, bringing the total to 15 percent.

Labor unions have also actively promoted HMO alternatives. The United Autoworkers organized a prepaid group practice in Detroit in the early 1960s, which has since merged with the Health Alliance Plan of Michigan that Ford helped to start. The Rhode Island AFL-CIO initiated the Rhode Island Group Health Association in 1968 to enroll members of the United Steelworkers, the International Association of Machinists, and the American Federation of State, County, and Municipal Employees in that state. The Communications Workers negotiated a nationwide HMO dual-choice option with the Bell System in 1971. The International Union of Electrical, Radio, and Machine Workers negotiated a similar provision with General Electric in 1970. And the International Longshoremen's and Warehousemen's Union on the West Coast encourages its members to join HMOs by not negotiating for more expensive benefits in non-HMO plans; consequently, a majority chooses Kaiser or other prepaid group plans.

Insurer involvement in HMO development deserves particular notice. Blue Cross/Blue Shield plans sponsor forty-three HMOs, which had about 858,000 members in 1980, an enrollment increase of 24 percent over 1979. The HMO of Minnesota, with 67,000 enrollees, is the second largest in the Twin Cities; Wisconsin Physicians Service's HMO, with 175,000 enrollees, is the largest of the Blue plans. Six new plans were put into operation in 1980, including one associated with the respected Lahey Clinic in Boston.

Three commercial insurance companies sponsor HMOs, and two of them plan major growth in their HMO programs. Connecticut General operates two HMOs—one in Phoenix and the other in Columbia, Maryland—with about 50,000 members, but has no plans for more. By contrast, both Prudential and the Insurance Company of North America (INA) plan to add new HMOs within the next year or so. Through its PRUCARE subsidiary, Prudential operates six HMOs, with an enrollment of about 120,000. Half of the enrollees are in Houston, where Prudential opened its first HMO in 1975. Its Chicago HMO, acquired last year, has 30,000 members; the remaining 30,000 are at Austin, Nashville, Atlanta, and Oklahoma City HMOs—all opened within the last two years. PRUCARE took from 1975 to 1979 to reach a total enrollment of 50,000, but it expects to add another 50,000 enrollees annually for the next few years. Through a subsidiary called INA Healthplans, INA has the largest share of the commercial insurers in the HMO market. Working principally through acquisition, INA has 500,000 enrollees in nine HMOs —300,000 of them in Los Angeles, where it acquired the well-established Ross-Loos Plan. Other acquisitions have been in Phoenix, Spokane, Miami, and St. Petersburg. The company started its own HMOs in Dallas, Tucson, and Tampa.

Although Prudential and INA see profitable opportunities in the HMO market, SAFECO—an innovator among commercial insurers—incurred losses at its United Healthcare subsidiary (formerly Northwest Healthcare), despite a promising start in Washington state and Northern California. Organized as a primary-care network, United suffered from the inability of some primary-care physicians to economize on specialist and hospital utilization.

Aetna Life and Casualty has taken a different step toward creating competition in the delivery of health care by developing a program, Choice, that tries to combine the strengths of both traditional health insurance and HMOs. The freedom to choose one's own primary-care physician is incorporated into Choice by allowing the patient, at the time of enrollment, to select physicians and hospitals for referral and specialty services from a list of those chosen for their quality, efficiency, and cost effectiveness. This component of the program combines the freedom to choose referral physicians with the HMO's ability to control the costs of specialty care by restricting the choice of providers. Aetna seeks out specialty physicians and associated hospitals known for their high standards and appropriate utilization of tests and surgery because at least three-fourths of claims costs are for these services. Choice will be available in the Chicago area in mid-1982. The company expects to extend the program to several additional areas within the year as well.

Alternative Avenues. While some coalitions, individual companies, labor unions, and commercial insurers have worked to promote HMO development and enrollment, others have focused on containing costs through utilization review, planning activities, and Professional Standards Review Organizations (PSROs). The Joint Health Cost Containment Program of the Greater Philadelphia Chamber of

Commerce/Penjerdel Council has developed a data base on hospital utilization for its thirty-seven member companies, enabling them to reshape benefit packages to encourage lower utilization and to make providers more conscious of the high cost of hospitalization. Penjerdel also educates hospital trustees to exercise more cost-conscious leadership and to develop better local health planning mechanisms as alternatives to HSAs.

Another coalition is the Fairfield/Westchester Business Group on Health, with twenty-four member companies including IBM, Mobil, and American Can. The Fairfield/Westchester Business Group seeks to emulate Penjerdel in gathering data on utilization and in improving area-wide hospital planning in Fairfield County, Connecticut, and Westchester County, New York.

The Michigan Cost Containment Coalition consists of representatives from the Big Three auto companies, the United Autoworkers Union, and Blue Cross. It worked with state legislators to develop and secure passage of a bill that makes HSAs responsible for planning bed reduction in Michigan hospitals.

The Boston University Health Policy Institute has helped establish a process for using hospital data to highlight utilization and cost problems. The institute is currently working with ALCOA in Blunt County, Tennessee, and with Du Pont in Wilmington, Delaware— where these companies are the dominant employers. The purpose of the project is to bring health care cost and utilization problems to the attention of the local hospitals. The institute meets with providers, presents the findings from its analyses, and discusses actions that can be taken to clear up problems. The emphasis of the project is on a cooperative effort between payers and providers. In contrast to PSROs, the project seeks, not to have physicians reviewed by their peers or singled out for how they practice, but to influence the way all providers practice and to provide information on how to do so more efficiently. Although it is too early to determine the effect of the project, the Health Policy Institute has gained the attention and support of local physicians.

The Professional Standards Review Organizations were originally started to review health care provided under Medicare, Medicaid, and the Maternal and Child Health Programs. The PSROs attempt to ensure quality care and to contain costs through a peer review system funded by the federal government. Interest in this form of utilization review has recently grown in the private sector.

The Midwest Business Group on Health, based in Chicago, has encouraged some of its fifty-six member companies to sign contracts with PSROs to review the quality and volume of services provided to the companies—but not the price. Projects are under way in Minnesota, where fifteen major companies including Honeywell, Control Data, and the 3M Corporation have signed with the Twin Cities Foundation for Health Care Evaluation. Plans covering 150,000 individuals will be reviewed under this contract. PSROs also perform review for individual companies not affiliated with coalitions.

For the past three years, Deere and Company has contracted with the Midstate Foundation for Medical Care in Illinois and with its Iowa counterpart to conduct both admission and concurrent stay review. The results have been significant: within the Midstate Foundation's area of responsibilility, in-patient days per 1,000 for Deere workers declined by 26.8 percent, the average length of stay declined by nearly one full day, and admissions per 1,000 declined by 14.0 percent; within the Iowa Foundation's area, in-patient days declined by 21.4 percent, admissions declined by 14.6 percent, and average length of stay declined by one-half day. The company is now looking for a PSRO in Wisconsin.

PSROs are subject to some criticism. The effectiveness of having providers review their own peers is often questioned. In addition, there are virtually no incentives to save money. A recent study by the Congressional Budget Office (CBO) has found that PSROs reduce hospital days for Medicare patients only slightly (saving little more than the cost of the review itself) and that much of the small reduction in government outlays involves transferring costs to private patients, whose charges rise in proportion. When these cost-shifting effects are accounted for, the CBO concludes, the costs outweigh the benefits.[4]

U.S. Administrators (USA), a California-based claims processing firm, does provide utilization review with an incentive to reduce costs. If costs are not consistent with industry norms, the physicians are not paid the excess. This firm works on an administrative-services-only basis and has gained attention for its rigorous review of all claims for both appropriateness and cost. Using a set of model-treatment screens (MTS) developed from a computerized data base by physician panels, USA identifies providers who overutilize, underutilize, or overcharge, or whose services fail to meet practice standards determined by the physician panels. USA has also been willing to assume the role of advocate for the patient against providers whose claims have been rejected by the insurer. In addition to the MTS, USA uses screens to check length of hospital stay, hospital ancillary charges, and utilization in prepaid group practices. USA's procedures can identify and bring pressure on outliers, but they are unlikely to change the prevailing style of medical practice significantly.

Negotiating to Reduce Costs. A different experiment in cost containment has been initiated by the business community together with hospitals, local government officials, Blue Cross, the New York State Health Department, and the federal Health Care Financing Administration (HCFA) in Rochester, New York. The major insurers—Blue Cross and the federal and state governments—guaranteed area hospitals a specified total revenue for five years. This community revenue ceiling was based on 1978 costs adjusted annually for inflation. State and federal regulators agreed to waive many regulations governing reimbursement for the same period, and the hospitals formed the Rochester Area Hospitals Corporation (RAHC), which agreed to share any savings below the revenue cap with the insurers. This Hospitals Experimental Payment Program (HEP) became effective in 1980. Although Rochester area hospital costs had risen more slowly than the national average for the past few years because of tight state reimbursement regulations, RAHC members managed to improve their financial condition in 1980 while keeping cost increases at about half the national average. This suggests that HEP may have had some impact.

Pratt & Whitney Aircraft Group has developed a program at its West Palm Beach plant that guides employees in their choice of physician rather than providing direct care. The company established a medical information service in response to employee complaints about high medical fees that were not covered entirely by the company health insurance plan. This service directs the employees to certain physicians and advises them about expected charges based on service and fee schedules provided by the physicians. Started as a program to save money for the employees, it now saves money for Pratt & Whitney as the employees use health care services in a more cost-effective way and thereby stimulate competition among providers. This initiative is especially interesting because it prevents reimbursement for inefficient services and thus rewards the more efficient providers.

Several attempts by labor unions to lower medical costs for their members are worth noting. The United Federation of Teachers Welfare Fund in New York contracts with retail pharmacies to pay the wholesale price plus a fixed service fee for prescription drugs. This example has been followed by other unions in New York and other cities and has been incorporated in national agreements covering auto and steel workers. The International Ladies Garment Workers Union offers a mail-order prescription service under its nationwide Health Services Plan. By having members send prescriptions to one of four large pharmacies, where they are filled in a semi-automated manner, the union achieves economies of scale that reduce prices.

Conclusions

Although not all of the private sector initiatives in the health care field have been mentioned, this survey does reflect the variety of programs that have been established in response to the rise in health care costs. In spite of all the voluntary activity, however, it is difficult to say whether these efforts will have the desired impact on costs.

Most of the initiatives lack incentives both for consumers to change their use of health care and for providers to alter their fee schedules or practice patterns. Outside Minneapolis–St. Paul, Hawaii, and perhaps California and Seattle, there are no significant competitive markets offering multiple choices to consumers in the private sector. Such markets are available only to employees of individual employers offering multiple plans. As a result of the federal HMO act, most major companies offer two choices in some locations. Many companies, however, have not found or cannot find qualified HMOs to offer their employees. The efforts of coalitions to promote HMOs and other alternative delivery systems have generally fallen short of what employers in the Twin Cities did years ago. Most coalitions are concentrating on more restricted ways of trying to contain costs. Some work to limit supply—serving on Health Systems Agencies to improve area planning or supporting legislation like Michigan's bed law. Some seek to limit demand—developing data on local practice patterns to identify outliers or contracting with PSROs for utilization review. These activities are increasing and will have some impact at the margin, but they will not change the incentives for either the consumer or the provider. Interestingly, insurers like INA, Prudential, and the Blues are doing more to change the marketplace by establishing new lines of business—developing their own alternative delivery systems.

The initiatives of individual companies are more intriguing than those of business coalitions and some even provide those necessary incentives. Employers like American Can, ETS, TRW, and Sun are offering employees a choice of plans and are providing incentives to choose plans with more cost sharing. Others—Mobil and the Mendocino County Schools Office—are encouraging employees to use their plans carefully by offering financial rewards. These experiments—if successful, as some have been—may spread and eventually cause some change in the system.

Although private sector initiatives are important and worth studying, changes in government policies may be needed to alter the health care system and reduce the escalating costs that are a by-product of that system. In the following sections, changes in state and federal health policy will be discussed.

377

State Health Policy*

In the 1980s the states are emerging as more prominent health policy makers. This is especially clear as the "New Federalism" places more responsibility on the states for designing, implementing, and, to a certain extent, financing health programs. Block grants and the new regulations for the Medicaid program offer states more flexibility in structuring and administering their programs. This flexibility, however, appears to be overshadowed by budget constraints. States are faced with increasing health care costs, decreased revenues, and diminishing federal support. These factors, accompanied by state laws which generally prohibit deficits, put severe pressure on the states to respond to short-term financial problems rather than to focus on long-term structural reform. While short-term responses to a budget crunch are inevitable, they do not constitute a firm basis for the development of long-range policies and programs. Consequently, there is a need to address the long-term evolution of state policies in health care delivery and financing.

A specific example of the emphasis on short-term considerations can be found in the Medicaid program. On October 1, 1981, the Health Care Financing Administration promulgated regulations that gave states more flexibility and control in administering their Medicaid programs. A preliminary survey of the state responses to this federal policy initiative indicates that a preponderance of state initiatives focus on scaling back eligibility, benefits, and provider reimbursement rates. There is little emphasis on reform in the delivery and financing of Medicaid services.

A few states are pursuing case management or preferred provider plans whereby the state would be a more cost-conscious purchaser of health services. Some states have instituted minimal cost sharing while others are attempting to pursue competitive bidding for laboratory services and medical devices. Under such plans states try to steer Medicaid patients toward more cost-conscious service providers. For example, in Wayne County, Michigan, Medicaid recipients will choose a primary care provider who will oversee the patient's total care. The state will be able to identify those providers who are high utilizers and will offer incentives to the providers to be conscious of quality as well as cost. Minnesota now requires volume purchasing through competitive bidding for medical equipment—that is, eye glasses and other such devices. Yet, these initiatives are receiving secondary priority in many state health programs.

---

* This section was written by Rosemary Gibson.

Examination of state initiatives comes at a crucial time in the development of health policy. Existing and proposed federal policies indicate that a new approach to the economics of medical care is emerging. This approach incorporates changes in the incentive structure to encourage consumers, providers, and insurers to be conscious of cost and quality in their choice and provision of medical care. Several legislative proposals have been submitted to alter tax incentives and program features that encourage the purchase of first-dollar health insurance coverage among both the employed and the dependent populations.

The success of market reform, however, is contingent upon state laws and policies. In preliminary AEI surveys of state policies we have found numerous laws that could inhibit the development of "pro-competitive" forces in health care. Some state laws governing premium taxes and financial requirements prevent different insurers from competing on an equal footing. Other state laws serve as entry barriers, especially occupational licensing that delineates the scope of practice of the new, emerging groups of medical service providers. These constraints may inhibit the development of alternative delivery mechanisms that are more likely to use these new providers effectively. For example, forty states have enacted statutes governing physician assistants that define the scope of physician supervision and diagnostic competence required for physician assistants to practice. Since some requirements are not clearly stipulated, physicians may be reluctant to use physician assistants and other auxiliary personnel.

The most pressing health care problem for the states is, and will continue to be, long-term care for the elderly. At present 42 percent of Medicaid expenditures is allocated for nursing home care. There has been an annual rate of expenditure growth of 20 percent from 1970 to 1979 for nursing home care. Noninstitutional alternatives to institutional care that cost less but maintain high quality should be considered, along with tax and investment incentives for private financing, insurance, and delivery of care. In addition, programs that profile and screen providers as a condition of participation in Medicaid and competitive-bid contracting are options worth considering.

A 1981 Budget Reconciliation Act provision gives states new flexibility under Medicaid in offering home and community based services. Four states, Louisiana, Montana, Kansas, and Oregon, have received waiver approval. Fifteen more states have requests pending. Oregon's program is the largest and most comprehensive. The Oregon program seeks to prevent or reduce inappropriate institutional care by providing the necessary support services to enable a person to remain in the community. The financial savings Oregon hopes to recover are twofold. Community care is substantially less expensive than institutional care; Oregon predicts that four people can be cared for at home for the cost of one institutionalized patient. Also, removing inappropriately institutionalized patients frees nursing home space, which can then be filled with patients from more expensive hospital settings. Louisiana's program is directed toward the same population, which is inappropriately placed in nursing homes, but provides many fewer services than Oregon's program. Wisconsin's program, pending approval, would rely on a screening process to prevent placement in institutions of Medicaid patients who could be adequately served in other settings. Caring for persons in less expensive community settings helps alleviate the "spend-down" problem, whereby patients enter nursing homes financially solvent, but exhaust their resources paying for institutional care and become eligible for Medicaid. Like Oregon, Wisconsin hopes to place patients in the most appropriate setting.

Federal Health Policy *

The federal government must not renege on its commitment to assist elderly and low-income individuals in protecting themselves against outlays for health care that are beyond their means. But meeting this obligation does not mean that current federal health-related tax, reimbursement, and regulatory policies must be left untouched. Indeed, these features of federal health policy are at the heart of spiraling cost increases; fundamental structural reforms in federal policy are a precondition for a truly economical deceleration in cost increases, rather than one that simply cuts costs by cutting benefits.

The cost of Medicare and Medicaid is doubling every four years, and is likely to amount to over $70 billion in FY 1983. With tax expenditures related to health care included, the federal government's "budget" for health care will be in the range of $100 billion next year.

In a desperate effort to contain this cost escalation when other major categories of federal spending such as national defense and social security are held "untouchable," the federal government has reached for feckless and cumbersome controls and, more recently, tried to shift the cost to lower levels of government, patients, providers, and employers. Meaningful reforms in government health policy have been sidestepped; as a result, costs have been not so much controlled or reduced as they have been hidden and shifted.

Medicare and Medicaid have both inefficient and inequitable features. In Medicare and Medicaid, costs are shared at the "back

* This section was written by Jack A. Meyer.

end," when people have incurred huge medical bills, but much less so for routine services at the "front end." Federal aid to the poor is inequitable, systematically excluding millions of people on the basis of family status. Open-ended tax subsidies encourage first-dollar insurance coverage for a wide variety of health services, which in turn has led to increased demand for services. We have stacked the deck against innovative health care delivery systems that promise to compete with the dominant delivery system, and we have entangled the health care system in a labyrinth of largely ineffective government regulations.

The following proposals are offered to reform health care: (1) a system of sharing costs that encourages people to economize on the use of routine health services, while offering greater protection on serious illnesses; (2) federal aid to low-income people that increases with increasing need, and vice versa; (3) within a given category of need, fixed dollar instead of open-ended federal subsidies to aid those unable to purchase adequate health insurance; and (4) fair competition among alternative health care plans for the consumer's dollar. Incorporating these changes into government policy will require a major overhaul of federal programs.

By reforming the current system of retrospective cost reimbursement, open-ended tax subsidies, and heavy reliance on planning and regulation, health cost increases might abate over time without jeopardizing the quality of care or access to it. But the growth in outlays will not be reduced immediately, while the increase in revenues may initially be minimal. Instead of a promising set of reforms, both the Reagan administration and its predecessors have offered a continuation of budget ceilings, rate caps, and cost shifting as they have striven for short-term savings. Such steps merely gloss over the built-in cost-generating features of government health care programs.

In Medicare and Medicaid, the Reagan administration has begun to scale back federal regulations, but has offered in their place only marginal budget cuts instead of structural reforms. These stopgap measures merely shift the costs of caring for the elderly and the indigent to patients, providers, and employers. This strategy allows the main costs of these programs to continue to rise while trimming their periphery and changing their form. In the end, this strategy leads to cutbacks in services to the groups in need and shifts from payment through taxes to higher out-of-pocket expenses and higher health insurance premiums.

For example, the 1983 budget proposed by President Reagan calls for achieving Medicare savings through such methods as an arbitrary 2 percent reduction in Medicare hospital reimbursement, a delay in coverage until the first day of the first full month of eligibility, and caps on physician reimbursement. Such steps do not achieve true economies, but rather mortgage the future of the groups in need by encouraging providers to boycott them.

I recommend the following specific steps for federal health policy: (1) cap the chief open-ended tax subsidy related to health by placing a ceiling on the amount of employer contributions to employee health insurance that can be excluded from an employee's income for federal tax purposes; (2) build a stop-loss feature into Medicare combined with a manageable measure of cost sharing for routine services; (3) convert Medicare to a program of premium subsidies that can be used for Medicare coverage or an alternative plan; these subsidies would be equal in real value to the average cost of serving elderly people; (4) replace the current Medicaid system with sliding-scale premium subsidies in which the very poor would be fully subsidized; (5) reexamine the Medicaid matching rate formula to ensure that states with greater needs receive greater federal assistance; (6) continue to deregulate the health care system; and (7) use antitrust laws to encourage fair competition among alternative health plans and providers.

Notes

[1] For further information see *An Analysis of Procompetitive Health Care Proposals* (American Enterprise Institute, forthcoming).

[2] Senator David Durenberger (Republican, Minnesota), Health Incentives Reform Act, S. 433; Congressman Richard A. Gephardt (Democrat, Missouri), National Health Care Reform Act, H.R. 850; and Senator Orrin G. Hatch (Republican, Utah), Comprehensive Health Care Reform Act, S. 139.

[3] Stephen C. Caulfield and Pamela L. Haynes, *Health Care Costs: Private Initiatives for Containment* (Washington, D.C.: Government Research Corporation, 1981), p. 88.

[4] Congress of the United States, Congressional Budget Office, *The Effect of PSROs on Health Care Costs: Current Findings and Future Evaluations* (Washington, D.C.: U.S. Government Printing Office, June 1979).

The Potential for Pharmaceutical Development and Regulation

William M. Wardell and Nancy Mattison

The Significance of Pharmaceutical Development and Private Sector Initiatives

The development and supply of new drugs is a component of health care that, while modest in its contribution to total costs, has the potential for reducing expenditures by displacing other, more costly forms of therapy. As a proportion of total national health care expenditures, the cost of drugs and drug sundries [1] declined over the past two decades from 13.6 percent in 1960 to 11.3 percent in 1970 and to 7.8 percent in 1980. In contrast, expenditures for hospital care increased from 33.8 percent of the total in 1960 to 39.5 percent in 1978. Indeed, by reducing the need for hospital therapy, new drugs may have slowed the rise in hospital costs. A recent study, for example, estimates that if cimetidine had been used in 80 percent of duodenal ulcer cases in the United States in 1977, $34 million would have been spent for drugs, saving $258 million in hospital costs and $30 million in surgeons' fees. Similar savings are expected from use of the recently approved hepatitis B vaccine: an analysis by the federal government's Centers for Disease Control estimates that this vaccine will eventually save $225 million in hospital costs annually.

Other contributions of new drug therapies to health care are more difficult to assess in monetary terms. The U.S. Food and Drug Administration (FDA) estimates, for example, that the use of the beta blocker class of drugs to prevent death from secondary myocardial infarction will save 7,000 to 10,000 lives per year in the United States. The development of vaccines effective against measles was followed by a drop in the number of reported cases from 83,452 in 1969 to 45,170 in 1978, and an intensive national effort is under way to eliminate measles in the United States completely by October 1, 1982.

Recently, new methods of drug delivery have contributed significantly to improvements in therapy. In 1981, for example, novel transdermal (stick-on) dose forms of nitroglycerine were introduced that extend the duration, convenience, and hence usefulness of this traditional but previously limited form of treatment for angina pectoris. In March 1982, the FDA approved a new type of implantable drug pump that is expected to lessen the need for hospitalization and extend the life expectancy of patients with liver cancer by more than two years.

Such advances in drug development are especially remarkable given that this is one of the few sectors of science in which the research process itself—not just marketing—is strictly regulated by government. The effects of regulation and the prospects for private sector initiatives in drug development can serve as instructive examples for other high-technology sectors of the health care industry, especially medical devices and diagnostic products. Decision makers charged with regulating recombinant DNA research can also benefit from these experiences.

From the broader perspective of technology and economics, the U.S. pharmaceutical industry is an example of a domestic high-technology industry with a history of successful competition in international markets. The U.S. pharmaceutical industry has consistently ranked among the top four national pharmaceutical industries in favorable balance of trade, reaching a $1.3 billion import-export surplus in 1981. In recent years, however, other drug-developing countries have challenged the preeminence of the United States in world pharmaceutical exports. Moreover, the number of new chemical entities introduced annually into clinical research by the U.S. industry (a measure of new drugs that may be available in five to ten years) declined from an average of fifty-five per year for 1965–1974 to twenty-eight per year for 1975–1979.

Inadequate incentives are but one of the complex reasons the U.S. pharmaceutical industry has become less competitive and innovative. Private sector initiatives that can improve the efficiency and productivity of drug development and regulation would enhance the quality of health care in the United States and help restore the economic viability of an essential high-technology industry.

Components of the Private Sector

The private sector organizations interested in drug development and regulation can be divided into four categories: industries, professional organizations, consumer groups, and health care providers. Table 1 lists some of the constituents in each category.

TABLE 1
Components of the Private Sector

Industries	Professional Organizations	Consumer Groups	Health Care Providers
Pharmaceutical manufacturers and associations: Pharmaceutical Manufacturers Association	*National:* American Medical Association American Society for Clinical Pharmacology and Therapeutics	*General interest:* Public interest research groups: Health Research Group American Association of Retired Persons	Health maintenance organizations
Generic manufacturers and associations: National Association of Pharmaceutical Manufacturers Generic Pharmaceutical Industry Association	American Society for Pharmacology and Experimental Therapeutics American Pharmaceutical Association American Society of Hospital Pharmacists Association of American Medical Colleges National Council on Drugs[a] United States Pharmacopoeial Convention	National Retired Teachers' Association *Specific interest:* Over 125 disease-oriented volunteer organizations including: American Cancer Society American Heart Association March of Dimes–Birth Defects Foundation Muscular Dystrophy Associations of America National Easter Seal Society American Lung Association	Health insurance companies and associations: Blue Cross Association National Association of Blue Shield Plans Hospitals and associations: American Hospital Association
Wholesale distributors and retail pharmacies and associations: Drug Wholesalers' Association National Wholesale Druggists' Association National Association of Retail Druggists	*Local institutional:* institutional review boards pharmacy and therapeutic committees		

[a] Member organizations include the American Dental Association, the American Hospital Association, the American Medical Association, the American Pharmaceutical Association, the American Society for Clinical Pharmacology and Therapeutics, the American Society for Pharmacology and Experimental Therapeutics, the National Medical Association, and the Pharmaceutical Manufacturers Association. Liaison organizations include the American Society of Hospital Pharmacists, The Proprietary Association, and the U.S. Food and Drug Administration.

Even from this partial listing, the number and diversity of private sector groups interested in drug development and regulation is striking. We should not expect a single, uniform approach from these organizations; such diversity should, however, permit a wide variety of private sector approaches to emerge and flourish.

The debate in Congress in 1982 over whether to extend the effective patent life for new drugs illustrates the variety of approaches and interests that arise both within and between private sector categories. Patent-life extension is strongly supported by the Pharmaceutical Manufacturers Association (PMA) and its member firms as a means of providing the financial incentives for further research and development. In comparison, the generic firms and their associations argue that this change is neither necessary to encourage innovation nor desirable from the standpoint of consumer costs. Consumer groups that do not represent patients with specific diseases—such as Public Citizen, the American Association of Retired Persons, and the National Retired Teachers' Association—agree with the generic manufacturers that longer patent life will seriously diminish price competition to the detriment of the consumer. By contrast, disease-oriented volunteer organizations generally favor more research, whether by the private sector or by government.

Although disagreements among the components of the private sector may impede efforts to foster private sector initiatives, they are not necessarily insurmountable barriers. In the sections that follow, we consider the feasibility of proposals for private sector initiatives in drug development and regulation, building where possible on the diversity of interests.

How Can Private Sector Participation in Drug Development and Regulation Be Increased?

While most drug development is already a private sector activity, some form of government control is exercised over all aspects of drug development and marketing, beginning long before the first clinical testing of a new chemical entity and continuing after marketing approval. Figure 1 illustrates the steps in the process and includes data on the average length of time required for each phase, the average research and development costs to the firms, and the mean patent life remaining after marketing approval. Private sector initiatives could be harnessed at several points in this process to influence both the time and the cost of drug development and to increase innovation.

The role of the private sector could be expanded in three ways. First, some of the existing regulatory functions of the government—

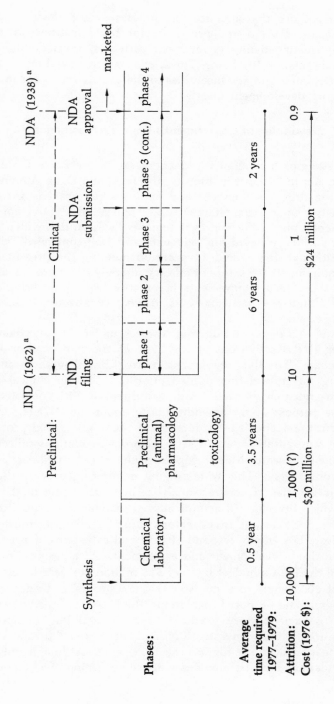

FIGURE 1

DRUG DEVELOPMENT IN THE UNITED STATES

	Preclinical:		Clinical		
Synthesis	Chemical laboratory	IND filing	phase 1 phase 2	phase 3 NDA submission	phase 3 (cont.) NDA approval phase 4 marketed
	Preclinical (animal) pharmacology → toxicology				

IND (1962)[a]   NDA (1938)[a]

Phases:

Average time required 1977–1979:	0.5 year	3.5 years	6 years	2 years
Attrition:	10,000	1,000 (?)	10	1	0.9
Cost (1976 $):		$30 million		$24 million

[a] Date statute passed by Congress.

NOTE: Average effective life of compound patent (from date of NDA approval): 1966, 13.6 years; 1981, 6.8 years.

SOURCE: This is a new figure compiled from our data base here at the Center.

particularly those that monitor the process—could devolve to the private sector. Second, the private sector could institute programs that supplement existing government activities, preclude the need for more regulation, or both. Third, changes in government policy and practice could provide incentives to the private sector for increasing its drug development efforts.

Devolution of Government's Regulatory Function

Since passage of the Kefauver Amendments to the Food, Drug, and Cosmetic Act in 1962, regulation by the Food and Drug Administration of the drug development and approval process has increased enormously. Under current new drug application (NDA) approval requirements, marketing approval requires "substantial evidence" of safety and efficacy based on "adequate and well-controlled" clinical trials. Although few would advocate abandoning the present legislative requirements for safety or efficacy, there is a legitimate question whether the FDA's requirements in practice have gone beyond the intent of Congress—particularly as to what constitutes "substantial evidence" of efficacy.

The FDA's regulation of drug research under the investigational new drug (IND) provisions of the 1962 amendments has also provoked debate. The IND regulations control clinical research and, by specifying the information needed prior to initiating clinical trials, preclinical research as well. Although there is little objectionable about the purpose of the amendments or about the IND regulations as written, the agency's interpretation of them has caused problems. The FDA's proposals for a new set of rigorous regulations collectively termed the Bioresearch Monitoring Program has generated particularly heated controversy. This wide-ranging monitoring program had its genesis in a series of congressional hearings, beginning in the mid-1970s, which investigated acts of alleged malfeasance committed by preclinical and clinical investigators, drug companies, third-party companies, FDA employees, and virtually all categories of people involved in drug development and assessment. As a result, Congress increased the FDA's budget by over $16 million per year to assemble a staff of 600 people to administer the new program. Under several sets of actual and proposed regulations, the FDA has broad powers to enforce "good laboratory practices" and the activities of sponsors and monitors, clinical investigators, and institutional review boards (including specifications for informed consent). Although only two such regulations have become final—those governing good laboratory practices in 1979 and institutional review boards in 1981—FDA policies and practices have in effect applied some of the provisions contained in the proposed rules.

Many believe the Bioresearch Monitoring Program constitutes regulatory overkill, and a variety of sources have offered proposals for replacing at least part of the FDA's monitoring role with private sector alternatives. These proposals apply both to the premarketing research-and-approval process and to the postmarketing phase.

The Premarketing Phase. Under existing regulations early clinical trials (phases I and II in figure 1) must be approved and monitored by both the FDA and an institutional review board. Various ad hoc task forces within or sponsored by government have been considering proposals that include the option of removing this task from the FDA. In such cases, it is proposed, local review boards could become more responsible for overseeing early trials. The primary advantage of this change would be to reduce duplicated efforts and to free the FDA to concentrate its limited resources on the later, pivotal studies required for NDA approval.

The idea has many supporters, including the FDA, which formally requested comments in September 1981. Responses from the private sector have been mixed. The Pharmaceutical Manufacturers Association favors a flexible system that would give the review board the option of refusing sole responsibility; in that case, the FDA would continue to approve and monitor early trials. The American Society for Clinical Pharmacology and Therapeutics and the American Pharmaceutical Association are two professional groups supporting this plan. While this option is favored by some pharmaceutical firms, others disagree with this suggestion, arguing that the FDA should continue to oversee trials of all new chemical entities and those entailing high risks. PMA, in contrast, has said that categorization of trials as "high" or "low" risk is not feasible.

Certainly there are some disadvantages to devolving responsibility to local institutional review boards. Many lack the specialized manpower to make such decisions and may be reluctant to act without FDA assurances that preclinical studies are adequate. An increase in applications to review boards coupled with a lack of expertise to assess preclinical data may overburden these groups, creating substantial delays. Issues of legal liability and insurance coverage may add to the review boards' reluctance to take on these additional responsibilities. Finally, the system could produce numerous FDA-like bureaucracies with widely varying, idiosyncratic requirements and differing degrees of competence. Multi-center studies might become impossible as a result.

Private sector initiatives, nevertheless, have already made definite progress. Several independent review boards have been set up for the express purpose of reviewing drug studies rigorously but expeditiously. One such commercial board has been started as a service of the Philadelphia Association for Clinical Trials (PACT). PACT was established in June 1980 to perform clinical research studies and related services on drugs and is composed of representatives from each of its twelve-member medical school/industrial research institutions. The independent review board provides services for sponsors lacking access to institutional review boards. Although PACT's clients to date have been primarily pharmaceutical companies, its services are also available to sponsors of medical devices and diagnostic products.

Closely related to the proposal to devolve control to review boards are recommendations to alter the IND application process. Under the current IND regulations, sponsors must file numerous documents with the FDA that include "adequate information" on preclinical investigations demonstrating proof of safety, "complete information" on preclinical investigations or marketed use of the drug abroad, statements of the qualifications of clinical investigators and monitors, and assurances of approval by a review board. If the FDA raises no objections, the trials may begin thirty days after filing.

Recommendations for changing this procedure have come primarily from the private-professional portion of the private sector. Specifically, the National Council on Drugs and some prominent clinical pharmacologists have proposed that the IND information-filing requirements for phases I and II be replaced by notification to the FDA that trials are about to commence. Safety would be maintained by making sponsors, monitors, and local review boards responsible for overseeing these trials and by notifying the FDA of any serious toxicity or adverse-reaction problems. A certified summary of phase I and II trial results would be submitted to the FDA with the phase III protocols. In effect, adoption of the proposals would create a system quite similar to those in Germany and the United Kingdom.

These recommendations are supported by the argument that early clinical trials are inherently safe; no deaths have resulted from phase I or II trials in the past twenty years. It is estimated that this change in procedure would reduce the FDA's IND workload by roughly 90 percent.

Although the established pharmaceutical industry has endorsed proposals of this type, it seems probable that they will be heavily opposed by consumer groups on the grounds that the welfare of trial subjects may be endangered. The review boards also are likely to express concern about legal liability.

Good laboratory practice regulations, part of the Bioresearch Monitoring Program, were proposed in November 1976 and became effective on June 20, 1979. They followed congressional hearings held in the mid-1970s and a series of FDA pilot inspections that created the impression (probably erroneous) that widespread and serious deficiencies existed in preclinical testing procedures and results. In anticipation of the final regulations, industry and the FDA informally began to follow the proposed regulations in the mid- to late-1970s. It is estimated that, as a result, the costs of preclinical research increased by as much as 25–50 percent. Evidence shows, for example, that the anticipatory effect of the good laboratory practice regulations contributed significantly in 1975–1976 to a 50 percent drop in the number of new compounds introduced into clinical research by the U.S. pharmaceutical industry.

Many observers of the drug development process believe that these regulations constitute expensive regulatory overkill. Replacing at least a portion of this FDA monitoring function with private sector self-policing is one way to solve this problem. Indeed, such an approach would conform to one of the FDA's primary objectives for FY 1983, to control expenses by stressing voluntary compliance rather than the more expensive regulatory-oversight activities.

A number of advisory committees comprising experts from outside government are maintained and routinely consulted by the FDA. A few of these—the Medical Device Classification panels, for example—are required by statute, but for the most part the FDA uses these groups at its discretion. The FDA appoints all such committees and is free to accept or reject their recommendations in whole or in part. The General Accounting Office (GAO) recommended, however, that the Commission on the Federal New Drug Approval Process examine the feasibility of changing the system by mandating that: (1) an advisory committee independent of the FDA assess NDAs, and (2) the FDA be required to take these evaluations into account when deciding whether to grant marketing approval. The GAO noted that this kind of arrangement already exists in other countries.

Germany offers a good example of how such an independent group of advisers functions. Section 25 (6) of the 1976 German Medicines Act requires the establishment of an expert advisory group, "Commission A." The members of the commission are appointed by the federal minister for youth, family, and health based on recommendations from associations of medical professions, professional societies of medical practitioners, dentists, veterinarians, pharmacists, lay and medical practitioners, and the pharmaceutical industry. In practice, the commission regularly includes not only medical practitioners and experts from academia, but also consumer and industry representatives—all from the private sector.[2] Under the law, the commission must evaluate all applications for marketing new drugs and make a recommendation to the BGA (Bundesgesundheitamt— the German equivalent of the FDA) for approval or denial of the application. In making its decision, the BGA must take the commission's recommendation into account and must justify any decision that contradicts the commission's recommendation. If a similar system were adopted in the United States, the FDA's decision-making autonomy might be reduced, and private sector representatives would supplement—though not replace—the FDA review process.

Involving the private sector to the same extent in the U.S. drug approval process faces numerous barriers, including statutory ones, that should be examined to determine what full implementation of private sector initiatives would entail. First, Congress would need to amend the Food, Drug, and Cosmetic Act, and no new drug laws or amendments have passed since 1972. Because an autonomous commission would require a drastic shift in regulatory philosophy, the prospects for such change are slight.

Second, if industry representatives were to be included in a U.S. commission, repeal of (or special exemption from) the provisions of the Ethics in Government Acts of 1977 and 1978 would be required. These statutes exclude from participation in government decision making all individuals whose objectivity might be compromised by financial ties to regulated industry. These conflict-of-interest laws and implementing regulations have already been a serious barrier to the appointment of highly qualified experts to FDA committees. Consumer groups strongly oppose proposals to relax these strictures; most notably, the Health Research Group insists that advisers have absolutely no financial ties with industry. This approach is diametrically opposed to that taken in Germany, for example.

The disagreement over commission composition, however, also extends in the other direction. Several individual pharmaceutical firms responded negatively to the 1977 recommendation of the Department of Health, Education, and Welfare's Review Panel on New Drug Regulation that the FDA's standing advisory committees include consumer representatives with voting powers. The basis for industry objection was that these individuals might not possess the scientific knowledge necessary to make such decisions. Instead, the PMA and a number of physicians and scientists suggested this problem could be mitigated by basing appointments on the recommendations of the disease-oriented volunteer organizations. These organizations have generally been supportive of drug research and development programs, in contrast to other consumer groups that tend to downplay research in favor of cheaper prices for generic drugs.

Although it is not feasible for the FDA's responsibility for marketing approval to devolve to the private sector, more extensive use of advisory committees in this process is a sensible and realistic goal. It has been suggested, for example, that scientific advisory committees, independent of the FDA, be given the statutory authority to resolve disputes between the agency and industry. The required change in law, however, and the question of committee composition would again be powerful impediments.

Statutory changes in the advisory system have won little support. Nevertheless, the FDA's use of advisory committees may have to increase because staff reductions precipitated by budgetary constraints may leave the agency no other option. Moreover, the current administration may encourage such involvement by the private sector.

The prospects discussed in this section for devolving some of the FDA's premarketing control appear mixed. On the one hand, wholly replacing the IND with FDA notification (for phases I and II) and mandating the use of advisory committees in the approval process seem the least likely of these proposals to be implemented. On the other hand, the change in political perspectives—both budgetary and regulatory—greatly increases the prospects for adopting some of the other proposals. The FDA is much more receptive now to proposals to (1) allow local institutional review boards the option of assuming greater control over early clinical trials, (2) stress voluntary compliance with good laboratory practice regulations rather than relying on legal action, and (3) make greater use of advisory committees.

Progress in increasing the role of the private sector depends as much on agreement on goals between the various private groups as on any other single factor.

The Postmarketing Phase. Of the FDA's postmarketing responsibilities, ensuring the quality of marketed products is the most likely to devolve to the private sector.[3] Although this is one of the agency's original and most important missions, and one it performs admirably, there is room for assistance from the private sector. The FDA and several private sector groups already agree that certain postmarketing enforcement actions can be replaced by voluntary compliance. Both budgetary constraints and the regulatory philosophy of the new administration, including FDA Commissioner Arthur Hull Hayes, have contributed to this shift in FDA emphasis. To prove the effectiveness of this alternative, the FDA has begun to record cases wherein voluntary correction of deficiencies made legal action unnecessary.

The FDA's Bureau of Medical Devices (BMD) demonstrates this shift in emphasis by allowing manufacturers the opportunity to cooperate voluntarily rather than encounter legal action. One such case occurred recently when BMD disagreed with Bausch and Lomb about the legality of a newly marketed bifocal soft contact lens. The manufacturer argued that the new lens was equivalent to an FDA-approved monocular lens; BMD argued it was not. According to the trade press, Bausch and Lomb voluntarily withdrew the device from the market rather than face FDA seizure of the lens and possible legal ramifications. For its part, the FDA agreed to allow Bausch and Lomb to bypass more rigorous approval procedures by filing a supplementary approval application. Such cooperative solutions, however, have not always been successful. A smaller lens manufacturer, for example, steadfastly refused to withdraw its product from the market and filed suit against the FDA when its lenses were seized.

The current philosophy assumes that industry will favor voluntary methods. Private groups that support this change include the United States Pharmacopoeial Convention, the generics' National Association of Pharmaceutical Manufacturers, and the Congressional Commission on the Federal New Drug Approval Process. Reducing these FDA postmarketing activities, it is argued, will free the agency to concentrate on the more important task of reviewing new drugs. Not surprisingly, strong opposition has been expressed by the Health Research Group, which fears a possible decline in drug quality and safety.

Private sector initiatives could be especially useful in helping the FDA prevent the marketing of unapproved generic drugs. The FDA has claimed that this is not a serious problem and that virtually all such products were removed from the market by mid-1981. But the explosion over the past decade in the number of generic manufacturers—some of which are extremely small operations—makes effective, nationwide monitoring by the FDA difficult, if not impossible, and there are examples of unapproved drug products causing serious harm. Monitoring becomes more complicated when the manufacturer does not directly market the drug, but sells it to a distributor that marks the product with its logo or name and sells it to a pharmacy.

Private sector policing to eliminate the sale of unapproved generics could occur at several points. In particular, either the distributor or the pharmacy—or both—could require proof of FDA approval before purchase. The Purchasing Group of the Rochester Regional Hospital Association follows such a system. The Purchasing Group, composed of representatives from twenty-eight nonprofit hospitals and extended-care facilities, requires as part of its bid specifications that the prospective product supplier submit copies of documents showing FDA approval as proof of the product's legality. Greater use of this simple procedure would reduce the burden on the FDA, at present the sole monitor of legal compliance.

These are but two ways for the private sector to help government in the postmarketing phase. In the case of compliance with good manufacturing practices and marketing approval regulations, the FDA itself has taken steps to encourage voluntary private sector compliance. The change in attitude can be expected to continue only as long as the components of the private sector—particularly industry—demonstrate that this alternative is reliable. Similarly, the example of monitoring the legality of generic drugs demonstrates that the private sector can quite effectively devise monitoring methods of its own. Such efforts should be especially welcome in the current political climate.

Private Sector Initiatives to Supplement or Obviate Regulatory Control

Private sector initiatives to supplement existing government programs and, potentially, to forestall the adoption of additional regulations are also fostered by the change in political perspective. Three aspects of drug development seem particularly amenable to private sector involvement: postmarketing surveillance, the funding of basic research, and drug information for patients. The private sector already participates in these areas, but we should re-examine the extent to which government objectives facilitate—or demand—more private sector involvement.

Government agencies have long been active in both the postmarketing surveillance of drugs and the funding of basic research. Budgetary constraints, however, have recently reduced government programs. If projects are to continue, an increase in private sector involvement seems essential.

Postmarketing Surveillance. The idea of improving postmarketing surveillance (PMS) in the United States has received attention from a number of sources for several years. The drug regulation reform bills considered by Congress since 1975 have included provisions for some form of PMS. The FDA has been active in sponsoring several PMS programs both within and outside the agency. The pharmaceutical industry, in turn, has undertaken some PMS studies of its own (spontaneously or at the FDA's request) and cooperated with the FDA in others. Most collaborative efforts have been limited to a specific drug (levodopa, azaribine, and various cancer drugs, for example) or, in the case of the three-year study by the Joint Commission on Prescription Drug Use, to attempts to define the characteristics of an effective PMS system. This joint commission is a good example of a congressional proposal funded by the private sector. Few concerted attempts have been made to institute a comprehensive system, although the scope of the FDA's Division of Drug Experience has been increased greatly in recent years, and the agency has funded university centers to collect and analyze PMS data.

If the emphasis on deregulation of drug development continues, there will be a strong social need to maintain and improve PMS. The idea of speeding up drug development and approval by replacing phase III studies for at least some drugs with phase IV studies, with postmarketing surveillance, has been a subject of discussion for several years. Many believe that the benefits of earlier availability of new drugs outweigh the safety risks, but agree that one of the main barriers to accepting PMS as an alternative is that existing PMS systems in the United States are not sufficiently developed to monitor drug efficacy nationwide. The opposition of some consumer groups and congressional representatives to the idea of a trade-off as well as the historically adversarial relationship of the FDA and industry are at least partly responsible for a lack of progress.

Given the political and technical difficulties inherent in installing a comprehensive PMS system, perhaps the best course of action would be to begin with a relatively small program. One such possibility, recommended by the GAO in 1981, is to require phase IV —rather than phase III—studies to validate the results of foreign efficacy and safety studies. This could have several advantages. First, it could illustrate the feasibility of PMS as a trade-off. Second, drugs already tested and marketed abroad would be available sooner in the United States than they are under the present system. And, finally, political opposition based on real or imagined safety risks might be lessened because safety and efficacy information would be more extensive for these drugs than for those just emerging from phase II studies in the United States.

There is little evidence that PMS activities of either the FDA or industry are expanding to focus on studies of drug efficacy as well as safety. In October 1981, the agency announced its intention to fund two PMS projects to be conducted in collaboration with private researchers entailing substantial FDA involvement in design. The Pharmaceutical Manufacturers Association has also announced funding for studies of PMS methodology. Both projects, however, seem intended to emphasize techniques for assessing safety rather than efficacy.

Both funding programs involve the private sector. Still, the PMS development process would be further facilitated if other groups in the private sector began or improved their own programs. Confidence in any PMS system—whether limited or comprehensive—will be strengthened by directly involving private groups other than industry. Physicians' and pharmacists' organizations, for example, could take an active role by helping with design, organization, and data collection in a PMS system. Particularly for drugs with restricted distribution, health care providers could perform some monitoring and data collection functions. Consumer organizations could contribute by disseminating information to the general public or, through the disease-oriented volunteer organizations, to the specific population for which the drug is intended.

The private sector may need to support more postmarketing surveillance programs, since the government has significantly reduced funding for such work. FDA funding of the Boston Collaborative Drug Surveillance Project, for example, declined from $685,710 in FY 1981 to $368,000 in FY 1982; support for the Boston Drug Epidemiology Unit has also been radically reduced. Each is a major independent PMS effort.

Looking at the overall picture of PMS, one can see that if new-drug approvals are increased, the total PMS effort—whatever its composition—should also be increased to detect potential trouble at an early stage.

Funding of Basic Research. Although in real terms government funding of basic research declined throughout the 1970s, reductions since 1980 have been particularly pronounced. Funding for the thirteen divisions of the National Institutes of Health (NIH), for example, increased by a yearly average of 5.6 percent between 1979 and 1981 and by 2.0 percent from 1981 to 1982; under the Reagan administration's proposed FY 1983 budget, the 1981–1983 average annual increase would be only 2.3 percent. These small increments do not allow the NIH budget to keep pace with inflation, estimated to be 8–10 percent per year for basic research.

Another measure of the decline is the number of grant and research activities included in the proposed FY 1983 budget. In 1981, Congress directed NIH to fund 10,000 trainees and 5,000 grant projects. Under the administration's proposed budget, however, the number of research trainees supported by NIH would decline from about 9,700 full-time equivalents in 1982 to 8,915 in 1983, and only 4,100 grants will be funded. Despite public statements by the administration of its commitment to basic research, actual government support for these activities has declined. The scientific community has expressed concern about the effect of these reductions.

The private sector—particularly industry—has been urged to compensate for reduced federal funding, and grants to private research centers in 1981 make it evident that industry is willing to play a greater role. Grants made in 1981 include:

- $6 million from du Pont to Harvard's genetics department for basic immunology research
- over $65 million from Hoechst to Massachusetts General Hospital for the establishment of a molecular biology department
- $3.9 million from Mallinckrodt to Washington University for hybridoma research
- $1.1 million from Celanese to Yale for basic research in microbial transformations
- $1.5 million from DNAX (a division of Alza) to Massachusetts General Hospital for cardiac-related immunology research
- $331,000 from DNAX to Stanford's Cancer Biology Laboratory for human monoclonal antibody research

Under the terms of most of these agreements, the research center retains patent rights that could eventually supplement funding through royalty payments. As of mid-December 1981, Stanford had signed licensing agreements with seventy-one firms for its recombinant DNA process patent. Stanford's annual income from royalties is expected to be about $1 million within four to five years.

Despite this impressive beginning, the total amount of such funding is small compared with previous NIH budgets for basic research, and serious doubts remain that industry can (or will) invest at a rate to offset losses of federal funds. Moreover, some observers argue that industry sponsorship will narrow the field of research by emphasizing only those areas of interest to industry.

No component of the private sector can match industry's resources for investment in the basic biomedical research that underpins drug development programs, although some do have strong investment incentives. In 1979 an average of 10 to 15 percent of the annual income of the disease-oriented volunteer organizations went to fund biomedical research. But this funding—about $110 million in 1978—is not enough to compensate for federal budget cuts. Moreover, in a time of high unemployment and general economic malaise, the voluntary contributions that constitute most of the income of these organizations are not likely to increase.

The valuable role of private sector initiatives as an alternative to government regulation is aptly illustrated by the private sector's response to the challenge of patient education. In September 1980, the FDA initiated a three-year pilot program mandating the distribution of patient package inserts (PPI) with ten designated drugs. Although the principle of better informing patients was not in question, most of the industry components of the private sector and several professional associations (the American Pharmaceutical Association and the American Medical Association, for example) strongly opposed this particular program. Opponents proposed alternatives and repeatedly argued that an effective program of patient education could be undertaken by the private sector without government interference.

With the change in administration, the federal government became much more receptive to these ideas. Despite attempts by some consumer groups to retain the PPI program, the pilot project was cancelled in December 1981. But the government's proposed PPI project could not have been rendered unnecessary without the strong programs already begun by the private sector.

Two overlapping private sector approaches to providing patients with drug-use information are those that disseminate information directly to the public and those that encourage or enable the physician or pharmacist to do so. Direct patient information is available in 2,000 of the 9,392 chain drug stores that are members of the National Association of Chain Drug Stores (NACDS). In many cases, consumers have access to a compendium of drug information in a notebook binder at the pharmacy. NACDS members intend to increase their public-information efforts in 1982. Other private groups have announced plans to make information more readily available. The publishing firm Medical Economics is developing a *Consumer Desk Reference* that will include manufacturers' information summaries reviewed by the FDA. In part, this is a response to the growing popularity among the general public of the firm's *Physician's*

Desk Reference to prescription drugs. The National Retired Teachers' Association and the American Association of Retired Persons are collaborating on a drug information system intended for use by the elderly. A project that may be more highly visible to the general public is the series of 3,000 "health fairs" stressing patient education that are planned nationwide. Directed by the National Health Screening Council for Volunteer Organizations, these events are staffed entirely by volunteers from professional organizations (the American Society of Hospital Pharmacists and the American Pharmaceutical Association, for example), the disease-oriented volunteer organizations, industry, and the media. Financial support is provided by over 100 corporations and fifty media businesses. Much of the funding for materials has come from a single large pharmaceutical firm, Ciba-Geigy.

Several additional efforts to improve patient education by physicians and pharmacists are already under way or complete. The United States Pharmacopoeial Convention announced its intention to put the material from its book *Dispensing Information* into a computer network being organized by the American Medical Association (AMA) for health professionals. The National Association of Retail Druggists and the American Society of Hospital Pharmacists plan a professional education program and manual for pharmacists to facilitate drug counseling of patients. By the middle of 1982, the AMA will have leaflets, based initially on *Dispensing Information,* available for physicians to give to patients on the twenty most used drugs. The AMA will launch a public campaign to promote the program, and industry, through the Pharmaceutical Manufacturers Association, has announced its support.

The FDA's response to these initiatives has been generally positive, though constrained by the legal questions of drug labeling. To help provide both the necessary coordination for these diverse programs and a focal point for government efforts, the FDA and the Department of Health and Human Services (HHS) approved a Committee on Patient Education. In January 1982 at its first meeting, the committee created the Patient Education Resource Center to coordinate programs on patient education.

Outside government, Ciba-Geigy has announced plans to provide $1.1 million in funding for an autonomous Joint Commission on Patient Information. This nonprofit organization will serve primarily to coordinate activities. The firm has proposed that all interest groups be members, including professional medical and pharmacy associations, school associations, consumer associations, regulatory agencies, pharmaceutical manufacturers, publishers, health insurers, and foundations. The FDA supports the proposal and intends to participate as a member.

The success of these patient-education programs should make extensive government regulation unnecessary, although some government oversight will still be needed. Moreover, the approach may show ways of reducing health care costs in the future. Nationwide information networks—perhaps computerized—might, after thorough testing and risk assessment, allow some self-diagnosis and serve as a reliable guide to self-medication. The growing popularity of national data networks and the in-home computer creates possibilities for patient education with far-reaching implications.

Increased private sector initiatives in designing and implementing postmarketing surveillance and patient education systems and in funding basic research are all encouraged by today's political perspectives on government regulation and spending. The response of the private sector to both the need and opportunity for greater involvement has been impressive. If the attention given since 1980 by the private sector to such activities as postmarketing surveillance and patient education continues, then the FDA may well be able to concentrate on coordinating rather than regulating these programs, a role certainly in keeping with the administration's political philosophy.

Government Incentives to the Private Sector

The decline in innovative activity in the U.S. pharmaceutical industry has stimulated the introduction of bills in the Ninety-seventh Congress dealing with patent-life extension and orphan-drug development. A common assumption underlying the proposals appears to be that innovative incentives will increase as industry's financial returns on research and development increase. Two possible methods of achieving this result are included in the bills. First, lessened regulatory requirements are intended both to reduce costs incurred in the premarketing phase and to facilitate earlier marketing of new drugs. Second, financial returns are increased by granting and/or increasing the length of time the firm has market exclusivity.

The patent-life restoration bills (H.R. 1937 and S. 255) have been the subject of contentious debates, particularly in the House of Representatives.[4] Under the terms of the bills, up to seven years would be added to the patent life of a new drug (and other products subject to premarket clearance) to compensate for the time spent in the premarket regulatory review process. According to analyses performed at the Center for the Study of Drug Development at the University of Rochester Medical School, the effective life of the compound patent on new drugs (that is, the life of the patent remaining after NDA approval) has declined from a mean of 13.5 years in 1968 to a mean of 6.8 years in 1981. Increases in the preclinical and clinical periods of drug development, both subject to regulation, and the regulatory assessment time itself account for most of this decline.

Among those supporting the patent-life extension bills are the research-based pharmaceutical industry, HHS and the FDA, and some universities (Johns Hopkins, for example). Whereas most of the discussion has focused on the potential impact on industry, the universities' perspective is particularly interesting in light of the increased industry-academe research connection discussed earlier. Under the terms of most of these agreements, the university (or research center) retains the patent rights to compounds discovered; the sponsoring industry has marketing and licensing rights. Extending the effective patent life would increase university revenues from patent royalties, perhaps stimulating additional academic research.

Opposition to patent extension has come from other portions of the private sector, particularly generic manufacturers and some consumer groups (the Generic Pharmaceutical Industry Association and the Health Research Group, for example). Each argues that additional financial incentives are unnecessary, that consumer costs will rise, and that the particular bills are not optimum in design.

"Orphan" drugs are those considered to be commercially unattractive to industry because they treat relatively rare diseases or conditions or have an especially small market. Such drugs face the same regulatory requirements as other new chemical entities, cost at least as much to develop, and can generate only a small financial return. The most recent orphan-drug bill introduced into Congress, H.R. 5238, is intended to stimulate research and development by removing some regulatory barriers and providing financial incentives, such as tax credits and market exclusivity for nonpatentable drugs. The bill has achieved some popularity: as of March 1982 it had 131 cosponsors.

Despite this political support, the pharmaceutical industry opposes the bill, arguing that the impediments to orphan-drug development are not necessarily financial. Clinical trials to prove efficacy, for example, are difficult to perform, given the small size of the target population. Industry has suggested, moreover, that regulatory changes to facilitate research and marketing can be implemented without statutory amendment of the Food, Drug, and Cosmetic Act and that the same policy ought to be applied to all drugs, not just orphan drugs.

Although there is little strong opposition to the bill, industry greatly favors nonlegislative initiatives. In August 1981, for example, the Pharmaceutical Manufacturers Association, perhaps stimulated by the prospect of government initiatives, established a Commission on Drugs for Rare Diseases to encourage research, in part by serving as a clearinghouse for information and as a liaison between independent researchers and potential sponsors. Paralleling this private sector initiative is the creation by HHS of a board to coordinate all government activities affecting development of orphan drugs and products.[5] Although it is too soon to draw any firm conclusions, the combination of effective private sector action and government cooperation may make legislation unnecessary.

The patent-life and orphan-drug legislation indicates that congressional sponsors believe that changes in regulatory practice alone are not sufficient inducements for innovation in drug development. Various private sector groups, however, have disagreed with this approach; the research-based pharmaceutical firms in particular have been decidedly lukewarm. In contrast, research-based firms have consistently favored the patent-life bills, while generic manufacturers fervidly oppose them, and other private sector components offer only conditional support.

On the surface, both the patent-life and parts of the orphan-drug bills coincide with the current government perspective by explicitly recognizing the role of the market in fostering innovation. On the whole, the orphan-drug bill, however, seems to contradict the dominant regulatory philosophy by adding yet another set of rules to those already governing the drug development and approval process.

Conclusions

These examples of private sector initiatives in drug development and regulation aptly illustrate several points. First, even in an area of health care that is already largely the responsibility of the private sector, there is still room for innovative initiatives from the private sector—initiatives that could have profound and diffuse consequences. Such efforts are not limited to the provision of additional funding, but range over the entire spectrum of drug development activities.

Second, cooperative efforts are essential—not only between government and the private sector but also among the various components of the private sector itself. Despite favorable political attitudes, there is no guarantee of unequivocal public and private support for further increases in private sector involvement. For instance, strong objections—and charges of agency "capture"—are likely if input from industry appears to outweigh that from other private sector organizations. The FDA can coordinate and balance private sector participation and foster a spirit of cooperation, but similar efforts among private organizations are also imperative. The example of patient education programs shows what can be done at both the government and private levels.

Third, some private sector alternatives to regulation face legal barriers. Many of the examples show that although significant changes can be made without congressional action, others require it. Attempts to alter the law provoke lengthy debate (as in the case of the patent-life extension bills), delaying the implementation of some initiatives. Ultimately, private sector involvement—whether under existing or revised statutes—may encounter a final impediment: challenges in the courts may determine whether (or to what extent) government can rely on private sector initiatives as alternatives to regulation.

We have not exhausted the possibilities for increased private sector involvement. By focusing on the most visible initiatives, we have illustrated the effect of changes in regulatory (and budgetary) philosophy. Without this change in political perspective, some of the private sector programs now showing great promise and achievement—such as postmarketing surveillance and patient education—might already have been eclipsed by government programs. At the same time, the potential for private involvement in other aspects of the process—including, perhaps, review board authority over early clinical trials and reliance on advisory committees—may never be fully realized without further and more basic changes in political attitudes and closer agreement on goals within the private sector.

Although the private sector already plays a primary role in drug development, the opportunities for increased private sector participation are extensive. Private initiatives could improve the efficiency and heighten the achievements of the processes of drug development and regulation. Private groups should be encouraged to continue to devise innovative solutions to existing problems.

Notes

[1] Prescription drugs account for 60 to 65 percent of drugs and drug sundries.

[2] The actual composition of the commission varies depending on the particular drug or drug class under study. The law requires that the commission members have specialized knowledge of the therapeutic category and/or individual drug.

[3] Postmarketing surveillance is discussed in the next section of the paper.

[4] S. 255 passed the Senate unanimously in July 1981.

[5] By including "products," as well as drugs, the board's activities extend to biologics, medical devices, and diagnostic products.

Youth Crime Prevention:
An Alternative Approach

Robert L. Woodson

Throughout the United States, people fear criminal violence. The latchkey is no longer out in friendly welcome to all who pass by. Now doors are locked and windows barred; now children are carefully instructed to note well which houses have a sign in their front window announcing that *this* house offers sanctuary if needed to children on their way to and from school; now signs are posted to warn potential intruders that this community participates in a Neighborhood Watch program. The welcome mat has disappeared from our doorsteps.

Americans are afraid, that much is clear. Public opinion polls report that two Americans in five are afraid to go out alone at night. People living in urban settings are more afraid than those living in the suburbs, and blacks and other minorities are more afraid than whites. And not without reason. According to a recent report prepared for the Twentieth Century Fund by Frank Zimring,[1]

- Males between the ages of thirteen and twenty compose only 9 percent of the delinquent population but account for more than half of all property crime arrests and more than a third of all offenses involving violence.
- Most young offenders who commit acts of extreme violence and pursue criminal careers come from minority ghetto and poverty backgrounds. So do their victims.
- Violent crime committed by youths has increased.

The question remains—of whom are we afraid? The answer, it seems, is that we are afraid of our children. Thus it should follow that the primary emphasis and the bulk of the money for programs to decrease youthful criminal activity should focus on minority low-income young men who have already committed, or are likely to com-

405

mit, a property offense or a violent offense. This, unfortunately, has not been the case. Instead, an estimated 80 percent of the $448 million spent by the Office of Juvenile Justice and Delinquency Prevention since its inception in 1974 has been spent on counseling and support to keep so-called status offenders out of institutions (status offenses are actions that would not be unlawful if committed by adults: for example, truancy, curfew violations, and incorrigibility). About 82 percent of the juveniles affected by de-institutionalization programs are white. Since most diversion programs are carried out by nonprofit organizations that typically do not serve urban minorities, the majority of children being "saved" are middle class. Relatively little has been done for the more serious delinquents and for the small group—some 4 percent—who are violent offenders. Yet these are the children we fear most, and it is only by diverting this group of young people from criminal activities that the ever-escalating rate of serious juvenile crime can be reversed.

There are some who point to the declining birthrate and predict a concomitant decrease in the rate of crimes committed by youths whether or not there is a change in the policies we adopt toward juvenile offenders. These prophets are not entirely wrong: as the number of youths decreases, the number of crimes committed by youths will also decrease (though not necessarily in proportion). What they fail to take into account, however, is that the birthrate among minorities is *not* declining. Nor do they note that the number of young urban black males between the ages of eighteen and twenty will increase 8 percent over the next fifteen to twenty years, or that 44 percent of the Hispanic population is under eighteen years of age —and neither of these figures includes youths among the uncounted illegal aliens.

Wish though we may, the problem of youth crime will not simply and quietly die of attrition—certainly not within the next two decades and probably not ever. Conditions affecting our children are constantly changing. Who would have dreamed even twenty years ago that courses instructing our fifth and sixth graders in the dangers of substance abuse would become a routine part of the regular curriculum? It is our responsibility as adults to help our children cope with the changes thrust upon them. It is also our responsibility as adults to examine the way we deal with the problem of youth crime.

Children cannot change public policy; grown-ups can. Not only has public policy failed in the past to address adequately the overall problem of youth crime, but it has also failed to meet the needs of those youths most in need of the help. Even in instances when the Office of Juvenile Justice and Delinquency Prevention (OJJDP) programs and funds were directed toward working with "hard-core" young offenders, the programs and methods espoused by OJJDP changed few, if any, present or potential offenders. These programs failed in large part because they addressed the problems and needs of middle-class youths and were inappropriate to the needs and interests of young minority men living in ghettos.

The primary contention of this paper is that past policies aimed at solving the problem of youth crime have failed. Equally important, it calls attention to several grass-roots initiatives that reduced the incidence of youth violence and crime. The failure of present strategies to confront the problem presented by the hard-core juvenile offender will be analyzed, and the ability of alternative grass-roots programs to "turn around" these youths will be described.

The Problem of Youth Crime

Like the weather, everyone talks a lot about youth crime, but no one seems to be able to do much about it. There is no consensus about which strategies work best, let alone about the philosophical bases underlying the different approaches used with youthful offenders. Indeed, though a variety of strategies and rationales have been studied intensively, no study has been able to prove conclusively that one type of intervention is more effective than another or even more effective than doing nothing at all. Strategies that appear to have had moderate success with status offenders or with middle-class youths have not been effective when applied to hard-core offenders, who are, for the most part, from low-income and minority backgrounds. As a result of past failures to reach these youths, a consensus appears to be forming toward hard-core offenders—to "lock them up and throw away the key." Thus, these children are punished for society's failure to deal with them effectively.

It need not be this way. In cities throughout the United States, individuals and neighborhood organizations working at the grass-roots level have managed to reach hard-core youths, work with them effectively, and reduce the crime plaguing their neighborhoods. Some of the strategies used in these grass-roots efforts are identical to strategies that failed when used by outsiders. Other strategies are innovative or unique to a particular organization. Despite their sometimes different approaches to the problems of youth crime, however, the various grass-roots organizations have two things in common: (1) the approach they take toward reducing youth crime has been developed within the community; it reflects and respects community values, mores, and needs and enjoys broad-based community support;

(2) each program draws on the strengths of the youths themselves as well as on the strengths of adult members of the community; everyone—youths and adults alike—participates equally and fully in achieving the program's goals. We shall now examine the reasons why the approach taken by grass-roots organizations succeeds where public approaches have often failed, and how the strategies used by local groups differ from those used by institutions.

Traditional Approaches to Youth Crime

Youths coming into contact with the juvenile justice system can usually be characterized as falling into one of three categories: (1) youths who are unaware of the rules; (2) youths who are "sick" and cannot comply; or (3) youths who are simply willful. If the youth has had insufficient opportunity to learn the rules or has learned the wrong ones, then his learning milieu must be altered and the child must be retrained. If a youth is psychologically incapable of behaving correctly, then he must be "cured." If, on the other hand, he is merely self-willed and obstinate, then he must be punished. These categories, and the strategies formulated to serve the needs of the children in them, underlie the three most widely used approaches to resolving the problems of youth crime: change the child's environment, change the child himself, or "get tough" with him.

Alter the Environment. Some social welfare professionals maintain that the environment in which the troubled youth lives is the root of the youth crime problem. They argue that violent and criminal acts among youth can be prevented and controlled only by addressing the complex social and economic problems within the child's immediate environment. This line of reasoning is the basis of two different approaches popular with social welfare bureaucracies. One approach consists of removing the child from his own home and, depending on the nature of the delinquent activity and where the child is in the juvenile justice process, placing him in a foster home or detaining him in a residential institution. The other approach calls for a massive overhaul of urban neighborhoods, job development and training, desegregation of public schools, and reform of the public welfare system. Both approaches assume that crime control will come as a result of breaking the link between the individual likely to commit crime and the criminogenic environment. Neither approach has demonstrated much success.

Child welfare systems have placed great emphasis on changing the individual by removing him from poor or questionable home environments and retraining him in artificial settings. Recent evidence indicates, however, that these alternatives to the child's home environment are often more harmful than helpful. It appears, in fact, that many children begin delinquent careers *because* of their experiences in the child welfare system. (The destructiveness of this approach is examined in the chapter in this volume on foster care.)

The second way to insulate youths from a dangerous environment is to rehabilitate the urban neighborhood itself and reorganize its institutional structure. This approach was attempted during the 1960s when programs funded by the Office of Economic Opportunity and inspired by the President's Commission on the Prevention of Juvenile Delinquency had as their goals delinquency prevention through removing social, educational, and economic barriers to achievement among youth. Unfortunately, however, these community organization efforts, which were directed toward establishing idealized democratic institutions, gave little consideration to the genuine needs of the local population and did not include the real involvement of the youths and their families. Instead, middle-class practices in social work were imposed on poverty-ridden communities. Not only did these programs fail to achieve their intended objectives, but the price tags for these efforts also ranged in the billions of dollars. Cost alone makes continuation of a similar effort unlikely at a time when the American economy is in trouble and the average taxpayer, feeling this economic squeeze, is unwilling to support such expensive urban development and system-changing approaches.

Change the Child. A different approach—the mental-health approach—to the problem of youth crime is based on the philosophy that delinquency can be prevented by directly altering the youth's behavior through such techniques as psychotherapy or counseling. This approach has been strongly supported by the Office of Juvenile Justice and Delinquency Prevention and has, indeed, achieved some success. The difficulty with this approach, however, lies in the fact that mental-health intervention strategies succeed only to the degree that the goals of the helper mesh with those of the person being helped. (For further discussion of the professionalization of the client, see the chapter on the importance of neighborhood grass-roots organizations in meeting human needs.) Mental-health personnel are often upper middle class, and their orientation is reflected in the norms, procedures, and cultural climate of therapeutic practice. Although traditional mental-health practices may be useful in addressing the problems of people who share the same or similar cultural values, they have made only limited inroads in providing effective services to those criminal justice clients most at risk—those who are poor, urban, members of a minority, and young.

A second, more serious, difficulty with the mental-health approach that limits its ability to serve poor and minority communities is its emphasis on medical disease or the model of pathological deviance. Low-income clients, their families, and even the community in which they live are looked upon as a kaleidoscope of interlocking pathologies. Clients are regarded as sick, their families undesirable, their community unwholesome. By refusing to acknowledge the client's very real strengths and by failing to provide the client with the skills he needs to survive in his so-called undesirable and unwholesome environment—in short, by undermining his ability to function successfully, in the name of helping him—these mental-health professionals frequently produce a "cure" worse than the original "disease."

Getting Tough with Young Criminals. With each apparent failure of traditional strategies to deal with the problem of youth crime, and with every press report of a young person committing a violent crime, demands are made that we "get tough" with young criminals. These demands include lowering the jurisdictional age limit and even continuing detention of certain youthful offenders beyond the completion of the sentences imposed by the courts.

The reasoning behind these demands is, at best, confused, albeit understandable. No one can blame a person who has been the victim of an assault, or whose friend or loved one has suffered injury at the hands of an attacker, for wanting revenge or advocating the severest penalties for the perpetrator of the attack. The desire to lash out at those who have hurt us is perfectly human—it is, in fact, the primary reason why some sort of judicial intervention between the attacker and the attacked is needed to ensure that the punishment meted out actually fits the crime. Fear of criminal activity and the desire to lock up offenders and throw away the key are equally understandable human responses to the problem of youth crime. We must not let our fears and our desires for retribution, however, blind us to the realities at hand.

Putting youthful offenders behind bars for perpetuity will *not* solve the problem of youth crime. First, statistics on population growth presented earlier in this paper show that every hard-core offender incarcerated will soon be replaced by another on the streets. Second, the incarcerated offender will, sooner or later, return to those streets, older, wiser in the ways of crime, and still more embittered.

The notion that the threat of increasingly harsh punishment will deter youths from criminal activity is equally faulty. Even in the cases in which the threat of such punishment becomes a reality for

410

one offender, there is little or no deterrent effect on the actions of other offenders. Anyone familiar with the environment of urban delinquents must realize that these youths have been subjected to threats and coercion for most of their lives. Threatening them with additional punitive harshness is analogous to threatening a kamikaze pilot with death. If a youth is conditioned to cope with armed gang members, if he has faced death daily on the streets and in the schools on his "turf," what inhibiting effect can a "get-tough" policy have?

We must not allow our psychologically understandable fears and desires to be translated into punitive public policy. If we do—if, in the words of James Wilson, we "fund our fears"[2]—then we, as a country, severely threaten the democratic constitutional guarantees that protect us all. And we would do so in support of a public policy that does nothing at all to alleviate the problem of youth crime.

Two-Track System of Juvenile Justice

Regardless whether the traditional approaches to hard-core juvenile offenders will be modified or a harsher, more punitive policy adopted, Americans are faced with a two-track system of juvenile justice that de-institutionalizes and rehabilitates one group of youths while incarcerating, in ever-increasing numbers, another group of young people.

A decade ago, racial minorities composed 30 percent of the inmates in state prisons and juvenile facilities. Since then, with little public notice, that number has jumped to nearly 60 percent. At the same time, when white youngsters are increasingly being removed from the criminal justice system through de-institutionalization, restitution programs, and diversion, the overall prison population is becoming increasingly black and poor. That this startling increase comes during a period of social and economic gain for most minorities is a source of growing concern for those involved in the criminal justice system.

Nothing in this paper argues against a policy of de-institutionalizing youthful offenders, which is a matter of justice and should be done. The fact is, however, that de-institutionalization has nothing to do with crime rates. Programs for de-institutionalizing youthful offenders foster, even if inadvertently, the separation of children by race and class.

Effective Help for the Youthful Offender

If we could put aside momentarily our thinking based on traditional approaches to the problem of youth crime, it would be easier to see that effective programs for youth cannot be those that in any way

411

demean—or segregate—people. Nor can these programs be ones that include domination, however well intended the efforts of people who are strangers to these youths' experiences.

Although largely unknown to the world of professionals, examples of effective programs for youths that operate on principles of reciprocity and accountability are not hard to find. In Philadelphia's ghetto, the House of Umoja has established an enviable record of success working with neighborhood youth who had previously been rejected as incorrigible and multideficient by schools, social welfare agencies, and juvenile authorities. In a place that outsiders usually consider a mere tangle of social pathology and criminogenic forces, Umoja has been able to call on the many real strengths of the community to achieve with its own troubled children what outsiders could not. In Chester, Pennsylvania, a few miles south, a similar project undertaken by amateur inner-city activists is showing equal success in strengthening the personal resources of community youth, measurably reducing the chance that they will become involved in criminal activities.

House of Umoja. Sister Falaka Fattah and David Fattah are, in some ways, just ordinary people who happen to live in West Philadelphia. As in the case with most of the other residents in this particular section of the "City of Brotherly Love," the Fattahs are black, low-income, and nonprofessional, although David is working, when his duties at the House of Umoja permit, toward a degree in business administration at Temple University. What sets the Fattahs apart is the fact that they are, besides being the parents of six sons, the psychological parents of over 500 young black men who are also residents of West Philadelphia. Single-handedly, the Fattahs were instrumental in helping Philadelphia lose its reputation as the youth gang capital of America.

Sister Fattah is a warm, pleasant, and affable person who looks younger than her mid-forties. Her conversation is sprinkled with constant references to the "kids," and she often adjusts her speech to speak in the vernacular to youngsters seeking information or advice. David Fattah is an intelligent, friendly, and committed person who has strong attachments to and knowledge of the plight of young blacks in the streets. As a former gang member who grew up in Philadelphia, David Fattah is one of the few adults who enjoys the complete trust and confidence of gang members from different parts of the city.

The Fattahs, like other parents in Philadelphia, were concerned about the daily slaughter of young black people in gang warfare on the city's streets. Their concern was intensified in 1969 when they learned that the eldest of their six sons was a fringe member of a street gang called Clymer Street. The activities of young gangs in Philadelphia became so violent in 1969 that the *Philadelphia Inquirer* dubbed it "The Year of the Gun."

After long hours of consultation with their son and the fifteen youths in the gang, the Fattahs extended an invitation to the group to come and live with them. Sister Fattah relates that the only commitment they made to the young people was to help them stay alive and to keep them out of jail. All the youths were between the ages of fifteen and seventeen. The leader (or runner) was being hunted by a rival gang. The police, too, were searching for him. So David Fattah and Sister Fattah, their six sons, and an elderly mother made room in their small, four-room house. Virtually all the furniture in the house had to be removed to accommodate mattresses that were used for sleeping and sitting. Sister Fattah began to teach the boys English, and David Fattah began coaching them in mathematics and economics. Television was also used as a teaching tool. Role playing was a means used to prepare the youths for job interviews and court appearances. At the end of the first year, according to Sister Fattah, "We were all alive, and no one went to jail, nor did any of the youngsters want to go home."

Despite some of the early difficulties, all the fifteen original members remained during the first year. A code of conduct was established, based on a set of principles that amounted to a constitution. It helped the youths to adjust and guided the conduct of daily life at the house. "Umoja," a Swahili word meaning "unity within the family," is made up of seven principles: unity of self, unity within the family, unity within the House of Umoja, unity within the neighborhood, unity within the black community, unity within the people in the world, and unity in the area of human rights for all people. At the House of Umoja there is rigid scheduling and a maximum of free time—planned activities and freedom of choice. New residents must obey the Fattah parents and the other Umoja siblings, who set limits and controls. Each youth's personal qualities and unique problems are also recognized.

If a young person is to compete in the world of work, his time frame must be consistent with that of the workplace. Gang youths are night people, rising late and staying up most of the night. To reorder their time frame, the House of Umoja adheres to a rigid daily schedule. At 6:00 A.M. everyone rises with the sun. A conference is held to set goals for the day, to discuss personal problems of the previous day, and to reach decisions. Between 7:00 and 7:30 in the

413

morning, the youths breakfast, choosing from a limited menu. The rest of the morning is spent at school or work. The time from 3:00 in the afternoon to 10:00 at night is spent pursuing personal goals and may be devoted, for example, to homework and personal friendships.

Every Friday night the entire group meets for the Adella, a meeting similar to a tribal council (in more traditional mental-health circles it would be called group therapy). This is a weekly review to resolve personal conflicts and settle family disputes. Any member may lead the discussion. Anyone found in violation of the code of conduct must determine his own punishment. If the group thinks the sanction is too lenient, it may suggest a more just punishment. The most severe sanction is to tell others on the street that the youth is not a person of his word. Even with the Adella, however, there are times when an individual problem must be handled one to one, usually by Sister Fattah.

The Adella and the individual counseling sessions are always conducted in the kitchen around food. Sister Fattah says that the children of Umoja seldom have had enough food. Because food symbolizes nurturance, she makes certain that there is always enough. She believes that young people will fight when they are drinking together, but they will seldom fight when eating together.

Every new youth accepted into Umoja starts at the bottom in accordance with the general policies put into effect ever since the house opened. As the youth demonstrates his capacity to control himself and shows that he is dependable and trustworthy, his status improves, which usually means a better job and increased responsibility. He cannot achieve this new status simply by remaining in the program. He must aggressively pursue positive goals and work toward self-improvement within the philosophical framework of Umoja's seven principles. Successful completion of the seven steps earns the youth a much sought-after prize—the right to change his last name to Fattah.

From 1969 to the present, the Fattahs have helped over 500 young men change their lives. The Umoja program is constantly evolving, its activities and approach constantly being altered to accommodate the changing needs and tastes of each new group that comes through the doors of the House of Umoja. In summary, Umoja has been successful in tackling one of the most perplexing problems facing the American public—the behavior patterns of violent youth.

Youth-In-Action. Chester, Pennsylvania, with a population of 53,000, has the appearance of a long-neglected community—neglected by private enterprise, government agencies, and the citizens of Chester.

Here can be found all the ingrained problems associated with urban density: poverty, high unemployment, lack of opportunities and resources, lack of local control over institutional decisions that affect the area, and crime, delinquency, drugs, and despair. Chester has the second highest crime rate in the state, with more than 50 percent of the crimes being burglary, larceny, or other property offenses. In addition to the fear generated by the serious law enforcement problem, the economic impact of crime in Chester has been devastating. The general unemployment rate is 17 percent and is estimated to be more than 20 percent in any given year for black males. Public assistance expenditures amount to more than $1 million per month in Chester.

As might be expected, the juvenile population of Chester is deeply affected by these economic and social ills. Of a total of 3,311 juveniles living in the city in 1976, 11 percent were arrested at least once and 210 were remanded to the juvenile justice system. Nearly 15 percent of Chester's children never complete high school. Chester, they say, is "no place to be somebody."

In spite of the deep social problems and in marked contrast to official inertia, a dynamic program for youth and community development has been started in Chester. It is staffed by volunteer nonprofessionals. Founded in 1968 through the energy and vision of Tommie Lee Jones, the organization was completely self-funded and was operated out of Mrs. Jones's home. Now incorporated as Youth-In-Action (YIA), the program receives a continuing grant from Sun Oil Company and some funds from the Law Enforcement Assistance Administration (LEAA). The various activities and programs that have been organized or influenced by Youth-In-Action in Chester are now strongly endorsed by the social service agencies of Chester and Delaware County, a testimony to the effectiveness of the efforts of the YIA.

Youth-In-Action first focused on the youth gangs multiplying in different areas of the city. The program worked with gang leaders and managed to bring together members of rival gangs to promote a spirit of peaceful coexistence and to eliminate the threat gang warfare posed for community security. YIA began to coordinate alternative youth groups that could diminish the attraction of gangs. The new groups also acted as mediators in gang disputes. Through the activities of YIA, the gang threat has been all but eliminated in the area.

Self-rehabilitation of former gang members, drug users, truants, and parolees takes place through peer counseling. The youths—working for self-development through service to the community and to

415

one another—counsel each other on school, family, and legal problems. The genuineness of the counseled youths' commitment to change develops from the support they receive from peer relations. The counselors are themselves youths who have been in trouble and received counseling.

The youth counseling program has become so effective that YIA has begun to take referrals from the Delaware County Child Care Services and other state youth agencies. Activities include an outreach program for drug users and legal assistance for those who want it. YIA also actively counsels and assists truants.

La Playa de Ponce. A third example of successful grass-roots intervention in the lives of troubled young people is a program run by Sister M. Isolina Ferré in La Playa, the port section of Ponce, Puerto Rico. Without any initial funding and armed only with a philosophical commitment to help in the unfolding of the human potential of community children, Sister Isolina began to help young people who were in trouble with the courts or who were school dropouts. Among these was a hard-core group that contributed disproportionately to the police statistics on crime and to the unsavory reputation of La Playa.

Sister Isolina's influence on hard-core delinquents was not originally mandated or enforced by the courts. It was grounded entirely in the ideals and concerted efforts of local people who began to see themselves as being responsible for the community's children. Although she did not have a residence for children, Sister Isolina began to build relations with young people who were in trouble and with their families and neighbors. She found that in many cases the schools had refused further contact with these "bad" children who were rejected and left to run wild in the streets. Sister Isolina began to organize alternative education programs by means of a small grant from LEAA. Many workshops were initiated to provide cultural enrichment, opportunities to learn employable skills, and, most of all, the social milieu that encourages young people to discover and take an interest in developing their own potential. Delinquents are "renamed" as young adults, as officers of clubs, as artists, skilled technicians, future parents, citizens, and the like. At the same time, adults of the area acquire new identities as advocate *intercesores*, board members, community planners, and activists. From the beginning the children were told that the equipment and tools of the workshops belong to their neighbors, not to the staff, thus eliciting the children's pride in them and developing their ability to care for things.

Before Sister Isolina began her work, it was considered unsafe to walk in La Playa at any time of the day or night. Now there is less stealing and less violence among Playeros involved with the program. In four years there has not been a homicide among the juvenile population in La Playa. The schools continue to report some damage to school property, but there is much less vandalism at the program centers and in the neighborhood itself. La Playa, being a port, was once notorious for the sale and use of hard drugs. Sister Isolina's programs, however, appear to have reduced such incidents. Some marijuana and glue are used by the youths, but few hard drugs are found in the area. Significantly, police records show a marked reduction in all categories of juvenile offenses in La Playa since the program has been in effect.

Programs like the ones just described can be found in many different cities where youth are at risk in potentially damaging environments. A recent Washington, D.C., conference, sponsored by the American Enterprise Institute, called together representatives of sixteen different grass-roots programs run by nonprofessional ghetto residents. These nonprofessional programs are working with that very category of youth considered most intractable by professionals. In addition to their encouraging success, these programs have demonstrated several common structural features, so it is tempting to attribute their success in reducing youth crime and gang warfare to those features.

In contrast to professional youth projects, urban neighborhood programs are conceived, organized, and maintained voluntarily by community people who are neither connected with the welfare bureaucracy nor trained professionally. In the beginning of the projects, basic economic support comes from the personal household budget of the leaders and is supplemented by neighborhood fund-raising efforts. As the projects mature, some active members subsequently go on to qualify as professionals, and public funds are sometimes obtained for established programs.

This independence from the institutional order is important because it guarantees the maximum feasible participation of youth in their own rehabilitation. Relations between the youths and adults are reciprocal and consultative. Communication is open—it is not constrained by bureaucratic precedents or the theories of outsiders. People of the so-called underclass are helping children of the underclass. The helpers themselves have experienced and surmounted the environmental dangers that threaten the children they counsel. They have achieved and can communicate the adult perspective needed for survival in the particular economic, cultural, and political realities of the ghetto.

417

In short, grass-roots helpers know more in a practical sense than their professional counterparts. Their knowledge is firsthand, not theoretical. It is geared to the specifics of a dangerous environment and the life of the youth at risk. Moreover, their commitment to helping the youths does not imply a disrespect for them. Rather, the counselors' commitment is rooted in a positive identity shared with the youths, which is reinforced and drawn on as a resource in the relationship. The chance for authentic reciprocal communication and flexible response is greatest under these conditions. Most youths in these urban programs not only make a successful personal adjustment, but also contribute actively to community revitalization in various community service roles.

Public Policy Guidelines and Recommendations

The guidelines presented here are based on the success that grass-roots organizations have had attacking youth crime. They are intended to provide a framework for evaluating existing policies and for developing new public policies and approaches for solving the problem of youth crime:

- Those who are close to or who are experiencing the problem to be addressed should play a primary role in its solution.
- The needs of the child should be satisfied first within the context of the family, either nuclear or extended, and within the culture that the child knows.
- If existing neighborhood facilities are unable to provide the services needed, every effort should be made to develop such a resource by educating and training neighborhood people and institutional representatives, with professional providers of services supplying technical assistance in a spirit of voluntarism.
- When the nature of the problem is such that outside professional assistance would be effective, service should be provided in such a way that those being helped can participate fully in the decision making.
- The goal of all assistance should be to strengthen existing social and kinship ties, social conventions, and cooperative networks to enable these associations to develop the capacity to address the immediate and long-range needs of the community. Physical facilities, information systems, and evaluative techniques should be geared toward building the capacity of neighborhoods to replace a street culture of violence and mayhem with the positive culture of community.

With these policy guidelines in mind, the following policy recommendations are offered for the prevention of juvenile delinquency.

Research. Research should shift its concentration from behavior-centered problems of individual deviant youths and their subculture to an inventory of strengths within populations at risk. The objective should be to assess the successful methods and techniques employed by those who have survived in high-crime communities. More attention should be given to the impact of economic conditions on populations at risk. More specifically,

- Research on deviant youths should cease to command the bulk of funding committed to the study of juvenile delinquency.
- Representatives of the target populations under study should be encouraged to play a greater role in conducting research.
- The technical skills possessed by professional research institutions should be shared with neighborhood people to enable them to assess the impact of their own activities and make more informed decisions about their own participation in various kinds of research.
- More studies should be devoted to the impact of the fear of crime and its corrosive effect on the behavior of neighborhoods. Less attention should be given to studies of victimization.
- Better methods and techniques must be found to assess neighborhood crime prevention efforts and to measure the results quantitatively.
- The effect of neighborhood-based crime prevention programs on the commercial life of the neighborhood should be measured. A closer relationship should be established between the neighborhood and the business community.
- Identification of subjects to be researched should emanate in part from the sector of the society experiencing the problem to which the study is addressed.
- Studies should be undertaken to determine the sanctions and rewards that effectively influence behavior within a given cultural environment. All current assumptions in juvenile justice practice should be critically reexamined.
- Juvenile offenders who are from poor families, who have been found guilty of a serious offense by the court, and who have been sentenced to a restrictive institutional setting, should be afforded the same quality of treatment as the children of more affluent families. The state should provide a voucher to the parents of these youngsters that would enable them to choose an insti-

tutional setting in either the public or the private markets. Viable alternatives must be made available.

Program Policy. The following list provides an agenda for youth crime programs.

- Nuclear and extended families that have successfully raised children in urban areas characterized by a high incidence of crime should be used as principal service providers to youngsters with a penchant for delinquency. Such families could also be used to assist other families in coping with stressful conditions. Local institutions serving populations at risk should play a primary role in the delivery of delinquency prevention services.
- The cultural and ethnic traditions that often represent the cornerstone of the social infrastructure of a neighborhood should be incorporated into the design of programs for controlling and preventing youth crime.
- Policies to de-institutionalize status offenders or to isolate them in restrictive institutions should be distinct from program policies to control and prevent serious youth crime. Separate legislative categories should be established for both purposes.
- The number of alternative behavioral options should be increased for youngsters living in populations at risk by reinforcing the stabilizing local institutions in the neighborhoods.
- Policy should move away from support of large-scale criminal-justice bureaucracies as the primary agent of reform and service delivery because of the perverse financial incentives to maintain caseloads as a condition of financial support.

Programs to deal with youth crime should be based on an analysis of policies that have worked, rather than on some presumed cause-and-effect relationship. Program initiatives should be derived from empirical studies of effective neighborhood-based approaches to the control and prevention of youth crime. Common elements that are identified should form the basis for major initiatives and should be shared with other neighborhood organizations and groups.

Notes

[1] Franklin E. Zimring, "Confronting Youth Crime," in Twentieth Century Fund, *Task Force Report on Sentencing Policy toward Young Offenders* (New York: Holmes and Meier, 1978), p. 4.

[2] James Q. Wilson, *Thinking about Crime* (New York: Vintage Books, 1975), p. 59.

Social Service Programs in the Public and Private Sectors

Andrea M. Haines, V. Ruth McKinnon, and
Patricia W. Samors

Introduction

Since the 1930s, the federal government has played a major role in ensuring that the basic human needs of families and individuals—such as health care, nutrition, and a minimum level of income—are met. There are numerous government social welfare programs, each created in response to one or more of these particular needs.

This chapter has two primary objectives. The first is to provide an overview of several federal programs that attempt to meet the fundamental needs of lower-income families. Medicaid, food stamps, and Aid to Families with Dependent Children (AFDC) are among the largest social service programs. Besides those, an array of other federal programs that do not involve such large outlays will be discussed.

The second purpose of this chapter is to present a number of examples of private sector initiatives that have objectives similar to those of the federal programs. The private programs are by no means pure substitutes for federal assistance—meeting the basic human needs of low-income or disadvantaged Americans must be done primarily through government efforts. The point of describing these private sector programs is simply to indicate that there are many private organizations trying to provide social services to individuals and families. Along with government assistance, they are a vital part of the effort to meet these fundamental needs.

Section I: Federal Programs

MEDICAID

Patricia W. Samors

In 1965 the Medicaid program was enacted to assist the states, through federal grants, in their efforts to provide medical care to low-income persons who are members of families with dependent children or

421

who are aged, blind, or disabled. Financial responsibility is shared by federal, state, and at times local governments, and the program is administered by the states. The federal government provides the states with open-ended matching payments for their expenditures, with the federal contribution (based on state per capita income) ranging from 50 percent to 78 percent. The categories of persons covered and the benefits to which they are entitled vary significantly from state to state.

By federal law, all AFDC and Supplemental Security Income (SSI) recipients are eligible for Medicaid, and approximately thirty states cover those persons who are unable to pay their medical bills but who do not qualify for Medicaid under either of the other programs. Even though this program is meant to provide medical care to low-income persons, a large portion of the poor population such as intact families, single persons under sixty-five, childless couples, and the working poor are ineligible for this aid because they do not qualify for AFDC or SSI.

Growth in the Medicaid program averaged 15 percent annually from 1975 to 1980 and was 21 percent in FY 1981.[1] This growth is reflected in federal outlays for Medicaid, which increased from $2.7 billion in FY 1970 to $16.8 billion in FY 1981.[2] The increase in the eligible population, the rise in per capita medical spending, and the greater use of nursing homes by the elderly caused the growth in spending for the program.

To reduce the escalation in federal spending on Medicaid and to improve the program's effectiveness, the Reagan administration proposed various legislative changes for FY 1982 and again for FY 1983. Adoption of the proposals in the FY 1983 legislation is expected to produce savings of $278 million in FY 1982, $2.0 billion in FY 1983, and $2.3 billion in FY 1984.[3]

The Omnibus Reconciliation Act of 1981 (P.L. 97-35) provided for a reduction in federal grants to the states of 3 percent in 1982, 4 percent in 1983, and 4.5 percent in 1984. The law, however, also established target rates of growth in medical costs to encourage states to limit Medicaid's rapid growth. Each year, those states whose rate of increase is less than the target (which is 9 percent for FY 1982 and equal to the actual medical consumer price index for FY 1983 and FY 1984) will be able to recover from the federal government an amount equal to the full reduction in the grant. The act provides added flexibility in that those states that experience high unemployment, maintain effective hospital cost control programs, or reduce fraud and abuse will be exempt from the grant reductions by an amount equal to 1 percent of the grant for each of these stipulations.

The 1983 Reagan budget proposes to reduce the high costs of Medicaid by emphasizing program efficiency, providing incentives to improve program effectiveness, and incorporating sufficient flexibility into the program to reduce unnecessary expenditures. More specifically, the changes would:

- require modest beneficiary copayments
- shorten the automatic extension period of Medicaid eligibility
- phase in full state responsibility for erroneous payments
- eliminate higher matching payments for particular Medicaid services
- reduce federal matching payments for optional services and beneficiaries
- provide a fixed payment to the states for the administration of Medicaid, food stamps, and AFDC
- allow states the flexibility to recover long-term care costs from beneficiary estates and relatives
- eliminate federal matching payments for state payment of beneficiary Medicare premiums

Even with these reforms and the anticipated savings, federal program expenditures are expected to rise to $17 billion in FY 1983, $18.6 billion in FY 1984, and $20.4 billion by FY 1985. Combined federal and state payments per Medicaid beneficiary are expected to exceed $1,400 in 1983 despite the proposed adjustments.[4] The average rate of growth in federal outlays, however, will be reduced. A critical review of the Reagan administration's FY 1983 budget proposals for health care is contained in this volume in the chapter on health care costs by Patricia W. Samors and Sean Sullivan.

Food Stamps

Andrea M. Haines

The food stamp program was authorized by Congress in 1961 as a small experimental program. Since that time it has grown to be the second largest income-tested in-kind transfer program (Medicaid is the largest) in the United States, with projected FY 1982 costs of $10.3 billion. The program serves more than 22 million persons. In a given month, one American in ten receives food stamps.

The Department of Agriculture (USDA) is responsible for food stamps, which are distributed through state and local welfare offices. The federal government pays the full cost of the food stamps and 50 percent of the administrative costs of the states. Eligibility is based on monthly income, and eligibility standards and benefit levels are set by the federal government and are uniform throughout the nation.

Pre-1981 Program Standards. Income eligibility limits are based on poverty thresholds determined by the Office of Management and Budget and are adjusted annually for inflation. Prior to the 1981 legislative changes, for a family to be eligible for benefits net household income after a standard deduction ($85 per month in January 1981) and a 20 percent earned income disregard could not exceed the applicable poverty threshold. Some households were also permitted to deduct from gross income work-related child care expenses, excess shelter costs, and certain medical costs for elderly or disabled household members. After deductions and disregards, some households with gross incomes up to 160 percent of the poverty level were eligible for food stamps. These deductions and the standard deduction are adjusted annually in January for inflation. In January 1981 the maximum combined deduction for excess expenses for shelter and dependent care for nonelderly, nondisabled households was $115 per month.

The amount of the food stamp benefit varies inversely with income—that is, benefits are higher for lower-income households. Households with no countable income received the maximum monthly benefit. Benefit levels are adjusted annually to reflect changes in the price of a market basket of foods included in the USDA thrifty food plan. (In theory, benefits can be adjusted downward to reflect a drop in the price of the goods.) The thrifty food plan is designed to provide a nutritionally adequate diet for low-income individuals or families.

Food stamp recipients must register for work and must accept suitable job offers. Mothers of children under twelve years of age and certain other categories of recipients are not subject to the work requirement. Failure to comply with the work requirement carries a minimum penalty of sixty days' lost eligibility.

Changes Introduced by the 1981 Omnibus Reconciliation Act. The reconciliation act restricts eligibility to households with gross incomes below 130 percent of the poverty line, except for households with an elderly member. Eligibility will be based on actual past earnings rather than projected income, and recipients will submit periodic income reports. Reports had been required only at the option of the state or if family circumstances changed. The new rules also decrease the earned-income disregard from 20 to 18 percent of household earnings, and they freeze other adjustments to income at their 1981 levels until July 1983.

The inflation adjustment in the USDA thrifty food plan will be delayed three months each year for the next three years—that is, the adjustments will be made every fifteen months instead of annually. The cumulative effect will be a savings equal to the cost of a nine months' inflation adjustment. Households having a member on strike will not be eligible for food stamps unless they were eligible before the strike. Benefits may not be increased to compensate for the loss of the striker's income.

The definition of "household" is expanded to include paying boarders and all parents and children living together, even if the parents are not married. If one parent is over sixty, the parents and the children may be treated as separate households.

First-month food stamp benefits will be prorated based on the date of application. Formerly, recipients had been able to receive an entire month's coupon allotment regardless of the date of application. The reconciliation bill also prohibits the use of federal funds for outreach programs to inform people of their eligibility for food stamps.

Changes mandated by the reconciliation act were expected to remove 1 million recipients from the rolls in FY 1982 at a savings of $1.7 billion.[5] Further changes have been proposed in the budget for FY 1983 to restrain the growth of this entitlement program. Under the new legislation:

- energy assistance payments would be counted as income
- special disregard of earnings would be eliminated
- benefits would be reduced by 35 cents for each additional dollar of income rather than the current 30 cents
- benefits would be rounded to the lower whole-dollar amount
- monthly benefits of less than $10 per household would be eliminated
- states would be responsible for all erroneous eligibility and benefit decisions by 1986

These policy changes are expected to reduce federal outlays by $2.3 billion in FY 1983 and $2.4 billion in FY 1984.[6]

The Issues in Reforming the Food Stamp Program. Predicting the cost of the food stamp program presents many of the same difficulties found in estimating the cost of related entitlement programs. Chang-

425

ing economic conditions—such as higher unemployment rates—can have a significant effect on program expenditures. Since food stamp benefits are based solely on income, reductions in programs such as AFDC, unemployment insurance, or public service jobs can lead to corresponding increases in food stamp expenditures.

Food stamp fraud and erroneous payments are also controversial topics. In 1981 erroneous food stamp issuance cost the federal government an estimated $1.1 billion.[7] Other issues that confront food stamp reform efforts include job search requirements, disparities in the treatment of certain kinds of income in determining eligibility, and the use of the consumer price index to adjust income guidelines.

AID TO FAMILIES WITH DEPENDENT CHILDREN

Andrea M. Haines

Under Title IV-A of the Social Security Act, the Aid to Families with Dependent Children (AFDC) program, funded jointly by the federal government and the states, provides monthly cash payments to poor families with dependent children. The federal government pays at least 50 percent of the program's cost, with a higher federal matching grant for states with a low per capita income. For example, the poorest state, Mississippi, receives a federal share of almost 80 percent. In FY 1981, an estimated $14.2 billion in state and federal expenditures provided aid to 11.1 million recipients, approximately 70 percent of whom were children.[8] Table A-1 (see the appendix following this chapter) shows the growth in both AFDC spending and the number of AFDC participants over the period 1960–1980.

Within broad federal guidelines, states set their own benefit levels and eligibility standards. Each state calculates a standard of need reflecting the cost of basic necessities for a given family size. After determining the needs standard, the state also decides what percentage of that need will be met in AFDC payments. These payments are adjusted to take into account family size and any outside income. Different components included in the needs standard and variations in the support level among the states lead to wide variations in benefits. In July 1980, thirty states met the full needs standard. The remaining states set maximum AFDC cash payments at some (lower) percentage of the standard of need.[9] Table A-2 in the appendix shows the average AFDC payment per recipient for the fifty states in 1970, 1975, and 1980.

In general, only single-parent families are eligible for assistance under AFDC. Twenty-six states do offer a program for two-parent

426

families in which the principal wage earner is unemployed, but participation is severely restricted (only 5 percent of all AFDC families in
December 1980 were covered under this program).

Aid to Families with Dependent Children is an entitlement program—that is, the government must provide benefits to all persons
who meet eligibility requirements. In this sense, spending for AFDC
is sometimes considered "uncontrollable." Because the government
cannot arbitrarily limit its funding of AFDC, another way to reduce
spending is to tighten eligibility requirements to remove the less
needy from the rolls. Other alternatives include reducing benefits to
recipients and increasing program efficiency.

Title XXIII of the Omnibus Reconciliation Act of 1981 made
several changes in the AFDC program that were expected to produce
savings of $1.2 billion of the estimated $8 billion federal share in
FY 1982. The administration estimated that over 650,000 of the 3.9
million families who receive AFDC payments would be affected by
the changes. Over 258,000 families (6.9 percent) would receive reduced benefits, and 400,000 families (10.7 percent) would no longer
be eligible.[10] The changes in the earned income disregard, the work
expense deduction, and the 150 percent eligibility ceiling are discussed elsewhere in this volume. In addition to the new rules, the
act also made a number of other changes and requirements, which are
summarized below.

Income and Resources. In determining eligibility for AFDC, the state
must consider the income and resources of any child or relative claiming the right to benefits under the program, including the income of
step-parents living in the same home as the dependent child. States
will have the option of including income and resources of other
nonrelated members of the household in determining eligibility. The
reconciliation act sets a $1,000 limit on resources (excluding debts or
other obligations on those resources) that a family may own and
still be eligible for benefits. The previous limit was $2,000. The
$1,000 limit excludes the value of the home and one automobile, and
the state may set a limit lower than $1,000. The secretary of health
and human services may prescribe limits on the amount of the value
of an automobile that may be excluded. States may also choose to
consider as income food stamps and rent or housing subsidies to the
extent these amounts duplicate food or housing components in the
state standard of need.

The act also requires that lump-sum payments be considered
as income over several months rather than only during the month
of receipt of the payment, as is now the case, and it provides a

427

formula for apportioning the lump-sum payment over time. The act also mandates the inclusion of the earned-income tax credit as earned income.

Work Programs. The reconciliation act authorizes three work programs for AFDC recipients. The first program allows states to institute required "workfare." A state may choose to establish a community work experience program to provide experience and training on projects that serve a useful public purpose. All recipients must participate as a condition of receiving aid, except those already employed more than eighty hours a month at the applicable minimum wage and those with children under three years of age. Parents of preschool children over three years of age must participate if child care is available. The state will coordinate the program with the work incentive (WIN) program to ensure that job placement has priority over participation in the community work experience program. Costs of materials, equipment, and supervision of the work will be assumed by the state.

The act also authorizes states to offer a work supplementation program. The states may make jobs available, on a voluntary basis, as an alternative to aid. The state can choose to provide jobs directly or to subsidize jobs in certain public or nonprofit entities. Wages earned under the work supplementation program are considered earned income. The states are authorized to lower benefit payments to categories of recipients eligible to participate in the work program but who refuse to do so.

The third jobs initiative in the reconciliation act is the work incentive demonstration program. States may apply to the secretary of health and human services for grants to operate a program designed to place welfare recipients in private sector jobs. The state is free to structure the program to suit its needs, resources, and labor market conditions. If the state plan is approved, the demonstration program will last three years, of which six months may be used for planning purposes.

Miscellaneous Eligibility and Reporting Requirements. The states may not make payments to pregnant women before the sixth month of pregnancy. The act also lowers the age limit of a dependent child from twenty to eighteen (or nineteen if the child is a full-time student completing high school or vocational or technical training). AFDC beneficiaries between sixteen and eighteen who are not in school must register to work. Strikers will not be eligible for AFDC.

As noted previously, some states offer an AFDC program for two-parent families where the principal wage earner is unemployed. Prior to the Omnibus Reconciliation Act of 1981, eligibility under this program was based on unemployment of the father. Eligibility is now based on the unemployment of the parent with the higher income during the twenty-four-month period preceding the application for aid.

The reconciliation act instituted retrospective budgeting and monthly reporting. A family's eligibility and benefits will be determined by the amount of income actually received during the month of application for aid rather than by the amount of anticipated income. To be eligible for aid, each family must report income and relevant changes in circumstances each month. (Some, but not all, states had already required monthly reporting.) States must correct overpayments and underpayments promptly. A state may reduce current payments to compensate for earlier overpayments, but it may not reduce benefits below specified levels.

Illegal aliens are not eligible for AFDC. If a legally admitted alien applies for aid, the state must take into account income and resources—after certain exclusions—of the alien's sponsor and the sponsor's spouse in determining eligibility. The sponsor's income and resources are deemed available for support of the alien for three years after the alien's entry into the United States.

Further reforms of the AFDC program that have been proposed for FY 1983 are expected to save an estimated $1.2 billion in FY 1983 and nearly $6 billion over the next five years. States should save an amount equal to roughly 85 percent of the federal savings.[11]

Instead of giving states the option of establishing community work experience programs, the reforms would mandate such programs. The proposed changes would also require applicants to look for jobs to be eligible for AFDC. The changes would eliminate the WIN program, provide benefits to two-parent families only if one parent participates in the community work experience program, and eliminate the parent's benefit when the youngest child reaches sixteen.

Other proposed changes would take into account sources of income—such as federal or state energy assistance payments or the income of unrelated adults in the household—that were not previously counted in determining AFDC benefits. Additional reforms include rounding benefits to the lower whole-dollar amount, prorating the first month's benefit, eliminating program overlaps, and gradually letting states accept full responsibility for incorrect AFDC payments. All of these changes are designed to strengthen employment incentives, streamline the program, and tighten eligibility requirements.

Title XX Social Services

Andrea M. Haines

In 1974 Congress added a new title to the Social Security Act that authorized a wide variety of social services for the low-income population. Although the federal government had provided funds to the states for social services to welfare recipients since the 1950s, the new Title XX provided much greater flexibility to the states in the planning and design of these programs. Title XX grants were based on state population, with a 75 percent federal share (90 percent for family-planning services). State and local funding sources provided the remaining matching funds.

The states were free to decide what services to offer and how to allocate funds among programs, with the condition that 50 percent of federal funds must be spent for services to AFDC, SSI, and Medicaid recipients. Services were to be selected with a view to achieving the five goals of Title XX: (1) self-support, (2) self-sufficiency, (3) protection of children and adults, (4) community- or home-based care, and (5) services to persons in institutions. Although the services provided varied from state to state and among regions within states, Title XX programs most often included child day care to enable AFDC recipients to work, companions for the elderly to prevent premature institutionalization, services for abused or neglected children, and services to persons with drug- or alcohol-related problems.

Each state developed a Comprehensive Annual Services Plan (CASP) detailing the services to be offered and made the plan available for public comment. The CASP could be revised to reflect suggestions made during the comment period, but such changes were not mandatory. Each state determined income eligibility levels, which could not exceed 115 percent of the state median income. Information and referral, protective services, and family-planning services were available to any person regardless of income level. A fee was charged for services to persons whose income exceeded 80 percent of the state median, and states had the option of charging fees for services to persons below the 80 percent level.

The 1974 legislation set the Title XX funding ceiling at $2.5 billion per fiscal year. In FY 1977–1981, this amount was supplemented by a $200 million appropriation each year for child day care that required no local matching funds. Congress enacted legislation in 1980 that would have raised Title XX spending to $2.9 billion in FY 1981 and would have increased the amount by $100 million each year to a total of $3.3 billion in FY 1985. State and local outlays for Title XX have increased from $0.7 billion in 1976 to $1.5 billion in 1981.

Social Services Block Grant. The Omnibus Reconciliation Act of 1981 established a new social services block grant to replace Title XX. The new grant program was funded at $2.4 billion for FY 1982, increasing to $2.7 billion in 1986. The FY 1982 funding represents a 23 percent decrease from the Congressional Budget Office (CBO) current policy base line.[12]

The new block grant allows the states even more flexibility in structuring the programs they offer. The requirement that 50 percent of federal funds be spent on welfare recipients is eliminated, as are the federal income eligibility restrictions. The states may transfer up to 10 percent of social services block grant funds to block grants for health services, health promotion and disease protection activities, and low-income energy assistance.

The reconciliation act still requires the states to prepare an annual services plan, but the citizen review process is less strongly emphasized. The new legislation does not mention the mandatory federal day care standards that had been part of the old Title XX.

Budget authority of $2.0 billion is being requested by the Reagan administration for the social services block grant in FY 1983—a 16.7 percent reduction from the FY 1982 level.[13] No further changes in the program are included in the current legislation.

SUPPLEMENTAL SECURITY INCOME

Patricia W. Samors

In 1982, 4.2 million aged, blind, and disabled persons are expected to receive cash assistance under the Supplemental Security Income (SSI) program. This program was created in January 1974 to replace state assistance programs receiving federal aid. Table 1 shows SSI outlays since 1973 and the number of recipients.

Although the number of recipients has remained relatively constant since 1974, federal outlays have steadily increased because of the rise in the average monthly benefit payment. These payments are automatically adjusted to reflect increases in consumer prices. Payments have increased from $140 per month for an individual and from $210 for a couple in FY 1974 to $265 for single recipients and $397 for couples in FY 1982.[14] Supplementary state payments,

TABLE 1

SUPPLEMENTAL SECURITY INCOME: OUTLAYS AND RECIPIENTS,
FY 1973–1983

Year	Outlays (billions of dollars)	Recipients (millions)
1973	2.0	3.0[a]
1974	2.3	4.0[a]
1975	4.8	4.5[a]
1976	5.1	4.3
1977	5.3	4.2
1978	5.9	4.2
1979	5.5	4.2
1980	6.4	4.2
1981	7.2	4.1
1982	7.9[a]	4.1[a]
1983	8.9[a]	4.1[a]

NOTE: In 1973-1980 the number for recipients represents those covered at the end of the year. In 1981-1983 the number for recipients equals the average number of monthly beneficiaries.

[a] Estimated figures.

SOURCES: Office of Management and Budget, *Appendix to the Budget* for FY 1983, p. I-K45; FY 1982, p. I-K53; FY 1981, p. 480; FY 1980, pp. 467-68; FY 1979, pp. 446-47; FY 1978, pp. 354-55; FY 1977, p. 367; FY 1976, p. 441. Office of Management and Budget, *The Budget for Fiscal Year 1976*, p. 140.

which are provided by forty-one states, can raise monthly benefits. In California, for example, single individuals receive $439 in combined state and federal payments and couples receive $815.[15]

In the program's initial years there was a significant number of payment errors. Over the years, however, the high error rates were reduced as program staff concentrated on cases in which errors were likely to occur and cross-checked payments against other benefit programs. Several legislative changes were proposed for FY 1982 and FY 1983 to further reduce errors and to slow the increase in federal spending. In the reconciliation act of 1981, Congress adopted the administration's retrospective monthly accounting proposal to meet these objectives. In addition, legislation was recommended to end federal special subsidies to three states still receiving the aid. Congress agreed to end the subsidies except to Wisconsin, but to phase out aid to that state by 1986.

Additional technical changes have been proposed for 1983 as a further attempt to reduce federal outlays, including prorating the first month's benefit, rounding benefits to the next lower dollar, restricting the definition of permanent disability, eliminating the $20 disregard for new beneficiaries, and recovering overpayments to individuals from social security benefits. It is estimated that these changes will save $78 million, $256 million, and $489 million in federal benefit payments in fiscal years 1982, 1983, and 1984, respectively.[16]

REFUGEE AND ENTRANT ASSISTANCE

Patricia W. Samors

Prior to the Refugee Act of 1980, the federal government responded to refugees* as they arrived in the United States—programs were temporary and were dismantled when no longer necessary. The number of refugees entering the United States is considerable, however, and in response to their growing numbers, the federal government created an ongoing program of refugee assistance. The passage of the Refugee Act in March 1980 was an attempt to coordinate refugee assistance into a permanent program.

Under the current program, states and local governments provide cash and medical assistance to the refugees through their regular AFDC, SSI, and Medicaid programs. The states also offer instruction in English and vocational training and provide education assistance through systems set up specifically for refugees. Under the Refugee Act, the states document their costs and notify the Office of Refugee Resettlement in the Department of Health and Human Services, which reimburses the states 100 percent for their expenditures. Each refugee is eligible for assistance for thirty-six months.

Since April 1980, over 135,000 Cubans and roughly 40,000 Haitians have been allowed to settle in the United States. The federal government provides for the reception and care of these entrants** under the Refugee Education Assistance Act of 1980. It also reimburses states for costs incurred in providing the Cubans and Haitians with medical care and social services once they are settled.

Federal expenditures for these two programs have fluctuated over the past several years as a result of the flow of refugees and

---

* A refugee is any person who has fled his country because of a well-founded fear of persecution on account of race, religion, nationality, membership in a particular social group, or political opinion.

** An entrant is a special classification given by the Carter administration to Cubans and Haitians who arrived in the United States between April 21, 1980, and October 10, 1980.

entrants and the recent cuts in social programs. In fiscal years 1979 and 1980, before the two acts were passed, outlays to provide assistance to needy refugees were $141 million and $368 million, respectively. In FY 1981 there was a sharp increase in the number of Cuban, Haitian, and Indochinese arrivals—as a result federal outlays rose sharply, to $726 million. In FY 1982, expenditures on refugee and entrant assistance are expected to rise further, to $849 million. The $670 million budget authority requested for FY 1982, however, is less than the $902 million requested for FY 1981. For FY 1983, the budget request has been reduced even further, to $532 million—covering both refugee and entrant assistance.[17]

Prior to April 1, 1981, any refugee was eligible for cash and medical assistance for thirty-six months. Under a new program, however, the Office of Refugee Resettlement has instituted a more restrictive policy whereby the period of aid to those refugees not categorically eligible for AFDC, SSI, or Medicaid is reduced to eighteen months. Those refugees not eligible for federal assistance, however, may apply to state or local general assistance programs to receive the additional eighteen months of coverage. Expenditures on those approved are refunded by the federal government. These new restrictions do not apply to social service assistance such as vocational, educational, or language training. These new regulations also apply to the Cuban and Haitian entrants who receive transitional assistance. After the initial eighteen-month period, if they are ineligible for federal assistance, they may also apply to the state or local general assistance program for additional benefits.

WOMEN, INFANTS, AND CHILDREN

Patricia W. Samors

In the early 1960s attention was focused on the lack of prenatal care for low-income women and its relation to increased health hazards to mothers and children. At the time, the Department of Agriculture (USDA) was providing surplus food to poor families through the Needy Family Food Program. The Children's Bureau of the Maternal and Child Health Program (within the Department of Health, Education, and Welfare), together with USDA, worked to provide increased allocations of certain selected foods to pregnant and lactating women and to infants and preschool children under the existing program. Over the next few years, the attempt to provide supplementary food to this group evolved through several phases. Initially, the USDA program was expanded. Then medical staffs at clinics and health centers were authorized to give prescriptions for supplementary foods to mothers and preschool children.

In the late 1960s a Commodity Supplementary Food Program (CSFP) was created for infants and preschool children and for pregnant, postpartum, and nursing mothers. The CSFP is the name given to the expanded USDA-donated food program. After two years, however, it became apparent that it was difficult for the women to transport the food from the distributing agencies to their homes, where there was inadequate storage space. Thus, in 1970, a pilot Food Certificate Program was initiated to test the feasibility of issuing food certificates for specific commodities that could be redeemed at retail food stores. In 1972 the Special Supplementary Food Program (later known as Women, Infants, and Children, or WIC) was enacted. Actual food donations continue under CSFP, although in only twelve states. WIC has become the primary supplementary food program.

Under WIC federal funds are allocated to each state health agency, which in turn works with local health agencies either under a subgrant or contract to administer the program. The local agencies are responsible for determining applicants' eligibility, certifying those who qualify, and providing the food vouchers. As an indication of the program's growth, in FY 1974 outlays were $14 million. They are expected to reach $994 million in FY 1982. It is further estimated that in each month of 1982 approximately 2.2 million pregnant, postpartum, or nursing women and infants and children under five will receive supplementary food assistance.[18]

Although most maternal and child health services were consolidated into a block grant by the Omnibus Reconciliation Act of 1981, WIC remained an independent program.[19] The Reagan administration has proposed to expand the block grant in FY 1983 to include the nutrition program. The Reagan budget request of $1.0 billion for FY 1983 would reduce total funds for the merged programs by approximately $250 million from 1982 levels.

ALCOHOL, DRUG ABUSE, AND MENTAL HEALTH

Patricia W. Samors

The Alcohol, Drug Abuse, and Mental Health Administration (ADAMHA) administers public health programs that focus on substance abuse and mental health. The programs include research, training, and services in each of these three health areas.

Mental health research is conducted by the ADAMHA to increase the understanding of major mental disorders, maladaptive behavior, and associated biological and biochemical processes. Drug abuse research is carried out to develop more effective methods of treating and preventing drug abuse and addictive behavior. ADAMHA also continues to perform research to determine the causes and consequences of alcohol use.

The training programs in mental health and drug and alcohol abuse attempt to increase the pool of skilled researchers and improve the ability of health service personnel to deal more effectively with the problems in their special areas. The final set of programs under ADAMHA's jurisdiction provides services such as making comprehensive mental health programs available to states and communities and setting up national and community prevention and treatment networks for drug and alcohol abuse.

The Omnibus Reconciliation Act of 1981 consolidated all of these services (except the mental health Community Support Program) into one block grant.[20] Under the block grant the states apply for funding to distribute among their different programs and communities as they see fit.

In FY 1982 the states are allowed either to choose the block grant or to continue under the previous system—every state except California has chosen to participate in the block grant. In FY 1983, however, federal support for the services will be provided only through the block grant.

The Reagan administration is requesting $433 million in budget authority in FY 1983 for the block grant, which is about the same level that was appropriated in FY 1982.[21] This amounts to a cut in the real funding level for these programs. In FY 1981, $540 million was appropriated for these services when they were not combined in the block grant.[22]

Low-Income Energy Assistance

Patricia W. Samors

Since FY 1980, energy assistance to low-income families has been provided to the states through a grant administered by the Department of Health and Human Services (formerly the Department of Health, Education, and Welfare, or HEW). It is estimated that about 6.5 million households will be served in FY 1982.[23] Under this grant, energy aid is available either as direct cash assistance to eligible households, as direct payment to fuel vendors, or as payment to public housing building operators.

In 1980 the energy program had several components, with funding totaling $1.55 billion. Under the program $805 million was administered by HEW and allocated to the states in the form of block grants; $391 million was provided directly to Supplemental Security Income recipients; and $254 million was allotted to the Community Services Agency (CSA), which ran an energy crisis assistance program. (Prior to 1980, funds for energy emergencies were available only through CSA).[24]

With the passage of the Crude Oil Windfall Profits Tax Act in 1980, roughly $3 billion was authorized for energy assistance. Yet only $1.85 billion was appropriated for the program for FY 1981. The funding consisted of a $1.76 billion grant distributed to the states and a $89.36 million set-aside to CSA.[25]

Since the 1960s, states have been able to participate in an optional federal grant program whereby they could obtain funds to meet the emergency financial needs of their low-income citizens. This program is funded under Title IV-A of the Social Security Act and calls for a 50–50 match in funds from the participating states. For FY 1982, as part of its effort to combine programs into block grants to the states, the Reagan administration proposed consolidating the low-income energy assistance and emergency aid programs into one flexible block grant. It was the administration's belief that this would enable the states to eliminate the duplicative administrative work required by both programs.

Congress, however, did not agree with this strategy and authorized $1.85 billion for the energy program alone.[26] The $1.85 billion is to be allocated totally to the states—CSA no longer exists. The funds are allotted on the basis of a formula in the Windfall Profits Tax Act of 1980 which takes into account energy costs, the number of low-income households, and heating degree days within each state.

Despite its failure in 1981 to merge the two assistance programs, the administration is once again proposing this combination in the FY 1983 budget. The combined request for budget authority is $1.3 billion for FY 1983.[27] The new proposal would reduce state reporting and compliance procedures from 32,490 to 16,000 man-hours. It would also reduce the number of regulatory requirements below the 1982 number—which was itself a reduction from the 1981 number.

OTHER PROGRAMS

Patricia W. Samors

Besides the programs already discussed, there are several other federal programs that provide assistance to different groups. Table 2 lists the programs and the budget authority requested for each in FY 1981 through FY 1983.

TABLE 2

FUNDING REQUESTS FOR PUBLIC SECTOR SOCIAL PROGRAMS,
FY 1981–FY 1983

(millions of dollars)

	Fiscal Year		
Program	1981	1982	1983
Child Nutrition Programs	3,464	2,847	2,826
Child Welfare Services	174	465	380[a]
Community Health Centers Program	325	375	417[b]
Community Services Program	550	336	104
Comprehensive Employment and Training Act (CETA)	7,143	3,023	2,400
Guaranteed Student Loan	2,535	2,752	2,485
Head Start	825	950	912
Indian Health Services	607	600	613
Nutrition Assistance for Puerto Rico and Territories	968	958	869
Rehabilitation Services and Research	964	1,000	637[c]
Services for Children, Youth, and Families	N/A[d]	1,200	923
Services for Elderly and Other Special Groups	777	765	774
Special Milk Program	119	28	—[e]
Trade Adjustment Assistance	1,481	144	10

NOTE: Funding requests for FY 1983 reflect Reagan administration proposals. Some of the figures for FY 1982 and FY 1981 reflect Reagan administration changes to the initial Carter administration budget requests.

[a] Under the Reagan administration proposals, in FY 1983 Child Welfare Services together with Child Welfare Training, Adoption Assistance, and Foster Care would be consolidated into the Child Welfare Block Grant.

[b] According to the Reagan administration's budget for FY 1983, this program would be converted into a block grant to states. The $417 million request includes funding for the community health centers program and for black-lung clinics, health care for migrants, and family planning.

[c] Under the Reagan administration proposals for FY 1983, budget authority for research for the handicapped would no longer be included in this figure.

[d] Figures for FY 1981 are not available.

[e] This program will be terminated effective for the 1982-1983 school year under the Reagan administration proposals.

SOURCES: Office of Management and Budget, The Budget for FY 1983, FY 1982, and FY 1981; Office of Management and Budget, Appendix to the Budget for FY 1983 and FY 1982; Office of Management and Budget, Major Themes and Additional Budget Details: Fiscal Year 1983.

Section II: Voluntary, Charitable, Nonprofit Organizations

There is a great deal to be learned about the make-up of the private sector organizations that provide social services and still more to be learned about the magnitude of their outreach. The following case studies are a sample of the vast array of volunteer and charitable nonprofit groups that provide countless services to individuals in need. The present study does not allow us to do justice to the diverse components of these programs. Nevertheless, the examples that follow serve as a small (though not necessarily representative) cross section of the kinds of activities and services found in the private sector.

BROTHERS REDEVELOPMENT, INC.

V. Ruth McKinnon

Almost ten years ago, four creative and community-minded residents of Denver, Colorado, channeled their energies into establishing what was to become a full-scale nonprofit organization for neighborhood preservation. Their idea was to provide housing development, rehabilitation, construction, and home counseling services to low-income, elderly, and disabled individuals in metropolitan Denver. They named the organization Brothers Redevelopment, Inc. (BRI).

They began by remodeling several owner-occupied homes and used the help of volunteers from the Mennonite Voluntary Service as well as several local church and community groups. As the requests for assistance increased and as BRI gained the ability to meet those needs, the staff expanded to its present size of twenty-eight.

Because of the group's ability to work well both on its own and in conjunction with other groups, local agencies have grown to depend upon BRI's expertise and organizational abilities. The demand for housing-related services has caused BRI to offer a significant range of services since its beginning ten years ago.

The home counseling service, for example, operates from a storefront office that opened in 1980 with seed money from the Public Welfare Foundation. The service offers pre–home purchase advice, guidance on home purchase and rehabilitation, and mortgage delinquency counseling. It provides home inspections for prospective home buyers and low-interest loans to low-income families in cooperation with the Colorado Housing Finance Authority.

In addition, BRI is involved in neighborhood revitalization, homeownership projects, the construction of new buildings, and energy conservation and property management. The Edgewater Plaza project

439

—a six-story, eighty-four unit apartment building in Denver—serves as an example of BRI's continuing effort to develop affordable rental housing for low-income, elderly, or handicapped individuals. BRI worked with the U.S. Department of Housing and Urban Development (HUD) to develop the complex, which provides subsidized housing for senior citizens as well as facilities for the handicapped. BRI's involvement as owner/sponsor of this particular housing project evolved in part because of the excellent public relations it enjoys with both state and city governments and private sector agencies. BRI is also involved in the daily operation of the project through its affiliated property management firm.

BRI's Volunteer and Training Program uses church, school, corporate, and community groups to help with minor home repairs, rehabilitation, weatherization, and painting. One of the program's most successful ventures started with an idea proposed by a local radio disc jockey who approached BRI and several local housing authorities and suggested joint sponsorship of a community-wide "paint-a-thon." As a result, 100 senior citizens' homes were painted. Equally important was the involvement of numerous groups of volunteers from a cross section of the community who contributed time and energy for this one specific purpose. Since then, the "paint-a-thon" has become an annual event, organized by BRI and supported by increasing numbers of community groups. In 1981 and 1982 the First National Bank of Denver sponsored the event, contributing the paint and coordinating public relations.

In 1981 alone, BRI accomplished much. As many as 348 projects were undertaken, using up approximately 20,000 hours of volunteer labor. BRI aided 350 clients through its home counseling program, a 100 percent increase from 1980. Fourteen housing acquisition, rehabilitation, and sales projects were completed in 1981—compared with nine the preceding year. The Edgewater Plaza housing unit, BRI's first major development project, was completed ahead of schedule and below projected cost.

Brothers Redevelopment, Inc., maintains ten working programs with an annual budget of approximately $2 million. Its funding flows primarily from such private sector groups as churches, banks, savings and loan institutions, corporations, oil companies, foundations, and individuals. BRI has also worked in conjunction with such public and quasi-public agencies as the Community Development Agency of the City and County of Denver, HUD, the Colorado Division of Housing, and the Colorado Housing Finance Authority. Funding is also generated from projects such as proceeds from the sales of homes and revenues from rental properties.

Over the past few years, BRI has grown steadily, in large part as a result of its increasing expertise in creating and implementing housing partnerships between the public and private sectors, and in part because of its use of volunteers to keep production and maintenance costs at a minimum.

CENIKOR FOUNDATION, INC.

V. Ruth McKinnon

The Cenikor Foundation, Inc., was established in 1968 as a nonprofit corporation to provide a center for rehabilitating people who have problems with drugs, alcohol, or the law. Because of the effectiveness of its program in these areas, Cenikor expanded to accommodate individuals in an intensive residential program. Cenikor's three residential facilities are located in Denver, Colorado, and in Fort Worth and Houston, Texas. The Houston facility, which also serves as the foundation's administrative headquarters, houses almost half of Cenikor's 300 residents.

Most residents are referred to Cenikor by the courts or social service agencies in various parts of the country. Cenikor's staff consists of qualified program graduates. In most cases, staff members have already received, or are in the process of obtaining, educational degrees and certification in the field of human services. They provide assistance to Cenikor residents in many areas—for example, personal and financial counseling, legal aid, and vocational rehabilitation. In addition, residents receive outside professional help whenever it is needed.

Stage 1 of the three-year program involves two years of concentrated counseling and personal rehabilitation. This full-time "treatment" phase emphasizes good work habits, decision-making skills, and building or rebuilding the individual's self-esteem. Group therapy sessions, which are scheduled on a regular basis, are conducted by the residents themselves. Although room and board are provided by the foundation, every resident is responsible for some type of daily job task.

During stage 2, or the "reentry" phase of the program, full-time residency continues, as well as involvement in group and individual counseling. The residents become full-time employees at outside jobs, however, and pay a monthly fee for room and board, at the same time budgeting any remaining earnings.

Financial support for the foundation is self-generated. Cenikor receives cash donations, goods, and services from various private sector sources which account for approximately one-half of its annual operating budget. The rest of the money comes from revenues generated by various small businesses operated by Cenikor residents. A six-member board of directors made up of local community leaders and program graduates manages the foundation.

Cenikor is a viable alternative for young, prison-bound first offenders. A typical example of the effectiveness of Cenikor's program is the case of a young Maryland resident who was put on probation in Cenikor's Houston facility. While a participant in the reentry phase of the program, he enrolled as a full-time student at the University of Houston. He is a member of the university's varsity football team.

Commitment to the program is stressed to all residents at the outset. Cenikor's philosophy urges residents to deal not only with symptoms but also, perhaps more importantly, with the underlying causes that brought them to Cenikor. Residents are encouraged to work—whether as an employee in the community, a contributor to the Cenikor community, or the prime mover in rebuilding a life.

The Children's Heart Institute of South Texas

V. Ruth McKinnon

The Children's Heart Institute of South Texas (CHI) is a nonprofit organization devoted to the task of providing early detection, diagnostic, and referral services to the children of rural Texas who suffer from various types of heart disease. The institute was founded by a Corpus Christi pediatric cardiologist who was concerned about the growing number of children among rural poor families lacking both the resources and the availability of simple diagnostic services for serious or potentially serious heart problems.

Of the 500,000 residents of the southern Texas area served by the CHI, as many as 10,000 children and adolescents (all under the age of eighteen) are known to have some type of heart condition requiring professional treatment. A medical facility in Corpus Christi is the closest place offering such specialized treatment, but distance from the facility as well as the cost of care make such service of little value to this segment of the population.

The Children's Heart Institute was established in 1972 with funding from both public and private sources. It operated initially under the auspices of the Driscoll Foundation Children's Hospital and has since established itself as an incorporated nonprofit organization.

The CHI operates thirteen satellite clinics at various locations in thirty rural southern Texas counties. A team composed of several physicians, social workers, nurses, and a psychologist sees as many as 8,000 individual patients each year and conducts 32,000 patient visits annually. The CHI provides a training program for its nurses, who receive certification as pediatric cardiology associates (PCAs) after six months of intensive instruction. By using the services of the PCAs in X-ray interpretation, electrocardiogram testing, and physical examinations, the institute estimates that such services can be provided at one-third the cost of conventional means. The institute also provides a practicum program for medical, premedical, and prenursing students, particularly those of the minority populations.

Patients who are most often referred by state and county health departments, clinics for migrants, Rural Health Initiative Clinics, and private practitioners in the various locations are first examined by the PCAs and then by the pediatric cardiologist on the team. If additional medical treatment is necessary, the child is referred to a larger medical facility to receive more complete medical attention. In addition, the CHI team provides the services of a psychologist who is available for family and/or individual counseling during and after the diagnostic procedure.

The institute works in partnership with various publicly and privately funded groups, serving as a link between diagnosis and detection, and direct medical care. Working with an average annual budget of $450,000, CHI receives funding from both public and private sources, including foundations, agencies, oil companies, trusts, and individuals. Contributions have also come in the form of free office and clinic space donated by several health agencies in the rural areas.

As the institute moves ahead in its attempt to provide diagnostic services to this particular group of people, it has become more and more aware of the need for preventive medicine. Thus, the institute must work closely with area agencies, including schools and community action groups, to increase and improve health services, with this emphasis on preventive health care. The institute also recognizes opportunities to expand or increase its services in selected critical areas: specialized testing for hypertension and arterial sclerotic heart disease; education related to obesity and cigarette smoking; research into the possible prevention of inherited heart problems; attention to migrant workers and their children; and transportation systems for both the CHI team as it travels to the various clinics, and for patients needing emergency care at selected urban health facilities.

443

Deep-Sea Diving Program

V. Ruth McKinnon

Conoco, Inc., in cooperation with Prison Fellowship, Inc. (a nation-wide church-related ministry to inmates and ex-offenders), and the Commercial Diving Center (CDC) in San Pedro, California, has recently funded a unique program to train former and current federal prisoners as divers for the offshore diving industry.

Several years ago, a Conoco executive launched a study to determine the need for divers worldwide. He discovered that as many as 500 replacement divers are needed each year and that the rigors of offshore oil production in deep waters required a special type of diver training. Some innovative thinking led the executive to conclude that, ironically, the more negative aspects of a prisoner's incarceration could provide the kind of individual who would be an effective diver: a person with strong physical and mental composure and the ability to function in a contained environment.

With the discovery of this untapped resource, Conoco channeled $62,500 through the Prison Fellowship to fund its Divers Program in 1979. Part of that money has been set aside as an endowment to maintain the new program, and it is anticipated that more money will be raised to continue funding the program. Special permission was sought and granted from officials at the Federal Bureau of Prisons for the interstate transporting of federal prisoners to the selected training facility at the CDC.

After undergoing a highly selective screening and testing process to determine both physical and mental stamina, two prisoners have been chosen to begin the thirty-two-week diving course. Both prisoners, confined for bank robbery under three- to five-year sentences, have a short time left to serve. Plans are under way for their paroled release to the custody of a future employer following their diver training. The successful training of these men should open an opportunity for other prisoners to take advantage of this specialized training.

In a broader sense, it is felt that programs like this one for deep-sea divers, and others—such as photographic technology or welding and fabrication, for example—can offer prisoners a chance to pursue a professional career and at the same time function as contributing members of society. Conoco, in fact, is already involved in a new vocational training program in which prisoners at a maximum-security prison operate a blending facility. A specialty plant, set up at the Somers, Connecticut, prison, trains thirty-five prisoners while significantly reducing the state's cost of sanitation chemical materials.

Grand Street Settlement Jobs Cooperative

Sean Sullivan

The Grand Street Settlement was founded on Manhattan's Lower East Side in 1916 to help meet the various needs of what was then largely an immigrant population, but is now primarily a black and Hispanic community. One-sixth of the area's residents are on welfare, and at least one-third of the young adults are unemployed. Many of them do not work or attend school or engage in other socially constructive activities.

Government job training programs have largely failed to provide these people with permanent unsubsidized employment opportunities. When a group of unemployed young adults came to Grand Street Settlement to seek help in finding work, the private business people on the settlement's board of directors responded by making jobs available in their firms, thus starting the Jobs Cooperative. Over an eighteen-month period the program operated informally, as the settlement's executive director worked with the board to place twenty-five people in jobs. Many of the original group who came seeking help worked as volunteers.

The early results led to funding through a private foundation and the Greater New York Fund/United Way, enabling the settlement to hire staff and develop a more formal program for the Jobs Cooperative. The program's first-year (1981) objectives were to improve the employment skills of 90 people, to improve the typing and office skills of 40 people, and to place 60 people in private sector jobs. The program's achievements far exceeded these objectives, as 176 people received employment skills training, 60 people received typing and office skills training, and 98 people were helped to find unsubsidized employment—mostly in the private sector. Employment skills training focused on developing positive work attitudes and values in job readiness workshops. Representatives from companies such as IBM and Bankers Trust helped to prepare participants for the demands they would have to meet in the workplace. Those judged to be "employment-ready" were referred to a job developer for help with job placement.

The job developer, with the help of the board of directors, created a network of private sector job opportunities, building on the original support of board member firms. Of the ninety-eight placements, eighty-five people were still employed at the end of the year and two others had returned to school. The high job retention rate is attributed to thorough screening of the applicants, including employment interviews and a battery of skills tests, the intensive workshop sessions, and follow-up counseling after job placement.

In its second year, the Jobs Cooperative is trying to concentrate its program more on the least employable. It is funded entirely by private contributions and depends on the local private business sector for support. The settlement's board of directors was instrumental in getting the program started by establishing the original network of job opportunities. The program also depends on the initiative of the unemployed young adults in the neighborhood, like those who first came seeking help. No stipends are paid to participants—they are motivated by the desire for a job. The program emphasizes job preparation and placement more than skills training, although it does teach office skills to some participants.

The Jobs Cooperative offers employers job applicants who have been readied for the world of work and follows up to see that those who are hired keep their jobs and perform well enough to ensure future employer support for the program. This locally created and operated program could easily be emulated by social service agencies in other neighborhoods.

MILE HIGH UNITED WAY

V. Ruth McKinnon

In 1978 the Mile High United Way agency in Denver, Colorado, initiated the Venture Grant Program, a three-year pilot program to aid new and/or struggling agencies with a history of difficulty in securing funding. During the three-year period, as many as forty agencies received grants ranging in amounts from $200 to $20,000 to foster more creative and nontraditional projects in the community. Although requests for grants totaled $3.4 million in 1980, only $168,000 was available for distribution. By the end of 1981 a total of $265,000 in grants had been awarded through the program.

As the pilot program neared completion, Mile High United Way decided to reevaluate the program to determine the feasibility of continuing it. In view of the promised federal cutbacks in the area of human services, it seemed more imperative than ever to extend the program and, at the same time, implement a new project focus.

In September 1981, Mile High United Way announced a modified version of the Venture Grant Program. Applications for funding were to come from groups of agencies seeking to combine efforts in focusing on a particular human service. Application to the program is made by submitting a letter to the Venture Grant Committee including the names of agencies involved, the amount of funding needed, and a brief explanation of the project. The projects must be joint ventures by agencies and should be able to deliver services at reduced costs.

Projects are selected for funding according to the following criteria: the need for service, the nature of the target group, the validity of the proposal, the creative potential of the project, and the project's potential for reducing duplication in the delivery of services.

The volume and types of applications that have been received thus far attest to the growing interest in the program. By early 1982, eleven agencies had been awarded grants under the new joint-venture format amounting to $131,794.

In 1982, the Denver Social Service Volunteers, Inc., for example, received a $22,000 award to continue its work of reducing the cost of publicly supported foster care by using the services of volunteers and placing children in Specialized Foster Care (SFC) homes. The Denver group, in a joint effort with two other groups, will use the venture grant to train and place twenty-five volunteers to work on a one-to-one basis in supportive roles with children and parents. The grant will also be used to find more SFC homes. By consolidating their efforts and more effectively managing this type of service, the participating groups projected that in the first year, 1982, they would save approximately $83,000.

NATIONAL ASSOCIATION FOR THE SOUTHERN POOR

V. Ruth McKinnon

The National Association for the Southern Poor (NASP) was established in 1968 through the efforts of Don Anderson, a young black lawyer. Anderson's concerns were focused on what he calls the "Black Belt" of the South—those communities having high percentages of very poor blacks. In such areas, where the median family income commonly falls between $2,000 and $3,000 annually, families most often live in tin-roof houses with cardboard insulation and no indoor plumbing.

Obviously, the difficulties and hardships facing these families are numerous. These families often find their local governments to be complex and difficult to understand. They may see only a handful of people making decisions that ultimately affect the entire community.

It was this problem in particular that inspired Anderson, while a student at the London School of Economics, to think about creating a nonprofit corporation for the purpose of organizing Black Belt neighborhoods into community groups. Establishing its headquarters in southern Virginia, the NASP has worked diligently over the past thirteen years to organize thirty such communities in parts of Virginia and eastern North Carolina.

The process is relatively simple. In response to a community's request for assistance, members of the NASP's staff of twelve move into a rural area and organize neighborhoods into self-help groups known as assemblies.

Each assembly works on the local level in a variety of ways, but concentrates on bridging gaps in communication between the local government and the more remote and illiterate members of the community. Assemblies have helped establish day-care centers, low-income housing, a discount clothing store, a mobile health clinic, a legal aid society, a nursery school program, and various types of cooperatives. They have also provided a bus for transporting the elderly and handicapped.

Individual needs are met as well. One assembly, for example, was instrumental in helping a man secure some much-needed health care, and another person was helped in finding a place to live after his own home had been destroyed by fire. Assemblies have also dealt with some sensitive community issues, such as the problems of segregated physicians' waiting rooms and high school curriculums that exclude black history courses.

Acting initially as an organizer, the NASP provides technical and practical assistance to neighborhoods. It helps local groups identify and solve problems. The assemblies are organized to become self-sufficient, with the NASP gradually lessening its direct involvement in the community and eventually withdrawing altogether. A NASP maintenance staff often remains for a period of time to continue to help the community in any way needed.

The strength of the NASP lies in its ability to facilitate solutions to existing needs in these communities. It tries to inform, organize, and educate community members—with the intention of leaving once several neighborhoods can function on their own as an organized and self-sufficient group.

Seed money for establishing NASP came from a Virginia realtor. More recently, funding has come from private foundations, churches, individuals, and corporations. The organization presently functions with an annual budget of $350,000.

The NASP is currently involved in a five-year expansion program, with the goal of establishing assemblies in the other six states of the Black Belt. Bringing together communities in these areas will be a yearlong project in each state, at a projected cost of $15,000 per assembly. The NASP will continue as a helper and an educator of those involved in expanding the NASP/assembly network across the rural South.

RECORDING FOR THE BLIND, INC.

Patricia W. Samors

With passage of the GI Bill following World War II, higher education was made available to a greater number of visually handicapped students. Yet the learning process for these students was hampered because of their inability to use conventional textbooks. Also, college-level reading materials were not readily available in Braille. Recording for the Blind, Inc. (RFB), therefore, was created in the late 1940s as a nonprofit organization to provide these students with necessary and usable educational reading materials.

Recording for the Blind, Inc., provides taped textbooks, at no cost, to visually and physically handicapped students at the elementary, secondary, undergraduate, graduate, and professional levels. RFB periodically publishes a catalog of recorded books that is distributed to schools, colleges, service agencies, libraries, and individual students throughout the country. To use these materials, interested students must register with RFB by completing a service application and a disability statement, confirmed by a qualified doctor. (Applicants are primarily individuals with visual and physical handicaps, but may also include those with learning disabilities such as dyslexia.)

After receiving an identification number, students may make requests for recorded books by mail or phone—usually to RFB's main New York office. If the requested book is already one of the 55,000 recorded volumes on file at the Master Tape Library in New York, it is duplicated and mailed to the student. If the book has never been recorded, however, RFB will obtain two written copies of the requested text from the student and forward them to one of RFB's twenty-eight studios for recording. As the text is being prepared, completed sections are sent ahead to the student. Once completed, the recording is added to the permanent collection of the Master Tape Library.

Recording for the Blind, Inc., uses the services of over 5,000 volunteers throughout the country. Volunteer reader-monitor teams record subjects in mathematics, computer science, economics, medicine, law, and management, among others. Using the second copy of the book being recorded, the monitor simultaneously proofreads the text, corrects errors, and checks each page for proper sound levels. Both the monitor and the reader must have total familiarity with the subject being recorded.

During the past two years, several improvements were made in the RFB program. Prior to 1980, for example, book orders were processed through a series of manual operations and the time needed to fill a student's request was often as long as ten or more days. With the implementation of a new computerized order-processing system, however, the turnaround time has been reduced to less than four days. In addition, RFB recently installed an incoming WATS (Wide-Area Telecommunications Service) line so students could have their orders processed immediately without the usual mail order delays. In 1980 alone, RFB distributed 77,000 recorded books to 14,000 borrowers.

ST. FRANCIS' FRIENDS OF THE POOR

V. Ruth McKinnon

There are thousands of homeless individuals in New York City. Every morning for the past fifty years 300 or more of these homeless and hungry men and women line up in front of St. Francis' Church at 135 West Thirty-first Street to receive fresh sandwiches and a cup of coffee from several Franciscan friars. The line is usually made up of young and old, of the coherent and the not-so-coherent. Some have stood in this same line every morning year after year. Others are merely passersby who happen to find their way into the line to receive free food.

A recent outgrowth of the bread line has been seen in efforts by the Franciscan brothers to house some of these displaced individuals, especially those with serious mental problems. About ten years ago the friars obtained some rent-free space in an old dilapidated welfare hotel. They used the space to provide limited medical and psychiatric services to the tenants. Professional staffing was provided by nearby Bellevue Psychiatric Hospital, the Visiting Nurses Association, and the city of New York's Human Resources Administration. Once the program was fully operational, the brothers felt that still more remained to be done.

Thus, St. Francis' Friends of the Poor was formed as a tax-exempt, not-for-profit corporation composed of a small group of Franciscan friars and lay persons. The group's intention was to raise enough money to purchase an old hotel and convert it into a residence to be used exclusively for the city's homeless. Through an intense mailing campaign, the group raised $300,000, primarily in the form of individual contributions of $5, $10, and $20. They supplemented the amount received through contributions with a low-interest loan from the Franciscan Province, and finally bought the old Beechwood Hotel for $550,000. They renamed it the St. Francis Residence.

The structure was renovated and redecorated at an additional cost of $250,000. In August 1980, the hotel opened its refurbished doors to 100 residents. Some occupants are walk-ins from the street; others come as a result of their contact with the bread line. A significant number are referred by the Bellevue Hospital. Some spend only a night at the residence; others stay for an indefinite period of time. All are charged $35 to $50 a week for their room, and 25 cents to 50 cents per meal.

Staff members include a full-time resident manager and assistant manager, as well as janitorial and maintenance personnel. New York City provides a full-time homemaker to oversee the resident-run kitchen staff. The city also provides a full-time social worker who supplies a variety of services, including art and exercise therapy. The State Department of Mental Health contributes the services of a part-time social worker. Several physicians from Bellevue provide much needed psychiatric and medical services to a large number of the tenants who have long-term histories of mental illness.

A Residents Council meets weekly to solve in-house problems as well as various tenant grievances. It is not uncommon for residents to make hospital visits to fellow residents or to shop for others less mobile than themselves. Birthdays are often celebrated at the residence.

The St. Francis' Friends of the Poor are presently working to purchase and renovate another building as their work with New York's homeless continues to grow. Neither the bread line nor the residence receives any federal, state, or local government funding.

Appendix

TABLE A–1

THE GROWTH OF THE AFDC PROGRAM, 1960–1980

	1960	1965	1970	1975	1980
Total cost (billions of dollars)	$1.0	$1.7	$4.9	$9.2	$12.5
Total recipients (millions)	3.0	4.3	8.5	11.3	10.8
No. of child recipients (millions)	2.3	3.3	6.2	8.1	7.4

NOTE: Cost figures represent combined state and federal expenditures.
SOURCE: For 1960-1975, *Social Security Bulletin, Annual Statistical Summary, 1980,* table 174, p. 232; for 1980, *Social Security Bulletin,* January 1982, table M-28, p. 48, and table M-29, p. 49.

TABLE A–2

AVERAGE MONTHLY PAYMENT PER AFDC RECIPIENT,
BY STATE, 1970, 1975, 1980
(dollars)

State	December 1970	December 1975	December 1980
Total	49.65	71.70	99.61
Alabama	15.20	29.61	39.07
Alaska	71.40	102.99	162.61
Arizona	32.00	40.60	63.70
Arkansas	25.00	39.18	51.30
California	53.95	85.98	147.14
Colorado	52.15	69.39	93.69
Connecticut	65.30	82.24	131.07
Delaware	36.25	63.15	82.28
District of Columbia	55.25	73.02	93.45
Florida	23.85	40.06	65.25
Georgia	28.45	33.39	53.87
Hawaii	64.95	103.54	126.05
Idaho	50.60	83.62	101.59
Illinois	58.55	80.03	90.98
Indiana	35.95	54.53	72.55
Iowa	52.30	87.27	112.80
Kansas	55.75	74.95	108.64
Kentucky	30.80	56.65	71.28
Louisiana	20.10	35.61	51.40
Maine	40.40	53.12	85.86
Maryland	43.65	59.04	87.62
Massachusetts	71.50	120.98	125.91
Michigan	53.80	88.43	127.88
Minnesota	72.05	91.22	127.60
Mississippi	12.10	14.38	29.83
Missouri	30.50	44.92	77.87
Montana	45.85	54.23	82.82
Nebraska	41.60	66.22	103.64
Nevada	30.85	51.55	79.27
New Hampshire	61.35	74.67	100.52
New Jersey	62.60	82.71	104.63
New Mexico	32.50	43.45	65.98
New York	77.90	106.84	123.24
North Carolina	30.90	54.85	64.48
North Dakota	61.50	82.01	107.81
Ohio	43.85	65.53	87.97

TABLE 2–A   (continued)

State	December 1970	December 1975	December 1980
Oklahoma	37.25	59.33	85.67
Oregon	46.85	85.07	99.11
Pennsylvania	63.10	87.12	101.53
Rhode Island	61.85	77.15	141.13
South Carolina	19.70	28.87	42.83
South Dakota	53.40	67.33	82.93
Tennessee	29.65	34.44	42.85
Texas	28.95	32.69	35.91
Utah	42.85	84.12	103.06
Vermont	61.35	81.27	117.07
Virginia	47.25	64.09	82.35
Washington	60.25	86.12	135.20
West Virginia	27.15	50.97	62.15
Wisconsin	64.20	99.44	138.06
Wyoming	42.25	62.53	102.74

SOURCE: *Social Security Bulletin, Annual Statistical Summary, 1970*, table 140, p. 134; *Social Security Bulletin, Annual Statistical Summary, 1975*, table 178, p. 188; *Social Security Bulletin*, November 1981, vol. 44, no. 11, table M-31, p. 51.

Notes

[1] Office of Management and Budget, *Major Themes and Additional Budget Details: Fiscal Year 1983*, p. 55.

[2] Congressional Budget Office, *Reducing the Federal Deficit: Strategies and Options*, Washington, D.C., February 1982, p. 136.

[3] Office of Management and Budget, *Major Themes and Additional Budget Details: Fiscal Year 1983*, p. 55.

[4] Ibid.

[5] Congressional Budget Office estimates, as cited in Harrison Donnelly, "Millions of Poor Face Losses Oct. 1 as Reconciliation Bill Spending Cuts Go into Effect," *Congressional Quarterly*, September 26, 1981, pp. 1834-37.

[6] Office of Management and Budget, *Major Themes and Additional Budget Details: Fiscal Year 1983*, p. 45.

[7] Ibid.

[8] Office of Management and Budget, *Appendix to the Budget: Fiscal Year 1983*, p. I-K47.

[9] Social Security Administration, Office of Research and Statistics, *AFDC Standards for Basic Needs: July 1980*, March 1981, p. 3.

[10] "Government Benefits Are Being Withdrawn," *Washington Post*, October 1, 1981.

[11] Office of Management and Budget, *Major Themes and Additional Budget Details: Fiscal Year 1983*, p. 52.

[12] Richard P. Nathan, *Background Material on Fiscal Year 1982 Federal Budget Reductions: A Background Document for the First Round of the Field Network Evaluation Study of the Reagan Domestic Program* (Princeton, N.J.: Woodrow Wilson School of Public and International Affairs, Princeton University, December 1981), mimeographed, p. 116. The Congressional Budget Office base line is CBO's projection of the amount needed to maintain program levels in FY 1982 at 1981 levels, based on 1981 spending adjusted for inflation.

[13] Office of Management and Budget, *The Budget for Fiscal Year 1983*, p. S-124.

[14] Congressional Budget Office, "Interactions among Programs Providing Benefits to Individuals: Secondary Effects on the Budget" (draft paper), March 5, 1982, p. 18; Office of Management and Budget, *Appendix to the Budget: Fiscal Year 1975*, p. 454.

[15] Congressional Budget Office, "Interactions among Programs Providing Benefits," p. 18.

[16] Office of Management and Budget, *Appendix to the Budget: Fiscal Year 1983*, p. I-K45, and *The Budget for Fiscal Year 1983*, p. 5-157.

[17] Office of Management and Budget, *Appendix to the Budget: Fiscal Year 1983*, p. I-K49; FY 1982, p. I-K57; and FY 1981, p. 483.

[18] Office of Management and Budget, *The Budget for Fiscal Year 1982*, p. 263.

[19] The programs consolidated into the Maternal and Child Health Services block grant include: Maternal and Child Health, Crippled Children's Service, SSI Disabled Children, Hemophilia Treatment Centers, Sudden Infant Death Syndrome, Lead-Based Paint Poisoning Prevention, Genetic Diseases, and Adolescent Pregnancy.

[20] The programs consolidated into the alcohol and drug abuse and mental health block grant include: Alcoholism State Formula Grants, Alcohol Abuse and Alcoholism Project Grants and Contracts, Special Grants for Uniform Alcoholism Intoxication and Treatment Act, Drug Abuse State Formula Grants and Contracts, Drug Abuse Projects Grants, and Mental Health Services.

[21] Office of Management and Budget, *The Budget for Fiscal Year 1983*, p. 5-135.

[22] Department of Health and Human Services, *The Fiscal Year 1983 Justification of Appropriation Estimates for Committee on Appropriations*, Volume IV.

[23] Department of Health and Human Services, Division of Policy and Evaluation, Office of Energy Assistance, March 31, 1982.

[24] Ibid.

[25] Ibid.

[26] Ibid.

[27] Office of Management and Budget, *The Budget for Fiscal Year 1983*, p. 5-159.

Child Welfare Policy

Robert L. Woodson

For the estimated half-million children in the foster care system in the United States, conditions appear to be getting worse. Attempts to improve the child welfare system have sometimes failed as the interests of institutions prevailed over those of their clients. These institutions should be challenged with new policies and practices, which emphasize the interests of families and children. In this chapter, the deficiencies of the current foster care system are highlighted, and the tendency of social agencies to keep children in high-cost foster care institutions indefinitely is explained. By contrast, mediating structures that stress the willingness and ability of families to adopt children have broken through the foster care holding pattern. This approach, which stresses placement in a permanent home rather than a "maintenance" or "custodial" approach, holds more promise for the well-being of children.

The Plight of the Children

It is the children of low-income families especially who become wards of the state. Child welfare practices, ostensibly enacted in their "best interests," have increasingly come under attack even by professionals in the field.[1] So many children raised in the child welfare system have gone on to commit crimes that it has been called a government-funded incubator of youthful offenders.

Some children come into the foster care system as a result of abuse or neglect by their parents, who are compelled to surrender custody by court decree. Others are voluntarily committed to out-of-home care by parents who are ill or otherwise incapacitated and cannot care for their own children. If the child in foster care cannot be returned home in a short time, authorities are expected to seek an adoptive home. Each year federal, state, and local governments spend over $2 billion for the care of these children. Since the 1960s, the number of children subject to such care has more than doubled.[2]

Many of these children are shunted from one home to another. Since foster care is supposed to be temporary, official policy is to discourage strong emotional ties between foster parents and foster children. Yet for these children, foster care often becomes an endless series of temporary havens. Many of them grow up without the sense of permanence and the psychological support necessary for sound development.

For some children, the state is the worst possible parent. Prolonged institutional care can injure and disorganize normal development.[3] Although everyone agrees that children should be moved quickly out of institutions, group homes, and foster care and into permanent, loving homes, the evidence shows that child welfare agencies are not accomplishing this goal. Nationwide, children spend an average of five to seven years in foster care. Few efforts are made to return them to their natural parents. Often children are placed in foster homes or institutions far from their parents' home, so that visiting becomes difficult and the parents and children become estranged. Because of such estrangement, the courts may then terminate the rights of parents who cannot afford to travel to visit their children. The hurt and rejection experienced by the children can be devastating. The child may feel abandoned when public systems take over responsibility for him.

Efforts to provide a permanent adoptive home for a child are usually insufficient, and adoption may be inadvertently discouraged. The body of administrative regulations that has grown up around child placement over the years act as barriers to adoption. The children who need homes and the families who want children often do not learn about each other. Applicants for a child may be rejected because they are considered too old, too young, or too poor, or because they are single or they belong to the wrong religion. Some prospective adoptive parents withdraw their applications rather than answer embarrassing questions about their personal lives. Handicapped individuals are routinely turned away. Moreover, the agencies receive more money if they hold onto children than if they place them in permanent homes.

Money for the care of child wards is often diverted. One agency accumulated a multimillion dollar portfolio while spending as little as $2.96 a day to feed and clothe each child.[4] Since this agency received $24,000 a year for each child in its care, placing children for adoption was less attractive than keeping the children and the income they brought in. In one year, four agencies were given $6 million to place 2,000 children, but they placed only ten.[5] While these cases may be exceptions, there is no doubt that the number of children in care has increased dramatically. In 1963, 37 in 10,000 children were in foster care; in 1969, 45 in 10,000 children; and in 1977, 77 in 10,000 children. Estimates of the present number, usually arrived at by extrapolation, range between 250,000 and 502,000. Regardless which estimate is accepted, more children are in foster care in the United States today than ever before.[6]

There is no effective means of monitoring the quality of services to children or the practices of various institutions. Large caseloads and voluminous paper work prevent workers from getting to know the children they supervise or maintaining communications with their families. Unprepared or unable to deal with family problems, they can do little to facilitate a child's return home. Nor are there any effective sanctions for poor performance by child welfare agencies.

Even a well-run institution, however, cannot replace a family or a home. A significant number of children who become wards of the state are injured by this "care." The mortality rate of foster children is twice the national average for children. Although only some 12 percent enter foster care for reasons of personal maladjustment, almost half of those in care show symptoms of poor adjustment and emotional distress.[7]

Our public policy provides perverse incentives for maintaining children within the foster care system. It often prevents good people within the system from acting in the best interests of the child. Their salaries, the agency's overhead, and related expenses are all based upon having children in care. Many dedicated professionals in the system have tried to change these practices, but they are faced with a system that discourages inquiry. Thousands of dedicated foster parents who provide love and care with little compensation for their efforts are also victims of the system.

Foster Care in Three Cities

New York City. In May 1977 the Office of the Comptroller of the Bureau of Municipal Investigation and Statistics of the City of New York conducted an audit of the nonprofit agencies providing voluntary foster care for dependent and neglected children. In New York, the approximately 29,000 children in individual family foster care cost $280 million a year, or nearly $10,000 per child. The majority of the children are cared for by thirty-five voluntary agencies funded by the city, state, and federal governments. More than half of the money goes for administrative overhead and social services. Many of these agencies depend entirely on tax dollars for their survival.[8] The auditors found that out of 35,657 children in all types of foster care (including group homes) in 1976, only 5,431 were discharged to permanent homes. The number released each year nearly equaled the number entering.[9] Many of these children spend the rest of their childhood in foster care. Of the children sampled, 29 percent have been in three or more foster homes, often with debilitating effect.

If a parent has abandoned a child, or if a child is severely abused or neglected, the agency is expected to seek the release of the child for adoption. In 110 cases reviewed by the city auditors, only eight were released in good time and only twenty-two others after many years of care.[10] New York state law requires that state adoption services have listings and photographs of all children eligible for adoption. Only 24 percent of the available children, however, are in fact listed; hence, many children are never made known to prospective adoptive parents.

Washington. The foster care agencies claim that many children are in foster care because of the lack of prospective parents. Minority and older children are said to be particularly hard to place, but a poll of prospective parents indicated that 30 percent of the parents wanted a child eight years or older and that the agencies' policies and attitudes had discouraged them.

The District of Columbia has a foster care system that serves more than 2,000 children, at an annual cost of $14 million.[11] A survey showed that most children entered care while very young and remained in care for very long periods. The median age at entrance was 3.0 years; the median time in care 7.3 years. Most children had experienced multiple placements.

Seventy-seven percent of the children in the sample were living in traditional foster family homes; 10 percent in institutions; 5 percent in group homes; 4 percent with relatives. The remaining 4 percent were runaways.

A disproportionate number of the youngest children were in institutions; 29 percent of all those under six, compared with 10 percent of all children. The District is forbidden by law to place any child under the age of six in an institution operated by the District unless medically necessary, but as many as eighty-five nonhandicapped children are in institutions.

Philadelphia. There are approximately 4,200 children being cared for by the city of Philadelphia at an annual cost of $60 million per year. Only 12 percent of them are being considered for return to their families. For children in foster care, the average length of separation from parents is almost six years. Adoption is planned for only 7.5 percent of the children. Of the 268 legally free children in private agency care, only eighty-six had adoption plans made for them. Only thirty were actually placed in adoption, and only three were referred to the Adoption Center of Delaware Valley, an organization that brings together prospective adoptive parents and children.[12] Failure to make plans to return the children to their parents or to place them in adoptive homes increases the cost of foster care services by several million dollars per year.

The city of Philadelphia's reimbursement arrangement is similar to those of Washington, D.C., New York, and other systems. The bulk of the $60 million goes to the agencies in support of a system that makes it more profitable for children to remain in the care of the public than to be adopted. The city pays the agencies $17.50 per day per child and only $7 to foster parents. For group or institutional care, it pays from $46 to $58 per day.

Social workers responsible for supervising foster homes and for providing needed services have an average caseload of 200 families.

Funds for children in institutional care all go to the public and private agencies. The figures given do not include medical, educational, or psychological services, which add a substantial amount to the total cost. One director of a foundling home received $44,592 a year in salary—50 percent more than allowed for this position—and psychiatrists and psychologists were paid as much as $65,000 a year in city funds for seeing children on a part-time basis.[13]

The Problems with Proposed Reforms

A system should be evaluated not by individual cases or by the intentions of the workers, even if they feel real compassion for children in need, but by the consequences of the actions they take. A pattern of injury may signify that a whole system of child care requires correction. The harm done to children by placing them in foster care has been public knowledge since the First White House Conference on Dependent Children, in 1909.

There are currently a number of proposals to reform the foster care system, some of which may be counterproductive. Reform is currently proposed in two ways. On the one hand, there are those who claim that more funds would provide more staff to keep track of cases, to keep up with paper work, to provide more services, and to pay more attention to the children. Children would not then be lost or shunted about in the system until they become emotionally disturbed, as they are now.

On the other hand, some policy makers address the huge burden of cost to the taxpayer. They assume that reducing the funding will reduce fraud in reimbursements and eliminate the financial incentives that keep children out of adoption. Putting less money into the system could, however, result in a perpetuation of the same faults—prolonged stays in foster care, lack of services, moving children about—only they would be carried out more efficiently. Thus, even with fiscal restraints, the children may be no better off. Neither a reduction in funds nor an increase in funds in itself constitutes an adequate policy.

There is no evidence that tinkering with the foster care system will ever make it become like a family to its children. Nor can the issue be resolved by an argument over public care versus private care; most private child care agencies receive the bulk of their support from the public agencies and therefore conform to the same rules and regulations.

Even Public Law 96–272, the Adoption Assistance and Child Welfare Act, which passed by a vote of 401–2 in the House and has been hailed by child advocates as a major reform, leaves much to be desired. It was designed to give financial incentives to states to manage foster care better, to return children to their families, and to encourage their adoption. Funds are made available to restore families and keep children at home and to recruit adoptive families, as well as for other purposes. The act relies, however, upon professional agency personnel to carry out the reforms. A different perspective may be required to make real improvements in the system.

The Reagan administration's position on foster care includes the following goals: to reduce burdensome federal regulations; to emphasize adoption assistance rather than service entitlements; and to switch from federal mechanisms to those of states and localities. These are significant changes that may well prove to be auspicious. To reverse the present trend in foster care, however, a new vision may be needed.

An alliance is forming between some child advocate groups and service delivery leaders to shift public intervention to preventive and protective services on behalf of children. A ceiling on spending would be acceptable to these groups if the funds could be spent for preventive and protective purposes. Would shifting public funds from one set of programs to another result in improvements, however, as long as the same professionals remained responsible for the services? Understandably, these professionals seek to legitimize their mission, but government policy should be concerned primarily with the needs of children and families. If these professionals insist on making use of existing structures, a family's opportunity to work out its own problems may be severely curtailed.

Another struggle in foster care turns on whether services and placement should be supplied by private agencies or by publicly operated agencies. This struggle between the "centralists" and the "privatists" is to some extent illusory. Both public and private agencies have been remiss in setting standards for removing children from their homes, and in their slowness in making assessments, in placement, in monitoring, in adoption, and in other ways.

A Mediating Structures Approach to Foster Care

By far the majority of children under eighteen who are separated from their biological parents are likely to be cared for informally by relatives and friends, without the involvement of the government. In *The Strengths of Black Families*, Robert Hill has described support networks as a particular strength of black families.[14] Others have arrived at the same conclusion, but their recommendations have been largely ignored. Their insights, however, support the ideas on public policy proposed by Peter Berger and Richard Neuhaus in *To Empower People: The Role of Mediating Structures in Public Policy*, which has been developed by the Mediating Structures Project of the American Enterprise Institute.[15] Applying the mediating structures idea to foster care leads to the proposition that the family—and no conceivable substitute—is the best vehicle for child care. Contrary to some authorities on child care and family welfare, the emphasis should return to individual families. Parents—and in particular parents who are poor and members of minority groups—should again be seen as the best advocates of their children's welfare, rather than being regarded with ambivalence and distrust.

The family should not, however, be too narrowly defined. Anyone willing and able to commit himself or herself to the care of children for a number of years should be included. A great variety of people who lead very different lives can be effective parents.

Family rights should be emphasized as much as children's rights. Parents deserve a fair hearing in custody cases, and in neglect and

461

abuse proceedings. Vague and ill-defined charges have sometimes led to the separation of children, usually to the detriment of the children.

This does not mean that parents should be allowed to view their children as objects of whim or impulse. To protect children against physical abuse in the home, a review board should be set up. It should be composed of community members (that is, people who are actually living in the community and are part of the community), as well as social workers and lawyers. Laws should be applied stringently to those guilty of abuse.

Support services should be made available to families in crisis. They should be largely in the form of practical assistance, to be obtained in the neighborhood whenever possible. The choice of counseling and therapeutic services, as well as other services, should be left to the discretion of the families themselves. The greatest possible choice should also be given to clients of professional services and agencies involved in foster care. These agencies should be held accountable to their clients and to community review boards. The best way to ensure choice and accountability is to make available to parents some kind of voucher to be used at their discretion. The intention here is not to denigrate these services, but to clarify their relation to the families they serve, in particular families in crisis. There is a real need for professional advice and services; a mediating structures approach to foster care is unlikely to do away with them.

In cases of adoption, where the role of professional services becomes particularly important, a community review board has a heavy responsibility. More than thirty states have some form of foster care review. A mediating structures approach would emphasize the role of these boards in relation to the roles of judges, administrators, child advocates, and others.

A national family policy on foster care should respect the existing pluralism of family life styles and child care practices. There is a great variety of American life styles, embodying widely different perceptions and goals. To be responsive to the different needs of these various families, adoption subsidies should be available, if needed, for each child taken by a family, whether the child had been in crisis or not. Such an allowance would resolve many of the controversies surrounding foster care. Its benefits would become dramatically evident, because it would encourage adoption by many foster families that could not otherwise afford to lose the money they receive for foster care.

Foster care policy must be freed of the pejorative myths that surround the black family. When the black community applies its own standards to the adoption of children, the results are astounding.

A Successful Initiative in Detroit. In 1969, Detroit had hundreds of children awaiting adoption in thirteen public and private agencies in the foster care system. Many infants were left unclaimed in the newborn ward of the general hospital and the city's maternal care homes. Although 58 percent of Detroit's illegitimate babies had black mothers, only one in fifteen children who were adopted was black.[16] A community group challenged the adoption practices of these agencies with some startling results. Homes for Black Children, originally funded by Detroit's United Way, has revolutionized adoption procedures in Michigan. A young black woman, Sydney Duncan, developed the organization in the belief that if black families have traditionally cared for children of unwed mothers, they would also formally adopt them. She saw that black families faced formidable barriers in their attempts to adopt children—barriers imposed by agencies with little understanding of the black experience. Applicants were discouraged by the endless paper work that was part of the application process. Questions about home ownership, sterility, and other matters intimidated many applicants.

By contrast, Homes for Black Children agrees to see all persons who inquire about adoption, at their home if they cannot come to the office (open two evenings a week for convenience). Duncan's group scrapped the traditional procedures, which required payment of fees for the adoptive study, and the traditional application, which contained questions about the moral, religious, personal, and social habits of the applicant. Many black families migrated from the South without the legal documents required by traditional adoption agencies. Homes for Black Children assists these families in securing birth certificates, marriage licenses, and other legal documents. Arbitrary income limits were discarded; instead the staff tries to determine whether a family can provide a warm, loving, and secure home.

The results of these policies are impressive. In the first year, Homes for Black Children placed 137 children, while the thirteen traditional agencies combined placed only 96. In its ten years of existence, Homes for Black Children has placed over 700 children in permanent adoptive homes.[17] As a result, the infant units in the Detroit General Hospital and in two maternal care homes have been closed.

In response to this success, Detroit's traditional social service agencies began to alter their practices and have increased their placement of black children. Now black children in Detroit move from foster care to adoption at the same rate as white youngsters.

Conclusions

The conclusions that follow with regard to child welfare policy should be obvious, but they bear repeating. No institution should gain financially from keeping children out of a permanent home. All incentives to do so should be removed. When it is necessary to remove a child from his natural home, every effort should be made to place him or her within the neighborhood or extended kinship group, or at the very least in a similar community or culture. This will require redefining the standards by which families are deemed worthy of becoming foster parents or adoptive parents, so that cultural pluralism is recognized and accepted.

Similarly, the definitions of "dependent" and "neglected" children should also be modified. Cultural and ethnic minorities should be given a greater share of the budgets allotted to child welfare. Regulations that tend to discourage natural or extended families from remaining together and helping each other should be exposed and eliminated. No one who wants to help a child should be prevented from doing so for reasons of race, ethnic background, income, or class. This is especially important with respect to "hard-to-place" children, usually older children from minority groups, who stand in jeopardy of growing into adulthood without ever experiencing family life. Finally, the law should be changed to require more accurate record keeping on the movement of children from institution to institution, both within and across state lines. Rules and regulations that provide a disincentive for finding these children permanent homes must be reviewed.

In short, many of the problems of child welfare could be overcome by recognizing—not thwarting—the cultural diversity of the American family and its ability to respond to the needs of its children.

Notes

1 Brigitte Berger, "Thoughts on Mediating Structures and Foster Care," unpublished paper (Washington, D.C.: American Enterprise Institute, 1981).

2 Controller General's Report to Congress, *Children in Foster Care Institutions/ Steps Governments Can Take to Improve Their Care*, Department of Health, Education, and Welfare survey, 1977.

3 "Children without Homes" (Washington, D.C.: Children's Defense Fund, April 1977); and David Fanshel and Eugene Shinn, *Children in Foster Care* (New York: Columbia University Press, 1978).

4 Nicholas Pileggi, "Who'll Save the Children?" *New York*, December 18, 1978, pp. 53-56.

5 Ibid.

[6] See Berger, "Thoughts on Mediating Structures and Foster Care."

[7] See the comments of Dr. Morris A. Wessel of the Yale University School of Medicine, in Richard Haitch, ed., *Orphans of the Living: The Foster Care Crisis*, Public Affairs Pamphlet No. 418 (1968), pp. 16-17. See also New York City Audit E78/426 (1978), p. iii.

[8] Office of the Comptroller, City of New York, Bureau of Municipal Investigation and Statistics, *Report on Foster Care Agencies, Achievement of Permanent Homes for Children in Their Care*, no. E77-403 (1976-1977).

[9] Ibid.

[10] Ibid.

[11] *Report on Foster Care*, D.C. Auditor's Office, March 1981.

[12] *Children without Families: A Report on Philadelphia Children in the Foster Care System*, Adoption Center of Delaware Valley, 1982.

[13] Ibid.

[14] Robert B. Hill, *The Strengths of Black Families* (New York: Emerson Hall, 1972). See also Robert B. Hill, *Informal Adoption among Black Families* (Washington, D.C.: National Urban League, 1977).

[15] Peter L. Berger and Richard John Neuhaus, *To Empower People: The Role of Mediating Structures in Public Policy* (Washington, D.C.: American Enterprise Institute, 1977), p. 2.

[16] "Homes for Black Children," *Ebony*, June 1976.

[17] Ibid.

Contributors

MICHAEL P. BALZANO is the director of government affairs for the Joint Maritime Congress in Washington, D.C., a visiting fellow at the American Enterprise Institute, and the former director of Action, the federal agency for volunteer service. He now advises public and private sector organizations on community initiatives. He is the author of *Reorganizing the Federal Bureaucracy: The Rhetoric and Reality, The Peace Corps: Myths and Prospects,* and *Federalizing Meals on Wheels: Private Sector Loss or Gain?*

MARLENE M. BECK is a research associate with the American Enterprise Institute. She served as director of volunteer services with the Meals-on-Wheels program of the Lutheran Service Society of Western Pennsylvania.

LANDRUM BOLLING is research professor of diplomacy at the Edmund A. Walsh School of Foreign Service, Georgetown University, and is an adviser to William J. Baroody, Jr., president of the American Enterprise Institute. He has served as president of Earlham College, as head of the Lilly Endowment, and as chairman and chief executive officer of the Council on Foundations. His writings include *Search for Peace in the Middle East* and *Private Foreign Aid: U.S. Philanthropy for Relief and Development.*

DENIS P. DOYLE is director of education policy studies and a resident fellow in education at the American Enterprise Institute. He has been a federal executive fellow at the Brookings Institution and was director of planning and program coordination for the Office of the Assistant Secretary, Office of Research and Improvement, Department of Education. He is the author of AEI's 1981–1982 high school debate analysis, *Debating National Education Policy: The Question of Standards.*

ANDREA M. HAINES is assistant director of the legislative analysis program at the American Enterprise Institute and former associate

467

editor of *Public Opinion* magazine. She has taught at Smith College and at Stanford University.

MARSHA LEVINE is a consultant on education policy and on private sector initiatives at the American Enterprise Institute. She was an education policy fellow in the Office of the Deputy Under Secretary of the Department of Education.

NANCY MATTISON, a research associate in the Department of Pharmacology at the University of Rochester School of Medicine and Dentistry, is studying the regulation of drug development and use in the United States and Western Europe. She has published two articles, with William M. Wardell, on cost-benefit, cost-effectiveness, and risk-benefit assessment in medical technologies.

V. RUTH McKINNON is a researcher at the American Enterprise Institute, specializing in the study of private sector initiatives. She was assistant to the dean of admissions, Gordon College, writer and editor at the Institute for International Development, Inc., and assistant to the associate director for health policy, Domestic Council, the White House.

JACK A. MEYER is director of the Center for Health Policy Research and a resident fellow in economics at the American Enterprise Institute. He has served as assistant director for wage and price monitoring with the U.S. Council on Wage and Price Stability and has held positions in the Department of Labor and Department of Housing and Urban Development. He is the author of *Health Care Cost Increases* and *Wage-Price Standards and Economic Policy*.

C. KENNETH ORSKI is president of the Corporation for Urban Mobility, an organization that seeks creative solutions to urban transportation problems through public-private cooperation. He was associate administrator of the Urban Mass Transportation Administration, director of urban affairs at the Organization for Economic Cooperation and Development, and vice-president of the German Marshall Fund.

RUDOLPH G. PENNER is director of fiscal policy studies and a resident scholar at the American Enterprise Institute. He was assistant director for economic policy at the Office of Management and Budget; deputy assistant secretary for economic affairs at the Department of Housing and Urban Development; and senior staff economist for the Council of Economic Advisers. He has written many books and articles on tax

468

and budget issues and contributes a monthly column to the *New York Times*.

PAUL L. PRYDE, JR., is president of Paul Pryde & Associates, a consulting firm specializing in problems of development policy and strategy. He is also the author of several works on urban enterprise zones.

PATRICIA W. SAMORS is a researcher at the American Enterprise Institute, specializing in health care policy, private sector initiatives, and wage-price controls. She was employed by the Department of the Treasury, Office of the Secretary, and by Nusac, Incorporated, a consulting firm to the nuclear energy industry.

WILLIAM A. SCHAMBRA is assistant director of constitutional studies at the American Enterprise Institute and coeditor, with Robert A. Goldwin, of *How Democratic Is the Constitution?* and *How Capitalistic Is the Constitution?* He is editing a collection of essays by the late Martin Diamond.

SEAN SULLIVAN is a consultant to the Center for the Study of Private Initiative and the Center for Health Policy Research at the American Enterprise Institute. He has served as assistant director and as senior labor economist for the U.S. Council on Wage and Price Stability.

WILLIAM M. WARDELL is associate professor of pharmacology and toxicology, assistant professor of medicine, and director of the Center for the Study of Drug Development at the University of Rochester School of Medicine and Dentistry. He is on the board of directors of the American Society for Clinical Pharmacology and Therapeutics and is a member of the National Council on Drugs.

JOHN C. WEICHER is a resident fellow at the American Enterprise Institute, specializing in the areas of housing and urban problems. He has served as deputy staff director of the President's Housing Commission, as deputy assistant secretary for economic affairs at the Department of Housing and Urban Development, and as director of the housing and financial markets research program at the Urban Institute. He is the author of *Housing: Federal Policies and Programs*, *Urban Renewal*, and *Metropolitan Housing Needs for the 1980s*.

ROBERT L. WOODSON is a resident fellow at the American Enterprise Institute and founder and president of the National Center for Neighborhood Enterprise. He is the author of *A Summons to Life: Mediating Structures and the Prevention of Youth Crime* and editor of *Youth Crime and Urban Policy: A View from the Inner City*.

A Note on the Book

This book was edited by Margaret Seawell, Claire Theune,
Gertrude Kaplan, Elizabeth Ashooh, and Donna Spitler of the
Publications Staff of the American Enterprise Institute.
The staff also designed the cover and format, with Pat Taylor.
The figures were drawn by Hördur Karlsson.
The text was set in Palatino, a typeface designed by Hermann Zapf.
Hendricks-Miller Typographic Company, of Washington, D.C.,
set the type, and R. R. Donnelley & Sons Company
of Harrisonburg, Virginia, printed and bound the book,
using paper made by the S. D. Warren Company.